国家出版基金项目
NATIONAL PUBLICATION FOUNDATION

THE
CHINESE
PATH

THE OPENING UP AND DEVELOPMENT OF PORTS IN CHINA

ZHU ZHEN

Translated by
Liao Hong, Gao Zhaoyang, Chang Wei

Proofread by
Chen Xiaowei

中国财经出版传媒集团
经济科学出版社
Economic Science Press

图书在版编目（CIP）数据

中国口岸开放与发展之路= The Opening Up and Development of Ports in China：英文/朱振著；廖红，高朝阳，常伟译. --北京：经济科学出版社，2022.3

（《中国道路》丛书）

ISBN 978-7-5218-3519-9

Ⅰ.①中…　Ⅱ.①朱…②廖…③高…④常…　Ⅲ.①通商口岸-经济发展-研究-中国-英文　Ⅳ.①F752

中国版本图书馆 CIP 数据核字（2022）第 048745 号

责任编辑：刘　博
责任校对：易　超
责任印制：王世伟

中国口岸开放与发展之路

The Opening Up and Development of Ports in China

朱　振　著

廖　红　高朝阳　常　伟　译

经济科学出版社出版、发行　新华书店经销

社址：北京市海淀区阜成路甲 28 号　邮编：100142

总编部电话：010-88191217　发行部电话：010-88191522

网址：www.esp.com.cn

电子邮箱：esp@esp.com.cn

天猫网店：经济科学出版社旗舰店

网址：http://jjkxcbs.tmall.com

北京季蜂印刷有限公司印装

787×1092　16 开　19.5 印张　575000 字

2022 年 5 月第 1 版　2022 年 5 月第 1 次印刷

ISBN 978-7-5218-3519-9　定价：90.00 元

（图书出现印装问题，本社负责调换。电话：010-88191510）

（版权所有　侵权必究　打击盗版　举报热线：010-88191661

QQ：2242791300　营销中心电话：010-88191537

电子邮箱：dbts@esp.com.cn）

Preface

The Chinese path refers to the path of socialism with distinctive Chinese characteristics. As Chinese President Xi Jinping points out, it is not an easy path. We are able to embark on this path thanks to the great endeavors of reform and opening up over the past 30 years and more, and the continuous quest made in the 60-plus years since the founding of the People's Republic of China (PRC). It is based on a thorough review of the evolution of the Chinese nation over more than 170 years since modern times and carrying forward the 5,000-year-long Chinese civilization. This path is deeply rooted in history and broadly based on China's present realities.

A right path leads to a bright future. The Chinese path is not only access to China's development and prosperity, but also a path of hope and promise to the rejuvenation of the Chinese nation. Only by forging the confidence in the path, theory, institution and culture can we advance along this path of socialism with Chinese characteristics. With this focus, *The Chinese Path Series* presents to readers an overview in practice, achievements and experiences as well as the past, present and future of the Chinese path.

The Chinese Path Series is divided into ten volumes with one hundred books on different topics. The main topics of the volumes are as follows: economic development, political advancement, cultural progress, social development, ecological conservation, national defense and armed forces building, diplomacy and international policies, the Party's leadership and building, localization of Marxism in China and views from other countries on the Chinese path. Each volume on a particular topic consists of several books which respectively throw light on exploration in practice, reform process, achievements, experiences and theoretical innovations of the Chinese path. Focusing on the practice in reform and opening up with the continuous exploration since the founding of the PRC, these books summarize on the development and inheritance of China's glorious civilization, which not only display a strong sense of the times, but also have profound historical appeal and future-oriented impact.

The series is conceived in its entirety and assigned to different authors. In terms of the writing, special attention has been paid to the combination of history and reality, as well as theory and practice at home and abroad. It gives a realistic and innovative interpretation of the practice, experience, process and theory of the Chinese path. Efforts are made on the distinctive and convincing expression in a global context. It helps to cast light on the "Chinese wisdom" and the "Chinese approach" that the Chinese path has contributed to the modernization of developing countries and solutions to human problems.

On the basis of the great achievements in China's development since the founding of the PRC, particularly since the reform and opening up, the Chinese nation, which had endured so much and for so long since the modern times, has achieved tremendous growth—it has stood up, become prosperous and grown in strength. The socialism with distinctive Chinese characteristics has shown great vitality and entered a new stage. This path has been expanded and is now at a new historical starting point. At this vital stage of development, the Economic Science Press of China Finance & Economy Media Group has designed and organized the compilation of *The Chinese Path Series*, which is of great significance in theory and practice.

The program of *The Chinese Path Series* was launched in 2015, and the first publications came out in 2017. The Series was listed in a couple of national key publication programs, the "90 kinds of selected publications in celebration of the 19th CPC National Congress", and National Publication Foundation.

Editorial Board of *The Chinese Path Series*

Contents

Chapter 1
Introduction

"Opening up" is a historical category, which has been a powerful impetus for social progress since ancient times. With its emergence and development in history, opening up carries different implications in different times, the degree of which is determined by the level and mode of production at the time. Opening up means mutual integration. Increasing openness establishes strong connections between the internal and external regions. Moving from seclusion to opening up is a dynamic evolution of expanding market space, promoting shared interests, optimizing resources allocations, and increasing growth momentum among different countries and regions.

Reform and opening up is the most defining feature and the largest dividend of contemporary development in China, as well as the gateway to empowering the country, enriching the people, securing the borders and befriending the neighbors. Histories of economic development and social practices in China and the rest of the world have borne witness to the fact that national strength, cultural prosperity and historical progress are all closely related to opening up, inclusiveness, reform, and innovation. Opening up has been the only path to both national and regional development. Ports function as the gateway to opening up, the platform of interconnections, the bridge for cross-border communications and the window for projecting positive national images. The opening of ports, which is a major component of opening up at both national and regional levels, is inextricably linked with the rise and fall of a particular economy.

Past, present and future are tightly interwoven. Only by reviewing the history can we learn from the past and do better for a more promising future. As an ancient Chinese line goes, "Only by getting to the peak of the high mountain can one see far and wide."[1] The reform and development of all things, including the opening of ports, are inseparable from specific geopolitics, human civilizations, cultural traditions, and

---

[1] From the poem *Ascending Clouds to the Mountain Top* by Liu Guo (1154-1206), a poet in the Southern Song Dynasty: "When the rain stops, the sun shines and the cold is dispelled. Only by getting to the peak of the high mountain can one see far and wide."

historical context. Thousands of years have passed and mankind has never stopped questing and aspiring for a better future. China is a great country nurtured by a brilliant civilization of more than 5,000 years. Studying the history of ports' opening and development in China, which spans almost 3,000 years from ancient times to the present day, provides a panoramic view of civilization and progress, prosperity and decline, exploration and resistance, as well as struggle and rise with the change of times and in the course of development. From the perspective of ports which are served as windows for readers to see China's endeavor to open up to the outside world and as platforms for partnerships and interconnectivity, the book is to unfold a long scroll of history, with a broad view and across time and space.

The CPC General Secretary Xi Jinping has stressed on many occasions that reform and opening up is a crucial move in making China what it is today and in achieving the Two Centenary Goals[1] and the great rejuvenation of the Chinese nation. Reform and opening up is a great feat of China. This book is to look back on the ports' opening up and development in contemporary China, with a focus on the practices and achievements of nearly 40 years since the start of the reform and opening up, as well as on the continuous exploration, reform, innovation and endeavor of more than 60 years since the founding of the People's Republic of China. From a broader perspective, a rational analysis shall be conducted with a historical view and a global vision. Present concerns should be approached with long-term considerations. Future developments should be planned based on the study of the past and a review of history. Efforts should be made to explore the practices, achievements, experiences, and implications of ports' opening up and development in ancient, modern and especially contemporary China, which is to be further interpreted in historical and social changes, in order to give a comprehensive rendition of the past, present, and future. All of the above are helpful in further strengthening the ports' overall planning from the top and practical operation at the bottom level, enhancing the modernization of ports' management, and ensuring growing confidence in the path, theory, system, and culture to unswervingly advance along the development path with Chinese characteristics.

---

[1] The Two Centenary Goals are to complete the building of a moderately prosperous society in all respects by the time the Communist Party of China marks its centenary in 2021 and to build China into a modern socialist country that is prosperous, strong, democratic, culturally advanced, and harmonious by the time the People's Republic of China celebrates its centenary in 2049.

1.1 Basic concepts, classifications, and characteristics of ports

1.1.1 Concepts and definitions of ports

Ports in China, in a narrow sense, refer to specific areas such as harbors, airports, stations and cross-border channels that are used for personnel, cargo, goods and means of transport to enter and leave the country, upon the approval of the central government or the provincial government with the authorization from the central government (the same below). State-appointed statutory bodies stationed at the ports perform duties of inspection, examination, quarantine for animals and plants, as well as supervision and governance in accordance with the law.

In a broad sense, apart from designated state-approved open areas such as those mentioned above, ports in China also include facilities and infrastructures associated with transportation, security control and inspection, as well as port towns inside the administrative areas where the ports are located or above the county level. Port towns emerge and prosper as a result of high traffic of personnel and goods, trading activities, industrial agglomeration and economic exchanges, all of which are brought by open ports. In this sense, ports in China have market and industry characteristics, responsible for supporting urban development. Ports and cities are integrated and inseparable. Statistics indicate that more than 80% of foreign direct investment in China is in cities with open ports. The opening of ports is the driving force behind many prosperous coastal, riverside and border cities.

1.1.2 Main categories of ports

According to different classification standards, ports in China are mainly classified into the following categories.

(1) *Classification by modes of transportation*

According to different modes of transportation, ports in China can be divided into water ports (including seaports, river ports), land ports (including highway ports, railway ports) and air ports. Water ports refer to special areas set up by the state along rivers, lakes, seas and boundary rivers (lakes and streams) for the entry and exit of personnel, cargo, goods, and means of transport, as well as for the docking and passing of international vessels. Land ports refer to special areas set up by the state in land border regions for the entry or exit of personnel, cargo, goods, and means of transport. Air ports refer to specific areas at the airports open to international routes for the entry and exit of personnel, cargo, goods, and aircraft.

(2) *Classification by rights of examination and approval*

By convention, ports in China can be divided into category-1 ports and category-2 ports, based on differences in the authorities' jurisdiction to examine and approve open ports. The category-1 ports are approved by the State Council while the category-2 ports, also known as the original second-class ports, refer to ports that are approved and administered by the people's government at the provincial level, during the period from the start of the reform and opening up in 1978 to 1998. The following are category-1 ports: ports open to vessels, planes, vehicles and other means of transport of foreign nationality to transport passengers and goods into or out of China through sea, land or air; ports for use only by Chinese vessels, planes and vehicles transporting passengers and goods out of or into the country by sea, land or air; spots on the sea within territorial waters where vessels of foreign nationality are allowed to enter or leave for the purpose of delivering goods. Category-1 ports are express ports, with direct access to overseas destinations for various means of transportation.

The following are category-2 ports: ports for loading and unloading, departure and delivery of shipping for Chinese vessels engaged in foreign trade where the formalities for exit and entry inspection and examination are conducted by personnel sent from other ports; ports where border trade in small amounts and contacts between people are carried out with local governments of neighboring countries; ports restricted to the exit or entry of the local residents in the border areas. It should be noted that in 1998, the State Council cleaned up category-2 ports which were approved by the people's governments at the provincial level, and withdrew authorization from the people's governments at the provincial level to approve category-2 ports. Category-2 ports are non-express ports with no direct access to overseas destinations for various means of transportation. The criteria for this division have been rarely in use now since the approval of category-2 ports has been stopped at the provincial level.

(3) *Classification by geographical locations*

According to different geographical locations, ports in China are divided into coastal ports, inland ports, and border ports. Coastal ports usually refer to the open ports approved by the central government in Beijing, Tianjin, Liaoning, Hebei, Shandong, Jiangsu, Shanghai, Zhejiang, Fujian, Guangdong, Hainan, and other provincial administrative regions. Inland ports usually refer to the open ports approved by the central government in Gansu, Qinghai, Ningxia, Shaanxi, Shanxi, Henan, Hubei, Hunan, Anhui, Chongqing, Sichuan, Guizhou, Jiangxi, and other provincial administrative regions. Border ports usually refer to open ports approved by the central government in Heilongjiang, Jilin, Inner Mongolia, Xinjiang, Tibet, Yunnan, Guangxi, and other provincial administrative regions.

(4) *Classification by degrees of openness*

According to varying degrees of openness, ports in China are divided into fully open ports and restricted open ports. The latter usually refers to one of the following: ports opening only to means of transport from the mainland of China to enter and leave the border; ports opening only to personnel, cargo, goods and means of transport from the mainland of China and neighboring countries to enter and leave the border; ports opening only within a specific period (e.g. seasonal). Fully open ports refer to fully functional ports approved by the central government with no additional restrictions for opening.

In addition to official open ports approved by the State Council, there are measures for opening temporary ports approved by the state port control authorities, allowing temporary entry and exit of personnel, cargo, goods, and means of transport from specific areas during the temporary opening period.

1.1.3 Main features of ports

As gateways for opening up and platforms for cross-border interconnection, ports in China are at the forefront of opening up. With functions of promoting political, economic, diplomatic, scientific, technological, cultural and tourist exchanges, they play an essential role in regional economic and social development. There is no opening up without ports. The level of ports' opening up and development keeps pace with the local economic and social development, consistent with the level of productive forces in a particular period. The degree of ports' opening up directly reflects the degree of openness to the outside world of a country or a region. Through ports' opening up, China goes global and the world gets to know about China. It can be seen that ports, as a special kind of resources, have salient political, economic, social and management attributes, with the following characteristics.

(1) *State sovereignty*

Ports are gateways for foreign exchanges set up by sovereign states in specific geographical locations according to the needs of opening up and development, examined, inspected, quarantined, supervised and managed by state statutory bodies. The power of opening, closing and governing ports, along with ports' executive power, tariff autonomy, inspection right and the like are important manifestations of state sovereignty.

The power to open, close and cancel ports belongs to the central authority and therefore should be approved by the central government. It is subjected to and at the service of the overall political and diplomatic situation of the country and the integral development strategy. The inspection organizations set up by the state and law enforcement authorities at the ports of entry and exit should govern in accordance with the law, providing services for legitimate entry and exit of personnel, cargo, goods, and means of transport; meanwhile, by joining relevant departments, the inspection organizations should prevent and combat illegal entry and exit, drug crimes and smuggling, spread of infectious diseases and epidemics, in order to safeguard the national border, maintain social security and defend national interests and state security.

(2) *Location specificity*

Open ports in modern and contemporary China usually require favorable locations and convenient transportation conditions. Geographical specificity, good natural conditions, rich resources, large hinterland economy, and other comparative advantages all contribute to the formation and development of the world's major ports and the cities they are in. A favorable location is both a prerequisite and a determinant of ports' opening up. Open ports in China generally have favorable locations, with a gradual shift from south to north, from east to west, from coast to inland as the norm, which is consistent with the route of China's regional economic development.

(3) *Direct involvement with foreign affairs*

The direct involvement with foreign affairs manifests itself in that the opening up of ports, especially border ports, involves the central government and local authorities, both domestic and overseas. For example, the opening up and operation of border ports involve bilateral diplomatic relations; water ports and air ports address issues concerning territorial land, water, and airspace sovereignty; issues from inspection, examination, quarantine, supervision, and management of personnel cargo, goods, and means of transport entering and exiting through the ports concern relevant domestic laws, regulations and international conventions as well as the international agreements signed into domestic laws. In addition, it takes consideration and determination from the national level in terms of the overall political, economic and diplomatic situation to answer the following questions: in our nation, which harbors, airports, stations, and cross-border passages can be opened up as ports, and which cannot; which ports can be fully opened and which ports should be opened up with certain restrictions; which ports should be given priority and which ports should be closed or canceled in due time.

(4) *Diversity of functions*

Ports of different transportation modes and types carry different functions. Even among the same type of ports, their functions may vary due to differences in location, resource reserve, and industrial development level, etc., which explains the competition and cooperation between port clusters in a particular region. In terms of the port administrations, inspection authorities, which are stationed at the ports for law enforcement, run and governed directly by the state, perform duties of control, inspection, quarantine, supervision and management on personnel, cargo, goods and means of transport crossing the border, in accordance with the law. Local governments related port-control sectors of county-level and above perform tasks including comprehensive management, coordination and services.

(5) *Engine for hinterland development*

Domestically, open ports are like "growth poles", functioning as the economic engine to the hinterland within certain administrative regions and generating combined effect to play an essential role in promoting economic and social development, adjustment of industrial structure, foreign trade and economic cooperation of port cities. The economic scale of port cities and their hinterland, the change of industrial structure and the closeness of connections between port and hinterland all have a profound influence on the long-term development of ports.

Internationally, since ancient times, opening up to the outside world, building international contacts and participating in world trades are integral to a country's economic and social development. Ports play an active part in the formation and development of the world market, connecting domestic and international markets and resources. As key platforms, ports play a leading role in international exchanges of personnel, culture, merchandise, technology, and capital.

(6) *Traffic efficiency*

To ensure safe, smooth, civil and efficient operation of ports, and provide convenience for the transport of passengers and personnel, specific requirements are formulated concerning business hours, regulations, arrangement, operation, and management. Failure to address congestion and clogging of personnel and means of transport that enter and leave the border, or public emergencies properly and timely once they occur may result in heavy economic losses and serious social consequences.

(7) *Cooperation and coordination*

As special national resources, ports' planning, construction, opening up, management and development should comply with and serve the national interests and overall strategy. Work at ports is multi-layered and multi-faceted, involving various departments and regions. Only through cooperation and coordination, can relevant port organizations (departments) give full play to the overall effectiveness. If they act in isolation, failing to support, cooperate, and comply with integral organization and coordination, the port traffic shall be obstructed with difficulties arising at border crossings.

1.2 Origin of ports in a modern sense

From a historical perspective of global ports' formation and development, the birth of ports is the inevitable result of cross-region commercial trades, cultural and technological bonds, as well as personnel exchanges, closely related to the specific geographical location, development of productive forces in a certain period, corresponding conditions of transportation and other specific factors.

Ports in the modern sense originate from "passes" on the land borders and harbors open to foreign trade in ancient times. China has a long history of establishing customs gates and opening ports, with the earliest records of the land barriers and coastal harbors dating back to the Western Zhou Dynasty (1046-771 BC), Spring and Autumn Period (770-476 BC), and the Warring States Period (475-221 BC), used for political, military and public security purposes. Tracing back to the Western Zhou Dynasty, commerce was listed as one of the "nine professions"[1] undertaken by royal officials. It was in this background that private businesses started to emerge. Nevertheless, for reasons of national security and defense, merchants and other traveling population were under strict control that "law enforcement agents shall conduct a strict inspection, ban outlandish clothing and be aware of foreign languages."[2] "Passes" with functions somewhat similar to modern ports had since come into being. As an ancient Chinese saying goes, "The moon of Qin shines yet over the passes of Han."[3] Here the "passes" refer to posts and gateways, predecessors of today's open ports.

Back to the Qin Dynasty (221-207 BC) and the Han Dynasty (202 BC-AD 220), "passes" on land and harbors at sea were set up and opened up, resulting in the birth of a

---

[1] From *Rites of Zhou* (Zhou Li).

[2] From *the Book of Rites* (Li Ji).

[3] From *The Two Poems on the Frontier* by Wang Changling (698-756) in the Tang Dynasty. The translation of the original text is: "The moon of Qin shines yet over the passes of Han, from all expeditions returned no man. If the Winged General of Dragon City were there, no Hu horses could ever cross Mt. Yin and survive."

Land Silk Road across Eurasia in Northwest and Southwest China, and a Maritime Silk Road across the oceans in the coastal areas of Southeast China. In modern times, China started to open up ports to the outside world after the First Opium War between China and Britain. The Qing government was forced to open five trading ports, namely, Guangzhou, Shanghai, Xiamen, Fuzhou, and Ningbo, according to the Sino-British Treaty of Jiangning (also known as the Treaty of Nanking), marking the birth of open ports in modern times.

1.2.1 Early world trade and the birth of land and waterway ports

Early world trade consisted of local trade and long-distance trade. Interregional trade was carried out mainly through land routes across the central Eurasian continent and sea routes along the Eurasian continental margin, with the help of the domestic transportation network, which was largely comprised of stagecoach routes and canals, and international maritime transport. Most goods were transported by both land and sea. Maritime trade can be traced back to ancient civilization, and trade ports were the earliest ports.

Shipping was then playing a central role in international trade, and international freight was mainly conducted by sea, both of which were impossible without open ports. From a historical perspective, many important ancient ports first appeared along the Mediterranean coast, e.g., the historical site of Port Messaria on the southern coast of Crete in Greece, which still exists today; Port Sidon and Port Tyre (in today's Lebanon) built by the Phoenicians in about 2700 BC on the eastern coast of the Mediterranean Sea; the famous Port of Carthage (in today's Tunisia) on the northern coast of Africa; the Port of Bilex on the western side of the Manichean Peninsula in ancient Greece; Port Alexandria built in 332 BC on the north shore of Egypt and Port Ostia (in today's Italy) built in the mouth of the Tiber River in ancient Rome by Alexander, King of Macedonia. These ports were all open to the outside world at that time.

The rise and fall of land trade largely depended on the social order, overall public security, and the maintenance and safeguarding of commercial roads in a country or a region. When most land routes were operated in good social order and under the control of a strong government, commercial transportation, commodity trading, and merchant safety were well-protected, with commercial trade flourishing as a result; on the contrary, when social disorder, turmoil, and unrest occurred in a country or region, it became largely difficult for commercial transportation, commodity trading, and merchant safety to receive fair protection, resulting in the decline of commercial trade.

9

During specific times, especially during wartime or under foreign invasion, land trade would be affected by various factors. With the decline of commercial land trade and even the interruption of the cross-border land transportation network, commercial trade would generally move to the sea. Due to different modes of transport and trade orientations, both counter-balance and interdependence coexisted between land and maritime trade, as could be seen from the evolvement of the Land and Maritime Silk Roads in China.

1.2.2 Birth of railway ports and air ports

In addition to the earlier land and water ports, with the development of science and technology, and the diversification of transport modes, cross-border railway ports and airports emerged after the 19th century. Following the completion of Britain's first railway in 1825 and its official opening to traffic, London-Paris Airlines launched regular international postal transport in June 1918. Countries around the world set up railway, highway and air ports at specific locations such as international land highway stations, intermodal railway terminals, international airports, and border trade centers.

With the opening of railways and railway ports, land resources were made easier to integrate and optimize, shortening the distances between different countries and regions with expanded markets and enhanced communications. After the First World War, early commercial airlines took off with a small number of air routes, operating mainly between important capitals of European countries and East Asia. It was not until the eve of the Second World War that transatlantic and transpacific air routes were opened. The operation of commercial airlines actually started in the 1940s and 1950s. Thanks to the development in meteorological services, radio communications, radars, and airport construction, aviation has gradually become an essential means of transportation. The birth of airplanes, as well as the opening of international routes and air ports turned "deep chasms into thoroughfares". It can be said that "the wilderness could not have been conquered without roads connecting inland and coastal areas, canals connecting rivers, trans-continental railroads and telegrams, steamships crossing the great rivers and coastal waterways, agricultural machinery cutting up the prairies, and repeating rifle conquering indigenous peoples."[1] The opening up and development of ports, therefore, bridged the gaps and connected the world.

The opening and development of various ports show a profound truth: the opening,

---

[1] Cf. Leften Stavrianos. *The World Since 1500: A Global History*, Eaglewood Cliffs: Prentice Hall, 1971.

rise or fall of ports are closely related to the opening up, rise or fall of a country, a region, and a city, for the rise and fall of ports are like the "barometer" of economic prosperity and decline. Ports prosper only when the nation thrives, and prospering ports bring booming trades. Open ports bring prosperity and development to regional economy while closed ports lead to backwardness and decline of regional development. The opening of ports and the development of export-oriented economy go through boom and bust together.

1.3 Geographical characteristics of land and water areas at China's open ports

As prerequisites, the geographical location, regional features and natural conditions of a country (region) determine and influence the opening up and development of ports in the country (region). The sequence of opening ports is closely related to specific geographical locations and regional features.

1.3.1 Geographical features of China

China is a large country with a large population and vast territory. Geographically, it is situated in the center of the Asia-Pacific region, sitting on the eastern tip of the Eurasian continent and off the west coast of the Pacific Ocean, facing the Pacific Ocean to the southeast and its junction with the Indian Ocean to the south, with the hinterland of the Eurasian continent in the north. With a vast territory of both land and water, China is a large regional country with both continental and oceanic characteristics.

China has the largest number of neighboring countries in the world. There are 20 countries directly adjacent to China on land and at sea, of which 14 are on land, namely North Korea, Russia, Mongolia, Kazakhstan, Kyrgyzstan, Tajikistan, Afghanistan, Pakistan, India, Nepal, Bhutan, Myanmar, Laos, and Vietnam, from north to south counterclockwise. The 6 neighboring countries at sea are South Korea, Japan, Philippines, Malaysia, Brunei, and Indonesia. Among these countries, Vietnam and North Korea are both land and maritime neighbors.

Historically, China has enjoyed a relatively stable territory and a clear border: stretching from Taiwan and the Penghu Islands in the southeast to Lake Balkhash in the northwest, from the Himalaya Mountains in the southwest to the Sakhalin Island in the northeast, from the South China Sea Islands in the south to the outer Hinggan

Mountains in the north. At the present, the four territorial endpoints of both land and sea boundaries in China are: Zengmu Ansha reef in Nansha Islands of Hainan Province as the southernmost point, the central line of the Heilong River main waterway at the northern end of Mohe County in Heilongjiang Province as the northernmost point, Pamir Plateau of the Xinjiang Uygur Autonomous Region as the westernmost point, the junction of central lines of main waterways on the Heilong River and the Wusuli River as the easternmost point. For thousands of years, this beautiful land has been a cherished home to generations of the Chinese nation.

With regard to its terrain and topography, China's contemporary territory spans 5,000 kilometers from east to west, crossing about 62 degrees of longitude and 5,500 kilometers from north to south, running about 50 degrees of latitude. Most areas are in the temperate zone, with only small regions in the tropical and subtropical zone and no regions in the cold zone. Due to the Himalayas orogeny, the terrain of China is high in the west and low in the east, roughly displaying a 3-level ladder-like land distribution from west to east, of which about 32% is highland, 26% plateau, 20% basin, 12% plain and 10% mountain area. Altitude gradually decreases from west to east, with generally high elevation in the northwest and low elevation in the southeast. The west is mainly dominated by mountains, plateaus, and basins while the east is dominated mostly by plains and hills.

With regard to geo-economic space and economic development, there is an evident gradual decrease from east to west of China. Conversely, the distribution of natural resources shows an apparent gradual increase from east to west. Coastal areas in the east have a more developed economy and a relative shortage of resources, because the overall distribution of resources is more favorable to the central and western regions, that is why the west areas with great advantages and potentials, enjoy a fuller space for development and adjustment.

1.3.2 Main characteristics of land territory in China

China has a land territory of more than 9.6 million square kilometers, accounting for 29.4% of the world's total land area. Next to Russia and Canada, China is the world's 3rd largest country, just ahead of the US (with a land area about 937 square kilometers). With a land boundary totaling more than 22,000 kilometers, Table 1–1 shows geo-relations of China's neighboring countries by land.

Table 1-1　　　Geo-relations of China's neighboring countries by land

Name of the neighboring country	World region	Neighboring provinces in China	Main geographical features	Major geo-relations
North Korea	East Asia	Liaoning and Jilin	Located in the northern part of the Korean Peninsula, a peninsular country.	Bordering South Korea on the south, China on the north and Russia on the northeast; surrounded by the sea on three sides, the Sea of Japan on the East (including the East Korea Bay) and the Yellow Sea on the southwest (including the West Korea Bay, off the coast of the Shandong Peninsula).
Russia	Eastern Europe and Northern Asia	Inner Mongolia, Jilin, Heilongjiang, and Xinjiang	Spanning the Eurasian, the largest country in the world. Sea area bordered by the Arctic Ocean to the north, the Pacific Ocean to the east, the Atlantic Ocean to the west, and the Baltic Sea and the Gulf of Finland to the northwest.	Clockwise, the adjacent sea areas: the Caspian Sea, the Black Sea, the Baltic Sea, the Gulf of Finland, the Barents Sea, the Kara Sea, the Laptev Sea, the East Siberian Sea, the Bering Sea, the Okhotsk Sea and the Sea of Japan.
Mongolia	East Asia	Inner Mongolia, Gansu, and Xinjiang	World's second largest landlocked country, surrounded by China and Russia.	No access to the sea, situated on the Mongolian Plateau in Central Asia, bordering China on the east, south and west, and Siberia in Russia on the north.
Kazakhstan	Central Asia	Xinjiang	World's largest landlocked country, spanning Asia and Europe, with the Ural River as its continental boundary.	Bordering Xinjiang on the southeast of China, Russia on the north, Uzbekistan, Turkmenistan and Kyrgyzstan on the south.
Kyrgyzstan	Central Asia	Xinjiang	A landlocked country, bordered by China on the southeast and east, Kazakhstan on the north, Uzbekistan on the west, and Tajikistan on the south.	Located in the hinterland of Eurasia and the northeastern of Central Asia, connecting Eurasia with the stronghold of the Middle East, no access to the sea.
Tajikistan	Central Asia	Xinjiang	A landlocked country.	Located between Afghanistan, Uzbekistan, Kyrgyzstan and China, the smallest in land area of the five Central Asian countries.
Afghanistan	West Asia	Xinjiang	A landlocked country, located in the heart of Asia, at the junction of West Asia, South Asia, and Central Asia, connecting the East and the West.	Bordering Turknrenistan, Uzbekistan and Tajikistan on its north, Wakhan Corridor bordering China and Pakistan on the northeast, and Iran on the west.

(continued)

Name of the neighboring country	World region	Neighboring provinces in China	Main geographical features	Major geo-relations
Pakistan	South Asia	Xinjiang	A coastal country, bordering India, China, Afghanistan, and Iran on the east, north, and west respectively.	Located in the northwest of the South Asian Subcontinent, bordering the Arabian Sea to the south and the Pakistan-controlled Kashmir bordering China.
India	South Asia	Xinjiang and Tibet	A coastal country, the largest country in the South Asian subcontinent, bordering China, Nepal, Bhutan, and Bangladesh on the northeast, Myanmar on the east, Sri Lanka to the southeast across the sea, Pakistan to the northwest, the Bay of Bengal to the east and the Arabian Sea to the west.	Land boundary between the eastern territory of India and the west of China unmarked, along with territorial disputes.
Nepal	South Asia	Tibet	A landlocked country, bordered by Tibet in China on the north and encircled by India to the east, west and south.	Located at the southern foot of the middle Himalayas, with the Himalayas as borderline with China.
Bhutan	South Asia	Tibet	A landlocked country, bordering Tibet in China on the northwest and the north, India and Shannan in China to the west, south and east.	Located in southern Asia, between China and India, on the southern slope of the eastern Himalayas.
Myanmar	Southeast Asia	Tibet and Yunnan	Located in the southeast of Asia and the west of the Indo-China Peninsula, a coastal country with the Andaman Sea to the south and the Bay of Bengal to the southwest.	Bordering Tibet and Yunnan in China on the north and the northeast, Laos and Thailand on the east, India and Bangladesh on the west, the Nujiang River, originating from Nagqu at the southern foot of Tanggula Mountains in China, flowing southward through Tibet and Yunnan in China to Myanmar to be called the Salween River (Thanlwin River).
Laos	Southeast Asia	Yunnan	A landlocked country in the northern part of the Indo-China Peninsula, bordering China on the north, Cambodia on the south, Vietnam on the east, Myanmar and Thailand on the northwest and southwest.	The Lancang River, originating in China, flowing into Myanmar and Laos, called the Mekong River, the largest river in Laos.

(continued)

Name of the neighboring country	World region	Neighboring provinces in China	Main geographical features	Major geo-relations
Vietnam	Southeast Asia	Yunnan and Guangxi	A coastal country located in the eastern part of Indo-China Peninsula in Southeast Asia, bordering Guangxi and Yunnan in China on the north, Laos and Cambodia on the west.	Bordering the South China Sea to the east and south.

Source: Compiled by the author.

1.3.3   Main characteristics of China's water areas

In terms of water areas, China is not only the main sea passage from Northeast Asia to Southeast Asia, but also an important link between the Pacific Ocean and the Indian Ocean. The eastern and southern parts are adjacent to the sea, namely the Bohai Sea, the Yellow Sea, the East China Sea, the South China Sea from northeast to south, joining the Pacific Ocean.

There are more than 5,800 natural rivers of all sizes in China, among which more than 1,600 have catchment areas of more than 1,000 square kilometers. In the inland river basins, the area of rivers out-flowing into the sea accounts for 64% of the total. On account of terrain high in the west and low in the east, along with most mountain ranges running west to east, many out-flowing rivers run from west to east into the sea. The six major oceanic basins from north to south are as follows: the Sea of Okhotsk basin (inflow from the Heilong River, the Songhua River and the Wusuli River), the Sea of Japan basin (inflow from the Tumen River and the Suifen River), the Yellow Sea basin (inflow from the Yalu River and the Huaihe River), the Bohai Sea basin (inflow from the Liaohe River, the Haihe River, the Luanhe River and the Yellow River), the East China Sea basin (inflow from the Yangtze River, the Qiantang River, the Yongjiang River, the Oujiang River and the Minjiang River), and the South China Sea basin (inflow from the Pearl River with its affiliations the Dongjiang, Xijiang and Beijiang Rivers, the Hanjiang River and the Lancang River). In addition, there are other waters including the Nujiang River flowing into the Andaman Sea, the Yarlung Zangbo River flowing into the Bay of Bengal, the Shiquan River and the Xiangquan River flowing into the Arabian Sea, and rivers in the east of Taiwan Island flowing into the Pacific Ocean, the Ertix River flowing into the Arctic Ocean, and the Tarim River, the largest inland river in Xinjiang. Meanwhile, there are more than 2,800 lakes of all sizes.

Only the Bohai Sea, the East China Sea and the South China Sea are marginal seas within the Chinese water areas. Ocean transportation has to pass through straits or waters of island chains to enter the Pacific Ocean and the Indian Ocean since there are no direct sea routes. China's coastal waters join the Sea of Japan via the Korean Strait in the north, enter the Pacific Ocean via the Ryukyu Islands waterways and the Bashi Channel in the east, and link the Indian Ocean through the Strait of Malacca in the southwest. This offshore area boasts important waterways within the Pacific Northwest, direct access to the Indian Ocean as well as many vital international sea lanes and key junctions. In particular, the Diaoyu Islands at the easternmost end of China are the gateway to the Pacific Ocean and the Indian Ocean, and the Nansha Islands at the southernmost end are the hub connecting the Pacific Ocean and the Indian Ocean. Both are strongholds of the national economy and military strategies, and two of the busiest zones of international shipping, most prone to conflicts. China's geo-environment and geo-characteristics determine its important strategic position as well as its vulnerability to foreign invasion, especially the impact of maritime forces, as an intersection of inter-regional contradictions and conflicts at the international level. Table 1–2 shows major Chinese offshore straits and sea channels. Table 1–3 shows major straits of the world and their connected oceans.

Table1–2　　　　　Major Chinese offshore straits and sea channels

Sea area	Channel name	Start	Transfer	Arrival
The Pacific Ocean	China, Japan, and South Korea Channels	China	Japan	South Korea
	North Pacific Channel	China	Japan	The US and Canada
	Central and South Pacific Channels	China	Guam and Hawaii	West coast of the US and the Panama Canal
The Indian Ocean	Northern Indian Ocean Channel	China	Strait of Malacca	Ports in South Asia, Suez Canal and Persian Gulf
	Central Indian Ocean Channel	China		East coast of Central African countries
	South Indian Ocean Channel	China		South Africa and West African countries
Offshore strait channels	Bohai Strait	Essential routes to and from the Bohai Sea and the Yellow Sea		
	Taiwan Strait	Marine transportation hub connecting China's north and south sea areas (the East China Sea and the South China Sea)		
	Strait of Wanshan Archipelago	Sea corridors for foreign exchange in the Pearl River Delta region		
	Qiongzhou Strait	Marine transportation hub connecting the mainland of China with Hainan Special Economic Zone (SEZ) and the only path connecting Guangxi coastal ports to other coastal areas		

Source: State Oceanic Administration, *P.R.C. China Marine Statistical Yearbook (2012)*, Beijing: China Ocean Press, 2013.

Table 1–3   Major straits of the world and their connected oceans

Strait name	Geo-location characteristics	Connected oceans
Strait of Malacca	Running between the Malay Peninsula and Sumatra Island, stretching from southeast to northwest, bordering the Andaman Sea to the northwest in the Indian Ocean and the South China Sea to the southeast; lying at the "crossroads" of Asia and Oceania, the Indian Ocean and the Pacific Ocean, serving as the linking path between Southeast Asia and South Asia, West Asia, Africa, and Europe, as well as the "lifeline" of oil transportation from West Asia and Africa to East Asia; about 1,080 kilometers in length, the widest in the northwest up to 370 kilometers, and the narrowest in the southeast only 37 kilometers.	Connecting the South China Sea with the Indian Ocean, known in Japan as the "lifeline of the sea" and now under the joint jurisdiction of Singapore, Malaysia, and Indonesia.
Strait of Hormuz	Lying in West Asia, connecting the Persian Gulf and the Indian Ocean, the only water channel to enter the Persian Gulf; Iran to the north of the strait and Oman to the south; one of the busiest waterways in the world, known as the world's key junction with important economic and strategic positions, and the only sea passage for oil transportation from the Middle East Gulf to the world.	Connecting the Persian Gulf and the Arabian Sea; an economic, cultural and trading hub between the East and the West since ancient times; regarded as the lifeline of the sea by the West.
English Channel (also known as La Manche Channel)	Separating the UK from France on the European continent, 560 kilometers in length and 240 kilometers in width, with the narrowest part known as the Strait of Dover, only 34 kilometers wide.	Connecting the Atlantic Ocean with the North Sea.
Turkish Straits (also known as the Strait of Black Sea)	An important gateway to the Black Sea and the only channel in the Mediterranean Sea, consisting of the Bosporus Strait, the Sea of Marmara, and the Dardanelles Strait; with a total length of 345 kilometers, stretching from northeast to southwest, as the demarcation line between Asia and Europe; the Bosporus Strait to the northeast and the Dadanelles Strait to the southwest, with the Turkish Inland Sea—the Sea of Marmara in between.	Connecting the Black Sea and the Mediterranean Sea, known as "the throat of the world"; regarded as one of the most important maritime passages in the world during the Cold War by the US and the Soviet Union; regarded as one of the crucial strategic points in Eurasia.
Strait of Gibraltar	Running between the southernmost of Spain and the northwest of Africa, the only sea passage from the Mediterranean coast to the Atlantic Ocean; the narrowest point situating between Point Marroquí in Spain and Point Cires in Morocco, only 13 kilometers wide; totaling about 90 kilometers in length, wide in the west and narrow in the east, the widest point in the west with a width of 43 kilometers and the narrowest point in the east with a width of only 14 kilometers.	The only passage connecting the Mediterranean and the Atlantic Ocean and the dividing line between Europe and Africa.
Mozambique Channel	The longest Channel in the world and an important passage between the South Atlantic and the Indian Ocean.	Connecting the South and North Indian Oceans.

(continued)

Strait name	Geo-location characteristics	Connected oceans
Bering Strait	Running between Cape Dezhnyov at the easternmost point of Asia and Cape Prince of Wales at the westernmost point of America, about 85 kilometers wide and 30-50 meters deep, as a waterway connecting America with Eurasia, and the Pacific Ocean with the Arctic Ocean; serving as the boundaries between two continents (Asia and North America), two countries (Russia and the US) and two peninsulas (Alaska Peninsula and Chukchi Peninsula); from a geopolitical point of view of the Western Pacific, the area covering Bering Strait, the Four Northern Islands, the Sea of Japan in the north, the Diaoyu Islands, Taiwan Island in the middle and the South China Sea and the Strait of Malacca in the south as both a guarantee for American interest and the lifeline of Japanese interests.	Lying between the Pacific Ocean and the Arctic Ocean, the only channel connecting the Arctic Ocean and the Pacific Ocean, also a key junction on the northern sea route in Russia connecting coastal ports in Eurasia.
Korea Strait	Lying between the Korean Peninsula and Kyushu Island in Japan; Korea Strait in the broad sense referring to the entire waterway between the Korean Peninsula and Kyushu Island Korea Strait in the narrow sense referring to the waterway between the Korean Peninsula and the Tsushima Island, which is 67 kilometers wide.	A key passage connecting the Yellow Sea, the East China Sea and the Sea of Japan.
Drake Passage	Lying between the southernmost tip of South America and the South Shetland Islands in Antarctica, 300 kilometers long and 900-950 kilometers wide, with an average water depth of 3,400 meters and the deepest depth of 4,750 meters, adjacent to Chile and Argentina; an important sea lane before the opening of the Panama Canal connecting the Pacific Ocean and the Atlantic Ocean, and the fourth largest ocean corridor of energy supply in the world, occupying a vital strategic position; playing a declining role in transportation after the opening of the Panama Canal, but still the nearest sea route from South America to Antarctica.	Connecting the Pacific Ocean and the Atlantic Ocean, an important channel for the two oceans to connect in the south, also the boundary between South America and Antarctica; Djibouti in the strait region regarded as a " strategic spot of vital military importance".
Bab el-Mandeb Strait (Mandab Strait)	Lying at the southwestern end of the Arabian Peninsula in Asia, between Yemen, which is to the southern end of the Red Sea and Djibouti on the African Continent; after the opening of Suez Canal, serving as a sea transportation hub of vital strategic position, from the Atlantic to the Mediterranean Sea, through the Suez Canal and the Red Sea to the Indian Ocean.	The vital channel connecting the Red Sea, the Gulf of Aden and the Indian Ocean.

Source: Compiled by the author.

1.3.4 Natural conditions for navigation in China

In the sailing era, the discovery and utilization of the monsoon were of great significance to maritime trade. China is a country with a typical monsoon climate and northerly winds prevail in the coastal areas in winter (usually from December to March of the following year). Caused primarily by the Mongolian and Siberian high pressure, the northerly airflows are constant in wind direction and strong in wind power, with an average strength of scale 4 to scale 5. In summer (usually from June to August) southerly winds prevail, unstable in direction and weak in power, with an average strength of scale 3 to scale 4. The southerly airflows in summer are mostly generated by the tropical marine air mass under the Pacific high pressure (southeast monsoon) and the low equatorial air mass in the Indian Ocean under the low Indian pressure (southwest monsoon). Spring (mostly April to May) and Autumn (mostly September to October) are the transitional periods when winter monsoons transform into summer monsoons and summer monsoons transform into winter monsoons respectively. Monsoon changes between seasons are significant and are affected by the corresponding land-sea distribution, terrain and topography.

In consideration of the navigation conditions in China's coastal areas, regular warm currents, coastal currents and monsoon currents abound in the sea areas. As for the warm currents, the North Equatorial Warm Current of the Pacific Ocean is divided into two streams as it approaches the eastern coast of the Philippine Islands. The small stream flows southward through the eastern coast of Mindanao Island. The large stream flows to the northwest or the north along the eastern coast of Luzon Island, and becomes the world-famous Kuroshio (also known as the Japan Current). The mainstream of Kuroshio flows northward and northeastward, in between the Taiwan Island and the Yonagunijima Island of the Ryukyu Islands, into the East China Sea, and then into the Pacific Ocean to reach the coast of North America through the Tokara Strait, which is between Yakushima Island, south of Kyushu Island and Amami Island in Japan. As for the coastal currents, they flow from north to south in the north of the Yangtze River estuary, and pass through the Bohai Strait from north to south all year round. Those along the Yellow Sea coasts are formed by the Bohai Sea coastal currents flowing southward around the Shandong Peninsula. As for the monsoon currents, the airflows vary with the monsoons. During the northeast monsoon period, currents mainly flow southward, and during the southwest monsoon period, they usually go northward. During the periods of seasonal changes, the flow direction and velocity are often unstable. These are navigation conditions which are basic to and influential on offshore and ocean voyages in the coastal regions of China.

1.4 Interdependence between China's open ports and their geographical space

The spatiotemporal order, layout, and development of open ports in China are closely related to the specific stages of development, topographic features, locations of the ports, transportation convenience, construction investments, operation and management difficulties, among others.

1.4.1 Terrain and topography as primary determinants and constraints of open ports

According to the historical law of opening up and economic development in China and other countries in the world, in most cases, ports and towns with more convenient conditions of transportation, richer natural resources, and larger hinterland area were more prone to opening up to the outside world and leading in development. Low elevation zones, coastal areas, and plains were generally opened up earlier compared with zones of higher elevation, hilly land, and basins.

With regard to the overall terrain and topography of China, due to the Himalayas orogeny, the terrain of China is high in the west and low in the east, roughly displaying a 3-grade ladder-like land distribution from west to east with a gradual decrease of altitude. The northwest is generally high in elevation whereas the southeast is low. The west is mainly dominated by mountainous regions, plateaus and basins while the east is dominated mostly by plains and hills. The first ladder includes the Plateau of Tibet and the Qaidam Basin, located to the south of the Kunlun Mountains and the Qilian Mountains, west of the Hengduan Mountains, and north of the Himalaya Mountains, with an average elevation of more than 4,000 meters. The second ladder includes the Inner Mongolia Plateau, Loess Plateau, Yunnan-Guizhou Plateau and the Junggar Basin, Sichuan Basin and the Tarim Basin, with an average elevation of about 1,000-2,000 meters. The third ladder is primarily composed of plains and hills, including the Northeast Plain, the North China Plain, the middle and lower Yangtze Plain and the East Liaoning Hills, Shandong Hills and the Southeast Hills, most of which are below 500 meters above sea level. The third ladder continues to extend to the ocean, forming an offshore continental shelf. The boundary between the first and second ladders is along the Kunlun Mountains–Altun Mountains–Qilian Mountains–Hengduan Mountains, and the boundary between the second and third ladders is along the Greater Khingan

Range–Taihang Mountains–Wushan Mountains–Xuefeng Mountains. Beijing is situated in the last platform of the lowest land ladder in China.

1.4.2 Vulnerability of open ports to constraints of the regional economy

Apart from influences of natural conditions as terrain and topography, open ports are influenced and restricted by the degree of regional economic development. Since the opening of the "five treaty ports" in modern times, due to historical reasons, the eastern coastal areas of China have greatly benefited from the convenience of marine transportation, which contributes to the operation of maritime affairs and exchanges with overseas countries. For a long time, due to the introduction of foreign capitals, cultures, technologies as well as their huge impacts, modern industries and commercial trades have enjoyed an early and intensive development, more advanced transportation, infrastructure, commodity trading, market services, etc. than the central and western regions, higher in labor productivity, degree of marketization and industrialization.

On the other hand, the central position of the western region on the Eurasian continent facilitates its direct contacts with Central Asia, Western Asia, and the European continent. As for economic development, from the east to west, there is an evident gradual decrease. Conversely, the distribution of natural resources shows an apparent gradual increase from east to west. Coastal areas in the east have a more developed economy and a relative shortage of resources, whereas the overall distribution of resources is more favorable to the central and western regions. That is why the west areas with great advantages and potentials have much room for development and adjustment.

It can be seen that China's topographic conditions and regional economic structure determine that the opening of ports should start from the coastal areas at a low elevation, with evident geographical advantages, convenient transportation and a more developed economy, and then expand gradually to the central hinterland and western borders in a graded manner. The historical practices of ports' opening up and development in China have proved that the rise or fall of ports are influenced by many factors, such as political, economic, social and natural conditions. On one hand, ideal natural conditions, preferred geographical locations, smooth transportation networks, vast economic hinterland, and flourishing regional economy all lay crucial foundations for the development of ports. On the other hand, the decline of ports can be attributed to factors including the shift of economic center, reorientation of foreign trade routes, shortage of hinterland resources, effects of wars, weak management system, ineffective policies and measures, work inefficiency and poor services at ports.

1.5 Historical view on the opening up and development of China's ports since modern times

Gong Zizhen, also named Gong Ding'an, a reformation-minded Chinese writer of the Qing Dynasty, pointed out in his essay "On Learning from History", which is included in the book *A Sequel of Ding'an*, "To know the Dao (the Way), one must first know the history. To destroy a nation, one must first destroy its history. To corrupt law and social order, one must first destroy the history. To suppress human talents and their enlightenment, one must first destroy their history. To destroy the ancestors of a nation, one must first destroy its history." Italian historian Benedetto Croce (1866-1952) put forward a great proposition in his book *History: Its Theory and Practice* in 1917: "All history is contemporary history." China's opening to the outside world in modern times began with the First Opium War between China and Britain. Along with ports' opening up came the sufferings of modern China.

1.5.1 Looking back: modern China in adversities

As an old Chinese maxim goes, a person is made stronger in hardships, just as trials and tribulations serve only to revitalize a nation. In spite of the fact that China had been the regional center of East Asia from the first unification of China in the 3rd century BC by the First Emperor of the Qin Dynasty Ying Zheng with the establishment of the basic structure of the political system for more than 2,000 years to the collapse of the Qing Dynasty in 1911, modern China had experienced "fluctuations which had never emerged in thousands of years".[1] Facing "ever-stronger enemies in thousand years",

---

[1] On June 30, 1895, Kang Youwei submitted a fourth written statement to the Qing Emperor, in which he wrote, if ocean-going routes had not been opened up in the world and western countries had not come to China, little changes would have happened in the next thousand years. However, with all this cross-border connectivity, it seemed that all of a sudden Western powers were coveting the Qing Empire...Not only did people outside the Qing government feel strongly about the change of the world, but many insightful government officials proposed that preparations be made for defense. So, *I Ching or The Book of Changes* was of great value for its sense of time, and *The Book of Guan Zi* was precious for its stress on observing neighbors. Guan Zi said, the survival or destruction of a country depended on its neighboring countries. If the country did not act properly, the neighboring enemy would win.... When a great dynasty unified a country, it was like a man lying in the chamber with the mosquito net and could have a good sleep. I read and knew about the Spring and Autumn Period and the Warring States Period in China, when various vassal states fought each other instead of being as centralized as the Han, Tang, Song and Ming dynasties. It was indeed a great change of times that had not occurred in thousands of years.

China encountered an incredibly dire historical situation of life and death and went through tremendous difficulties for its rebirth. It was tragic that the Chinese nation suffered gravely in this catastrophe. A weak state with almost collapsed traditional culture, the old China's backwardness led to its being exploited and bullied. It was also revolutionary that Chinese people strived to survive, risked their lives to resist foreign aggressions, and endeavored to rejuvenate the nation after a long and arduous struggle. History always repeats itself. The development of China and the world since modern times is a thought-provoking mirror that should be respected, remembered and never betrayed.

Shakespeare once said: "What's past is prologue." In March 2014, Chinese President Xi Jinping visited Germany and made a speech at the Körber Foundation, stressing that: "History is the best teacher, as it faithfully records the footprints of each country, and provides inspirations for the future development of each country. In the period of more than 100 years from the Opium War in 1840 to the founding of the People's Republic of China in 1949, China was plagued by incessant wars and conflicts. The alteration of internal warfare and foreign invasions brought unbearable sufferings to the Chinese people. The war of aggression against China waged by Japanese militarists alone caused more than 35 million casualties among the Chinese army and people. This tragic history has left unforgettable memories of pain to the Chinese people."[1] Lenin once said that forgetting the past means betrayal. History should not be forgotten, nor should the past be dwelled upon. Instead, it is necessary to face the future with lessons learned from the history, and look forward to new achievements. The foundations for today's constant progress are the importance attached to the history, reflections on the past and lessons drawn from prior experiences.

1.5.2 Profound influence of the opening up and development of ports on China in modern times

Ports, as the gateway and window to the opening up of a country (region), a bridge for foreign economic and trade cooperation and social exchanges, and an important junction connecting the internal and external markets and resources, serve as the "catalyst" and "incubator" in promoting economic and social development.

The opening of China's modern ports began in the First Opium War between China and Britain in 1840, which was a violent collision between the western industrial civilization and the oriental adherence to the unchanging theory of "nature does not

---

[1] http://cpc.people.com.cn/n/204/0330/c64094-24773108.html.

change, neither does the way", and also a barbaric conquest of the traditional agricultural society by the new industrial revolution. After the defeat, the Qing government was forced to sign the Treaty of Nanking with Britain and open five coastal port cities in Guangzhou, Shanghai, Xiamen, Fuzhou and Ningbo as trading ports. Since then, Britain, France, the United States, Germany, Russia, Japan, and other countries had forced China to open other ports one after another under various unequal treaties and charters. Due to external pressures and changing situations, an increasing number of treaty ports and non-treaty ports had been opened up in China, gradually spreading from coastal and border areas to areas along rivers and even the vast inland areas. Since the founding of the People's Republic of China, especially since the reform and opening up, China's open ports have played an important role in the process of reform and opening up, greatly promoted cooperation and exchanges with other countries in the world, and made remarkable achievements.

In the late modern times, the earliest open ports in China's coastal and border areas, along with cities where these ports were located, were not only where foreign productive forces were first introduced with the early development of the modern economy, but also the "growth poles" connecting domestic and foreign markets and promoting the development of the hinterland. In addition, their ports served as the main hub for domestic and international trade and transportation. Great changes have taken place in Chinese society since 1840 due to ports' opening up in China's coastal areas and the influences of port cities. Positive interactions between open ports and their hinterlands have greatly promoted the development of the regional economy and society. Today's open ports are the continuation and development of those in the past. History still plays a vital role in the opening up and development of ports today, and the latter will undoubtedly have a significant impact on China's future development.

1.5.3 Historical lessons from the last century for China's development

China was deteriorating after the late Qing Dynasty, which might be an external manifestation that the fully developed oriental civilization of agriculture and farming had turned from prosperity to decline. The oriental civilization of agriculture and farming always emphasized the importance of agriculture while belittling commerce, valuing self-sufficiency and national integration, whereas the western industrial civilization attached great importance to mercantilism, foreign trade, and world market. Material plundering and external colonial expansion used to be the key words of the western civilization. In the transformation from agricultural and farming civilization to industrial civilization, which was a specific historical development stage, the Qing Dynasty closed the borders and locked the country for a long time. Lacking both knowledge and understanding of the outside world, the rulers were self-assured to be governing a "celestial empire", with both arrogance and prejudice towards the western countries. Ignorance of the outside world and failure to improve the governance of internal affairs lay at the root of the national disgrace which China had suffered in modern times. As an old saying goes, "False tranquility of one day results in a great disaster for hundreds of years." Beginning with the First Opium War, the oriental agricultural and farming civilization led by China was bitterly defeated by the western modern industrial civilization led by Britain, which plunged China into a semi-colonial and semi-colonial society for several hundred years. This century-long shame is the best historical lesson to be learned.

In contrast to China's decadence in modern times, Britain and Japan were two typical examples among both eastern and western countries that flourished at sea and became sea powers through reform. In the past 500 years, despite an island country, Britain became the leader and protagonist of modern history, as the first modern country in the world with centralized maritime, industrial and colonial hegemonies. From the Industrial Revolution to the 20th century, Britain was a glorious world power for 200 consecutive years, building an unprecedented empire on which "the sun never sets", exerting profound influences on most countries across five continents through colonial activities around the world. Japan, also an island country, always subjected itself to the powerful countries in history, believing in beggar-thy-neighbor and territorial expansion. After the Meiji Restoration, Japan broke away from Asia and joined Europe, going through westernization, industrialization, and capitalization. No efforts were spared to launch a series of aggressions and expansions against its Asian neighbors, which led Japan on the way of imperialist aggression to militarism and expansionism, with the ambition of conquering East Asia and invading the rest of the world. History always repeats in a new situation with a new form. As Alan Beattie, an economist at the former Bank of England says, it is undoubtedly of great value to study the history of a particular period of time in the past, and the events or crises that occurred only once in a century. Similar circumstances and situations may occur in different historical periods, and comparative studies of history are of great significance to policymakers.

Chinese people believe that history is thought-provoking and adversity is spirit-lifting. With a look back on the past century and a look forward to the great cause of the national rejuvenation, ups and downs in history and reality are like ebbs and flows.

How should people in China today view the past with self-examination and introspections in a historical, dialectical and comprehensive manner? How to conform to the general trend of world development, find the niche in the globalization, take pragmatic actions towards progress, enrich the people and strengthen the country with an international outlook, strategic thinking, and clear vision? Countries rise and fall in cycles of boom and bust, which has far-reaching significance and profound implications for the Chinese people who have experienced epoch-making transformations and changes of dynasties. Great wisdom transcends time. Many events today have their historical counterparts, while many historical events are reflections of the reality.

The unforgettable past is a guide for the future. "The rises and falls of ancient times are deeply remembered in the heart. The gains and losses of the current times are never left behind" and "The smart changes with the times and the wise acts based on the facts."[1] Only by remembering the historical experience, reflecting on historical lessons and warnings and responding with wisdom and deliberation, can past lessons be learned for understanding the present. History should be studied for progress today. No efforts should be spared to achieve the Two Centenary Goals and realize the Chinese Dream of the great rejuvenation of the Chinese nation.

1.6 Attention from the CPC Central Committee and the State Council after the founding of the People's Republic of China

Han Feizi the ancient sage said: "Affairs should be addressed locally, while power should be centralized; A wise ruler has all the power, whom officials far and near come to serve."[2] After the founding of the People's Republic of China, both before and since the start of the reform and opening up, open ports in different historical periods were in different domestic and foreign situations, with dissimilar objectives and tasks, varying in scales and numbers, bringing different political influences, economic benefits, and practical effects. However, in view of the indispensable role of open ports in promoting economic and trade cooperation, enhancing cultural, scientific and technological exchanges, and facilitating interactions and communications, the Central Committee of

---

[1] From the twelfth essay of the second volume of *On Salt and Iron* by Huan Kuan, an essayist in the late Western Han Dynasty.

[2] From *Han Fei Zi·Yang Quan* (On Authority).

the CPC and the State Council have always attached great importance to ports in all periods of development, laying a solid foundation for a healthy, sustainable and rapid development of planning, construction, opening, operation and management of ports.

1.6.1 Before the reform and opening up

As early as 1973, with the approval of Mao Zedong, the State Council issued the "Notice on the Situation of Ports and Opinions for Improvement", which put forward clear and specific requirements for further improvement of ports in China. In the early years of reform and opening up, the State Economic Commission had carried out domestic and foreign investigations on ports and put forward policy proposals to the State Council, laying a solid foundation for strengthening the organization, leadership, and administration of ports after the reform and opening up.

1.6.2 From the start of reform and opening up to the 18th CPC National Congress

Since the start of reform and opening up, the State Council had strengthened the organization and leadership of ports. In 1978, the State Council promulgated "Notice on Strengthening the Organization and Leadership of Harbors" and established the Leading Group and Office of the State Council. The coastal provinces (autonomous regions and municipalities directly under the central government) also strengthened the organization and leadership of ports. In early 1984, the State Council issued the "Notice on Further Strengthening the Leadership of Port Work", renaming the Harbor Leading Groups of the State Council as Port Leading Group of the State Council, headed by Li Peng, then Vice-Premier of the State Council. After that, ports in China were under the direct leadership of Li Lanqing and other division leaders of the State Council. In 2003, then Premier Wen Jiabao of the State Council proposed at the Central Economic Work Conference to "optimize the port management system and improve customs clearance efficiency". In July 2006, when visiting the General Administration of Customs, Wen Jiabao stressed that the customs should give full play to its leading role as a functional department of port management, continue to deepen the reform of port management system and strengthen the guidance, coordination, and management of ports.

1.6.3 After the 18th CPC National Congress

After the 18th National Congress of the Communist Party of China, the opening and development of ports entered a new historical stage. President Xi Jinping, General Secretary of the CPC Central Committee, Premier Li Keqiang of the State Council, Member of the Standing Committee of the Political Bureau of the CPC Central Committee, and other leading members of the CPC Central Committee attached great importance to port work, inspected the ports on a number of occasions during their local visits and gave important instructions on port work, charting the courses of development for the time being and the time to come. In December 2014, in accordance with the "Decision of the Central Committee of the Communist Party of China on Several Major Issues Concerning Comprehensively Deepening the Reform", as well as decisions and arrangements of the State Council, to implement that "efforts should be made to promote cooperation in customs clearance between inland areas and coastal and border areas, so as to realize exchanges of information, mutual recognition of supervision, and mutual assistance in law enforcement between port management departments in all areas", the State Council issued "Notice to Promote Construction for Greater Customs Clearance", as a starting point for promoting the modernization of a comprehensive port management system and its governance capacity. In April 2015, the State Council promulgated "Opinions of the State Council on Improving Port Administration to Support Foreign Trade Development", emphasizing the need to optimize port services, promote stable growth of foreign trade, strengthen port constructions, and facilitate the transformation and upgrading of foreign trade, in order to deepen port cooperation, improve the environment for foreign trade development and expand the opening of ports. The level of opening up to the outside world should be improved to consolidate the port foundation, expand the capacity for economic and social development, and strengthen the organization and leadership of the port operation.

In June 2015, the State Council approved the establishment of an inter-ministerial joint meeting system for port work, with one of the State Council leaders in charge of ports as the convener of the joint meeting, the Minister of Customs and the Deputy Secretary-General of the State Council assisting in port work as the deputy convener, and leaders of relevant sectors as members of the joint meeting. This arrangement further strengthened the organization and leadership at the national level, with enhanced inter-departmental cooperation, improved efficiency, and promoted safety and convenience. In 2016, Premier Li Keqiang, in his report on the work of the central government, made deployment requirements for the construction of ports as the "single window" in international trade.

In conclusion, from the 18th National Congress of the CPC onward, with the great attention from and correct leadership of the CPC Central Committee and the State Council, a series of new visions, thoughts and strategies on governing the country put forward by General Secretary Xi Jinping was put into practice in port operation. New principles of innovative, coordinated, green, open and shared development were implemented and closely centered on the overall political, economic and diplomatic situation in China. Greater awareness, conscious actions and a sense of responsibility contributed to the strengthening of the top-level design, with attention to the overall coordination. Persistence in reform and innovation was combined with a focus on practices and explorations, for making a new leap at the new start. Open ports have played an active role in serving and promoting the implementation of national strategies such as the Yangtze River Economic Belt and the coordinated development of Beijing–Tianjin–Hebei region, as well as international cooperation programs like the Belt and Road Initiative. Positive results have been achieved in terms of port reform, innovation and development. Entering a new stage of development, ports have made remarkable contributions to the economic and social development of the country and all its regions.

Chapter 2
Open Ports in Ancient China and Their Development

In China's history of several thousand years, three revolutions fundamentally changed China's political system and social structure. The first great revolution took place in 221 BC, the same year Ying Zheng, the First Emperor of the Qin Dynasty, unified China and founded the first united centralized feudal state in Chinese history. The second revolution took place in 1911, in which revolution led by Sun Yat-sen overthrew the Qing government, ended the feudal rule and established the Republic of China. The third revolution took place in 1949 when the Communist Party of China led people of the whole country to end the semi-feudal and semi-colonial society and founded the People's Republic of China. In ancient, modern and contemporary times, ports which were open to the outside world in different historical periods vary, so do their development paths, both bearing distinctive features of the times.

2.1 Development of sea and land transportation during the pre–Qin period

According to historical records, tracing back the origins of China's current territories, the Yellow River basin and the Central Plains were first developed by the Han ethnic minority; the coastal areas by Laiyi, Xuyi, Huaiyi, Dongyi and other ethnic groups; the Yangtze River, Pearl River, and Minjiang River basins by the Miao and Yao ethnic groups; Tibet and Qinghai by the Tibetan ethnic minority; the southwest by the Yi and other ethnic groups in the area; the northeast by the Donghu ethnic groups; Inner Mongolia and other northern areas by the Xiongnu, Xianbei, Rouran, Turks, Uyghur and Mongolian; the northwest by the Hui ethnic minority and other northwestern ethnic groups; Hainan Island by the Li ethnic minority, and Taiwan Island by the Gaoshan ethnic minority. China's territory today is the outcome of concerted efforts made by all ethnic groups of the Chinese nation, who braved thorny paths, hacked their ways through mountains[1], expanded borders, cultivated lands, communicated with one another and created civilizations.

In terms of marine traffic in the pre-Qin period, with the development of shipbuilding and offshore navigation technology, China started friendly exchanges with neighboring countries such as Korea and Japan. According to *Legends of Mountains and Seas*, "The Gai Kingdom[2] is to the south of the Yan State and the north of Japan, which belongs to the Yan State." In the Spring and Autumn Period and the Warring States Period, Chinese people had already known the East China Sea route to Japan from China's coastal ports via the Korean Peninsula. Ancient Chinese people conducted exchanges by the sea with people in Korea and Japan, bringing advanced technologies and tools of production, as well as the coastal culture of North China, which promoted the development of Korean and Japanese civilizations.

In terms of land transportation in the pre-Qin period, there was an ancient Silk Road connecting the nomad tribes in northwest of China according to archaeological discoveries, running from the Hexi Corridor to the northern foot of the Tianshan Mountains, over the Altai Mountains and through the Amu Darya and the Iranian Plateau, and ultimately to the Mediterranean. This early Silk Road coincided with Zhang Qian's route to the West in the Han Dynasty. However, during the Spring and Autumn Period and the Warring States Period, policies, currencies and measurements varied among different vassal states. Cross-regional exchanges of goods and merchandise were thus restricted, and heavy taxes were levied at commercial and traveling "passes". All of the above affected the opening up, the internal reform and the development of agriculture, farming, industry and commerce.

---

[1] From *Historical Records: Five Emperors*: "If there were any rebels in the world, Yellow Emperor would go on expeditions to suppress them. After the enemies were put down, the army would leave for another place. Mountains were hacked to make ways, and the army would never settle in one place." "Yellow Emperor went east to the East China Sea and climbed Mount Maru and Mount Tai. He went west to Kongtong and climbed Jitou Mountain. He went south to the Yangtze River and climbed Xiongshan and Xiangshan mountains. He went north and expelled the Xunyu tribe. After meeting with his lords at Busan, Yellow Emperor built a city at the foot of the Zhulu Mountain. He migrated everywhere and had no fixed residence."

[2] The Gai Kingdom is in the east of Kaema Highlands in North Korea today.

2.2 Shaping of trading routes of the Land Silk Road in the Han Dynasty

China, the birthplace and hometown of silk, is the first country in the world to breed silkworms and weave silk. Silk, which the fairest clothes are made of, is the representative of the earliest Chinese merchandise exported by both sea and land. The transportation of silk opened up the famous Silk Road. Back to as early as the Western Han Dynasty, Zhang Qian's journey to the Western Regions opened up the road to the West on land, while in the sea area Guangzhou Port was opened up for trade with Southeast Asia, West Asia and the coastal countries of the Indian Ocean. During the heyday of the Western Han Dynasty, the central government dispatched officials directly to conduct sizable overland border trade and overseas trade.

The word "Western Regions", first appearing in the book *Records of the Historian* (*Shi Ji*) written by Sima Qian, was a general term referring to the areas west of Yangguan Pass and Yumen Pass in Gansu Province, or in fact the "Northwest state" beyond the direct jurisdiction of the Han Dynasty. The word is used in broad and narrow senses nowadays. In the narrow sense, "Western Regions" refer to the vast area west of Yangguan Pass and Yumen Pass, east of the Congling Mountains[1] and south and north of the Tianshan Mountains. In the broad sense, "Western Regions" refer to regions, besides those in the narrow sense, including central and western Asia, the Indian Peninsula, eastern Europe, and northern Africa. The Western Regions, with its special geographical location, became the hub of transportation and communication between the East and the West in ancient times.

2.2.1 Major roads connecting the East and the West opened up by Zhang Qian's journey to the Western Regions

In the Qin and Han dynasties, the Xiongnu (the Huns) established the most powerful regime of all ethnic powers around the Central Plains. Around the 3rd century BC, the Xiongnu rose from north and south of the northern desert, next to Donghu on the east, which was to the north of the Xar Moron River, Dingling on the north, which was near Lake Baikal, Selenga River on the west, and the Great Wall on the south,

---

[1] A joint name for the Pamirs Plateau, Kunlun Mountains, and the western slope of the Karakoram Mountain Range today.

which was built by the states of Qin, Zhao and Yan in the Warring States Period, establishing a powerful nomadic regime on the northern grasslands. Since its establishment, the Western Han Dynasty had been threatened and harassed by the northern Xiongnu for a long time. Despite measures taken at that time in exchange for temporary peace along the border, such as *Heqin* (making peace with rulers of ethnic groups in the border areas by marriage) and the opening of border markets, there was no guarantee for long-term external security. From the reign of Emperor Wen and Emperor Jing to the reign of Emperor Wu of the Han Dynasty, the state was rich and powerful. Emperor Wu made active plans to fight off the Xiongnu. Therefore, finding out more about the Xiongnu through on-spot investigations, making connections and alliances with countries in the Western Regions, opening up the Hexi Corridor, and spreading kindness and authority of the Han Dynasty became top priorities. In this circumstance, Zhang Qian was sent to the Western Regions.

Before the Han Dynasty, due to obstacles presented by high mountains, deserts, and wars, dynasties established in the Central Plains had not found a smooth road to the West. Emperor Wu of the Han Dynasty, for the sake of eradicating Xiongnu's threats to the inland, decided to send delegates to the Western Regions and expand territories by virtue of national wealth, financial abundance and military strength. In 138 BC, Zhang Qian was sent to the Western Regions. Going through tremendous hardships and difficulties, he entered Yanqi, Qiuci (now Kuqa) and Shule (now Kashgar) via Cheshi Kingdom (now Turpan Basin). He climbed over the Congling Mountains and arrived at Dayuan[1], Kangju[2], Darouzhi[3], and Daxia[4]. The first mission took him 13 years to return to Han. In his second mission, he arrived in Wusun kingdom[5] via the Hexi Corridor under the jurisdiction of the Western Han Dynasty and conducted friendly interactions with Dayuan, Kangju, Darouzhi, Daxia, Anxi[6], and Shendu[7].

---

[1] The specific location of the state of Dayuan was in the Ferghana Basin, which was in the border area of Uzbekistan, Tajikistan and Kyrgyzstan, and now in the eastern part of Uzbekistan. The capital of Dayuan was the city of Ershi, the city of Ashart in Turkmenistan today.

[2] Now between the Lake Balkhash and the Aral Sea, in Turkmenistan.

[3] Now in Tajikistan and Kashmir of Afghanistan.

[4] Located in the south of the Amu Darya and north of Hindu Kush, now in the northern part of Afghanistan.

[5] It is located in the southeast of Lake Balkhash, the Ili River Basin and the Amu Darya in Central Asia.

[6] The Parthian Empire of Persia, now in Iran, in the middle of the Silk Road and a critical position connecting the East and West.

[7] The first Chinese translation of the name of ancient India, which was later in Chinese classic literature also translated as Sindhu, Sindu, Xintou, Xindu, Shindu, Tianzhu, Xiandou, India, etc. It is located west of Pamir, including the South Asian Subcontinent east of the Indian River.

Over more than 30 years, Zhang Qian had carried out diplomatic missions twice to the Western Regions and once to Yunnan. He was knighted as Bowanghou (Marquess of Broad Vision) and credited in history with the achievement of "Zaokong"[1]. "Zao" means "to open", and "kong" means "to smoothen". "Zaokong" therefore means to open up, in this context, a smooth pass to the outside world connecting the central state with countries in the Western Regions for communications, interactions and exchanges, and a major traffic route linking the East and the West across the Eurasian Inland. This East-West road later became what is known as the Silk Road, providing favorable conditions for the opening up of the central state, which was an unprecedented achievement.

The East-West road, which was opened up by Zhang Qian's journey to the Western Regions, started from Chang'an and ran westward along the Hexi Corridor via Wuwei, Zhangye, Jiuquan and Dunhuang. It was then divided into two roads. One was called the South Road, which started from Yangguan Pass, stretching westward along the north foot of the Kunlun Mountains and through Loulan (later called Shanshan, now in the northeast of Ruoqiang), Yutian (now Hotan), Shache, Puli (now Taxkorgan), over the Congling (the Pamirs Plateau) to Darouzhi, and then going southward to Shendu and westward to Anxi, reaching the east coast of the Mediterranean. The other was the North Road, which started from Yumen Pass, ran westward along the South Tianshan Road, via Chesheqian Kingdom to Yanqi, Guhei (now Aksu), Shule, over the Congling to Dayuan, and went northwest to Kangju and Aorsi and southwest to Darouzhi, Anxi, reaching Daqin (the ancient Roman Empire) in the Mediterranean.

After the opening of this important East-West road, diplomatic corps sent by the Han Dynasty to the West Regions and trade caravans were in an endless stream. Silk, iron, and other commodities from the East were exchanged with spices, jewelry and other specialties from the West through bartering and trading. Economic and cultural exchanges between the East and the West experienced an unprecedented boom, and the world civilization made advances through integration. Thus, an international commercial route across Eurasia came into being. The brilliance of Chinese civilization spread to not only the north and south of Tianshan Mountains but also to the south of the Black Sea and the Caspian Sea, to blend with the glory of Western European civilization.

---

[1] From *Biography of Zhang Qian* in *History of the Former Han Dynasty*, "After Zhang Qian opened up the road to Western Regions, many envoys sent abroad were called 'Bowanghou.' Good relationships had been established and foreign countries trusted them."

After Zhang Qian's mission to the Western Regions opened up the Silk Road, the road witnessed not only hardships in the initial period, but also peaceful and prosperous scenes where " the frontier gates were closed, people were many, and cattle and horses were everywhere". In the meantime, the stories of Ban Chao and his son travelling to the Western Regions three times[1] and Gan Ying's visit to Daqin[2] were passed down to later generations. Ban Chao and his son Ban Yong held themselves responsible for Western Han's territorial expansions. Ban Chao gave up his literary pursuits and joined the army. He was dispatched to pacify the countries in the Western Regions and to develop the areas further. He held several posts, one was being the Guardian of the Western Regions and was knighted as Dingyuanhou (Marquess of Securing the Remote). His contributions to the promotion of Sino-Western friendship, the exploration of the Asia-Europe passageway and the maintenance of the Silk Road were among the greatest after Zhang Qian. Despite that Zhang Qian, Ban Chao, Gan Ying, and others went to the Western Regions for military and political purposes, they unexpectedly opened up a land trade and transportation route across the Eurasian continent, which was the world-famous

---

[1] In the 1st century, the Xiongnu rebelled because Wang Mang lowered their political status and diplomatic benefits. The Silk Road was in war. With conflicts arising between the Hans and the Xiongnu, the road to the West was blocked. In 73 (16th year of Yongping in Eastern Han Dynasty), Emperor Mingdi of the Han Dynasty decided to resume his jurisdiction over the Western Regions. Ban Chao was dispatched with a group of officials to pacify the Western Regions. They arrived in Shanshan, Yutian, Shule, Kangju, Shache, Rouzhi, Qiuci, Yanqi and other countries, to which point "more than 50 countries in the Western Regions pledged allegiance". Both the north and south silk roads were unobstructed, and the long-term political and economic relations between the Han Dynasty and the Western Regions was restored to begin a new stage of development for the Silk Road.

[2] According to *Biography of Parthia in Western Regions, History of the Later Han Dynasty*: In the 9th year of Yongyuan under Emperor Hedi's reign, Gan Ying was sent by the Guardian Ban Chao to Daqin. When the army arrived at Tiaozhi to cross the sea, a boatman in the west of Parthia told Gan Ying, "The sea is vast and deep. Boats can cross the sea in 3 months with a tailwind. Otherwise, it may take up to 2 years with a headwind. Therefore, all boats need to stock food for three years. People on the sea tended to become homesick, which led to many deaths." After hearing this, Gan Ying and his army stopped. They departed from Qiuci, passing Tiaozhi, Anxi and other kingdoms, reaching the coast of West Sea (now the Persian Gulf) in the western frontier of Anxi. Due to a long time of sailing and high waves, Gan Ying and his army failed to reach Daqin, but the expedition improved people's understanding of the Central Asian countries at that time. While Gan Ying was looking for Daqin, Daqin was also looking for China, hoping to obtain silk and other commodities through direct trade with China. With the help of the Indian Ocean monsoons, the merchants of Daqin opened up the port of Alexandria in Egypt, which was under the rule of the Roman Empire at that time, as well as a sea route to China apart from the land route in Anxi, opening up a new path for Sino-Western trade.

"Silk Road"[1] to Central Asia, South Asia, West Asia, Europe and even Africa.

2.2.2 Opening up of the Silk Road and its main routes

By the time the Silk Road got its name in modern times, this trade route had already existed for ages. The introduction of Chinese silk fabrics to the West started very early in history. In the 3rd century BC, Greece and Rome called China "Seres" or "the country of silk". At that time, Chinese silk had been transported to India and Europe along Central and West Asia. The opening up of the Silk Road became an important path for China's opening to the outside world, connecting for the first time the Chinese civilization with the ancient Indian civilization, the ancient Arab civilization, and the ancient Roman civilization, which was a major advancement in the development of human society. This road was regarded intersection of ancient Eastern and Western civilizations connecting Asia and Europe. With the development of the times, the Silk Road gradually became a general term referring to the passages for political, economic and cultural exchanges between ancient China and the West.

The Silk Road took shape in the Han Dynasty. According to historical records, it started in the east from Chang'an (now Xi'an, the capital of the Western Han Dynasty, which extended eastward in the Eastern Han Dynasty to Luoyang, the capital of the country), via Longxi, Guyuan, Jincheng County (now Lanzhou) in the Central Plains, passing Guzang (now Wuwei), Zhangye, Jiuquan, Anxi and Dunhuang in the Hexi Corridor, and reaching Yumen Pass and Yangguan Pass from Dunhuang. This original part of the Silk Road was the entry point and gateway to the Western Regions. There were two routes, the North Road and South Road from Yumen Pass and Yangguan Pass to the Western Regions. According to the *History of Western Regions in History of the Former Han Dynasty*, "There were two roads from Yumen Pass and Yangguan Pass to the Western Regions. The South Road started from Shanshan and went westward along the north of Nanshan and the west of Bohe River, and then to Shache. The South Road stretched to the west over the Congling, going outside of Darouzhi and Anxi."

---

[1] The name of "Silk Road" was first used by a German geographer Ferdinand Freiherr Von Richthofen in his book *China* published in 1877, referring to the land passageway opened up by Zhang Qian that started from Chang'an, going through Gansu and Xinjiang to Central and West Asia, and connecting countries in the Mediterranean. The road was named after silk products, which had the greatest influence among the goods transported to the west on this road. Its main course was set in the Han Dynasty, including three routes, namely the South Road, North Road, and Middle Road. The Silk Road in a broad sense was a general term referring to all long-distance routes for commercial trade and cultural exchanges, which started to form back in ancient times, traversing the Eurasian Continent, and even including North Africa and East Africa.

Specifically, the South Road stretched beyond the southwest of Yangguan Pass, running along the northern foot of the Altun Mountains to Yixun (now Mulan), Qiemo, Jingju (now Minfeng), Yutian, Pishan, Shache. Then it went through the Mintaka Pass via Puli (now Taxkorgan) and over the Congling, Yuros (now Zhambyl in Kazakhstan). It then went westward along the northern foot of the Hindu Kush Mountains and the upstream of the Panj River to Darouzhi and Anxi.

According to another record in the *History of Western Regions in History of the Former Han Dynasty*, "After passing the Cheshi Kingdom, the North Road went westward along the Beishan Mountain and the Bohe River to Shule. It climbed over the Congling to Dayuan, Kangju and Aorsi." Specifically, after going through Yumen Pass, crossing Bailongdui in the west and passing Loulan in the Tarim Basin, the North Road took a northward detour in the Cheshi Kingdom (now Turpan), and then moved southwest to Weixu on the north edge of the Taklimakan Desert (Wusha and Ketar on the northern shore of the Bosten Lake), Yanqi, Qiuci (now around Kuqa area in Xinjiang), Gumo (now Aksu), Lieutenant (now Akqi) to Shule (now Kashgar). It then extended westward from Shule, through Juandu (now Wuqia) and across the Pamir Plateau to Dayuan and Kangju. From Kangju the road stretched northwest to Aorsi (located in the northeast of the Aral Sea, later called Lite), south to Darouzhi, and southwest to Anxi and furthest to Lifen in Daqin (also called Lixuan, in Alexandria of Egypt).

After its opening up, the Silk Road became an important economic and cultural tie connecting ancient world civilizations. Through the Land Silk Road, a major artery of transportation linking Asia, Europe, and Africa, China not only communicated and developed relations with India, Persia, Babylon, Egypt, Greece and Rome but also conducted economic and cultural exchanges with remote Africa. Nevertheless, in ancient times, land transportation between countries was often blocked due to wars and turmoils, which prompted people to explore the route of trade and cultural exchanges by sea, and the Maritime Silk Road gradually emerged and developed.

2.2.3 Other silk roads on land

In addition to the official Silk Road bound for the northwest opened up by Zhang Qian on his mission to the Western Regions, there were other silk roads on land. The typical ones were the Grassland Silk Road going from the Central Plains northward to the Mongolian Plateau, and then westward via the northern foot of the Tianshan Mountains into Central Asia, as well as the Southwest Silk Road from Chang'an to India via Chengdu.

(1) *The Grassland Silk Road*

The Grassland Silk Road referred to the great passageway of business and trade connecting the Mongolian Plateau with Eurasia. It started from the Central Plains, went north over the Great Wall along the ancient Yin Mountains (now Daqing Mountain) and Yanshan Mountain, and traversed the Mongolian Plateau, the south Russian Steppe, and the north of Central and Western Asia to the European continent north of the Mediterranean. As an essential part of the Silk Road, also called the "Tea Road" and the "Fur Road", it greatly promoted the interdependent economic relationship between the Central Plains and the Grassland area.

From the Qin and Han dynasties to the Tang (618-907) and Song dynasties (960-1279), the Grassland Silk Road was under continuous development and expansion. In the Yuan Dynasty (1271-1368), the post system was established centering around Shangdu and Dadu, and main post roads such as Tiligan, Muxian and Naxian built an advanced transportation network connecting Mobei with Siberia and stretching westward to Europe via Central Asia, eastward to the Northeast, and southward to the Central Plains, starting from which point the Grassland Silk Road entered a period of all-around prosperity. During the Ming (1368-1644) and Qing dynasties (1644-1912), the Grassland Silk Road was on a gradual decline due to the wars in the grassland areas and the prosperity of the Maritime Silk Road in the Ming Dynasty.

(2) *The Southern Silk Road*

The Southern Silk Road, also called Shu-Sindhu Road, Tea-Horse Road, and Mountain-Valley Silk Road, was a passageway starting from Chengdu, passing Yunnan, Sichuan and other regions in southwest China, and stretching abroad via Myanmar to connect India and Central Asia. The Southern Silk Road consisted of three main roads: Lingguan Road, Wuchi Road and Yongchang Road. The road was divided into the east and west branches beyond Chengdu. The east branch was the so-called Wuchi Road, which ran along the Minjiang River to Bodao (now Yibin), passing through Shimenguan Pass, Zhuti (now Zhaotong), Hanyang (now Hezhang), Wei (now Qujing), Dian (now Kunming) to Yeyu (now Dali). The west branch was called Lingguan Road, which stretched from Chengdu to Yeyu, via Linqiong (now Qionglai), Yanguan (now Ya'an), Zuo (now Hanyuan), Qiongdu (now Xichang), Yanyuan, Qingling (now Dayao), Dabonong (now Xiangyun). The two branches met in Yeyu and then went southwest to Sindhu via Bonan (now Yongping), Xitang (now Baoshan), Dianyue(now Tengchong) and Shan State (now Myanmar). In Shan State, the road was divided into land and sea routes to Sindhu.

Formed in the Han Dynasty, the Southern Silk Road was under the governance of the Nanzhao and Dali local governments in Yunna during the Sui, Tang and Song dynasties. After the Song and Ming dynasties, due to the prosperity of the Maritime Silk Road, the Southern Silk Road, like other land-based silk roads, was on a gradual decline. During more than 2,000 years of existence, the Southern Silk Road had witnessed incessant ethnic migrations, commercial trade, missionary work, and military activities. In the 20th century, especially during the Anti-Japanese War, the sea passage of the home front was cut off. The Yunnan-Burma Highway and the Sino-Indian Highway opened along the Southwest Silk Road were unprecedentedly busy, which became the lifelines to the home front and played an important role in transportation.

2.3 Formation and the main routes of the Maritime Silk Road in the Qin and Han dynasties

2.3.1 Foreign navigation exchanges in Qin and Han dynasties

According to historical records, the Baiyue, Jiuyi and Dongyi people who lived in the coastal areas of the Bohai Sea, the Yellow Sea and the East China Sea in the summer were all good at navigation with material conditions and navigation ability. There is a large clockwise circulation in the North Pacific Ocean and its adjacent waters originating from the North equator of the Pacific Ocean and enters the Taiwan Strait through the northern part of Luzon Island and the eastern part of Taiwan region, and converging in the Zhoushan Islands. In the east sea to Tsushima, there is a diversion northward from the southern part of Kyushu, Japan to form the Tsushima current. The current flows through the Tsushima Strait into the Sea of Japan and then returns to the Pacific Ocean through the Tsugaru Strait. For Chinese coastal ancestors who had mastered navigation technology at that time, it was possible for them to use the direction of the North Pacific Great Circulation to drift across the sea and realize a long voyage.

During the Spring and Autumn Period and the Warring States Period, the coastal voyagers of Yan and Qi States started from Shandong and Liaodong Peninsulas to Japan via the Korean Peninsula, opening up a left-handed circulation route to the west coast of Japan via the southeastern end of Korea and a direct route to Japan's Kitakyushu via Tsushima. With the increase of navigation activities in the initial period of China's maritime undertakings such as Xia, Shang and Zhou dynasties, some ports emerged such as Jieshi Port, Huang Port, Chui Port, Langya Port, Panyu Port, and so on. During the pre-Qin period, the ancestors living in the Lingnan region had shuttled in the South China Sea and even the coast and islands of the South Pacific Ocean, which laid the foundation for the formation of the Maritime Silk Road.

After the unification of China by the Qin Dynasty, the waterways between the north and south, the east and west took shape, creating a peaceful environment for offshore navigation. During the 12 years from the unification of the whole country to his death, the first emperor of Qin made five cruises, including four patrols to the coastal areas, reaching the east of the Bohai Sea, Huangchui, Zhifu (chefoo, today's Yantai), Langya, Jieshi, Kuaiji (now Shaoxing), and the South China Sea (now the East China Sea). In particular, Emperor Qin dispatched Xu Fu and others to take a sea-voyage eastward for seeking the overseas Penglai, the Buddhist abbot, Mount Yingzhou and immortal medicines, promoting the navigation to the sea, which not only pushed China's maritime cruise into a new historical stage but also helped Japan to achieve a leap in the economy. Japan entered the Yayoi period featured with the use of metal tools and farming culture, and Sino-Japanese exchanges in the Han Dynasty developed from non-official trade to official exchanges.

In the Western Han Dynasty, especially under the reign of Emperor Wu, a pioneering emperor with gifts and bold strategies, in order to consolidate coastal defenses and smooth navigation, naval troops were sent for many times, and seven cruises sailed out to the sea, preaching the great national strength of the Han Dynasty. These activities opened up two sea lanes southward from Yangtze Estuary to Guangdong and Guangxi provinces and northward from Shandong province to eastern part of Liaoning province. Since then, the Maritime Silk Road had been extended eastward and westward to foreign countries with a voyage of tens of thousands of miles. In the Western Han Dynasty, the strategy and management of the Korean Peninsula were strengthened, and the navigation routes in the northern sea areas were smoothed, which greatly promoted the navigation activities between China and the Korean Peninsula, and the Japanese archipelagos. It also linked the shipping route from the Yalu River estuary in the north to the Beilun estuary in the south of China's coastal areas. The sea lane had been extended eastward to Japan, westward to India Peninsula, southward to South Ocean Islands, and northward to Korea. Throughout the Han Dynasty, the coastal areas were relatively developed in the economy, and the central government set up the corresponding management agencies. According to *History of the Former Han Dynasty—a Record of Emperor Ping*, in the first year of his reign, there was an official specially designated for collecting sea tax (Haicheng) and an official in charge of fruit production and trade (Guocheng) in royal finance[1]. Since the Han Dynasty, China's marine development and management had been in the leading position in the world and did not change until the early Ming Dynasty.

2.3.2 Formation and the main routes of the Maritime Silk Road

The Maritime Silk Road was closely related to the rise and fall of the Land Silk Road. The Land Silk Road was cut off from time to time with limited animal transport capacity and high cost, while sea transportation was busy with low cost and large volume. Besides, the coastal areas of Wu, Yue, Qi, and Lu were rich in silk, and people were good at shipbuilding in Hepu, Panyu, Minyue (now Fuzhou), Yongjia (now Wenzhou), Kuaiji, Langya, Donglai (now from Laizhou to Fushan, Shandong province) and Bohai (now Cangxian county, Hebei province). In addition to the Land Silk Road, the navigation in the south in Emperor Wu of Han Dynasty was smooth, which promoted the great development of the maritime traffic to the west of the Indian Ocean, and the maritime Silk Road took shape and developed.

The Maritime Silk Road is generally believed to start from Guangzhou, Jiaozhou (now Guangzhou and northern Vietnam) on the southeastern coast of China, which went along the coast of the Central South Peninsula and crossed the Strait of Malacca to enter the coast of the Indian Ocean and the Persian Gulf, reaching the same destination as the Land Silk Road. According to the records of the *Geography of History of the Former Han Dynasty*, there were mainly the South China Sea route and the East China Sea route. Starting from Xuwen, Hepu, and barriers of Rinan, the South China Sea route stretched westward into the Indian Ocean via the South China Sea Channel and traded with the Roman Empire through India. At that time, the Roman Empire also actively sought for direct contact at sea with China in the silk trade. In addition to South China Sea routes, there were also East China Sea routes from Shandong and the Liaodong Peninsulas to the east, through the Korean Peninsula to the Japanese archipelagos. The Maritime Silk Road was a transport route connecting China with the world. China's silk and other commodities were not only transported to Central Asia, West Asia, Europe and other places through the land-based transport routes across the Eurasian continent but also sold to other countries through the maritime transport routes. With the further

---

[1] Haiceng was taking charge of sea tax and Guocheng was taking charge of fruit production and trade. Both are official titles of royal finance in the Han Dynasty.

development of southern China and the center of the economy moving to the south, the maritime routes have become more and more developed and went further and further away from the South China Sea to the Arabian Sea and even as far as the east coast of Africa.

2.4 Major coastal ports and their development during the Qin and Han dynasties

The formation and development of ports in the Qin and Han and later dynasties were restricted by many factors such as geographical locations, political situations, economy, shipbuilding technology and navigation skills. Especially with the transfer of the economic center from the north to the south in China's major economic zones, the opening up and development of ports were directly affected. Looking back on history, in the different periods of feudal China, the political and military centers were in the north for a long time. During the Qin and Han dynasties, China's major economic zones and the national economical center were in the Central Plains and Hanzhong areas in the north of the Yangtze River, while the southern part of the Yangtze River was still in a primitive state of a vast territory with a sparse population. At that time, major coastal ports in China were Panyu, Hepu, Xuwen and Rinan Port in the south, Mashijin and Sanshanpu Port in the north.

2.4.1 Panyu Port

Panyu Port, namely Guangzhou Port, is located at the estuary of the Pearl River, near the South China Sea where the Dongjiang, Xijiang and Beijiang rivers converge into the sea with a deep and broad hinterland. The port offers maritime transport to Guangxi, Hunan, Guizhou, and Yunnan by going up the Xijiang River or to the Ganjiang River along the Beijiang River by crossing the Dayu Range; or by crossing Qitian Range to join the Xiangjiang River and turn into the Yangtze River to get to the Yellow River, arriving at destinations in the eastern, northern, northwestern and southwestern China. The port also leads to southern Jiangxi Province and western Fujian Province along the Dongjiang River. The favorable shipping conditions are most suitable for an ideal foreign trade port. Panyu Port was formed in the pre-Qin period and has been one of the ports along the Silk Road since 230s. In the early Western Han Dynasty, due to the limitation of the scale of ships and navigational technology, it was impossible to cross the Mulantou riffle at the northeastern corner of Hainan Island and the Qizhou Ocean at the southeastern side. It was mainly coastal navigation, not yet ocean navigation.

According to historical records, as early as the Warring States Period, Panyu had traded with its neighboring countries. As the place where Nanhai County was based in the Qin Dynasty, Panyu was one of the commercial towns in China and the distribution center of precious tropical specialties as well as the overseas trade hub of China. In the Han Dynasty, there were land and sea routes for foreign trade. The land route was mainly the Silk Road in the northwest, while the center of sea route was in Guangzhou where most imported goods were distributed here. In the Tang and Song dynasties, Panyu became the largest port in China and the world-famous oriental port. In the Ming and Qing dynasties, it became the only major port for China's foreign trade, a unique one in the world's maritime transport history that has been prosperous for more than 2,000 years known as the "eternal oriental birthplace of the Maritime Silk Road".

2.4.2 Hepu Port

Hepu bears the meaning of rivers flowing into the sea. In ancient times, Nanliu River used to be called Hepu Waters. The ancient Hepu Port was located in Beihai of Guangxi province today and was one of the main ports of the Maritime Silk Road in the Han Dynasty. It was the predecessor of present Beihai Port and was located at the crossing of rivers and seas, the southernmost part of Guangxi, in the central position of Beibu Gulf. Facing Southeast Asia, it bordered the southwestern part of China to the north and Beibu Gulf to the south, holding the Qiongzhou Strait and Beibu Gulf Strait and guarding the routes of countries from the west to China. It was an ideal place for ocean currents, monsoons and sea routes in southern China, as well as an outlet of the Nanliu River. It enjoyed prominent geographical advantages in land and sea transport, a vast hinterland, convenient transportation, economic and cultural prosperity and abundant export resources. Its land transport can be linked with the southwest, southeast and Central Plains, while maritime transport can be connected with Southeast Asia and South Asia, extending to western Asia and Europe.

After the Nanyue Kingdom was put down in the sixth year of Yuanding period in the Han Dynasty (111 BC), Emperor Wu set up Hepu County. During the Western and Eastern Han dynasties, Hepu County was located in the artery of communications between Lingbei, Jiaozhi, Hainan counties, and other counties connecting foreign countries. It was also the hub connecting Lingnan, Cangwu, and Jiaozhi counties in the west. Jiaozhi was the political, economic and cultural center in the southwest of Lingnan, playing the same role as Cangwu, the political and cultural center in the northwest of Lingnan. Hepu County in the middle effectively controlled Lingnan, with a pivotal role among the three counties to the south of Jiaozhi. In the Han Dynasty, Hepu was the political center of Lingnan with favorable conditions for maritime transportation and foreign trade.

Before the Qin Dynasty, there had been sailing activities in Hepu and non-governmental trade on the sea. The Maritime Silk Road in the Western Han Dynasty started here. During Qin and Han dynasties, the vessels sailing from Panyu Port to Qiongzhou Strait would have to get supplies of freshwater and cargo at Xuwen Port due to poor cruising capability before they sailed to Hepu Port. Then they would cross the Beibu Gulf to reach the Indian Ocean with the aid of the southwest monsoon, through Jiaozhi, Rinan and the Tunguan, Rahma, Chenli, Bagan, Kanchi, Pizon and other ancient countries, and took a long voyage to Yichengbu Kingdom (now Sri Lanka) and other places. In the Han Dynasty, the prosperity of Hepu Port exceeded that of Panyu Port, and the Indian Ocean route starting from Hepu Port was one of the longest ocean routes in the world at that time. Since the Three Kingdoms period, due to the southward movement of the political and economic centers, Panyu Port had been closer to the central area along the north of the Yangtze River or the coastal north, and its status was gradually rising. By the time of the kingdom of Wu, it was able to build the vessels with large capacity and mastered the navigational technology against the wind. Moreover, new offshore ocean routes have been gradually opened up, and ocean-going ships were no longer required to sail along the coast of Hepu. By the Eastern Jin Dynasty, the position of Hepu Port was declining day by day and replaced by Panyu Port; thus, the largest seaport in the south was transferred from Hepu Port to Panyu Port.

2.4.3 Xuwen Port

Xuwen port was one of the first ports of the Maritime Silk Road in the Han Dynasty, along with Hepu and Rinan Ports. Located in the southernmost tip of Leizhou Peninsula, across the Qiongzhou Strait and Hainan Island, defending the Qiongzhou Strait, Xuwen was surrounded by the sea on three sides, and its land and sea position was superior, interconnected with each other, both as a trading port and coastal fortress. The officials were stationed there in the Han Dynasty in charge of military administration and foreign trade. According to records from *Geography of the Han Dynasty*, "Starting from barriers of Rinan, the fleets of envoys, merchants and interpreters sailing from Xuwen and Hepu Ports could arrive at Tunguan after five months; another four months at Rahma; another 20 days or so, at Chenli; and after more than ten days on foot, at Bagan. Then sailing for another two months, they would arrive at Kanchi whose folk culture was similar to Zhuya. The kingdom covered an immense area with a large population and was rich in exotic objects which were presented as tribute to the Chinese Imperial Court since Emperor Wu of the Han Dynasty. Official interpreters with their guides would make deals with local people, bartering gold, dried fruit and other treasures they brought from China for pearls, colored glazes, rare stones and other exotic things. On the long journey, the fleets would visit various countries and trade with them. In addition to providing all kinds of food and escorting ships, those countries would meet and see off Chinese envoys and load or unload the cargo for mutual benefits. Sometimes the fleet might be robbed and crews killed by pirates and might be trapped or wrecked in the storm. It would take several years for the people to return home if they were lucky, bringing pearls as big as some six centimeters to the emperor. At the first year of the reign of Emperor Ping of the Han Dynasty (1-5), Wang Mang assisted the emperor in governing the country. To show off his authority and benevolence, Wang Mang would send envoys to give abundant gold and other gifts to Kanchi and asked for rhinoceros. The return journey of the fleets would start from Yichengbu Kingdom (Sihadvipa, now Sri Lanka), south of Kanchi. They would then arrive at Pizong after eight months; another eight months at Rinan and finally get to the boundary of Xianglin to be back to their own country." This document describes the maritime exchanges and trade between the Han Dynasty and Southeast Asia and South Asia in the middle and late Western Han Dynasty. The above-mentioned ocean routes from Xuwen, Hepu to the Indian Ocean in the Western Han Dynasty were the earliest and the most authoritative historical records about the ancient Maritime Silk Road.

In comparison, Hepu Port was superior to Xuwen Port in terms of geographical location, natural conditions, economic basis, transportation, and navigation. The two ports are located near Hainan Island and convenient in transport with foreign countries on land and sea. For the traffic routes, three channels were connecting the Central Plains during the Qin and Han dynasties. The first one was the Lingqu channel connected with the Lijiang River and the Xiangjiang River, both were the tributary of the Pearl River and the Yangtze River. Since the Qin Dynasty, it had been one of the most important routes to the Central Plains. The second one was the Linhe channel (Jiuyi channel). This channel ran along Hejiang River from the Xijiang River tributary, crossing the watershed and arriving in Xiaoshui, a branch of Xiangjiang River. The third one was the

Yelang Channel (Jiang Channel). Going along the Xijiang River or through the Liujiang River and the Hongshui River, the channel could reach the ancient Yelang Kingdom—Yanghe County (now Kaili, Guizhou province). Wuchi Channel also connected the Yelang Kingdom with Bashu.

2.4.4 Rinan Port

Rinan Port was located in Rinan County, the southernmost of the nine counties in the South China Sea set up by Emperor Wu of the Han Dynasty, and it is now a county of Guangzhi province in Vietnam. It is among one of the first harbors of the Maritime Silk Road from the southern coastal areas to Southeast Asia and South Asia. In the early Han Dynasty, Rinan was the most developed and important port of departure of the Maritime Silk Road. Because it was the southernmost county in the Han Dynasty, it was also called the "barrier". Also, it was the nearest county to Southeast Asia and South Asia, so it was where wealthy merchants and envoys at home or abroad mostly arrived and left. Ships of the Han Dynasty set off from Panyu, Xuwen and Hepu ports and left Rinan as an outward voyage. According to historical records, in the 9th year of Yanxi, Emperor Huan of the Eastern Han Dynasty, Roman Emperor Marcus Aurelius sent envoys to offer ivories, rhinoceros' horns and hawksbills via Rinan Port, where foreign envoys landed for their first visit to China. After that, because Jiaozhi, Jiuzhen, and Rinan were under the jurisdiction of the Han Dynasty again and the central government was too far to govern this area, the rebellions of ethnic groups frequently occurred, which were not conducive to the development of Rinan Port. As a result, it was eventually forced to close down.

2.4.5 Mashijin Port

Mashijin Port is today's Lushunkou. Located in the east of Mount Mashi (called General Mountain in ancient times, now Mount Laotie in Lushun), it was named as Mashijin. In the Warring States Period, it was Liaodong County belonging to the Yan Kingdom. In the Northern Wei Dynasty, Lushun was known as Tazhu or Tajin, and in the Jin Dynasty, it got the present name and became an important port for North-South navigation. In the Tang Dynasty, it was called the Duli Town. In Liao, Jin and Yuan dynasties, it was renamed as Shizikou. In the 4th year of Hongwu period in the Ming Dynasty, Zhu Yuanzhang sent Ma Yun and Ye Wang to guard Liaodong by boat from Shandong Province. Because of the smooth sailing on the sea, he changed its name into

Lushunkou, and the name has been used up to now. Located on the boundary between the Bohai Sea and the Yellow Sea, facing Dengzhou in Shandong Province across the sea, it is a significant military and commercial port linking the Central Plains and northeastern China with a history of more than 2,000 years.

2.4.6   Sanshanpu Port

Sanshanpu is today's Dalian Port which is located in the southern tip of Liaodong Peninsula, bordering the Bohai Sea in the west and the Yellow Sea in the south. It is named after Sanshan Island at the mouth of Dalian Bay. Since the Han Dynasty, Sanshanpu has been a vital port in navigating from Shandong Province to northeastern China, Korea and Japan. The two ports mentioned above belonged to Tashi County (now Jinxian County of the Dalian City). From the Warring States Period to Qin and Han dynasties, it was under the governance of Liaodong County. In the Han Dynasty, Tashi and Wenxian were established there, while in the Tang Dynasty, Andong Capital Protectorate was set up. In the Liao Dynasty, there were Suzhou and Fuzhou there. Suzhou was changed into Jinzhou in the Jin Dynasty. In the Yuan Dynasty, Wanhufu Prefecture in Jinfuzhou was set up, and Jinzhouwei Prefecture was established in the Ming Dynasty, and Jinzhouting Prefecture in the Qing Dynasty. In 1945, Luda City was established, and it was renamed as Dalian City in 1981.

2.5   Development of external transport by land and sea during the Wei, Jin, and Southern and Northern dynasties

In the Wei, Jin and Southern and Northern dynasties, there were rebellions here and there and the country was split, with perennial wars and changing regimes. It went through three stages: the Three Kingdoms, the Sixteen Kingdoms of the Eastern Jin Dynasty and the confrontation period of the Northern and Southern dynasties. Similarly, the western countries were undergoing constant changes: the rise and decline of the Sassanid Empire, the division of the Roman Empire, the regime changes of the Indian Empire and the rise of the Turks. All of these ultimately led to the evolution of the rise and decline of the Silk Road.

2.5.1 Development of the Land Silk Road

Since Zhang Qian's mission to the Western Regions, the land routes of ancient Chinese and Western traffic generally stretched into the Western Regions through the Hexi Corridor, and reached Central Asia across Congling and extended westward. When the Hexi Corridor or a certain section of the route was blocked, people would have to travel by other routes. During the Wei, Jin and Southern and Northern dynasties, because of the long-standing confrontation between different regimes in China, the transportation between them and the Western Regions took different routes. The turbulence in the Hexi Corridor which was the main route of the Silk Road and the Western Regions affected the transportation between China and the West. During this period, different regimes existed and constantly changed the eastern end of the Silk Road, while the western end extended to Constantinople. The Silk Road was roughly divided into the Longyou Route as the eastern section, Western Regions Route as the middle section and the western section to the west of Congling.

The Hexi Corridor was the path to enter the Western Regions via Wuwei, Zhangye, Jiuquan and Dunhuang. It was the key path stretching from the hinterland of the Central China to Xinjiang, Central Asia, West Asia, South Asia and Europe and the vital route linking the East and the West. Longyou Route started from Chang'an to the Hexi Corridor via Liangzhou North Route and Liangzhou South Route. Liangzhou North Route extended from Chang'an via Luoyang, running westward along the Jinghe Valley, past Guyuan and Jingyuan, then across the Yellow River to arrive at the Hexi Corridor. This route was the most convenient among all routes. Liangzhou South Route winded from Chang'an, moving westward along the Weishui River, across the Yellow River into the Hexi Corridor via Baoji, Tianshui, Longxi, Lintao and Jincheng. In addition to the two routes above, there was a middle one. This route started from Chang'an, through Longxian, extending west to Longguan Pass and Dazhenguan Pass, across Longshan Mountain, going northwest through Lueyang, Weixi to Jincheng, and then across the Yellow River to the Hexi Corridor.

In the Wei and Jin dynasties, the "Zhongxin Route" was added to the western section of the Silk Road on the basis of the Han Dynasty. It started from Dunhuang, through Yumen Pass towards the Cheshihou Kingdom, and then moving westwards along the northern foot of the Tianshan Mountains. During the Eastern Jin Dynasty, the Western Region Route changed with the political changes of the Central Plains, the Hexi Corridor, and the Western Regions. With the ancient kingdom of Shanshan being starting point, the Southern Route of the Western Regions stretched from Dunhuang, heading west ward along the Shule River, across the Bailongdui Desert near Lop Nur and going southward to Yuni city in Shanshan (today's Ruoqiang in Xinjiang). During the Hon and Wei Dynasties, Shanshan's national strength was strong, and its capital Yuni city became the hub of the main channel of the Southern Route. After Yumen Pass, the Southern Route no longer went via Loulan, but southward to Shanshan along the northern foot of the Altun Mountain. The Middle Route of the Western Regions traveled westward through Dunhuang and Yumen Pass, joining the North Road of the Han Dynasty at Loulan and going westward. In the Wei, Jin and Southern and Northern Dynasties, a large number of Buddhist monks such as Kumarajiva from India and Central Asia came to China along these routes, spreading Buddhism and promoting cultural exchanges. Meanwhile, Chinese Buddhists such as Faxian went to the West Regions for Buddhist scriptures, contributing to the spread of Chinese culture at the same time.

2.5.2 Development of external maritime transport

During the Three Kingdoms period, the Wu Kingdom was located on the southern coast and enjoyed an advantage in overseas transportation with flourishing offshore shipping. Wu sent officials Zhu Ying and Kang Tai as envoys to Funan and other Southeast Asian countries to "promote Chinese culture" for more than ten years. After coming back, Kang Tai wrote *An Introduction of Foreign Countries of the Wu Kingdom*, and Zhu Ying wrote *A Record of Exotic Things in Funan*, providing information of overseas countries. The king Sun Quan sent fleets of thousands of soldiers sailing northward to support Gongsun Yuan in Liaodong against the Wei Kingdom, and Wei Wen was assigned to lead fleets of thousands of soldiers southward to fight against Yizhou (now Taiwan, China) and Tan (now Hainan, China). Moreover, in the Wei, Jin and Southern and Northern dynasties, Chinese and foreign Buddhist monks traveled between China and India by sea, and the Chinese navigation continued to develop. It can be found that the Chinese fleet had sailed as far as to the Persian Gulf at that time.

Generally speaking, before the rise of the Sui and Tang dynasties, although the internal vassal factions led to divisions and regime changes, the jurisdiction of the Chinese kingdoms over the Western Regions were well inherited. And the northern regimes such as the Wei, Western Jin, pre-Qin and Northern Wei basically maintained their jurisdiction over the Western Regions, while the Silk Road on the land remained open generally. At the same time, the Maritime Silk Road also developed, and China kept its relations with the East and the West of the world, enjoying close exchanges and friendly trade relations with Central Asia, West Asia, South Asia, Europe and North Africa on land and by sea.

2.6 Development of external transport by land and sea during the Tang and Song dynasties

The Tang and Song dynasties, especially the Tang Dynasty, were the most open and enlightened periods in ancient China, when one of the major opening-up policies for the imperial court was to facilitate the transportation between China and foreign countries, clear out the blocked routes and expand overseas trade. In addition to the development of land trade in the northwest, the maritime trade along the southeast coast flourished at the same time. Through the Land and the Maritime Silk roads, the economic and cultural exchanges with the Western Regions and the South China Sea areas were becoming more and more frequent and many merchants were engaging in business along the routes.

2.6.1 Land Silk Road in the Tang Dynasty and development of external transport

Compared with the Han Dynasty, the Land Silk Road in the Tang Dynasty somewhat changed. It started from Chang'an, via the Hexi Corridor, through the Tarim Basin, and across the Pamir Plateau. It was generally divided into two directions. One passed through the northern Pamir Plateau and Fergana to reach the Amu Darya and Syr Darya between today's Uzbekistan and Kazakhstan. The other crossed the south of the Pamir Plateau and split into two further routes, the south one moving towards North India and the west one to Afghanistan. In addition, the trade route towards Central Asian countries such as Tajikistan, Turkmenistan and Afghanistan went westward to Persia (now Iran), and split into two. The one traveled northwest to Constantinople, the capital of ancient Eastern Rome and today's Istanbul; the other headed southwest to Iraq, through the Syrian Desert, to cities on the eastern coast of the Mediterranean, and across the sea to Rome. On the Silk Road connecting China and the West, Persia was the only country to go through and for transshipment. It is also the hub of the north and south routes of the Silk Road. Actually, Persia had a particularly close relationship with China during the Tang Dynasty.

During the Zhenyuan Period of the Tang Dynasty (785-805), Jia Dan explored in detail the main routes of traffic between China and foreign countries and summed up the seven routes from the border to foreign countries. "The first one is from Yingzhou into Andong, the second one from Dengzhou to Koryo and the Bohai Sea, the third one from Xiazhou to Datong and Yunzhong, the fourth one from Zhongshouxiangcheng (today's Baotou) to the Uighur, the fifth from Anxi to the Western Regions, the sixth from Annan to India, and the seventh from Guangzhou to overseas countries. The mountains, settlements and places near and far were all mentioned. All prefectures and counties have their own names, some of which were not recorded before, maybe because they were named by local barbarians".[1] However, during the Kaiyuan Period in the Tang Dynasty (713-741), especially after the An Lushan Rebellion, due to the fact that a large number of border soldiers in Hexi and Longxi were withdrawn to suppress the rebellion, the border defense was weak. The Tubo Kingdom took advantage of the situation to invade and capture Longxi and Hexi, and cut off the land transport and the Silk Road between the East and the West. Thus, the East and West transportation was transferred from the land to the sea, and overseas trade had flourished unprecedentedly.

2.6.2 Maritime Silk Road in the Tang Dynasty and development of foreign exchanges

In the Tang and Song dynasties, China's maritime routes were well developed, facilitating its contacts with many other countries. The seas and oceans were the vital channel for foreign exchanges in the Tang and Song dynasties. The central government attached great importance to navigation management, shipbuilding, foreign trade, and navigation technology. According to the *Geography Records* of *New History of the Tang Dynasty*, Chinese merchant ships have sailed from the Indian Peninsula to the Persian Gulf and the trade between China and the Indochina Peninsula, Malay Peninsula, Malay Islands, Indian Peninsula, and Arab Peninsula was well developed. In the Tang Dynasty, China had grown to be a major navigation country in the western Pacific Ocean and the Indian Ocean, reaching the advanced world level in shipbuilding and navigation technology. It was indeed a time of great prosperity since the Qin and Han dynasties in terms of promoting land-based exchanges with other countries, industrial and commercial development and maritime trade, opening up of ports, expansion of

---

[1] *Geography Records*, Vol. 43 of *New History of the Tang Dynasty*.

eastern and Western Ocean routes, shipbuilding technology, navigational capacity and shipping management. It was the heyday of the development of ancient Chinese navigation.

The Maritime Silk Road was an important trade route between China and the Arab Empire during the Tang Dynasty. It started at Guangzhou, traveling southward along the eastern coast of today's Vietnam to Kunlun Island, heading southwest through today's Singapore Strait, moving southward to Java then westward from the Strait to Sri Lanka via Sumatra and the Nikpa Islands, along the western coast of the Indian Ocean to the Indian Estuary, sailing westward across more than 20 small countries, through the Persian Gulf to Abadan on the western end of the Gulf. If going upward the Euphrates River, it could reach Basra and then Baghdad by land, the capital of the Arab Empire; and sailing along the Arabian Peninsula, it could reach the Jeddah Island in the Red Sea and then to Egypt. Jia Dan recorded in his book *The Route from Guangzhou to Overseas Countries* that the route was so called because it started from Guangzhou, past the Malay Archipelago, the Malay Peninsula, Indonesia and Southeast Asia, via Sri Lanka and the west coast of India to arrive at Hormuz[1]. Then it sailed westward to Dares Salaam of Tanzania in East Africa, linking the Malay Archipelago, the Malay Peninsula and Indonesia or Southeast Asia, West Asia and East Africa.

In the Tang Dynasty, people from foreign countries and regions came to China for trade by sea. China conducted frequent exchanges with Japan, Silla, the Island Countries in the South, India, the Lion Kingdom (also known as Shiziguo, today's Sri Lanka), Persia, Arabs and so on. Chinese and foreign merchant ships, with monks who went to India to study Buddhism scriptures, frequently sailed between China, India, Arabia and other places, witnessing the prosperity of overseas transportation in the Tang Dynasty. At that time, people from all countries of the South and West Asia came to China by sea. They sailed from the Persian Gulf via India, rounding the Malay Peninsula, arrived at Guangzhou, and then landed on the ports such as Jiaozhou in the Lingnan area, Quanzhou and Fuzhou in Fujian, Yangzhou, Mingzhou, Wenzhou and Songjiang in Jiangsu and Zhejiang. At the turn of the 7th century and the 8th century, the influence of the Umayyad Caliphate in Arabia expanded greatly, reaching the Pamir

---

[1] It was close to Minab in the Persian Gulf to the southeast of Iran, near the Strait of Hormuz. The abandoned site was on the north coast of the Hormuz Island, choking the mouth of the Persian Gulf. It was the hub of ancient traffic and trade, and is now replaced by the port of Abbas on the opposite coast. Hormuz was also one of the destinations in Zheng He's voyages in the South Seas to as far as Africa.

Plateau to the east and bordering China in the Tang Dynasty. This provided favorable conditions for communication between Arabia and China. Through the Land and Maritime Silk Roads, envoys of the two countries were visiting each other in a constant stream, and business contacts were frequent. At that time, the business of Arabia was booming, especially its regular maritime trade with China. The navigation strengths of the two empires were basically on a par.

2.6.3   Opening up in the Song Dynasty and development of land and maritime transport

(1) *Land transport development*

At the end of the Tang Dynasty, wars along the Silk Road in the northwest broke up frequently, and the grasslands and oases were destroyed by years of war. Tubo crossed the Kunlun Mountains, went northward and occupied most of the Western Regions. The regime in Central Plains could not control the Hexi Corridor or even the northwest regions. The economy of the northern region was severely hit, and the production of silk and porcelain continued to decline. Merchants were reluctant to go far away for the sake of security, and people enjoyed no peace in production and life. Foreign trade declined, and the Silk Road in the northwest was eventually abandoned. After the Tang Dynasty, the economic center of China moved southward gradually, and the relatively stable foreign trade in the South increased significantly, which promoted the prosperity of the Southern Silk Road and the Maritime Silk Road.

(2) *Development of external maritime transport*

During the Tang and Song dynasties, neighboring countries and nationalities of the East and the West were not so developed as China in all respects, but they were growing and on the rise. The advanced culture, science and technology of China attracted businessmen, envoys and overseas students who came from Asian, European and African countries to China. Japan, Korea (Silla) and other Eastern neighbors and Arab countries sent people to study and establish contacts, and conduct foreign trade in China out of the need for maritime and land trade, cultural exchanges, spreading religions or learning technologies. The land and maritime exchanges were frequent. This period was the time of unprecedented development and prosperity of maritime transportation and foreign trade in Chinese history. The imperial court welcomed foreigners to China for business and adopted an open, encouraging and lenient policy towards cultural exchanges, maritime trade and overseas communication management.

The major maritime trade partners were Arab countries in the West and neighboring countries such as Koryo and Japan in the East. The imperial court approved opening ports for trade in Guangzhou, Quanzhou, Mingzhou, Yangzhou, Hangzhou, Zhenjiang, Jiangning (now Nanjing), Hongzhou (now Nanchang) and other places at different times. Among them, the foreign trade at Quanzhou and Guangzhou ports was the most prosperous. Quanzhou Port was one of the largest commercial ports in the world and the largest port in the East at that time. There was a time of "the people from all continents gathering in the city"[1] and "the merchants of all nations coming along the rising tide of the sea".[2] As a gathering place for world businessmen, Guangzhou presented a prosperous scene of "the endless stream of people from different countries". Mingzhou was specially designated as a port for trade with Koryo and Japan and developed rapidly. During this period, Chinese people traveled across the world by sea and established routes over Asia, Europe and Africa.

Throughout the Song Dynasty, rulers had been attaching importance to the economy and opening to the outside world. However, due to external constraints, the pattern of "strong sea route and weak land route" in foreign trade had existed. The Southern Maritime Silk Road had been developing continuously. China maintained close relations with more than 50 countries in Southeast Asia, South Asia, the Middle East and Africa sailing from Guangzhou Port. The maritime trade flourished, while north-west Land Silk Road trade gradually shrank. In the Song Dynasty, special management agencies for maritime trade had been set up. At that time, all the cargo ships leaving ports for maritime trade were required to apply to the *Shibosi* for inspection. They were also required to receive inspection when arriving at the ports and to pay duty for the goods. The imperial court had special provisions on these items.

Japan and the Korean Peninsula in Northeast Asia which were adjacent to the land

---

[1] Bao He, "Seeing off Commissioner Li to Quanzhou", *The Complete Collection of Poetry in the Tang Dynasty*, Vol. 208.

[2] In the Song Dynasty, Li Bing wrote in his *Ode to Quanzhou Overseas Transportation Trade in the Song Dynasty* that in the shadow of pines and cypresses stretched the Sanzhou Road, and along the rising tide of the sea came the merchants of all nations. Li Bing, whose literary name was Hanlao and style name Yunkan, was born in Rencheng Jizhou (Jining, Shandong Province). He passed the imperial examinations in 1106, held the post of the Assistant Minister of Military Service, Counselor of Political Affairs and Minister of Administration. He lived in Caixiang of East Street, Quanzhou, in his retirement.

and sea of China had opened the North Routes[1], South Island route[2], South route[3], and the Maokouwa route[4]. In addition, a sea route had been opened from Sakhalin Island, where the Moho people lived in Northeast China, crossing the northern edge of the Pacific Ocean, the Sea of Okhotsk and the Sea of Japan along the east coast of Sakhalin Island, with the current moving southward to Zezhuo Island (also known as Iturup Island), and finally arriving in Liugui State (the southwestern coast of present-day Kamchatka Peninsula).

2.7 Open ports and their development during the Tang and Song dynasties

In the sailing age, in order to ensure the safety of navigation, it was necessary to shorten the voyage to the nearest port and consider the convenient loading and unloading of the bulk cargo along the way when sailing to foreign countries or before crossing the Yellow Sea and the Strait of Malacca. Therefore, the layout of the coastal open ports extended from the north and south ends of the coast to the middle. With the

---

[1] One of the northern routes started from Dengzhou (now Penglai in Shandong Province), across the Bohai Sea along the eastern side of Liaodong Peninsula to Yalu River Estuary, entering Koryo along the west coast of the Korean Peninsula to Kyushu and other places in Japan. The other was from Wendeng in Shandong, southeast bound across the Yellow Sea, to Baekje at the southwestern end of the Korean Peninsula, and then to Liancourt Islands or Dokdo Islands (southwest of the Jindo Island Jeollanam-do in Korea), Danluo (Cheju Island), Dusma (Tsushima Island), Yizhi (Ikijima Island), Zhusi (or Zhuzi, today's North Kyushu), and other places, and finally arrived at Nambo (today's Osaka).

[2] The South Island Route started from Yangzhou, Chuzhou (now Huai'an in Jiangsu Province) or Mingzhou (now Ningbo in Zhejiang Province. It was known as Mingzhou in the Tang and Song dynasties, Qingyuan in the Yuan Dynasty, and Ningbo in the early Ming Dynasty). It crossed the East China Sea directly towards the Amami Great Island south of the mainland of Japan, then northward via Arnabo Island (Okinawa), Yejiu Island (also known as Yijiu Island, Ujiu Island), Domi Island (Seed Island), Samoa Coast (Samoa) and other places, to Hakata Port and Nampo Port.

[3] The South Route started from the Yangtze River Estuary (Chuzhou or Mingzhou), crossing the East China Sea, towards Sika Island (the Goto-Retto today, including Kashima Island, Hiradoshima Island, Fukueshima Island and Hisakashima Island). The destination of the south and the north routes was Sika Island.

[4] The Maokouwei-Japan Route. Maokouwei (now Kraskino Port, Russia) was known as Yanzhou, 100 miles southeast of Dongjing Longyuan Prefecture in the Bohai State (now Baliancheng, Hunchun, Jilin). This route started from Maokouwei sailing southeast to Nengdeng (Ishikawa Shikawa Peninsula) and Kagawa (southern Shikawa Prefecture) in central Honshu, Japan. Or it was from Maokouwa sailing southeast across the Sea of Japan, directly to Tsukiyoshi Tsumura Harbor (Fukuoka), the gateway of the Taizai Prefecture, where all ships sailing for foreign countries were anchored.

improvement of navigation technology and economic and social changes, especially the northern ethnic groups moving to the south in the Song Dynasty, the northern ports declined, and the southeastern ports flourished. Ports were gradually opened one by one from north to south. Thus, the configuration of four major trading ports, namely Guangzhou, Quanzhou, Mingzhou and Yangzhou, came into being during the Tang and Song dynasties. In the Tang Dynasty, the ports with booming foreign trade were mainly Guangzhou, Quanzhou, Mingzhou, Yangzhou, Jiaozhou (Annan)[1], Dengzhou and Mizhou. After the An Lushan Rebellion, the traffic on the northwest Silk Road was blocked, so the Maritime Silk Road began to play an important role.

From the Western Han Dynasty to the Yuan Dynasty, emperors generally encouraged foreign trade with an open mind and the Song Dynasty was the only one that did not carry out the policy of "restraining commerce" for a long time. It had a strong sense of opening to the outside world and was a major maritime trade country at that time. The ports in the Song Dynasty were roughly divided into three main port clusters, namely clusters of Guangnan Provincial District, Fujian Provincial District and Liangzhe Provincial District. In Guangnan Provincial District, there were main ports such as Guangzhou Port as well as other ports such as Hepu, Qiongzhou, and Qinzhou. In Fujian Provincial District, the main port was Quanzhou Port and the surrounding ports of Zhangzhou and Fuzhou. The main port in Liangzhe Provincial District was Mingzhou Port, and the peripheral ports were Hangzhou, Wenzhou, Yangzhou, Jiangyin, Zhenjiang, Huating and Mizhou.

2.7.1 Development of Guangzhou Port and its peripheral ports

From the Spring and Autumn period to the Tang and Song dynasties, Guangzhou Port had always been an important port for "a number of Chinese and foreign merchants and enjoying the advantage of shipping". Guangzhou Port was the first port to establish the management system of foreign shipping.

(1) *Development of Guangzhou Port in the Tang Dynasty and the establishment of the management system of foreign shipping*

In the 2nd year of Kaiyuan in the Tang Dynasty (714), to strengthen port

---

[1] Jiaozhou used to govern places like Vietnam now. In 624, the 7th year of Wude in the Tang Dynasty, Jiaozhou was set as the military government. In 679, the 4th year of Yifeng, it was named as the Annan Military Commanding Administration, and Jiaozhou was called "Annan" since then.

management, Emperor Xuanzong set up *Shibosi* (Bureau for Foreign Shipping)[1] which specialized in overseas transportation, trade, and port management. With the increasing number of ships arriving and leaving, the maritime trade and the port markets gradually increased, and the director of Bureau for Foreign Shipping had been promoted to *Yafanboshi*, a specially designated official position by the central government at the ports. Since then, in Guangzhou Port, the governor of Lingnan was responsible for the internal affairs and Yafanboshi was in charge of the foreign business. In the Tang and Song dynasties, there were many port management laws, such as *Six Codes of the Tang Dynasty*, *Laws of the Tang Dynasty*, *Orders of the Tang Dynasty* and *Articles on Foreign*

---

[1] Shibosi or Bureau for Foreign Shipping was a government agency set up at each seaport in the Tang, Song, Yuan and early Ming dynasties to administer maritime trade. It was in charge of foreign trade between the states by sea, and special officers were appointed, roughly equivalent to the present customs and port authorities. Emperor Xuanzong of the Tang Dynasty set up a port office named Office of Foreign Shipping in Guangzhou as the predecessor of the Bureau for Foreign Shipping. The Song court attached great importance to overseas trade, and in the 4th year of Kaibao (971) in Guangzhou, Bureau for Foreign Shipping was resumed, in charge of maritime trade. In the first year of Chongning, Emperor Huizong set up Bureau for Foreign Shipping in Hangzhou, Mingzhou (now Ningbo), Wenzhou, Mizhou (now Jiaoxian County, Shandong), Xiuzhou (now Songjiang County, Shanghai) and other places, responsible for checking ships in and out of ports and merchandise, acquisition of proprietary products, managing foreign merchants and so on. In the early years of Jianyan (1127-1130), Bureau for Foreign Shipping of Fujian Province and Zhejiang Province were disbanded, and their rights were taken over by Transport Department. The court of the Yuan Dynasty followed the system of the Song Dynasty, and Emperor Shizu had the Bureau for Foreign Shipping set up in Guangdong Province, and the Emperor Wuzong abolished the Bureau for Foreign Shipping from 1308 to 1310. Emperor Renzong lifted the ban and established the Bureau for Foreign Shipping in Quanzhou, Guangzhou, and Qingyuan, in charge of issuing certification of public inspection of ships, inspecting ships and managing ships at the ports. In the Ming Dynasty, the Bureau for Foreign Shipping was set up in all the cities along the coast, in charge of overseas tributes and foreign trade. In the 3rd year of Hongwu (1370), the Bureau for Foreign Shipping of Huangdu Taicang was disbanded; In the 7th year of Hongwu (1374), the Bureau for Foreign Shipping in Quanzhou, Ming Zhou, and Guangzhou were revoked. During the reign of Emperor Jiajing, only the Bureau for Foreign Shipping of Guangdong was reserved. In the early Qing Dynasty, the policy of seclusion was carried out, and the ban was lifted in the 22nd year of Emperor Kangxi (1683). Four ports of trade were opened in Guangzhou, Zhangzhou, Ningbo, and Yuntaishan (now Lianyungang). In the 24th year of Emperor Kangxi (1685), all the bureaus for foreign shipping were abolished; and four customs offices were established instead in Jiangsu, Zhejiang, Fujian and Guangdong provinces. In the 22nd year of Emperor Qianlong (1757), the emperor witnessed an endless stream of foreign merchant ships in Suzhou during his inspection tour to the south which alerted him. He ordered that all other customs except Guangdong Customs be revoked and only Guangdong Port of trade be allowed. After the Opium War, the Imperial Maritime Customs Service took charge of customs affairs, and largely staffed at senior levels by foreigners. The system of Bureau for Foreign Shipping began in the Tang Dynasty, flourished in the Song Dynasty, and gradually shrank in the late Ming Dynasty. In the Qing Dynasty, the customs were established, and the Bureau for Foreign Shipping was abolished. It was in charge of inspecting ships of foreign trade, collecting commodity tax, government monopoly and managing trade.

Shipping at Guangzhou which were made in the 3rd year of Yuanfeng in the Song Dynasty (1080). All of them had made explicit provisions on cargo certification, inspection, ship registration, taxation, and foreign merchant management in and out of the port. Subsequently, the status of maritime trade was becoming more critical and surpassed the land trade. According to the *Old History of the Tang Dynasty*, more than 20 countries in the South conducted foreign trade with China. During the mid-Tang Dynasty, owing to the An Lushan Rebellion and the Huang Chao Uprising, the political situation was turbulent, and the war brought great damages. Coupled with problems of Guangzhou port officials, such as corruption and extortion, the forced purchase of foreign goods for private profit, and the excessive levy of taxes, all of which resulted in the abuse of the shipping management, thus the port declined and never flourished again at the end of the Tang Dynasty. The navigation activities between the East and the West were in a slump at that time.

(2) *Development of Guangzhou Port in the Song Dynasty and the management system of foreign shipping*

In the Song Dynasty, the court attached great importance to Guangzhou's role as the maritime trade gateway to Southeast Asia and Arabia countries. In the 4th year of Kaibao in the Northern Song Dynasty (971), shortly after the Southern Han Dynasty was exterminated, the Bureau for Foreign Shipping was established in Guangzhou again, and the local officials were appointed as the director of this agency, mainly responsible for "the management of ships entering and leaving ports, port supervision, enforcement of prohibitions, inspection of goods, collection of customs duties, and assuming the functions of monopolizing imported goods and receiving envoys and businessmen from various countries".[1] With the flourishing of overseas tributes in the Song Dynasty, the volume of overseas trade was much larger than that in the Tang Dynasty. The ports with the Bureau for Foreign Shipping also expanded from Guangzhou to Quanzhou, Mingzhou, Hangzhou, Xiuzhou (now Jiaxing, Zhejiang), Mizhou (now Jiaozhou, Shandong) and later Shibowu (Marine Tax Collection Agency) was set up in Wenzhou, Qinglongzhen (Qingpu, Shanghai), Miaopu (now Haiyan, Zhejiang), Jiangyin and other places, and the management system of foreign shipping had gradually been improved. Especially in view of the shortcomings of the previous dynasties, the court of the Song Dynasty took various measures to strictly select and appoint officials with integrity, reward honesty, and severely punish corrupt

---

[1] *History of the Song Dynasty: Records of Officials*, Vol. 167.

officials, so the Guangzhou Port restored its former prosperity.

It should be noted that in the early Northern Song Dynasty, before the reunification of Zhejiang and Fujian, Guangzhou was the main port for maritime trade with the West. The foreign trade of Guangzhou Port had been prosperous again, and the port still maintained its status as the largest maritime trade port in the Southern Song Dynasty. Guangzhou Port was always the top one among many city ports. At that time, 70% of the imported spices were landed in Guangzhou, while Mizhou was the leading foreign trade port in the northern coastal areas.

(3) *Peripheral ports of Guangzhou Port in the Tang and Song dynasties*

In the Tang and Song dynasties, the main peripheral ports of Guangzhou were Bijing, Qiongzhou, Jiyangjun, and Wananjun. Bijing, the Rinan Harbor in Rinan county in the Han Dynasty, was located at the Lingjiang River Estuary in today's Hue, Vietnam. From the Han Dynasty to the Tang Dynasty, it was a necessary passage for navigation in the South. Its main function was to provide shelter for ships during their voyage. Qiongzhou (today's Haikou Port), Jiyangjun (today's Sanya Port) and Wananjun (today's Wanning Port) were located in Hainan Island. These three ports had come into being in the Tang Dynasty. Besides, Qiongshan, Chengmai, Lingao, Wenchang, and Lehui in Hainan Island all saw the foreign shipping.[1] Ships from Guangzhou and Quanzhou also often came here for trade.

2.7.2 Development of Quanzhou Port and its peripheral ports

Quanzhou, otherwise named "City of Carp", "City of Zaytun" and "Wenling" (warmer place), is known as a "treasure house of diversity of cultures, a historic city on the west side of the Taiwan Straits". It is located in southeastern Fujian at the estuary of

---

[1] Zhao Rushi, a geographer in the Southern Song Dynasty, mentioned "Danbo" (ships of the local Dan people) when he recorded Hainan's commerce and shipping management in the entry of "Hainan" in his *A Record of Local Tribes* (*Zhu Fan Zhi*), "Qiongzhou...consists of five counties: Qiongshan, Chengmai, Lingao, Wenchang and Lehui. They all have maritime trade ships. These ships are divided into three categories, the superior being Bo, the middling Baotou, the next Danbo. At the Customs office, officials measured the size of the ships, recorded it and set the tax standard. The local officials and army are fed on this tax." Zhao Rushi (1170-1231), with the literary name of Boke, the eighth son of the Song Emperor Taizong, served as an executive of Bureau for Foreign Shipping in Fujian Province from Jiading (1208-1224) to Baoqing (1225-1227) period of the Song Dynasty. In 1225, based on literature collected, he compiled *Zhu Fan Zhi* of two volumes. The first volume was the general situation of more than 50 countries from Japan in the East to Morocco of North Africa in the West. The second volume recorded the products with the origin, production, use, and distribution, with an appendix of *Hainan Geographic Records*. His work was an important document to study maritime transportation and foreign trade in the Song Dynasty.

Jinjiang River, with Fuzhou in the north, Xiamen in the south and Taiwan in the east. There are both riverbanks and bays. More than 1,300 years old, Quanzhou Harbor had been the world's largest for 400 years in the history of navigation, equally famous as Alexandria Port in Egypt. It is also the only "starting point of the Maritime Silk Road" recognized by the United Nations.

(1) *Development of Quanzhou Port and its management system of foreign shipping during the Tang and Song dynasties*

In the Tang Dynasty, Quanzhou Port was one of the four largest trading ports with Guangzhou, Mingzhou, and Yangzhou. In the Song Dynasty, Quanzhou was located in the center of the coastline under the jurisdiction of the Song Dynasty, at the intersection of the East China Sea route and the South China Sea route. Quanzhou Port connected Guangzhou in the south with Mingzhou in the north. From Quanzhou, ships could sail directly to the South China Sea, Africa in the west, Japan in the east, and Koryo in the north. Quanzhou also served as a market for transshipment and a production base for export commodities along the southeast coast. In addition to its superior geographical location, after the wars between Song and Jin triggered the southern moving of the Song court to Hangzhou, although Mingzhou was closer to Hangzhou, it was not easy to carry out large-scale maritime trade because of its vulnerability to the threat of the invasion of the Jin troops. Quanzhou Port had sufficient space for development and good traffic conditions compared with Mingzhou Port, and Quanzhou had developed quickly to be the peripheral port of the capital (Hangzhou) for its advantages of being secure in chaos. A large volume of maritime trade in ports in north Fujian was transferred to Quanzhou, contributing greatly to the rapid prosperity of Quanzhou Port and the rapid development and rise of the port. In 1087, the imperial court established Bureau for Foreign Shipping in Quanzhou. The departments in Fujian, Liangzhe (Mingzhou), Guangnan East (Guangzhou) were regarded as the "three best known Bureaus for Foreign Shipping" and were the most important shipping management departments. They managed more than 80% of the country's foreign trade. In the Song Dynasty, there were many ships and businessmen and dozens of thousands of Asians and Africans at Quanzhou Port. Traveling southward from Quanzhou, through today's Vietnam, Malaysia, Singapore, Indonesia, Myanmar, India, Sri Lanka, Pakistan, and other places, ships could reach the Persian Gulf coast and the Arab countries of North Africa.

(2) *Peripheral ports of Quanzhou Port in the Song Dynasty*

The peripheral ports of Quanzhou Port in the Song Dynasty mainly included ports of Houzhu, Anhai, Weitou, Shijing, Fuzhou, and Zhangzhou. Houzhu Port, located at the Quanzhou Bay, was the main peripheral port of Quanzhou. Anhai was located in the south of Quanzhou city and used to be called Wanhai. It was renamed Anhai in the Song Dynasty. Anhai was opposite to Shijing across the bay, which saw foreign ships gathering. Weitou, located at Weitou Bay in the southeast of Quanzhou, was a necessary harbor for foreign ships to anchor, with a branch port reaching the Shijing. Fuzhou was located in the east of Fujian Province, the lower reaches of Minjiang River and the coastal areas, also known as Rongcheng, Sanshan, Dongyue, Zuohai or Yecheng. Fuzhou Port had been opened earlier than Quanzhou Port. Fuzhou city was called Dongye in the Han Dynasty. It had been an important seaport on the southeast coast for a long time. Fuzhou Port became more and more important in the Song Dynasty. Zhangzhou was located in the southeast of Quanzhou, facing Xiamen in the east and Taiwan across the Taiwan Strait, bordering Guangdong in the south and southwest, Quanzhou Plain in the northeast and Fujian in the northwest. It was an important coastal town between Fujian and Guangdong. Sailing from Zhangzhou Port, ships could travel downward the Jiulong River, past Haicheng Port in the southeast, via Haimen Island (Haishan) and Jiujiang and Xiamen Island. Zhangzhou Port had already been a trade port in the south of Fujian in the Northern Song Dynasty and remained as a prosperous port in the Southern Song Dynasty as the peripheral port of Quanzhou Port.

2.7.3 Development of Mingzhou Port and its periphery ports

Mingzhou is today's Ningbo in Zhejiang Province, located in the middle of the coastline of mainland of China, at the south wing of the Yangtze River Delta. There are Zhoushan islands as its natural barriers in the east, bordering on Hangzhou Bay in the north with dense river network and Sanmen Bay in the south, connecting Shaoxing in the west and linking Sanmen and Tiantai of Taizhou. It has been the political and economic center of the east of Zhejiang. In the Qin Dynasty, three counties were established there, namely Yin[1], Ji[2] and Gouzhang[3], all belonging to Kuaiji Prefecture, which was called Yuezhou in the Sui Dynasty. In the 26th year of Kaiyuan of the Tang Dynasty (738), four counties were set up in Minzhou, namely Xiamao, Cixi, Fenghua, and Wengshan. In the Five Dynasties and the Ten States Period, it belonged to Wuyue State. In the 1st year of Changqing (821), the governor's office was moved from

---

[1] The county jurisdiction is Baidu Village, Xiwu Street, Fenghua today.

[2] The county jurisdiction is Tongao Village, Wuxiang Town, Yinzhou District today.

[3] The county jurisdiction is Wangjiaba Village, Cicheng Town, Jiangbei District today.

Yinjiangqiao to Sanjiangkou (the junction of Fenghua River, Yuyao River, and Yongjiang River). In the 1st year of Jianlong in the Northern Song Dynasty (960), Mingzhou was called Fengguojun. In the first year of Qingyuan in the Southern Song Dynasty (1195) it was upgraded to Qingyuan Prefecture. In the Yuan Dynasty, it was called Qingyuan Lu. In the 14th year of Hongwu in the Ming Dynasty (1381), Mingzhou Prefecture was renamed Ningbo Prefecture to avoid the name of the emperor with the meaning of "stable sea makes calm waves". This name is still in use today.

(1) *Development of Mingzhou Port and its management system of foreign shipping in the Tang and Song dynasties*

Mingzhou Port had distinct geographical advantages. It was backed by western Zhejiang, northern Zhejiang and the Yangtze-Huaihe River basin, with a vast economic hinterland connecting the Yangtze River, Huaihe River, Bianhe River in the north and the sea in the east. It was the hub of navigation and inland river shipping. It was also the nearest port and main trading port to sail to Japan and Koryo from the middle and late Tang Dynasty to the Song Dynasty. According to *Geography of Siming (Mingzhou) in Qiandao Period* (1165-1173) by Zhang Jin, although Mingzhou was not a metropolis, it was the place where the sea routes converged. There were Fujian and Guangzhou in its south, Japan in its east, and Koryo in its north. The businessmen and ships were gathering here, and the goods were abundant. In the Five Dynasties when Central Plain was in turmoil, some ports suffered heavy losses from wars. For example, Yangzhou Port had become ruins, and Guangzhou Port had been stagnant. However, under the rule of Qian Liu, King of Wuyue State, Mingzhou Port had remained stable for decades, and maintained maritime exchanges with Japan, Koryo, and Arab regions, thus promoting the transfer of maritime trade with Japan and Koryo from the northern ports to Mingzhou Port.

In the Song Dynasty, foreign shipping routes were mainly divided into the East China Sea and the South China Sea routes. The main port of the East China Sea route was Mingzhou (Ningbo), and the main port of the South China Sea route was Guangzhou. In the 2nd year of Duangong period in the Northern Song Dynasty (989), the imperial court set up the Bureau for Foreign Shipping in Hangzhou, which had jurisdiction over the Mingzhou *Shibowu* (Marine Tax Collection Agency) and was responsible for handling relevant licensing procedures for the trade of merchant ships to overseas countries. In the 2nd year of Qiandao period in the Southern Song Dynasty (1166), because of the gradual transfer of the main port of navigation trade to Quanzhou, the Bureau for Foreign Shipping of Liangzhe was abolished. Only five *Shibowu* were kept in Mingzhou, Hangzhou, Wenzhou, Huating (Songjiang in Shanghai today) and Qinglongzhen (northeast of Qingpu county in Shanghai today). In the Song Dynasty, the Jin troops invaded the south. To prevent the Jin of the eastern Liaoning from invading, the Song Dynasty demanded that all the ships going to Japan and Koryo should no longer take the Bohai Sea route from Dengzhou, but should choose Mingzhou Port. The port became the only one for leaving and arriving of the East China Sea route to Japan and Koryo. In Southeast Asia, ships from such countries as Champa (now Vietnam), Dupo (now Java or Sumatra), Samboja (now Sumatra) and Arab Empire in the west often came to Mingzhou for trade, and the port had been developed rapidly. Although Mingzhou was attacked by Jin soldiers during the Southern Song Dynasty, the harbor was quickly restored to prosperity as described in histoical records "thousands of sailing ships, and merchants from all over the world".[1]

(2) *Peripheral ports of Mingzhou Port*

The peripheral ports of Mingzhou port were mainly Hangzhou Port and Wenzhou Port. Hangzhou was located in the north of Zhejiang Province, the lower reaches of the Qiantang River and the southern end of the Beijing-Hangzhou Grand Canal. It was a famous city in the southeast of the Northern Song Dynasty. In the Southern Song Dynasty, Hangzhou was set as the temporary capital and was promoted to Linan Prefecture as the political and cultural center of Southeast China at that time. Because of the status of Hangzhou, merchants at home and abroad gathered here at that time. Wenzhou was located in southeastern Zhejiang, the lower reaches of the south coast of Oujiang River, called Ouyue in ancient times, historically known for papermaking, shipbuilding, shoe leather, embroidery, and lacquerware. It was also one of the birthplaces of Chinese celadon. Wenzhou Port was the choke-point of the cargo transportation in and out of southern Zhejiang and northern Fujian. It had been an important port in the Northern Song Dynasty and was set as a foreign trade port by the imperial court. In the Southern Song Dynasty, maritime trade was quite developed, and it was the main supporting port of Mingzhou Port to Japan and Koryo.

---

[1] The quotation is from the local chronicles in Southern Song Dynasty, *Geography of Siming (Mingzhou) in Qiandao Period (1165−1173)*, with twelve volumes, written by Zhang Jin and others. The book was based on *Geography of Mingzhou in Daguan Period*, which was rewritten and completed in 1169. Siming was Mingzhou at that time, which is located in Ningbo, Zhejiang Province today.

2.7.4 The development of Yangzhou Port and the formation of Shanghai Port

Yangzhou, also known as Guangling, Jiangdu, Weiyang and so on in ancient times, was located between the Yangtze River and Huaihe River, in the central part of Jiangsu Province. It was adjacent to Yancheng and Taizhou in the east, the Yangtze River in the south, Zhenjiang across the river, Nanjing in the southwest, Huaian and Chuzhou in the northwest. It had the reputation of "the first Canal City in China".

(1) *Development of Yangzhou Port in the Sui, Tang and Song dynasties*

Since the opening of the Grand Canal in the Sui Dynasty, Yangzhou (called Guangling at that time) had been situating at the intersection of the Yangtze River and the Grand Canal. Upstream there were Anhui, Jiangxi, Hunan, Hubei, Sichuan and other hinterland provinces. Downstream ships could sail directly overseas, with the advantages of water transportation through rivers and canal as well as maritime transportation. Besides, at that time Yangzhou was rich in natural and material resources. The surrounding mineral resources and agricultural and sideline products were abundant, with superb arts and handicrafts. The hinterland merchandise was collected and traded actively. The external policy of the Tang Dynasty always advocated protection of the maritime trade. As a result, Guangling became a gateway city with various kinds of commodities gathering here, making it a wealthiest place. Yangzhou Port was once prosperous as an important seaport in the Tang Dynasty. Many foreign merchants lived here. Overseas students and monks from Silla, Japan and other places all arrived at and left from Yangzhou Port. At the end of the Tang Dynasty, with turmoil of wars everywhere, Yangzhou was plundered and burned, and the city was in ruins with sparse population and constant wars. From the late Tang Dynasty to the Song Dynasty, changes in the geographical environment caused several changes in the lower reaches of the Yangtze River and the sediment flowed down the river, depositing on the bank. As the estuary of Yangtze River and the coastline moved eastward, Yangzhou city and Yangzhou Port had become farther away from the estuary, losing their basic conditions as a harbor, and failed to flourish and never recovered.

(2) *Formation of Shanghai Port*

Later, Qinglongzhen, Huating, Taicang and Shanghai ports in the lower reaches of the Yangtze River rose one after another, and Shanghai Port finally came into being under the influence of the rise and fall of Qinglongzhen and the changes of shipping routes.[1] It should be noticed that Shanghai Port was originally a fishing village on the banks of the Huangpu River. It was located in the upper reaches of Huangxiepu River near Huating (Songjiang) seashore and upward along the sea, and it used to be called Huatinghai. In the Song Dynasty, traders gathered there, and then it was called Shanghai. After the decline of Qinglongzhen, although Jiangwan and Yaohuang (now Yuepu) had the conditions for harbor formation, they were not as good as Shanghai for its advantage of being on the bank of the Huangpu River. Hence, Huangpu bank gradually became an important port at the estuary of the Yangtze River from the Southern Song Dynasty. Nowadays, the development of Shenzhen Port and Shenzhen Special Economic Zone is quite similar to that of Shanghai. Because of its superior geographical location and special institutional arrangement, Shenzhen has become the window of the reform and opening up of China and developed to be an influential international city.

2.7.5 Development of Dengzhou Port and its peripheral port of Banqiaozhen in Mizhou

Located at the northernmost end of Shandong Peninsula, Dengzhou was close to the Bohai Sea. It was the "choke-point" of the Bohai Strait, with the Yellow Sea on its southeast and facing the Liaodong Peninsula across the sea. It was the main port of the Tang Dynasty sailing to Liaodong, the outer to Koryo and Japan, and was the landing point for the envoys of Koryo and Japan. It was also an important trade port and military port in the northern Tang and Song dynasties. Especially in the Tang Dynasty and the early period of the Northern Song Dynasty, it has become the largest port in the north.

(1) *Development of Dengzhou Port during the Tang and Song dynasties*

In the 4th year of Wude in the Tang Dynasty (621), the government of Dengzhou was set up in Wendeng County, and that is why the port got the name. In the pre-Qin

---

[1] In the Song Dynasty, Qinglongzhen was adjacent to Wusong River, leading to Suzhou directly, to Huating through Guhuipu, and westward to Xiuzhou (now Jiaxing) via Dayingpu. It enjoyed convenient water and land transportation. After the middle of the Tang Dynasty, Qinglongzhen gradually became a harbor, one of the few ports for Wu and Yue regions to trade with the north and to foreign ships to be anchored there. In the second year of Chunhua in the Northern Song Dynasty (991), *Shibowu* was established in Qinglongzhen, under the jurisdiction of *Shibosi* of Zhejiang Province. In the Northern Song Dynasty, Qinglongzhen Port was a port of departure for Fujian, Guangdong and northern parts of Vietnam, with rich merchants and business tycoons gathering there. And Qinglongzhen was then considered well comparable to Hangzhou. In the Southern Song Dynasty, because Qinglongzhen was close to the Yangtze River and Huai River Region, and its position became more and more important. Its economic, political and military status kept rising and reached the peak of its development. Later on, Wusong River was gradually weakening and the harbor was destroyed by war and reduced to ruins at the end of the Song Dynasty, so the port was transferred to Shanghai.

period, Huanggang and Zhaogang were under the jurisdiction of Dengzhou. In the 3rd year of Shenlong period in the Tang Dynasty (707), Dengzhou government moved to Penglai, and its port was officially called Dengzhou Port. During the Tang and Song dynasties, Dengzhou was one of the centers for silks and hemp textiles production in China. There were also abundant gold and commodities in Dengzhou, and there were more foreign exchanges and shipping routes at sea. There were at least four routes departing from Dengzhou Port to overseas and coastal areas. The first one was the route to Koryo and Balhae State[1] on its north across the Bohai Sea; the second one was the way to Japan via Koryo across the Bohai Sea; the third one was to cross the Yellow Sea via Cheju Island to Japan; the fourth one was to travel southward to Yangzhou and Mingzhou ports. The first three routes were the only passages to Koryo and Japan. There were many merchants gathering here and ships anchoring here, and people having fun day and night. The port witnessed the impressive sight like "thousands of flags at sunrise, and dozens of thousands of lights at sunset". In the late Northern Song Dynasty when the war with Liao and Jin dynasties broke out, Dengzhou became an important frontier coastal defense site where heavy troops were stationed, and urgent messages were sent by the beacon fire to give border alarm from morning to night because it was close to the northern territory of the Jin Dynasty. In the 7th year of Xining in the Northern Song Dynasty (1074), the Song government imposed a sea ban and closed the port of Dengzhou. In the Southern Song Dynasty, when Jin soldiers captured Dengzhou, the port collapsed.

(2) *Peripheral port of Dengzhou: Banqiao Town in Mizhou*

The Banqiao Town is now in Jiaozhou, Shandong Province (used to be called Jiaoxian County). In the 16th year of Kaihuang in the Sui Dynasty (596), Jiaoxi County

---

[1] The Balhae State (698-926) was a regime dominated by the Mohe ethnic group in the history of East Asia, whose area coverage was equivalent to that of present Northeast China, the Northeast Korean Peninsula and a part of the Russian Far East. In 698, Da Zuorong, the leader of the Sumo Mohe, established his regime in Dongmou Mountain (now Dunhua in Jilin Province) by calling himself "the King of Zhen State". In 713, Xuanzong, the Emperor of the Tang Dynasty, conferred the title of "King of Bohai Prefecture" and the title of "Governor of Kuhan Prefecture" on him. In 762, Tang imperial decree upgraded Bohai into a state. The capital of the Bohai State was first stationed in Jiuguo (now Dunhua in Jilin Province), and then moved to Xiande (now Helong in Jilin Province), Shangjing Longquan (now Ning'an in Heilongjiang Province), Dongjing Longyuan (now Hunchun in Jilin Province) and Shangjing Longquan. The Bohai State established its political and economic system according to the Tang Dynasty constitution. During its heyday, it had jurisdiction over 5 provincial capitals, 15 prefectures, and 62 provinces. Its culture was deeply influenced by the culture of the Tang Dynasty and enjoyed the reputation of "prosperous country of Haidong". In 926, it was destroyed by the Khitan Kingdom. Balhae State lasted 229 years, ruled by 15 kings.

under the jurisdiction of Mizhou was set up here. In the 6th year of Wude in the Tang Dynasty (623), it was renamed Banqiao Town which was merged into Mizhou. In the 3rd year of Yuanyou in the Song Dynasty (1088), it was renamed Jiaoxi County, so it was also named Banqiao Town. In the Tang Dynasty, a port was set up here, which was intended to be a coastal defense site in the Yellow Sea rather than a trading port. After the closure of Dengzhou Port in the Song Dynasty, the port moved southward to Banqiao Town. After the opening, the port had been a sea passage for a long time. Businessmen from home and abroad gathered here, establishing ties with each other. Banqiao Town was the port of collection and distribution. Inland goods were transported to the south of the Yangtze River or overseas from here. In the 3rd year of Yuanyou Period in the Song Dynasty (1088), the Bureau for Foreign Shipping was set up in Banqiao Town to strengthen the management of the port and navigation trade.

2.8 Development of external transport by land and sea during the Yuan Dynasty

Both Yuan and Qing were feudal dynasties established by nomadic people of the north in the Central Plains, while the Yuan Dynasty established the largest feudal empire in human history. Throughout the Yuan Dynasty, Temujin and his successors had annihilated more than 40 countries and conquered more than 720 ethnic groups in more than 50 years, with a conquered population of 600 million, and established the largest country in human history. According to historical records, the territory of the Yuan Dynasty was stable with an area of more than 35 million square kilometers, with a maximum area of more than 45 million square kilometers, accounting for more than 80% of the world's land area at that time. Its territory ranged from the Korean Peninsula in the east to Poland and Hungary in the west, to the Russian and Siberia in the north, and to the Indochina Peninsula in South Java. Vasily Vladimirovich Bartold (1869-1930), a famous Orientalist of the Soviet Union, once said that the founding of the Genghis Khan Empire was a unique case in the world in a sense. It united the civilized countries of the Far East and South Asia under a dynasty regime, which was unprecedented. Genghis Khan was written into the annals of history as "the conqueror of the world". The descendants of Temujin had successively created the Khanate of Chahetai, the State of Ilhan, the Kipchak Khanate and later the Khanate of Timur. Almost all of Asia and Europe became the territory of the Yuan Dynasty, which was so unprecedented that no one came after it. That was more than three times of the size of China today, and now the entire land area of Asia (including islands) are less than 44 million square kilometers.

Because of the vast territory under his rule, Genghis Khan and the rulers of the Yuan Dynasty after him attached great importance to the use of various means of transportation to communicate with each other, and promoted the development of foreign transport by means of the post system, thus establishing a large-scale, well-organized, highly efficient post system with land stations as the main, supplemented by water, which covered a wide range of Korgo in the east, Siberia in the north, Annan (today's Vietnam) in the south, the Baltic Sea in the west and Hungary (Kipchak Khanate), and as far as the Persian Gulf (Chahatai Khanate) in the southwest. The Yuan Dynasty encouraged foreign trade, vigorously launched overseas trade, and constantly increased exchanges. This helped smooth the old Land Silk Road which had been blocked for many years, and the Maritime Silk Road became increasingly prosperous. Although the Yuan Dynasty survived for a short period of time, rising and falling within only 90 years, as a vast empire spanning Asia and Europe, it inherited the Song Dynasty system and expanded territory, and played a very prominent role in the history of China.

2.8.1 Development of external transport by land and sea in the Yuan Dynasty

The foreign trade of the Yuan Dynasty was mainly at sea, but the main passage of the Land Silk Road connecting Asia and Europe to the West was also smoother than in the previous dynasties.

(1) *Land transport development*

There were mainly the south road and the north road crossing the boundary. The north road started from Dadu (now Beijing) to the west, through Dunhuang, Hami to Alima (now Huocheng, Xinjiang) and Chorasmia (now Uzbekistan and Turkmenistan in the lower reaches of the Amu Darya), Crimea to the Black Sea, and then to Constantinople (now Istanbul, Turkey). The south road started from Constantinople to the east across the Asia Minor Peninsula, crossing the Iranian Plateau to Kurumus (today in Hormuz, Iran) to move northward into Central Asia and West Asia, across the Congling Mountains to Lost Har (Gushule, now Kashgar in Xinjiang), and passed Khotan (now Hetian, Xinjiang), Lop Nor, Dunhuang to finally go eastward to the capital of the Yuan Dynasty. The endpoint of the Silk Road Dadu (now Beijing), called Khan

Bali (meaning the capital) then, had developed into the largest city in the country.

(2) *External navigation at sea and Shibo system*

In the Yuan Dynasty, China's navigation and shipbuilding technologies were ahead of the world. After the Yuan Dynasty ruled the Central Plains, it first took advantage of the strength of the sea vessels to control the sea, destroyed the restoration forces in the Southern Song Dynasty along the coast, and unified China. With the prestige of the Mongolian army's Iron Knights sweeping across the Asian and European countries, it controlled the maritime trade relations with Asian, European and African countries. There were several major routes for overseas trade in the Yuan Dynasty. The Eastern Route reached Japan and Koryo; the southern route reached the countries of the South Ocean and the Indian Peninsula; the western route connects Central Asia, Persia and the Arabian Peninsula and then went to the eastern Mediterranean and the coast of East Africa. Although due to political reasons, the Yuan Dynasty had "four prohibitions and four openness rules" on foreign trade, all of these showed that foreign trade had become an important source of wealth for the Yuan government, which had to allow merchants out at sea and rely on the support of shipping.

After the founding of the Yuan Dynasty, Kublai Khan and other rulers followed the Song Dynasty system by attaching great importance to the development of overseas trade to attract overseas countries to trade in China. Ships were encouraged to go to sea, and the specialized administration organization—*Shibosi* was set up. In the 14th year of Zhiyuan in the Yuan Dynasty (1277), Shibosi was set up in Quanzhou, Qingyuan (now Ningbo), Shanghai and Ganpu (now north of Hangzhou Bay). In the 23rd year of Zhiyuan in the Yuan Dynasty, the Shibosi was set up in Wenzhou Port, Hangzhou Port and Guangzhou Port, and then the departments of some of the ports were adjusted.[1] However, it was responsible for the management of ships entering and leaving the sea and for levying appropriate tariffs on imported goods. Those entering and leaving foreign trade ports such as Quanzhou, Qingyuan and Guangzhou were not only foreign merchants from Southeast Asia, Arabia, Persia and other countries and regions along the Mediterranean coast but also merchant ships from coastal areas such as Fujian,

---

[1] In the 30th year of the Yuan Dynasty (1293), Hangzhou Shibosi and Wenzhou Shibosi were abolished and merged into Qingyuan Shibosi. In the 1st year of Dade (1293), Shanghai Shibosi and Ganpu Shibosi were merged into Qingyuan. Finally, Shibosi was established in Qingyuan, Quanzhou, and Guangzhou. At this time, Guangzhou Port had retreated to the second place, and Quanzhou in Fujian Province had become a prosperous port since the Yuan Dynasty.

Guangzhou, Jiangsu, and Zhejiang. The volume of maritime trade was far beyond any previous era, and the booming of overseas maritime trade earned for the Yuan Dynasty a tremendous amount of income every year.

2.8.2 Major ports of the Yuan Dynasty

Major ports for foreign trade in the Yuan Dynasty include Quanzhou Port, Guangzhou Port, Qingyuan Port and their peripheral ports.

(1) *Quanzhou Port*

Quanzhou, also called Zaytun city, is named after all kinds of Zaytun trees around the city. Quanzhou Port had been developing rapidly since the Southern Song Dynasty. By the turn of the Song and Yuan dynasties, Quanzhou Port had become the same as Guangzhou Port, where most of the seagoing ships entered and left. During the war of Song and Yuan dynasties, Quanzhou Port did not suffer heavy losses, and foreign navigation trade was continued. By the 15th year of Zhiyuan in the Yuan Dynasty (1278), Kublai Khan's imperial edict notified that foreign boats were allowed here to trade so that many foreign countries came to do business through Quanzhou Port. Thus, it became the largest international trade port in China and in the East. Marco Polo, an Italian who came to China at that time and had served in the Yuan Dynasty for 17 years, wrote about his Eastern experiences in his book *The Travels of Marco Polo*, and thought that the port of Zaytun was one of the world's largest harbors. Ibn Battuta, a Moroccan traveler who came to China after Marco Polo, also regarded the port as one of the largest seaports in the world. From what they wrote, we could see that the prosperity of Quanzhou Port in the Yuan Dynasty was unprecedented.

(2) *Guangzhou Port*

Guangzhou was the last stronghold before the fall of the Southern Song Dynasty. After suffering from the war, Guangzhou Port was severely destroyed. Ships were destroyed by fires, which had a great influence on the development of Guangzhou Port. When Quanzhou Port was prosperous after the Yuan Dynasty, Guangzhou Port was restored. However, the port had trade ties with only neighboring countries in the South Seas region, and the volume of foreign trade was significantly reduced.

(3) *Qingyuan Port*

Qingyuan Port, known as Mingzhou Port in the Song Dynasty, whose navigation trade was basically the same as that in the Southern Song Dynasty, still occupied a prominent position of the maritime trade in the Yuan Dynasty. The Wenzhou Port and the Ganpu Port near Qingyuan Port set up the *Shibosi*, and later merged with Qingyuan city. Shanghai Port in the north of Ganpu Port, formerly a small town in Huating County, Xiuzhou, had gradually developed into an important shipping and trade port on East Zhejiang Road of Jiangsu and Zhejiang provinces due to the divergence of trade and customs. Besides, Liujia Port of Taicang and Zhigu Port (today's Tianjin Port, renamed Tianjin in the 2nd year of Jianwen Period in the Ming Dynasty) were all major ports at that time.

2.9   Development of external transport and trade management during the Ming Dynasty and Zheng He's voyages to the Western Ocean

After the establishment of the Ming Dynasty, the policy of emphasizing farming and rewarding farming and weaving was carried out internally. The opening up to the outside world went through the periods from Hongwu in the early stage to Xuande and Zhengtong. It carried out the policy of opening up, combining conciliation with the prevention and tributary trade. However, at the later stage, it transferred to the closing-door policy due to the lack of national strength and the frequency of border conflicts.

2.9.1   Policy of maritime prohibition and the tributary system in the Ming Dynasty

In the early Ming Dynasty, the external environment was complex, and the sea was not peaceful. In order to prevent the attack of the remnants of the Yuan Dynasty from the sea and the harassment of the Japanese invaders, Zhu Yuanzhang, the founding emperor of the Ming Dynasty, advocated the ban on maritime trade, which was not intentionally self-closing, but restrictive control measures to ensure the peace of the border of the sea. In fact, the ban on maritime trade was for private ships, not terminating for the tributary ships controlled by the imperial court. It only allowed the government to monopolize foreign trade but not private free trade. Foreign countries were to pay tribute following the former policies of the Song and Yuan dynasties, and the only legal form of overseas trade of China linking overseas countries was limited to the tribute trade.[1] The policy of opening to the outside world in early Ming Dynasty was minimal and relatively closed. The maritime prohibition formulated by Emperor Zhu Yuanzhang was followed by his successors. This policy was carried out with instability, hurting the benefit of some bigwigs involved in the smuggling trade and making the game of power more fierce within the rulers over the maritime prohibition. In the late Ming Dynasty, restricted overseas trade policy was adopted.

The Ming Dynasty, as a regional power, jointly formed an East Asian order and tributary system featuring a "center-edge" structure with its neighboring countries. The premise of the tribute at that time was that the tributary states should accept the recognition and conferment of the local king by China, and held all kinds of activities of foreign submission to the Ming Dynasty in due course. According to the research of Japanese scholars, Hamashita Takeshi,[2] the tributary system of East Asia under the leadership of China had three characteristics: firstly, the suzerain (China) provided international security, and the regional disputes did not resort to force to resolve; secondly, the tributary trade protected by the tributary system was a special tax-free grace, which was very attractive to foreign trade; thirdly, the tributary system pursued the idea that the Ming emperor's benevolence enlightened the whole world and embraced the foreign-vassal culture, and the tributary states could contact other tributary regions within the tributary system, while China acted as a medium for the exchange between them.

---

[1] The two-way top-down and bottom-up foreign trade of the Ming and Qing dynasties were usually known as " feng-gong trade" or "tributary trade" in which the Chinese emperor conferred titles on the rulers of kingdoms or entities concerned, who respected or accepted his authority and paid tribute to the rulers via envoys to China. In return the Chinese court would usually accept and react to this kind of visit by giving these envoys substantial gifts. In the first year of Hongwu Period in the Ming Dynasty (1368), the emperor opened up coastal ports and accepted tribute from foreign countries whose rulers had been conferred titles on by the Chinese emperor and allowed them to trade in China. In the feng-gong trade system, paying tribute was supposed to be one of the main relationships and trade the subsidiary. But at many times, foreign countries came for trade with China in the name of paying tribute. Most of the tribute missions visited with merchant ships coming along with them. The main purpose was to trade, selling and purchasing goods and products, and completing transactions. During the Hongwu Period in the early Ming Dynasty, Ningbo, Quanzhou, and Guangzhou had opened up the tributary trade to Japan, Ryukyu, Champa, Siam and some western countries, that was, to allow merchant ships of tributary countries to trade at these three ports.

[2] [Japan] Hanshita Takeshi, *International Opportunities in Modern China: Tribute Trade System and Modern Asian Economic Circle*, Beijing: China Social Science Press, 1999, pp. 30-40.

2.9.2 The Shibo system and the management of foreign trade in the Ming Dynasty

In the 3rd year of Hongwu period in the Ming Dynasty (1370), the Shibosi of Ningbo, Guangzhou, and Quanzhou in the Song and Yuan dynasties were restored to meet the needs of tributary trade. Moreover, it stipulated that Ningbo Port be opened to Japan, Quanzhou Port to Ryukyu, and Guangzhou Port to Champa, Siam, Western countries, and other ports (harbours) were not allowed to trade beyond the rules. In the 4th year of Hongwu (1371), it exempted all taxes on overseas ships. In the 7th year of Hongwu (1374), because of the Japanese invasion, sea prohibition was strictly imposed. The Shibosi of Quanzhou, Mingzhou, and Guangzhou were closed down, the private entrepreneurs banned, and the sea prohibition was enforced strictly. Anyone who dared to trade with foreign merchants privately would get severe punishment.[1] All these resulted in the shrink of foreign trade. However, ships from foreign countries were allowed to pay tribute with the certificate of *"Kan he"*[2] and trade on the basis of the system, which was also called the Kan-he trade system.

In the 1st year of Yongle period, due to the increasing number of overseas

---

[1] From *Records of the Ming Dynasty, the 27th year of Hongwu.*

[2] Kanhe, a permit issued by the Ming government to allow tributary state ships to come to China for tribute and trade, was in duplicate, and one half called Kango, the other half a Dipu or Kangofu, a trading license, with seam seals printed in the middle. The Ming Dynasty Libu (Ministry of Rites, usually in charge of examinations, diplomacy, sacrificial rites, feasts and tribute) kept the Kango, and the tributary state held a Dipu. In the 16th year (1383) of Hongwu in the Ming Dynasty, the Ministry of Rites issued a prospectus to Siam, Chenla, Champa, Java, Malacca, Japan, Saltanah Sulu (East King, West King and Tong King), Cochin, Borneo, Ceylon, Zhanli, Sumatra, Maguindanao, Calicut and other countries, and stipulating that all vessels and envoys who came to China to pay tribute must hold a national certification. Each tributary state was awarded 200 Kango pieces by the Ministry of Rites, with four basebooks, 100 Kango pieces with one name and two basebooks to be kept by the imperial storehouse, another 100 Kango pieces with one name and one basebook to be given to the tributary state, and the last one to the relevant Secretary of Administration. At the same time, the Ming Dynasty also stipulated different time limits for overseas countries to pay tribute, restricting the number of ships, ports of entry and the routes for the transportation of tributes to Nanjing the then capital. Each of the tribute ships from various countries to China should bring one Kango with the names of the tributary envoys and the ship's personnel, the number of tributary articles, etc. When overseas tributary vessels entered designated ports, the Secretary of Administration of the place would go to inspect, check and verify with the officials of the Shipping Department of the municipality. If the investigation and verification were consistent, the ship would be allowed to unload the cargo into the post house to be opened. Otherwise, it would not be accepted, and would be punished for counterfeit or arrested as "pirates". When the tributary ship returned, it was to record the objects returned by the Ming Dynasty on the investigation and bring them back to the country. The implementation of the Kango trade system enabled the Ming government to place overseas trade under the strict control of the feudal dynasty, and to ensure the implementation of the sea ban and strengthening of the coastal defense policy.

tributaries to China, the Shibosi was restored in Ningbo, Quanzhou, and Guangzhou, and the Shibosi of Ningbo was requested to set up Anyuan Post House, Quanzhou Laiyuan Post House, and Guangzhou Huaiyuan Post House, to be in charge of the reception of tributary officials. The tribute trade reached its peak at this stage. Table 2–1 shows incomplete statistics of tribute trading with South China Sea countries in the Ming Dynasty.

Table 2–1　　　　Incomplete statistics of tribute trading with South China Sea countries in the Ming Dynasty

Country name	Number of visits	Country name	Number of visits
Annan	11	Siam	31
Champa Kingdom	29	Chenla	8
Maguindanao	1	Myanmar	53
Malacca	22	Sulu	4
Samudra	19	Pangasinan	3
Brunei	10	Luzon	1
Borneo	3	Pahang	3
Java	36	Lambri	9
Lampung	2	Aru	4
Laos	14	Nakur	2

Source: Edited by the author.

The Shibo system in the early Ming Dynasty could be summarized into three phrases: verification by Kan-he, punishment of smuggled goods, and fair trade. They were all about the management of tributary trade and were very conservative. In the late Ming Dynasty, due to the increase of military expenditure and the insufficiency of fiscal revenue, in the Zhengde Period and thereafter, the imperial government began to divide the imported seagoing ships from Guangzhou Shibosi to foreign trade ports, from material tax to monetary tax, from dividing tax to taxation and from import tax to export tax. While expanding fiscal revenue, a relatively complete tariff system was gradually formed which laid the foundation for the customs system of the Qing Dynasty. Originally, the duty of "fair trade" of the Shibosi was transferred to carry out by brokers gaining the official approval who was responsible for negotiation and transaction. They gradually obtained the privilege of monopolizing the maritime trade market and formed the later system of compradors.

In the mid-Ming Dynasty, sea prohibition was loose. Since the strict implementation of the closed-door policy and the cessation of regular maritime trade during the Jiajing Period, the people in the southeastern coastal areas had been living in poverty and risked their lives against the rules. Smuggling trade among people living in the sea, Japanese pirates, overseas merchants and other pirates had continued. At that time, pirates in Southern China featured complex characters. Private overseas trade was becoming more and more popular with an increasing ban. Offshore smuggling trade was mainly in the coastal areas of Jiangsu, Zhejiang, Fujian, and Guangdong. Ocean-going ships were private merchant ships that went directly to Japan, Korea, Ryukyu and other southeast Asian countries.

2.9.3 The seven voyages of Zheng He: achievements and impact for later generations

(1) *Regions of Zheng He's voyages*

In the Ming Dynasty and even in the history of China's opening up to the outside world, voyages of Zheng He from the 3rd year of Yongle Period to the 8th year of Xuande Period in the Ming Dynasty (1405-1433) were passed down. In order to show the military power and its prosperity, advocate virtues and make other countries respect and accept its authority and influence, Emperor Yongle sent Zheng He, a Chinese navigator and diplomat, to lead his fleet to the Indian Ocean, sailing to more than 30 countries and regions in Asia and Africa, from the southern Indochina Peninsula to the eastern part of Africa across the entire Indian Ocean and the South Pacific, which not only pushed tributary trade to its heyday, but also promoted the unprecedented prosperity of the Maritime Silk Road. It has been regarded as the greatest feat in the world maritime history in the 15th century. Table 2–2 shows the dates and major countries or regions reached by Zheng He's seven voyages around the Indian Ocean.

Table 2–2　　Dates and major countries or regions reached by Zheng He's seven voyages around the Indian Ocean

Order	Time span	Sailing vessels and numbers	Main purpose	Major countries or regions to be visited (▲ destination countries)
1	From November of the 3rd year to September of the 5th year of Yongle Period (1405-1407)	62 treasure ships with 27,800 people	Restoring the exchange of tribute ships with Western countries and open up shipping routes	Champa, Java, Sumatra, Palembang, Malacca, Lambri, ▲ Calicut, Palembang

(continued)

Order	Time span	Sailing vessels and numbers	Main purpose	Major countries or regions to be visited (▲destination countries)
2	From September of the 5th year to summer in the 7th year of Yongle Period (1407-1409)	249 treasure ships with unknown passengers	Establishing friendly relations via southeast Asia and India	Champa, Java, Siam, Malacca, Lambri, Kayal, Cochin, Qambari, Ahmedabad, ▲Calicut, Ceylon
3	From December of the 7th year to June of the 9th year of Yongle Period (1409-1411)	48 treasure ships with 27,000 people	Establishing friendly relations via Southeast Asia and India	Champa, Java, Siam, Malacca, Sumatra, Ceylon, Kollam, ▲Calicut, Lambri, Ahmedabad
4	From Winter of the 11th year to July of the 13th year of Yongle Period (1415-1415)	63 treasure ships with 27,670 people	Sailing to the Persian Gulf and keeping close contact with West Asian and East African countries	Champa, Java, Palembang, Malacca, Ceylon, Cochin, Calicut, Pahang, Kelantan, Aru, Lambri, ▲Hormoz, Maldive, Mogadishu, Brawa, Malindi
5	From the autumn and winter of the 15th year to July of the 17th year of Yongle Period (1417-1419)	The number of treasure ships and their accompanying personnel unknown	Sending envoys to other countries	Champa, Java, Palembang, Malacca, Pahang, Sumatra, Ceylon, Cochin, Calicut, Aden, Mogadishu, Malindi, Brawa, ▲Hormoz, Sulu, Ra's Sharwayn, Malindi
6	Form the autumn of the 19th year to August of the 20th year of Yongle Period (1421-1422)	The number of treasure ships and their accompanying personnel unknown	Escorting envoys of 16 countries, such as Hormoz, back home	Champa, Ceylon, Siam, Malacca, Sumatra, Bengala, Calicut, Cochin, ▲Hormoz, Aden, Phofar, Zeila, Maldive, Lambri, Aru, Mogadishu, Brava, Malindi, Gumbari
7	From December of the 6th year to July of the 8th year of Xuande Period (1431-1433)	100 treasure ships with 27,550 people	Communicating with overseas countries to expand Emperor Xuande's influence and attract foreigner merchants	Champa, Java, Palembang Malacca, Siam, Sumatra, Aru, Nakur, Lide, Lambri, Ceylon, Bengala, Maldive, Kollam, Gambari, Kayal, Cochin, Calicut, ▲Hormoz, Dhofar, Zeila, Aden, Mogadishu, Juba, Mecca

Source: Edited by the author.

(2) *Profound influence of voyages of Zheng He*

The voyages of Zheng He were a symbol of the heyday of ancient Chinese navigation. It fully showed the developed civilization of China to the world and exerted a far-reaching influence on later generations. Firstly, the range of activities and sailing routes of Zheng He's fleet connected all the routes of Asia and Africa in a comprehensive vertical and horizontal pattern, forming a smooth Asian-African maritime traffic network between the Western Pacific and the Indian Ocean. Secondly, the good and orderly organization and management of the sea-going fleets provided a satisfactory reference for later generations. Thirdly, Zheng He's voyage paved the way for the great geographical discovery in the East. Zheng He's Nautical Charts and Star Drawing Operation System summarized the technical experience of China's navigation since the Song and Yuan dynasties, were pushing the quantitative navigation to a new historical period and making great contributions to the later transoceanic navigation.

(3) *Reflections on the competition between Zheng He's voyages and the global oceangoing voyages*

The voyages of Zheng He were more than half a century earlier than the "great geographical discovery". Zheng He's first voyage to the Atlantic Ocean (1405) was 87 years earlier than Columbus' arrival at the New World in America in 1492, 92 years earlier than Da Gama's arrival in Calicut, India (Kozekot) in 1497 and 114 years earlier than Magellan's global voyage in 1519. He was indeed a forerunner of "great geographical discoveries". Joseph Needham, an expert in modern science and technology in Britain, said in the *Science and Civilisation in China*, Around 1420, the Ming Dynasty's sailors may have been better than any other Asian country in history, or even better than any other European country of the same era. Even all European countries united, they still could not surpass China in navigation.

However, since Zheng He's ocean voyages were forced to stop, China had retreated to the mainland, and Europeans had come to dominate the sea. This has had a strategic impact on the course of world history. American historian, Stavriyanos, pointed out that when the Chinese withdrew from the ocean-going sailing competitors in the mid-15th century, the Portuguese quickly controlled the huge trading areas from East Africa to Malacca, and even established commercial bases in Macao on the Chinese coast. The fact that the Portuguese opened the trade route to China instead of the Chinese to Europe marked a fundamental turning point in the history of the Third World. It determined which parts of the earth would constitute the Third World that was dependent on others and which parts would become the first world of expansion and development.[1]

---

[1] Cf. Leften Stavrianos, *Global Rift: The Third World Comes of Age*, Pennsylvania: William Morrow & Co., 1981.

2.9.4 Major ports in the Ming dynasty and their development

In the Ming Dynasty, the most important coastal ports from north to south were mainly Liaodong (Jinzhouwei), Zhigu and Laizhou, Dengzhou, Huai'an, Songjiang, Ningbo, Taizhou, Wenzhou, Fuzhou, Xinghua, Quanzhou, Zhangzhou, Chaozhou, Huizhou, Guangzhou, Leizhou, and Qiongzhou. In the late Ming Dynasty (after the 1st year of Longqing Period in 1567), the sea was opened at Yuegang Port of Haicheng, and allowed to "trade in Eastern and Western oceans".[1] There were mainly Jiaozhi, Champa, Siam, Xiagang, Caliba, Cambodia, Patani, Palembang, Malacca, Achie, Paheng, Johor, Indragiri, Gresik, Banjar marsin and other ports in the Western Ocean, while the Eastern Ocean were mainly Luzon, Sulu, Burial, Sayao, Dapitau, Maluku, Brunei, Jilong, Danshui and other ports. Private trade vessels from Yue Port had a wide range of trade. At that time, the trade points to the Western Ocean were mainly concentrated in Pattani, Banten and Batavia ports, and the main destinations to the Eastern Ocean were Luzon and Japan. Throughout the Ming Dynasty, when the sea prohibition was strict or relaxed from time to time, domestic trade and commerce were generally not prohibited, and there were certain restrictions on the sea trade, and the opening of coastal ports was limited.

Reviewing the actual development of external transportation and trade both on land and sea from the Qin and Han dynasties to the Ming Dynasty, we can clearly realize that no matter which dynasty or era, the one that wants to open to the outside world and develop foreign trade is inseparable from a strong and unified central government, a stable and open social environment, and a smooth and safe land-sea cross-border

---

[1] Generally, historians believe that the terms of "Western Ocean" and "Eastern Ocean" were formed before the Yuan Dynasty and should have something to do with the foreign Maritime trade in the Southern Song Dynasty. By the early Ming Dynasty, these terms had been widely popular and followed a clear boundary and definition. According to Wang Ermin, a historian from Taiwan region, when Chinese overseas merchant navigators sailed to the Eastern and Western Oceans, their starting points were mostly Quanzhou, Fuzhou, Jinmen, and other places. Quanzhou was taken as the center. The east of the meridian was called the "Eastern Ocean", and the west of the meridian was called the "Western Ocean", which was different from what they mean today. In the Yuan Dynasty, the navigation areas were divided into the Great Eastern Ocean, the Little Eastern Ocean, the Great Western Ocean and the Little Western Ocean. The Eastern and Western Oceans were roughly separated by the Lambri (Aceh) of the Strait of Malacca, and the South Pacific Ocean, east of the Lambri was the Eastern Ocean. The Eastern Ocean was divided by Borneo (Brunei), the Great Eastern Ocean to the west, and the Little Eastern Ocean to the east, and the west of the Lambri was the Western Ocean. In the Ming Dynasty, to the west of Jiaozhi, Cambodia and Siam were today's Malay Peninsula, Sumatra, Java, Lesser Sunda Islands, India, Persia, Arabia and other places for the Western Ocean, including Champa, Siam, Java, Malacca, Sumatra, Calicut, Bengala and other places. Today, Japan, Ryukyu, the Luzon Islands, the Philippines, the Sulu Islands, Kalimantan, and the Moluccas belong to the Eastern Ocean.

passageway. The Land Silk Road was opened up since Zhang Qian's mission to the Western Regions, and it declined in the late Ming Dynasty; the Maritime Silk Road with foreign transportation, trade and cultural exchange centered on the South China Sea which had been opened up since the Emperor Wu of Han Dynasty overthrew the Nanyue Kingdom; the Maritime Silk Road route was expanded to the world and entered a period of great prosperity in the Ming Dynasty. After the Opium War, the coastal ports of China were forced to open up. Since then, the Maritime Silk Road had declined.

The rise and decline of land and sea ports' opening up were closely related to the development of transportation and trade both on land and sea. And the rise and decline of navigation were closely linked with the development of ports. In particular, there were three peaks in the development of navigation and shipbuilding industry in ancient China. It started in the Qin and Han dynasties at its early age, flourished in the Tang and Song dynasties, and thrived in the Yuan and Ming dynasties. The flourishing period lasted from the 14th year of Zhiyuan Period in the Yuan Dynasty when the Shibosi was restored to Zheng He's voyage to the Western Ocean in the 8th year of Xuande Period in the Ming Dynasty (1433), lasting for 156 years. From the 8th year of Xuande Period in the Ming Dynasty to the 12th year of Daoguang Period in the Qing Dynasty (1840), China's navigational career had changed from prosperity to decline, which lasted for 407 years. From the beginning of the First Opium War to the time before the founding of the People's Republic of China in 1949, the development of navigation and the opening of ports in China entered the period of stagnation. After the founding of the People's Republic of China, the opening up and navigation development of China's ports entered a time of revitalization.

Chapter 3
Open Ports, Foreign Trade, and Their Development during the Qing Dynasty and Modern China

3.1 Opening policy and foreign trade management of the Qing Dynasty before the First Opium War

From its founding in 1644 to its fall in 1912, the Qing Dynasty lasted for 286 years. In the Qing Dynasty, there were two periods of maritime prohibition and two different opening policies were implemented in different periods.

3.1.1 Policies of maritime prohibition and sea trade in the Qing Dynasty

(1) *Two prohibitions of maritime trade*

The first prohibition was from the 12th year of Emperor Shunzhi (1655) to the 23rd year of Emperor Kangxi (1684), which lasted for 29 years. Its primary purpose was to prevent the Zheng's anti-Qing forces in the southeastern coastal areas. The Qing government issued a number of bans of maritime trade and orders of migration of coastal dwellers[1], covering coastal areas of Shandong, Jiangsu, Zhejiang, Fujian and Guangdong provinces, especially Fujian and Guangdong. It was reiterated that "no boat is allowed to enter the sea, and no goods are permitted to be shipped across the border. Sailing ships are prohibited to harbor in ports". "From now on, any merchants who sail into the sea without permission and exchange grains and other goods with foreigners will be executed to death whether they are government officials or local civilians. Their goods will be confiscated by the local government, and the properties of the offender's

---

[1] In the early Qing Dynasty, the "prohibition of the maritime trade" and the "orders of migration of coastal dwellers" required that coastal residents of Fujian, Guangdong, Jiangsu, Zhejiang and Shandong provinces be forced to move 25 km inland. Those who violated the law were severely punished, and navigation and trade, fishing and cultivation of coastal land were prohibited. The coastal area was destroyed as a depopulated zone within 15 or 25 km, which was a catastrophe to the development of navigation and overseas trade in coastal areas.

families would be given to the informant. If local officials and military officers do not carry out the order, they will be dismissed and severely punished".[1] With the completion of the reunification of Taiwan in the 23rd year of Kangxi and the gradual stabilization of the Qing Dynasty, the Qing government announced the removal of migration order from the coastal frontier for the sake of national economy and people's livelihood. In that year, Emperor Kangxi ordered the abolition of the national maritime prohibition and opened up trading with Europe at the request of Dutch businessmen for tribute, restoring the development of the maritime trade. The second maritime prohibition was between the 56th year of Emperor Kangxi (1717) and the 5th year of Emperor Yongzheng (1727) for around 10 years. The primary purpose was to prevent the Ming descendants who migrated to Southeast Asia at the turn of the Ming and Qing dynasties and during the period of reunifying Taiwan from gathering forces overseas against the Qing Dynasty. This maritime ban was mainly aimed at domestic ships instead of foreign ones. The routes for Chinese ships to sail to Southeast Asia were blocked, but those for foreign vessels to enter China for trade were not closed.

(2) *Policies of opening to the outside world at two different stages*

Before the Opium War, the Qing Dynasty's policy of opening to the outside world experienced two stages. The first stage, from the sea trade policy in 1684 to the middle of the 18th century, was a relatively healthy period of foreign exchanges, especially before the mid-Kangxi period. From the late Kangxi period to the reign of Yongzheng period, China's exchanges with Europe were suspended because of the "conflicts between religions and rites", but the overall foreign exchanges and trade remained normal. The second stage lasted from the 22nd year of the reign of Emperor Qianlong when it was stipulated that Guangzhou was the only port for foreign trade, to the first Opium War. During this period, Emperor Qianlong began to restrict the customs, and issued the policy of "Priority to coastal defense over trade." Then during the Jiaqing and Daoguang periods (mid-19th century), the policy with the ideas of "prohibition" and "prevention" was developed, which not only strictly restricted Chinese merchants' shipbuilding and navigation to the outside world, but also strictly restricted western science, technology, commodities, and technologies to come to China. Xenophobia and a long-term close-door policy of seclusion,

---

[1] *Factual Records of the Ancestors of the Qing Dynasty*, Volume 102, *Classical Cases of Laws and Regulations in Guangxu Period of the Qing Dynasty*, Volume 776, and *Historical Materials of Ming and Qing Dynasties*, Volume 2.

eventually led to a forced opening of China with fleets and bombs of western countries led by Britain since the 1840s.

(3) *Objective analysis*

From the founding of the Qing Dynasty to the First Opium War, there were only 29 years of ban on maritime trade out of the 196 years, and in the rest of the time the Qing government implemented the opening policy to foreign countries. Sino-foreign trade had not been interrupted. The Qing government mainly adopted a policy of mollification to comfort foreign countries, instead of strict prohibition on foreign trade. After the First Opium War, under the threat of the British and other Western invaders, the gateway of the Qing Dynasty had to be opened, ruling out the possibility of any maritime bans. Looking around at the open ports of Britain, the Netherlands and other western countries at that time, in order to achieve trade protection, only domestic ships were allowed to enter and leave the ports, and imported goods were only allowed to be loaded and transported by domestic ships or vessels of the goods-producing countries. However, these so-called civilized and robbery-like western countries forced other countries to open their doors through various means of colonial expansion and armed aggression, so that they were allowed to enter and exit freely and practice trade monopoly, such as the Anglo-Dutch War on the Sea, the Sino-British Opium War, the "Perry's Expedition" in which the United States forced Japan to open ports to trade during the Meiji Period.

3.1.2 Establishment of the customs in charge of foreign trade in the early Qing Dynasty

When Emperor Kangxi ceased the maritime prohibition in the 23rd year of his reign, the Qing government announced that Macao in Guangdong (later transferred to Guangzhou), Zhangzhou in Fujian (later transferred to Xiamen), Ningbo in Zhejiang and Yuntaishan in Jiangsu (later transferred to Shanghai) were the ports for foreign navigation and trade. However, in the early years of Emperor Qianlong's reign, merchant ships from Britain and other countries gradually got in and out from Guangzhou Port, and seldom went to Xiamen and Ningbo ports. This was due to the favorable position and trade condition of Guangzhou, which was formed naturally without mandatory regulations by the government.

In the 24th year of Emperor Kangxi (1685), the Qing government established Provincial Shipping Departments including Guangdong customs (based in Guangzhou), Fujian customs (based in Fuzhou), Zhejiang customs (based in Ningbo) and Shanghai customs (based in Shanghai) in order to abolish the Bureau for Foreign Shipping system, as Municipal Shipping Departments could not meet the needs of development. All of these newly-established departments were mainly responsible for the management of foreign trade, the collection of foreign currency and cargo taxes, port management, and administrative affairs of the ports and opened Guangzhou, Ningbo, Xiamen and Shanghai ports as the foreign trade ports, and allowed non-governmental trade beyond the coastline.

3.1.3 Specific ports for restricting the entry of foreign merchants

Considering the political, military, coastal defense, trade management and other factors, the Qing government, following the old practice of the tribute and trading system of the Ming Dynasty, clearly stipulated that foreign merchant ships from different countries came to China from different ports. To be specific, Myanmar and Nanzhang (formerly called Chenla, now Laos) came into China from Yunnan, Vietnam from Guangxi, and Ryukyu from Fuzhou and Quanzhou in Fujian, Siam (now Thailand) and other countries from Guangzhou, Japan from Ningbo, Kyakhta (Maima Chin) was exclusively open for Russian land borne trade. Although there were limited ports of entry and exit for foreign merchants, they were not completely restricted to one city, one port or one place. Foreign businessmen could trade at any ports such as Guangzhou, Quanzhou, Ningbo, Shanghai and Zhoushan ports along the coasts of Guangdong, Fujian, and Zhejiang.

As the number of British ships in and out of Guangzhou port increased, in the 54th year of Emperor Kangxi (1715), the British East India Company set up a commercial center in Guangzhou as a base of activities with China. Britain's trade with China was in the hands of the East India Company until its trade monopoly was abolished in 1834. From the 20th to the 22nd year of Emperor Qianlong's reign (1755-1757), the East India Company, which had not been to Ningbo for many years, suddenly sent a large number of armed vessels to Dinghai and Ningbo for three consecutive years. After Emperor Qianlong received reports from Zhejiang and Guangdong officials, in order to prevent the emergence of a "state within a state" occupied by foreigners in China's coastal areas, he took necessary measures against the aggressive ambitions of the United Kingdom. Then the imperial court immediately ordered British merchant ships to "trade only in Guangzhou and stop going to Ningbo". In the 22nd year of the reign of Emperor Qianlong (1757), the imperial court explicitly stipulated that only Guangzhou Port was allowed to trade with foreign countries for the reason that the troubles would be made when domestic coastal residents lived with foreign businessmen. Actually in 1702, the "Thirteen Foreign Trade Companies", which were authorized by the government and managed by the Guangdong customs, began to appear. Guangzhou became the port and center for foreign trade between China and western countries at that time. Objectively speaking, although the British ship was limited to the Guangzhou Port, the volume of trade with China increased year by year.

3.2 Regular trade between China and Britain before the First Opium War

Before the Opium War, in the foreign trade relations between the Qing Dynasty and western countries, Britain occupied the leading position, and the United States came second. The first time that British ships arrived in China's Sea areas was in 1635, and there was no progress in Sino-British trade in the following 50 years. In 1685, when Emperor Kangxi repealed a maritime prohibition, foreign businessmen were allowed to trade freely in Xiamen, Zhangzhou, Ningbo and Yuntaishan. However, it was not until 1699 that the British merchants reached an agreement with local officials of Guangzhou to obtain a number of trade facilitation conditions in China. The British East India Company set up a trading house in Guangzhou and was committed to importing industrial goods such as wool textiles into the Chinese market. Due to differences in consumption concepts and habits between China and the West, the wool textiles exported to China from Britain did not sell well in the next 50 years, and the business suffered losses. Between 1700 and 1757, the volume of British trade with China was small. During the period from 1757 to 1840 when Guangzhou became the only port for maritime trade with Europe and America and the First Opium War broke out, Britain's Industrial Revolution and capitalism developed rapidly to maturity. As the first country in the West to realize the industrial revolution, the direct consequence of the British Industrial Revolution was the improvement of production efficiency. With the dramatic increase of industrial products, monopolizing imports of tea, silk and other commodities from China, dumping industrial commodities to China and changing the long-term trade deficit became the top priority for Britain at that time.

3.2.1 Introduction to the British East India Company

From the 16th century to the 19th century, Portugal, the Netherlands, Britain,

France, and other countries established the "omnipotent company" one after another which monopolized the trade of colonial countries, plundered their wealth with economic, political, military, and judicial functions. The British East India Company, established by British merchants in London in 1599, was granted chartered rights and monopoly powers to trade in the East by the British Royal family. The so-called "East India" is not the eastern part of India, but a general name for the eastern world, including India and China.

In the Ming and Qing dynasties, Guangzhou was China's most important open port. In 1698, French merchants set up the first trading facilities in Guangzhou. In 1715, the British East India Company set up its branches in Guangzhou. By 1837, the number of British businesses in Guangzhou had increased to 156. Subsequently, Spain, the Netherlands, Denmark, Sweden, the United States, and other countries also had their business operations in Guangzhou. After the British East India Company stabilized the Chinese market, the company strove to monopolize the tea trade status at all costs owing to the fact that the Chinese tea was prevalent in the UK and its profits were high (more than 100%). As a notorious colonial expansion machine in modern history, the British East India Company had been closely linked with the expansion of British interests in the East from its establishment, development to its end, and had always been privileged by the British government. It had grabbed a huge monopoly through such barbaric means as monopolizing trade, selling opium and publicly plundering. The unfair huge profits provided sufficient funds for Britain's development from commercial capitalism to industrial capitalism and laid a solid foundation for Britain's transition from a national state to a world colonial empire and the establishment of world hegemony.

3.2.2 Trade situations between the UK (East India Company) and China

By the 1870s, the amount of tea purchased by Britain through the East India Company accounted for 33% of China's tea exports per year, 54% of China's total exports between 1781 and 1800, and 80% of total exports at its peak between 1801 and 1810, and then declined. From 1760 to 1833, the value of the tea imported from China accounted for more than 69% of the total value of the main commodities imported from China by the East India Company annually. With the lowest 69.2% (1780-1784) and the highest 94.1% (1825-1829), tea trade increased British revenue and helped Britain to become the world trade center in the West.

In the early years of Sino-British navigational trade, only woolen fabrics and cotton fabrics were the traditional commodities that Britain exported to China. Metallic products (lead, tin, and copper) grew rapidly in the late 18th century, but there was no improvement in the 19th century. On the contrary, with the mechanization of production, the prices were falling, and the total value of the British export products was decreasing. During 1830-1833, the average annual amount of tea imported directly from China to Britain was worth 5.61 million taels of silver. The average annual amount of three major commodities (wool textiles, cotton, and metals) from Britain was about 2 million taels of silver, that was less than half of the price of tea imported from China (tea accounting for 80% of the total value of goods imported from China to Britain). Between 1761 and 1800, Britain sold 13,062,000 pounds of goods in China but paid 33,996,000 pounds for tea. China's surplus was 20,934,000 pounds, and Britain made up for it by 62,802,000 taels of silver. In 1820, it was estimated that the net loss of British merchants in the past 20 years was 1,688,103 pounds, which was a situation of import surplus for a long time and the trade with China was maintained mainly by the delivery of silver to China.

3.3 Major coastal ports and their transportation development in the early Qing Dynasty

Before the Opium War, China's domestic and international situations were generally in peace and stability. Coastal ports and cities developed smoothly. In addition to the continued prosperity of traditional ports and cities such as Guangzhou and Ningbo, ports such as Shanghai, Xiamen, Tianjin, and Niuzhuang sprang up. Within the coastal areas from Liaodong Bay in the north to Hainan Island in the south, the provincial seagoing vessels took the base on the harbors of the province, with ships coming and going from south to north, forming a busy coastal transport line.

3.3.1 Guangzhou Port and its peripheral ports

Guangzhou port was a well-known port for foreign trade in the Qing Dynasty, and its shipping had spread all over the north and south provinces during the reign of Yongzheng and Qianlong. Ships from the port could reach Dengzhou, Laizhou, Yantai, Shidao, Jiaozhou in Shangdong, Yingkou and Jinzhou in Liaodong, Tianjin and other ports at the turn of spring and summer. They could reach Gaozhou, Leizhou, Qiongzhou, Yazhou and other ports after autumn and winter. Although Guangzhou was the national foreign trade center, the Qing Dynasty stipulated that silk, tea and other exports were not allowed to be transported by coastal waterways, but from inland and inland rivers to Guangzhou; thus the coastal shipping industry of Guangzhou was not as developed as Shanghai and Xiamen. According to records, there were more than 200 seagoing ships, with a total load of about 40,000 tons. There were more than 400 ships outside the Pearl River Estuary and Huizhou, and 300-400 salt transportation ships. There were 700 seagoing ships in Chaozhou Port outside Guangzhou Port, with a total load of about 100,000 tons. There were about 1,600 merchant ships in Guangdong Province, with a total load of about 200,000 tons.

3.3.2 Ningbo Port and its peripheral ports

Ningbo Port was one of the four ports opening to the outside world in the early Qing Dynasty. There were about 700 ships with a load of about 80,000 tons. In its peripheral ports, there were about 100 ships in the Zhapu Port, with a carrying capacity of about 10,000 tons. There were 300 seagoing ships in Wenzhou and Taizhou, with a load of about 15,000 tons. There were about 1,000 seagoing ships in each port of Zhejiang, with a load of about 100,000 tons. Besides, each year there were more than 1,000 sea vessels from Zhejiang and Shanghai, Shandong, Liaodong, Fujian, Guangdong, Taiwan and other regions. More than 4,000 inland river vessels and the port's annual freight volume were about 200,000 tons.

3.3.3 Shanghai Port

Shanghai is located in the junction of rivers and seas, the middle point between the north and south coastal center, endowed with the richest south of the Yangtze River as its hinterland and a dense network of waterways and rivers. It could reach as far as Japan and the western countries. Despite the late rise of the port, it developed as the hub between the North and the South sea routes in the Qing Dynasty. During the Jiaqing period, it became the country's largest port and the hub of the sea. There were about 3,500 to 3,600 ships in Shanghai and about 5,300 ships sailing in and out of Shanghai Port each year, with a throughput of no less than 3 million tons per year. It was one of the world's largest ports at that time.

3.3.4 Xiamen Port and its peripheral ports

Xiamen is situated at the junction of Quanzhou and Zhangzhou, guarding the entrance to Taiwan and Penghu, as the gateway of Fujian Province and the important passage of the South-North Sea route. Xiamen was one of the fastest-growing and most prosperous ports after the lifting of maritime trade ban during the reign of Kangxi. As one of the four major trading ports listed by the Qing government, Xiamen Port had contacts with the north and south coastal ports, and there were ferry routes to Taiwan region, north routes and south routes primarily from Xiamen Port. One could sail directly to Lumen, Changhua, Danshui in Taiwan region. The north route could reach Jinzhou, Laizhou, Jiaozhou, Dengzhou, Tianjin, Shanghai, Zhapu, Ningbo, Wenzhou, and other ports. The south route could reach Zhangzhou, Nan'ao, Guangdong, and Malacca. There were 500 merchant ships in Xiamen Port, with a load of about 100,000 tons. The merchant ships in its peripheral ports Zhangpu and Zhaoan were about 40,000 tons. Quanzhou harbor, including merchant ships about 300 tons in Jinjiang, Hui'an and Nan'an, had a capacity of about 40,000 tons. There were about 100 seagoing ships in Fuzhou Port, with a load of about 15,000 tons. There were more than 300 seagoing ships in each port of Taiwan region, with a capacity of about 20,000 tons. There were about 1,500 vessels in the above ports, with a load of about 220,000 tons.

3.3.5 Tianjin Port

Tianjin Port is a major port in North China, located in the confluence of tributaries of the Haihe River, along the coast of the Bohai Sea, and sailing far to Jiangsu, Zhejiang, Fujian and Guangdong provinces. As the North-South intercourse, Tianjin was the gateway to the sea for Beijing. After the ban was lifted during the reign of Emperor Kangxi, there were frequent maritime business contacts between Jiangsu, Zhejiang, Fujian, and Guangzdong. Tianjin strengthened maritime trade with ports in the Bohai Bay, such as the ports in Shandong and Liaoning, which facilitated fast development of the port of Tianjin. The harbor had about 700 ships in addition to some 300 regular grain carriers in the Bohai Sea, with a capacity of about 170,000 tons.

3.3.6 Niuzhuang Port

Niuzhuang Port, located in the east of Liaohe River at its mouth, was a northern port that was revived in the Qing Dynasty. Because the route between Tianjin and Niuzhuang was more convenient than the Dengzhou line, the need for Niuzhuang Port to transport grain to Tianjin Port and to provide government relief food made Liaodong an important food base in Tianjin. Due to changes of river courses and other factors, the port city gradually moved to the mouth of the Liaohe River, and the Niuzhuang Port was replaced by the Yingkou Port. According to the incomplete statistics in the above-mentioned historical records, before the Opium War, there were about 10,000 merchant ships along the coast of China, with a load of about 1.5 million tons. In addition to inland river vessels and ocean-going merchant ships, there were about 200,000 vessels of large and small sizes in China, with a load of approximately 4 million tons. In 1814, there were only 21,500 ships with a capacity of 2.4 million tons in Britain, and the United States had a load of 1.35 million tons in 1809. On the whole, China was not weaker than the western navigating powers then.

3.4   Large quantities of smuggled opium from Britain to China

Britain began its gold-standard policy in the 18th century, while the Qing Dynasty adopted silver as its currency. Since all trade between China and Britain was converted to silver, Britain needed to buy silver from Europe for trade with China, and its profits were hurt by the purchase and sale of gold and silver. Besides, the tax rate for imported goods from Britain was 20% which made Britain dissatisfied. However, because Chinese silk and tea would bring high profits to British businessmen, Britain had to maintain tea trade with China and actively seek various means to make up the trade balance. Because of the long-standing trade surplus between China and Britain, Britain had to pay a lot of silver every year to buy Chinese tea, silk, and other goods. The British government was eager to change the situation of long-term import surplus and annual outflow of silver and hoped to achieve the purpose of occupying the Chinese market and plundering China's wealth.

3.4.1   Serious impact of Britain's massive smuggling of opium on China

Britain had sought to sell all the goods on the Chinese market, of which the greatest profit was the smuggling of opium from Anatolia and the British colony of India into China by the British merchants from the mid-18th century. Opium production in the British colony of India was large and profitable, with the profit margins estimated to be close to 200% per box at the lowest and close to 400% per box at the highest. British merchants first transported cotton and woolen goods to North America for sale, in exchange for local wheat for sale in India, and then sold wheat for opium and smuggled it into China for tea and other commodities, thus forming a British starting point and terminal point, via North America, India and China, through multi-angle trade and commodity exchange. Buying and selling, Britain had made profits for many times and poured much wealth into the great business cycle in Britain. Besides, British capitalists were not satisfied with the normal trade between China and Britain, they also strongly advocated the British royal family to launch a war of aggression against China, preparing to open the Chinese market by force. In the 28th year of Qianlong (1773), the East India Company decided to smuggle opium to China in large quantities. Since 1780, it had transported and monopolized all opium by itself and controlled the right to smuggle opium to China.

The smuggling of opium to China brought the British bourgeoisie, the British-Indian government, East Indian Company and opium traffickers staggering profits. It was the lifeblood of British trade and the British-Indian colonial government and a major source of tax revenue for Britain. In the ten years before the Opium War, the opium trade brought huge income to British businessmen and the British-Indian government. Britain changed from an import surplus to export surplus, which changed the long-term disadvantageous situation of Britain-China trade. For China, the situation was just the opposite. Opium poisoned a lot of people's health, which had never happened in China's history of over three thousand years. It had broken the long-term advantage of foreign trade and made China change from a country that enjoyed a trade surplus for more than 200 years to a country of import surplus.

The massive smuggling of opium and the spread of opium-smoking and drug-trading in China were far-reaching and harmful to China. As a result, the massive outflow was up to 6 million taels of silver a year, resulting in appreciation of silver and depreciation of copper cash, as well as extreme financial exhaustion, empty national treasury, shortage of military salaries and marginal defense costs. All this had led to severe social decay and sufferings of people's physical and mental health. It also caused severe damage to productive forces and plunged industry and commerce into recession along the southeast coast. Due to the increasing number of opium addicts from officials to civilians, the sharp shrinkage of social productive forces, the depression of industry and commerce, and the intensification of social contradictions, political, economic, financial and military crises had posed a serious threat to the Qing government.

3.4.2 The Qing government's policy of opium banning and the destruction of opium in Humen

The large amount of opium smuggling trade in Britain brought much serious harm to Chinese society, drawing much attention from the Qing government. For the sake of national interests and survival, the Qing government decided to implement the policy of opium ban and had promulgated eight bans from 1821 to 1834. In December 1838, Lin Zexu, the Governor-general of Huguang (Hunan and Hubei provinces), at the order of Emperor Daoguang, served as the imperial commissioner and was sent to Guangdong to carry out opium ban. In March 1839, Lin Zexu arrived in Guangzhou and ordered foreign opium traffickers to hand over all opium and promised not to sell it again. In June, he destroyed most of the opium belonging to the British. In August 1839, Lin Zexu banned all trade with Britain, sent troops into Macao, and further deported the British.

After the news of opium seizure and destruction in Humen spread to Britain, the British government and merchants regarded China's anti-opium action as an infringement on private property. They launched a declaration of war against China in order to expand colonialism, open the door of the Chinese market, plunder the Chinese market and safeguard the interests of opium merchants. In October 1839, the British Cabinet decided to "send a fleet to the Chinese Sea" on the grounds that business was blocked and British lives were threatened. In January 1840, according to the decree of Emperor Daoguang, Lin Zexu announced the formal closure of the ports and permanent severance of trade with Britain. In April of that year, the British Parliament, under the influence of Queen Victoria, finally decided to adopt military action against China. In June of that year, more than 40 British ships and 4,000 soldiers set out from India to the Chinese sea, marking the beginning of the First Opium War. According to Rhoads Murphy, an American historian, the underlying reason for Britain's troop deployment was to seize free trade opportunities with China through armed invasion so that goods could enter the Chinese market in large quantities directly.

The First Opium War in 1840, often referred to as the First Anglo-Chinese War or the "Trade War", was the beginning of modern Chinese history and a typical contest between the backward agricultural empires and the newly-developed industrial countries. Before and after the First Opium War, the development between China and Britain was different. Before 1800, China was ahead of Britain. Despite the beginning of the Western Industrial Revolution and the rapid economic growth, China maintained the same upward momentum. Its share of the world's manufacturing industry miraculously increased from 32.8% in 1750 to 33.3% in 1800. After 1800, Britain surpassed China. Due to the development of Western machinery industry, China's share of the world's manufacturing industry declined from 33.3% in 1800 to 29.8% in 1830, and then to 19.7% in 1860. Britain, on the other hand, surged from 4.3% in 1800 to 9.5% in 1830, surpassing China as the world's Number One for the first time in 1860 with a 19.9% share.

The artillery fire of the Opium War forced China to open the door, and China's social and economic patterns had undergone profound changes, gradually descending to a semi-colonial and semi-feudal society. As Marx said, "A great empire, with a population of almost one-third of humankind, is artificially isolated from the world, regardless of the times and the status quo, and therefore strives to deceive itself with the illusion of imperial perfection. Such an empire is doomed to be defeated in a desperate duel. In this duel, the representative of the stale world is fierce morality, while the representative of the most modern society is to obtain the privilege of cheap buying and expensive selling"[1] "Complete isolation from the outside world was a prerequisite for the preservation of old China, and when this isolation was broken by violence through Britain, it was inevitably followed by disintegration, just as the mummy carefully preserved in a sealed coffin must disintegrate when it is exposed to fresh air."[2] The First Opium War between China and Britain was a watershed in modern Chinese history. Since then, China had gradually entered a semi-feudal and semi-colonial society.

3.5 The First Opium War, the Sino–British Treaty of Nanking and its influence

The First Opium War was China's first war against western capitalist powers. The British army launched this war with a clear aim and demanded that China ceded territory and paid indemnities, resumed trade and opened its door. Before the war, Britain had spent a year and a half collecting military intelligence and reconnaissance along the coast of China, surveying and drawing military maps of waterways, rivers and gulfs along the route in the name of fact-finding and sightseeing tours, to ensure that it could defeat the Qing government with fewer surprise attacks and at a lower cost. Britain won with fewer forces. The asymmetrical war between an agricultural country and an industry one was doomed at that time. During the First Opium War, the Qing government broke down and bowed its head to seek peace. As a result, China's grand

---

[1] Marx, *History of the Opium War, Collected Works of Marx and Engels*, Beijing: People's Publishing House, 1995, p.716.

[2] Marx, *Chinese Revolution and European Revolution, Collected Works of Marx and Engels*, Volume 1, Beijing: People's Publishing House, 1995, p. 692.

image as a great power to the outside world for thousands of years had plummeted. From then on, Westerners and even neighboring countries completely changed their ideas about China as a "Celestial Empire", and began to treat it with contempt and a sense of superiority of Eurocentrism.

3.5.1 Sino-British Treaty of Nanking and its severe impact

On August 29, 1842, Britain's threat to divide China's power by military force was compromised in the form of treaties and agreements. The Qing government was forced to accept all the British proposals and terms and signed the first unequal treaty in modern China, the Treaty of Nanking (also known as the Treaty of Jiangning) on the flagship of the British Army. The main contents of the treaty were as follows: Firstly, China was to cede Hongkong Island to Britain, which resulted in the loss of part of its territorial sovereignty. Secondly, Guangzhou, Xiamen, Fuzhou, Ningbo, and Shanghai were opened as treaty ports, where the British were allowed to set up consulates, resulting in the loss of trade sovereignty at the trading ports. Thirdly, China was to pay an indemnity of 21 million Spanish Carolus dollars to the United Kingdom. Fourthly, the United Kingdom and China jointly negotiated the tax policy on imports and exports of goods in China, and the independent tariff of the Chinese Customs became an agreed tariff, resulting in the loss of customs tariff sovereignty. Fifthly, British businessmen were free to trade with Chinese businessmen, not restrained with "public rules", resulting in the loss of foreign trade management. Sixthly, the British had consular jurisdiction. Crimes committed in China were not subjected to Chinese law. Britain had ordered China to cede territory and pay indemnities, allowing trade in five ports and seizing privileges such as tariff rights, consular jurisdiction and one-sided most-favored-nation treatment, which had seriously damaged China's independence and sovereignty.

3.5.2 Forced unequal treaties with other foreign powers following suit of Britain

After the signing of the Treaty of Nanking, the United States, France, Germany, Russia, and other countries followed Britain in succession, taking the opportunity to obtain privileges, forcing the Qing government to sign a series of unequal treaties. Britain continued to grab privileges to maintain its dominant position in China. In October 1843 (the 23rd year of Daoguang Period), the British government forced the Qing government to sign the General Regulations under which the British Trade was to be conducted at the Five Ports of Canton, Amoy, Foochow, Ningbo, and Shanghai and Supplementary Treaty of Hoomun Chai (Treaty of the Bogue). As an additional treaty to the Treaty of Nanking, the Treaty of the Bogue increased consular jurisdiction, one-sided most-favored-nation treatment, and other provisions. The British, acting on consular jurisdiction, violated the law of China and flouted it. It was particularly harrowing that the ports of trade under the treaty became the cities that the Qing Dynasty could not defend in the war between China and foreign countries. In November 1845, China and Britain signed the Shanghai Land Regulations, which established the first concession in modern China and set a precedent for foreign aggressors in the concession in China, playing a bad leading role.

Other powers did not want Britain to take everything, and they signed unequal treaties with China one after another. In July 1844 (the 24th year of Daoguang Period), China and the United States signed the Treaty of Peace, Amity, and Commerce, with Tariff of Duties (Treaty of Wanghsia). This treaty enabled the United States to enjoy all the privileges obtained by Britain under the Treaty of Nanking and its additional treaties, except for the indemnity of the cession of territory and had become a model for other foreign powers to sign unequal treaties with China. In October 1844, France signed Treaty of Commerce and Navigation (Treaty of Whampoa) with China, which enabled France to obtain all the privileges in the Treaty of Wanghsia except for the indemnities for land-cutting in the Treaty of the Bogue and Treaty of Nanking, further undermined China's judicial, customs and territorial autonomy, and laid the foundation for foreign missionaries to preach in China. In March 1847, Sweden, Norway, and China signed the Treaty of Peace, Amity and Commerce and had obtained the same privileges enjoyed by Britain, France, and the United States in China.

From 1842 to 1850, the Qing government had signed a series of unequal treaties with foreign powers, which enabled them to "legally" open a large number of concessions at treaty ports and use them to sell opium, organize smuggling, dump commodities, seize resources and even commit crimes. Port diversion rights were deprived, and foreigners controlled China's port diversion business, seriously undermining China's sovereignty of the territorial sea and inland waters. After the loss of autonomy in foreign trade, opium smuggling was gradually "legalized" and aggravated the destruction of China's economy and even endangered the survival of the nation. With unequal treaties as the amulet, foreign powers dumped industrial commodities into China and plundered its resources and energy. The traditional natural economy in the coastal areas began to disintegrate, and China's sovereignty over the territory, territorial sea, jurisdiction, tariff, and trade was more severely damaged. The failure of the Opium War and the signing of a series of unequal treaties, such as the Treaty of Nanking, had brought about fundamental changes to Chinese society. Since then, China had experienced a century of hardships and agonies.

3.6 Treaty ports opened to the outside world on the basis of unequal treaties in modern China

According to the Treaty of Nanking, China opened five coastal ports, i.e., Guangzhou, Fuzhou, Xiamen, Ningbo and Shanghai to the United Kingdom as treaty ports. The British were allowed to stay with their families and set up concessions under their direct management, so that they could enjoy freedom of doing business and of residence. Since then, the Qing Dynasty ended the practice of "one-port trade" in Guangzhou and was forced to carry out "five-port trade", which resulted in the system of treaty ports in modern China, abolished only in January 1943 with the annulling of Sino-US and Sino-British extraterritorial jurisdiction.

3.6.1 Formation of treaty ports

The so-called treaty port, literally speaking, refers to specific areas such as the port or the city, of a country (or a region) opening to foreigners in order to serve foreign trade, economic contacts and personnel exchanges. Port trade was initially a common practice in international trade, but in modern history, capitalist powers forced China and other countries to open some ports and cities to foreigners by means of unequal treaties, trading regulations and forceful intervention with an excuse to facilitate trade, which was forced to open by the agreement between the central government and foreign governments. These were called "trading ports" or "treaty ports" or "open ports by agreements". To dilute the Sino-Western relationship implied in the word "treaty", the more inclusive term "trading port" was usually used. The cities where the trading ports were located were usually referred to as port cities. The emergence of trading ports indicated that China's social and port opening had entered a new historical stage of development.

After the First Opium War and before the founding of the People's Republic of China (1842-1948), China entered a complex era of foreign aggression during the 100 years of the existence of the system of treaty ports. On the one hand, the powers used a series of wars of aggression against China, unequal treaties or regulations to seize all kinds of legal and illegal privileges in order to maximize their interests. On the other hand, after China was humiliated by successive territory cession, indemnities, deprivation of power, and forced open ports and trade portals, profound changes gradually took place within China. As the major window for the development of modern China's economy and society, the opening of trade ports was the major form of opening up to the outside world in modern China. With the formation of the treaty port system, the modernization of China had also begun its difficult process.

3.6.2 Unequal treaties forced to be signed and the treaty ports opened accordingly

(1) In the 1850s, the Qing government suffered serious domestic strife and foreign aggression since the opening of the "five ports" for trade. During this period, the Qing government was forced to sign a large number of unequal treaties with foreign powers and opened a large number of treaty ports. The peasant uprising of the Taiping Rebellion broke out in 1851, which effectively attacked the feudal rule of the Qing Dynasty and the invasion of foreign forces, directly and severely threatened the rule of the Qing government, and directly facilitated the collapse of the society. As the ancient Chinese saying goes, the leak of the house is on rainy days, and blessings do not come in pairs but calamities never come singly. From 1856 to 1860, when the Qing Army and the Taiping Army were in the fierce battle in the middle and lower reaches of the Yangtze River, Britain and France jointly launched the Second Opium War. The Qing government was unable to put down the rebellion or resist foreign aggression and was forced to sign the Treaty of Tientsin and the Convention of Peking with the foreign powers again. Furthermore, Russia occupied a large area of Northeast and Northwest China, which greatly damaged China's territorial integrity and had a far-reaching impact on future generations.

Firstly, in the 1st year of Xianfeng Period (August 1851), the Qing government and Russia signed the Treaty of Kuldja. This was the first unequal treaty signed by the Qing government and Russia. According to the provisions of the treaty, Ili and Chuguchak (Tacheng) were opened as treaty ports, which were exempt from tax trade, and Russia established consulates in Ili and Chuguchak to take care of the interests of Russian merchants and possessed consular jurisdiction. Russian merchants could build "trade pavilions" (commercial stations, also called trade circles) in Ili and Chuguchak. From the second half of the 18th century to the first half of the 19th century, land-borne trade between China and Russia was mainly concentrated on the border city, Kgakhta. After the Opium War, Russia's trade in Kgakhta was in a disadvantageous position in the Chinese market competition. The Russians turned their eyes to the northwest of China and expanded the trade in the area by various means, and finally achieved it. From then on, Russia began to open the door of Northwest China by land route. In the western part of China, from the border between China and Russia to the Great Wall, the Russian people enjoyed the right of duty-free trade, but the Chinese people did not enjoy this right. The trade inequality between Chinese and Russian merchants in Xinjiang became increasingly apparent.

Secondly, in July 1854 (the 4th year during the reign of Emperor Xianfeng), the Qing government signed the New Code of Shanghai Land Regulations with Britain, France, and the United States, which made the Shanghai concession a "country within a country" in China, which, as a result, was followed by other concessions, and the foreigners demarcated the concessions at various treaty ports.

Thirdly, in May 1858 (the 8th year during the reign of Emperor Xianfeng), the Qing government and Russia signed the Treaty of Aihui (also called the Treaty of Aigun). According to this agreement, China ceded more than 600,000 square kilometers of land to Russia from the north of Heilong River to south of the Khingan Range. About 400,000 square kilometers of land from the east of the Ussuri River to the coast of China was designated to be "co-managed" by both China and Russia. Russia enjoyed the navigation rights of Heilong River, Ussuri River and Songhua River and seized the passage from Heilong River to the Pacific Ocean, where other foreign ships were forbidden to sail, which led to a large-scale plundering of northeastern China by Russia. After the signing of the Treaty of Aigun, the Qing government refused to ratify it until the conclusion of the Convention of Peking between China and Russia in 1860.

Fourthly, in June 1858, the 8th year of Emperor Xianfeng, the Treaty of Tientsin was signed between China and Russia, the United States, Britain, France. The treaty between China and Russia stipulated that Russia be allowed to open trade at ports in Shanghai, Ningbo, Fuzhou, Xiamen, Guangzhou, Taiwan, Qiongzhou and other ports opening to other countries; Russia may establish consular offices, enjoyed consular jurisdiction and one-sided most-favored-nation treatment and stationed at these ports, and dispatched troops to berth at these ports, and allowed the Russian Orthodox to preach freely in China; and Russia was free to expand land-borne trade without restriction. It was agreed that the two countries would send personnel to investigate.

According to The Sino-US Treaty of Tientsin, the United States was allowed to trade at newly opened ports as Guangzhou, Chaozhou, Xiamen, Fuzhou, Taiwan, Ningbo and Shanghai, enjoy the same preferential tariff treatment and expand the one-sided most-favored-nation treatment. In the past, the US trade with China was limited to five ports along the southeastern coast, but now the US had the right to trade in Taiwan and the Yangtze River basin. With the opening of treaty ports, US warships could cruise and patrol all the waters of China, and enjoyed all the privileges that countries such as Britain and France seized during the Second Opium War. The Sino-British Treaty of Tientsin stipulated that Niuzhuang (later called Yingkou), Dengzhou (later called Yantai), Taiwan (later based in Tainan), Chaozhou (later called Shantou), Qiongzhou, Hankou, Jiujiang, Zhenjiang and Nanjing should be added as treaty ports, allowing British merchant ships to enter the ports along the Yangtze River and the river for business, and British warships to enter the ports. The British had the rights to travel and do business in the mainland. The British minister stationed in Beijing and the Qing government paid Britain 4 million taels of silver in compensation. That treaty made Britain seize more privileges of aggression against China. According to the Sino-French Treaty of Tientsin, Qiongzhou, Chaozhou, Taiwan, Danshui, and Nanjing would be added as treaty ports. France could build houses and install various facilities at any treaty ports. Chinese local officials should protect them, entitle them to consular jurisdiction, one-sided most-favored-nation treatment, and established consular officers at trading ports so that they could be based in Beijing in the long term and French warships could be berthed at various treaty ports, together with China's compensation of 2 million tales of silver to France, allowing inland river navigation and commerce, which made France further invade and plunder China.

In addition, in November 1858, the Qing government signed the additional regulations of Tientsin Treaty with Britain, the United States, France, and other countries. It included that the customs employed British employees to assist the tax authorities and the customs would levy a tax of 5% on the imports and exports. When foreign goods were sold to the mainland, or British companies bought local products from the mainland for export, only 2.5% of the transit dues had to be paid. Likin Tax would not be paid and "foreign medicine" (opium) was allowed as import trade. Since then, the autonomy of the Chinese customs fell into the hands of the British for half a century, which also marked China's further deepening of semi-colonization.

(2) The Qing government launched a westernization movement in the 1860s to revive and revitalize the imperial court with the conclusion of peace with foreign powers and the suppression of the Taiping Rebellion in 1864. During this period, the American Civil War ended in 1865, the Meiji Restoration started in Japan in 1868, the Suez Canal officially opened in 1869, and Germany and Italy were unified in 1870. In addition to Britain, France and the United States, other powers, such as Russia, Germany,

Denmark, the Netherlands, Spain, Portugal, Belgium, Italy, Austria, Japan and other countries, continued to make use of the Qing government's decline and incompetence to carry out diplomatic blackmail, seizing a large number of aggressive rights and interests. The details are as follows.

Fifthly, the Qing government signed the Convention of Peace and Friendship, Additional Convention: Peace and Friendship, War Indemnity, Additional Treaty of Commerce and Navigation (also called the Convention of Peking) respectively with Britain, Russia, and France in October 1860. According to the Convention of Peking between China and Britain, Tianjin was opened as a commercial port, while a district in Kowloon was ceded to the Britain, and the British were allowed to recruit Chinese laborers for export. Britain was compensated 6 million taels of silver for its military expenditure and 2 million taels of silver for the loss of British merchants, and claimed the indemnity must be deducted from customs tax, forcing the Qing government to appoint the British Horatio Nelson Lay as the Inspector General of the Customs in 1861, and had since then fulfilled the ambition of the British people who had long dreamed of controlling the customs in China. According to the Convention of Peking between China and France, Tianjin was opened as a commercial port, and France was allowed to recruit Chinese laborers for export. French missionaries were allowed to buy land and build houses in various provinces, and 8 million taels of silver were compensated. To permit the export of Chinese laborers was, in fact, the plundering and trafficking of "contracts" by the powers for overseas colonization or labor in the America, Southeast Asia and other places. The fate of these Chinese laborers was as tragic as that of African slaves. The Convention of Peking between China and Russia stipulated that China's territory of 400,000 square kilometers in the east of the Ussuri River shall be incorporated to Russia and the border between China and Russia in the western part of the country should be along the mountain range, the river and the route of China's permanent Kalun (post), and that Kashgar (today's Kashi) should be opened as a commercial port, and consular officers may be set up in Kulun and Kashgar. It was reiterated that Russia enjoyed consular jurisdiction in China, stipulating tax-free trade between the two countries' frontiers and allowing Russian businesses in Kulun (today's Ulan Bator) and Zhangjiakou. In addition, Russia was granted the privilege of expanding trade by land and expanding its aggressive forces to southern Xinjiang, which was one of the unequal treaties in modern history that seriously damaged China's sovereignty and territorial integrity.

Sixthly, in March 1861 (the 11th year of Emperor Xianfeng's reign), China and

Britain signed the Yangtze Trade Regulations and the Agreement on Concession in Kiukiang. It enabled Britain to obtain "one-sided inland waterway shipping rights" and to trade and reside in the Jiujiang concession, and gradually deprived China of judicial and legislative power over the treaty ports.

Seventhly, in June 1861 (the 11th year of Emperor Xianfeng's reign), China and Russia signed the Treaty of Khanka. Russia invaded most of the Lake Khanka west of the Ussuri River and a large part of China's territory southwest of the Lake Khanka by demarcation.

Eighthly, in September 1861 (the 11th year of Emperor Xianfeng's reign) China and Germany signed the Treaty of Friendship Commerce and Navigation and the Agreement: Rules of Trade, with the Tariff of Imports and Exports, Transit Dues. The treaty stipulated that Prussian and German be allowed to do business, lease and live at ports of Guangzhou, Chaozhou, Xiamen, Fuzhou, Ningbo, Shanghai, Zhifu, Tianjin, Niuzhuang, Zhenjiang, Jiujiang, Hankou, Qiongzhou, Taiwan and Danshui. German warships could sail into Chinese ports. According to this treaty, Germany gained all the rights and interests seized by the powers in China since the Opium War without a single shot.

Ninthly, in October 1861 (the 11th year of Xianfeng's reign), the Qing government signed the Provisional Treaty of Commerce in Yangtze Region and the Treaty of Commerce in Yangtze Region with Britain and other countries. The ports along the Yangtze River had been expanded from Britain to foreign traders.

Tenthly, in October 1864 (the 3rd year of Tongzhi's reign), China and Russia signed the Treaty of Tarbagatay. Russia changed the direction of the Sino-Russian border through the threat of force and diplomatic blackmail, redefined the border between the western part of China and Russia. The west of the new territories and its annexes, property, etc., were forced to cede to Russia, through which Russia grabbed about 440,000 square kilometers of territory in the northwest frontier of China.

(3) In the 1870s, during the Westernization Movement of the Qing Dynasty, enterprises were established for the purpose of "seeking strength" while "seeking wealth". The Western powers gradually strengthened their economic and cultural aggression against China by means of unequal treaties and privileges. As a semi-colonial country, China was further involved in the capitalist world market. The details are as follows.

The eleventh is that, in October 1874 (the 13th year of Emperor Tongzhi's reign), Engagement between Japan and China Respecting Formosa (present-day Taiwan, China) . It stipulated that Japan should withdraw its troops from Taiwan and compensate Japan for 500,000 taels of silver, recognizing that Japan's invasion of Taiwan of China was an act of "protecting the people and benevolence". This agreement led Japan to an intensified invasion of Ryukyu, forcing Ryukyu to break off its vassal relations with China. After Japan annexed the Ryukyu, it was renamed as Okinawa County.

The twelfth is that the Yantai Treaty (also called the Chefoo Convention) was signed between China and Britain in July 1876 (the 2nd year of Emperor Guangxu). Yichang, Wuhu, Wenzhou, and Beihai were added as treaty ports. Datong, Anqing, Hukou and Shashi along the Yangtze River would be opened to allow foreign ships to berth and load passengers and cargo. Foreign cargo would only pay transit dues when entering the mainland of China, but all the inland taxes would be exempted. The British would send personnel to Yunnan to investigate and prepare to negotiate the border and trade regulations between Yunnan and Myanmar. The British were allowed to enter Tibet for "fact-finding tours". Through this treaty, Britain, after opening the portal along the Yangtze River and its ports, gained the right to invade Southwestern of Yunnan and Tibet in China from India.

(4) Looking back on the 1860s-1890s, especially the 1880s, there were no other large-scale wars except the Sino-French War. However, as China's neighboring countries became colonies, the border areas adjacent to these neighboring countries had become objects of coveting by foreign powers, such as Xinjiang, Mongolia, Northeast China, Qinghai and Tibet to Russia; Yunnan, Guangxi, Fujian and other places to France; Yunnan, Tibet and other places to Britain; and Taiwan, Ryukyu and other places to Japan. China's land and sea territory became the target of foreign invasion, and the long border line had been in war. China's territory and sovereignty had been seriously damaged once again.

The thirteenth is that, in 1881 (the 7th year of Emperor Guangxu's reign), China and Russia signed the Treaty of Saint Petersburg (also called the Treaty of Ili). In accordance with this agreement, Russia returned the occupied Ili area, and China ceded the areas west of the Khorgos River and north and south of the Ili River to Russia. Suzhou (Jiayuguan), Uliastai, Urumqi, Turpan, Hami, Qitai (Gucheng) and Kobdo were opened as treaty ports, and Russia was allowed to establish a consulate in Jiayuguan and Turpan and increased the land-borne trade channel from Xinjiang to Jiayuguan. As a matter of fact, the import trade tax had been decreased by 1/3. When opening Songhua River, Russian merchants could trade along the river. Sino-Russian border trade within a hundred miles was not taxable. Russian businessmen in Inner Mongolia trade were still tax-free. In Xinjiang, it was "temporarily not taxable", which made Xinjiang entirely under the political, economic and military pressure of Russia.

The fourteenth is that, in October and December 1882 (the 8th year of Emperor

Guangxu's reign), China and Russia signed the Attached Treaty of Ili and the Treaty of Kashgar by redefining the frontier issue in the Treaty of Saint Petersburg, in which Russia demarcated the northern Russian border along the Tianshan Mountains of Kashgar to which China belonged, and seized a large part of Chinese territory at the same time.

The fifteenth is that, in October 1883 (the 9th year of Emperor Guangxu's reign), China and Russia signed the Protocol of Tarbagatay. This led to Russia's occupation of the vast territory of the western part of the Tarbagatay by its one-sided survey of this area.

The sixteenth is that, in June 1884 (the 10th year of Emperor Guangxu's reign), China and Russia signed the Protocol on Boundary in the Kashgar Region. Russia coerced the Qing government to assign Chinese territory to Russia in the Aksai area of northern Kashgar and laid a foundation for the further occupation of Chinese territory south of the Uzbel Pass.

The seventeenth is that, in June 1885 (the 11th year of Emperor Guangxu's reign) China and France signed the Vietnam Accord (also called the Sino-French New Convention or the Li-Patenotre Convention). Although the Qing government won the great victory of Zhennan Pass in the Sino-French War, it begged for peacemaking and suffered defeat in the end. The treaty recognized Vietnam as France's protectorate which made Vietnam a base for further French aggression against China. It stipulated that two ports should be designated as treaty ports on the borders between China and Vietnam in Yunnan and Guangxi, allowing the opening of ports and trade, the French to live and establish consulates and to enjoy the same privileges as other trading ports.

The Eighteenth is that, in 1887 (the 13th year of Emperor Guangxu's reign), the Qing government signed the Sino-French Supplementing Convention of Commerce, the Sino-British Agreement of Opium Trade at Hong Kong, the Sino-Portuguese Treaty of Peking and the conference protocol. Longzhou, Mengzi, Kowloon, and Gongbei were opened to trade, but Gongbei Port was declared to be "ports opened voluntarily" by the Qing government in the same year. In particular, Portugal established its legal status in Macao through the Sino-Portuguese Treaty of Peking, which was the first treaty stipulated by the Chinese government over 300 years after Portugal occupied Macao. After 1928, the Chinese government declared that the treaty was abolished and that Portugal held Macao lost treaty basis actually.

(5) In 1890s, foreign powers' plundering China became more and more crazy, starting to carve up China with impunity. From 1842 to 1894, the Qing government opened 37 ports to the outside world all along the Southeast coast, and the border areas

to the hinterland of China. After the Meiji Restoration, Japan suddenly became a new power in East Asia. After the Sino-Japanese War in 1894, the capitalist powers further increased their aggression against China and partitioned the sphere of influence. The Qing government was forced to implement the "open door" policy, and the number of open treaty ports increased rapidly. Between March and June in 1898, the powers divided nearly half of China's provinces into their own "spheres of influence" through various treaties within three months. Such division reached its climax when the Boxer Protocol of 1901 was signed. It was not until 1910 that the wave of foreign forces forcing the Chinese government to open ports petered out.

The Nineteenth is that, in March 1890 (the 16th year of Emperor Guangxu's reign) and December 1893 (the 19th year of Emperor Guangxu's reign), the Qing government and Britain successively signed the Convention of Calcutta, the Additional Article Re-traffic in Opium-Supplementing Agreement of Chefoo and the Regulations Regarding Trade Communications in Tibet and Sikkim. The border between Tibet and Sikkim was stipulated so that Sikkim was utterly separated from China. Chongqing and Yichang were successively opened as treaty ports, and the trade between China's Tibet and India was duty-free within five years.

The twentieth is that, in 1894 (the 20th year of Emperor Guangxu's reign), China was defeated after the outbreak of the Sino-Japanese War in 1894. China was forced to sign the Treaty of Shimonoseki between China and Japan in 1895 (the 21st year of Emperor Guangxu's reign). The treaty stipulated that Shashi, Chongqing, Suzhou and Hangzhou should be added as treaty ports and that the whole island of Taiwan and all its affiliated islands, Penghu Islands and the Liaodong Peninsula should be ceded to Japan. It allowed Japan to set up factories and import various machines at any of its treaty ports in China and compensated Japan for its military expenditure of 200 million taels of silver. The treaty made the foreign powers in China set off a wave of capital export and the division of spheres of influence.

The twenty-first is that, in 1895 (the 21st year of Emperor Guangxu's reign) and 1897 (the 23rd year of Emperor Guangxu's reign), the Qing government successively signed the Convention Relating to Burmah and Thibet with Britain and the Sino-French Exchange of Identical Notes Agreeing upon Certain Stipulations of Commerce with France. It opened Wuzhou, Sanshui, Hekou, Simao and Tengyue as treaty ports.

The twenty-second is that, from 1898 to 1899 (the 24th year to 25th year of Emperor Guangxu's reign), Germany, Britain, Russia and France forced the Qing government to open Qingdao, Weihaiwei, Dalianwan (Qingniwa) and Guangzhouwan (Zhanjiang) as treaty ports by occupying and leasing the Treaty of Kiaochau, Weihaiwei, Lvshun, Dalian and Guangzhouwan.

(6) In the early period of 20th Century, the Eight-Power Allied Forces invaded China, and in 1901, the Boxer Protocol of 1901 was signed by the Qing government with other countries. This became the most humiliating page in the history of the treaties in the late Qing Dynasty. It also marked the basic end of the process of semi-colonization in China and the establishment of the ruling order of the semi-colonial and semi-feudal society. Later, the Qing government and other countries signed unequal treaties on trade, shipping and ceding power. The main characteristics of the open trade ports in this period featured the following. From the geographical distribution, except for some coastal ports and ports along the Yangtze River, the other open trade ports were mainly distributed in northeast China and Yunnan, Guangxi, Tibet, and other border areas. Because the northeast was located in the heart of Northeast Asia and the region was rich in forest and mineral land resources. It was a relatively developed economic region for modern China's industrialization, urbanization, port and railway transportation, and commodity agriculture. It had become the focus of contention among Britain, Japan, Russia, the United States and other powers. Therefore, big powers advocated opening the whole part of northeast China and setting up more treaty ports. From 1894 to 1911, the Northeast area had opened as many as 24 commercial ports as treaty ports.

The twenty-third is that, in September 1902 (the 28th year of Emperor Guangxu's reign) China and Britain signed the Supplementing Treaty of Commerce and Navigation (also called the Mackay Treaty), which stipulated that Changsha, Jiangmen, Huizhou, Anqing and Wanxian County should be added as treaty ports. The British may join China's stock companies to develop mineral resources in China. The United Kingdom could navigate and rent ports in China's inland rivers freely, and the rights were no different from those of Chinese ships. China's inland rivers, which prohibited British ships, should also ban China ships.

The twenty-fourth is that, in October 1903 (the 29th year of Emperor Guangxu's reign), China and the United States signed the Treaty of Commercial Relations, and China and Japan signed the Supplementary Treaty of Commerce-Supplementing Treaty of Peking, opening Jiangmen, Changsha, Fengtianfu (Shenyang), Andong (Dandong) and Dadonggou as treaty ports.

The twenty-fifth is that, in 1905 (the 31st year of Emperor Guangxu's reign), the scramble between Russia and Japan for northeast China was heating up. During the Russian-Japanese War, Japan defeated Russia with the support of Britain and the United States and other western powers. Russia "transferred" all railways from Dalianwan,

Lvshunkou and Changchun to Dalian and other related rights and interests to Japan. In December of that year, China and Japan signed the settlement forcing the Qing government to recognize Japan's privileges in the Northeast from the hands of Russia, and stipulating in the contract that it should open the 16 ports such as "Fenghuangcheng, Liaoyang, Xinmintun, Tieling, Tongjiangzi, Fakumen in Fengtian Province; Changchun (Kuanchengzi), Jilin City, Harbin, Ningguta, Hunchun, Sanxing (Yilan) in Jilin Province; Qiqihar (Tsitsihar), Hailar, Aihui, Manzhouli in Heilongjiang Province" as treaty ports.[1]

The twenty-sixth is that, in April 1906 (the 32nd year of Emperor Guangxu's reign), China and Britain signed the Additional Convention Respecting Tibet. It is required to open Gyangze, Gedake, Yadong as trade ports. Without the prior consent of the Britain, other countries should not interfere with the rights and interests of Tibet.

The twenty-seventh is that, in January 1907 (the 33rd year of Emperor Guangxu's reign), the Suifenhe Port was opened to the outside world according to the Notes to Russia for Protocol of Taxation.

The twenty-eighth is that, in 1909 (the 1st year of Xuantong's reign), Japan forced the Qing government to sign the Sino-Japanese Gando Convention by virtue of the so-called Gando issue, which stipulated that Longjingcun, Juzijie, Toudaogou and Baicaogou should be opened as treaty ports. Table 3-1 shows the treaty ports opened according to unequal treaties and trade regulations in modern China, and Table 3-2 shows the opening time of National customs during 1860-1910.

Table 3-1   Treaty ports opened according to unequal treaties
and trade regulations in Modern China

Serial number	Name of port	Province	Contract time	Actual opening time	Main basis for opening
1	Guangzhou	Guangdong	1842	July 27, 1843	Sino-British Treaty of Nanking in the 22nd year of Emperor Daoguang's reign
2	Xiamen	Fujian	1842	November 1, 1843	Sino-British Treaty of Nanking in the 22nd year of Emperor Daoguang's reign
3	Shanghai	Jiangsu	1842	November 17, 1843	Sino-British Treaty of Nanking in the 22nd year of Emperor Daoguang's reign
4	Ningbo	Zhejiang	1842	January 1, 1844	Sino-British Treaty of Nanking in the 22nd year of Emperor Daoguang's reign

---

[1]   Zhu Dexin, eds., *Collections of Chinese and Foreign Covenants* (1689-1949), Harbin: Heilongjiang People's Publishing House, 1991, p.379.

(continued)

Serial number	Name of port	Province	Contract time	Actual opening time	Main basis for opening
5	Fuzhou	Fujian	1842	July 3, 1844	Sino-British Treaty of Nanking in the 22nd year of Emperor Daoguang's reign
6	Ili	Xinjiang	1851	April 4, 1852	Sino-Russian Treaty of Kuldja in the 1st year of Emperor Xianfeng's reign
7	Tarbagatay (Tacheng)	Xinjiang	1851	April 4, 1852	Sino-Russian Treaty of Kuldja in the 1st year of Emperor Xianfeng's reign
8	Chaozhou (Shantou)	Guangdong	1858	January 1, 1860	Treaty of Tientsin in the 8th year of Emperor Xianfeng's reign
9	Zhenjiang	Jiangsu	1858	May 10, 1861	Treaty of Tientsin in the 8th year of Emperor Xianfeng's reign
10	Hankou	Hubei	1858	January 1, 1862	Treaty of Tientsin in the 8th year of Emperor Xianfeng's reign
11	Jiujiang	Jiangxi	1858	January, 1862	Treaty of Tientsin in the 8th year of Emperor Xianfeng's reign
12	Dengzhou (Zhifu, Yantai)	Shandong	1858	January 16, 1862	Treaty of Tientsin in the 8th year of Xianfeng's reign
13	Danshui (Taipei)	Taiwan	1858	July 28, 1862	Treaty of Tientsin in the 8th year of Emperor Xianfeng's reign
14	Taiwan (Dagou, Tainan)	Taiwan	1858	October 1, 1863	Treaty of Tientsin in the 8th year of Emperor Xianfeng's reign
15	Qiongzhou (Haikou)	Guangdong	1858	April 1, 1876	Treaty of Tientsin in the 8th year of Emperor Xianfeng's reign
16	Jiangning (Nanjing)	Jiangsu	1861	March 22, 1899	Treaty of Tientsin in the 8th Year of Emperor Xianfeng's reign and revised Yangtze Trade Regulations
17	Tianjin	Zhili	1860	January 20, 1861	Sino-British Convention of Peking in the 10th year of Emperor Xianfeng's reign
18	Niu Zhuang (Yingkou)	Fengtian	1860	April 3, 1864	Sino-British Convention of Peking in the 10th year of Emperor Xianfeng's reign
19	Kashgar	Xinjiang	1860	April 5, 1861	Sino-Russian Convention of Peking in the 10th year of Emperor Xianfeng's reign
20	Kulun (Urgo)	Mongolia	1860	July 11, 1861	Sino-Russian Convention of Peking in the 10th year of Xianfeng's reign
21	Kyakhta (Maima Chin)	Mongolia	1860	—	Sino-Russian Convention of Peking in the 10th year of Emperor Xianfeng's reign
22	Yichang	Hubei	1876	April 1, 1877	Yantai Treaty between China and Britain in the 2nd year of Emperor Guangxu's reign

(continued)

Serial number	Name of port	Province	Contract time	Actual opening time	Main basis for opening
23	Wuhu	Anhui	1876	April 1, 1877	Yantai Treaty between China and Britain in the 2nd year of Emperor Guangxu's reign
24	Wenzhou	Zhejiang	1876	April 1, 1877	Yantai Treaty between China and Britain in the 2nd year of Emperor Guangxu's reign
25	Beihai	Guangdong	1876	April 2, 1877	Yantai Treaty between China and Britain in the 2nd year of Emperor Guangxu's reign
26	Suzhou (Jiayuguan)	Gansu	1881	April, 1881	Revised Treaty of Ili between China and Russia in the 7th year of Guangxu's reign
27	Turpan	Xinjiang	1881	April, 1881	Revised Treaty of Ili between China and Russia in the 7th year of Emperor Guangxu's reign
28	Uliastai	Mongolia	1881	April, 1881	Revised Treaty of Ili between China and Russia in the 7th year of Emperor Guangxu's reign
29	Khovd	Mongolia	1881	April, 1881	Revised Treaty of Ili between China and Russia in the 7th year of Emperor Guangxu's reign
30	Hami	Xinjiang	1881	April, 1881	Revised Treaty of Ili between China and Russia in the 7th year of Emperor Guangxu's reign
31	Urumqi	Xinjiang	1881	April, 1881	Revised Treaty of Ili between China and Russia in the 7th year of Emperor Guangxu's reign
32	Qitai (Gucheng)	Xinjiang	1881	April, 1881	Revised Treaty of Ili between China and Russia in the 7th year of Emperor Guangxu's reign
33	Gongbei	Guangdong	1887	April 2, 1887	Sino-Portuguese Treaty of Peking and conference agreement in the 13th year of Emperor Guangxu's reign; the announcement of its opening was in the same year
34	Kowloon	Guangdong	1887	April, 1887	Sino-British Agreement of Opium Trade at Hong Kong in the 13th year of Emperor Guangxu's reign
35	Longzhou	Guangxi	1887	August 24, 1889	Supplementing Convention of Commerce between China and France in 13th year of Emperor Guangxu's reign
36	Mengzi	Yunnan	1887	August 2, 1889	Supplementing Convention of Commerce between China and France in 13th year of Emperor Guangxu's reign
37	Chongqing	Sichuan	1890	March 30, 1891	Sino-British Additional Article Re-traffic in Opium-Supplementing Agreement of Chefoo in 16th year of Emperor Guangxu's reign
38	Yadong	Tibet	1893	May 1, 1894	Sino-British Regulations Regarding Trade Communications in Tibet and Sikkim in the 19th year of Emperor Guangxu's reign

(continued)

Serial number	Name of port	Province	Contract time	Actual opening time	Main basis for opening
39	Suzhou	Jiangsu	1896	September 26, 1896	Sino-Japanese Treaty of Shimonoseki in the 21st year of Emperor Guangxu's reign
40	Hangzhou	Zhejiang	1896	September 26, 1896	Sino-Japanese Treaty of Shimonoseki in the 21st year of Emperor Guangxu's reign
41	Shashi	Hubei	1896	October 1, 1896	Sino-Japanese Treaty of Shimonoseki in the 21st year of Emperor Guangxu's reign
42	Hekou (Manhao)	Yunnan	1896	January, 1897	Sino-French Supplementing Convention of Commerce in 21st year of Emperor Guangxu's reign
43	Simao	Yunnan	1896	January, 1897	Sino-French Supplementing Convention of Commerce in 21st year of Emperor Guangxu's reign
44	Wuzhou	Guangxi	1897	June 3, 1897	Sino-British Convention Relating to Burmah and Thibet in the 23rd year of Emperor Guangxu's reign
45	Sanshui	Guangdong	1897	June 4, 1897	Sino-British Convention Relating to Burmah and Thibet in the 23rd year of Emperor Guangxu's reign
46	Tengyue	Yunnan	1897	May 8, 1902	Sino-British Convention Relating to Burmah and Thibet in the 23rd year of Emperor Guangxu's reign
47	Qingdao	Shandong	1898	July, 1898	Sino-German Convention Concerning Lease of Kiaochau in the 24th year of Guangxu's reign
48	Weihaiwei	Shandong	1898	July, 1898	Sino-British Convention Concerning Lease of Weihaiwei in the 24th year of Emperor Guangxu's reign
49	Dalianwan	Fengtian	1898	1898	Sino-Russian Treaty on Rental Land in the 24th year of Emperor Guangxu's reign
50	Guangzhouwan (Zhanjiang)	Guangdong	1899	1899	Sino-Franch Convention Concerning Lease of Guangzhouwan in the 25th year of Emperor Guangxu's reign
51	Jiangmen	Guangdong	1902	April 22, 1904	Sino-British Mackay Treaty in the 28th year of Emperor Guangxu's reign
52	Huizhou	Guangdong	1902	—	Sino-British Mackay Treaty in the 28th year of Emperor Guangxu's reign
53	Changsha	Hunan	1902	July 1, 1904	Sino-British Mackay Treaty in the 28th year of Emperor Guangxu's reign The Qing government announced its opening in the same year

(continued)

Serial number	Name of port	Province	Contract time	Actual opening time	Main basis for opening
54	Anqing	Anhui	1902	September 5, 1902	Sino-British Mackay Treaty in the 28th year of Emperor Guangxu's reign
55	Wanxian	Sichuan	1902	1902	Sino-British Mackay Treaty in the 28th year of Emperor Guangxu's reign
56	Andong (Dandong)	Fengtian	1903	March 1, 1907	Sino-Japanese Supplementary Treaty of Commerce-Supplementing Treaty of Peking in the 29th year of Emperor Guangxu's reign
57	Dadonggou	Fengtian	1903	March, 1907	Sino-Japanese Supplementary Treaty of Commerce-Supplementing Treaty of Peking in the 29th year of Emperor Guangxu's reign
58	Fengtianfu (Shenyang)	Fengtian	1903	April 11, 1908	Sino-US Treaty: Commercial Relations and Sino-Japanese Supplementary Treaty of Commerce-Supplementing Treaty of Peking in the 29th year of Emperor Guangxu's reign
59	Tieling*	Fengtian	1905	September 10, 1906	Sino-Japanese Convention Concerning the Three Provinces in Northeast China in the 31st year of Emperor Guangxu's reign, which stipulated its opening by China
60	Mintun* (Xinminfu)	Fengtian	1905	September 10, 1906	Sino-Japanese Convention Concerning the Three Provinces in Northeast China in the 31st year of Guangxu's reign, which stipulated its opening by China
61	Tongjiangzi*	Fengtian	1905	September 10, 1906	Sino-Japanese Convention Concerning the Three Provinces in Northeast China in the 31st year of Guangxu's reign, which stipulated its opening by China
62	Fakumen*	Fengtian	1905	September 10, 1906	Sino-Japanese Convention Concerning the Three Provinces in Northeast China in the 31st year of Eeperor Guangxu's reign, which stipulated its opening by China
63	Jilin City*	Jilin	1905	January 14, 1907	Sino-Japanese Convention Concerning the Three Provinces in Northeast China in the 31st year of Emperor Guangxu, which stipulated its opening by China
64	Kuanchengzi* (Changchun)	Jilin	1905	January 14, 1907	Sino-Japanese Convention Concerning the Three Provinces in Northeast China in the 31st year of Emperor Guangxu's reign, which stipulated its opening by China

(continued)

Serial number	Name of port	Province	Contract time	Actual opening time	Main basis for opening
65	Harbin* (Longjiangfu)	Heilongjiang	1905	January 14, 1907	Sino-Japanese Convention Concerning the Three Provinces in Northeast China in the 31st year of Emperor Guangxu's reign, which stipulated its opening by China
66	Manzhouli*	Heilongjiang	1905	January 14, 1907	Sino-Japanese Convention Concerning the Three Provinces in Northeast China in the 31st year of Emperor Guangxu's reign, which stipulated its opening by China
67	Qiqihar*	Heilongjiang	1905	May 28, 1907	Sino-Japanese Convention Concerning the Three Provinces in Northeast China in the 31st year of Emperor Guangxu's reign, which stipulated its opening by China
68	Fenghuangcheng	Fengtian	1905	June 28, 1907	Sino-Japanese Convention Concerning the Three Provinces in Northeast China in the 31st year of Emperor Guangxu's reign, which stipulated its opening by China
69	Liaoyang*	Fengtian	1905	June 28, 1907	Sino-Japanese Convention Concerning the Three Provinces in Northeast China in the 31st year of Emperor Guangxu's reingn, which stipulated its opening by China
70	Aihui	Heilongjiang	1905	June 28, 1907	Sino-Japanese Convention Concerning the Three Provinces in Northeast China in the 31st year of Emperor Guangxu's reign, which stipulated its opening by China
71	Sanxing* (Yilan)	Jilin	1905	July 1, 1909	Sino-Japanese Convention Concerning the Three Provinces in Northeast China in the 31st year of Emperor Guangxu's reign, which stipulated its opening by China
72	Hunchun*	Jilin	1905	January 1, 1910	Sino-Japanese Convention Concerning the Three Provinces in Northeast China in the 31st year of Emperor Guangxu's reign, which stipulated its opening by China
73	Ningguta*	Heilongjiang	1905	January, 1910	Sino-Japanese Convention Concerning the Three Provinces in Northeast China in the 31st year of Emperor Guangxu's reign, which stipulated its opening by China
74	Hailar*	Heilongjiang	1905	January, 1910	Sino-Japanese Convention Concerning the Three Provinces in Northeast China in the 31st year of Emperor Guangxu's reign, which stipulated its opening by China

(continued)

Serial number	Name of port	Province	Contract time	Actual opening time	Main basis for opening
75	Gyangze	Tibet	1906	April 27, 1906	Sino-British Convention of Calcutta in the 32nd year of Emperor Guangxu's reign
76	Gedake	Tibet	1906	1906	Sino-British Convention of Calcutta in the 32nd year of Emperor Guangxu's reign
77	Suifenhe	Heilongjiang	1907	January 14, 1907	Sino-Russian Notes to Russia for Protocol of Taxation in the 33rd year of Emperor Guangxu's reign
78	Longjingcun	Jilin	1909	November 2, 1909	Sino-Japanese Gando Convention in the 1st year of Emperor Xuantong's reign
79	Juzijie (Yanji)	Jilin	1909	November 2, 1909	Sino-Japanese Gando Convention in the 1st year of Emperor Xuantong's reign
80	Toudaogou	Jilin	1909	November 2, 1909	Sino-Japanese Gando Convention in the 1st year of Emperor Xuantong's reign
81	Baicaogou	Jilin	1909	November 2, 1909	Sino-Japanese Gando Convention in the 1st year of Emperor Xuantong's reign

Notes: (1) This table is sorted according to the time of signing the treaty or regulation, when the time of signing was the same. The order is arranged based on the actual time the ports were open.

(2) According to the chart, if there were more than one treaty, the treaty which directly led to the opening of ports or the most important one is listed.

(3) The province in which it was located refers to the province in which it was located at that time, rather than the actual location today.

(4) Hong Kong and Macao became free ports in 1843, which were not listed in the table because they were not open to the outside world according to any treaties.

(5) The Sino-British Treaty of Tientsin stipulated that Taiwan region open only two ports of Tainan and Danshui (Taipei). In fact, Gaoxiong (Kaohsiung) and Jilong (Keelung) ports were also opened at the same time.

(6) The Sino-British Yantai Treaty provided for the opening of treaty ports in Yichang, Wuhu, Wenzhou and Beihai. Besides, six berthing wharves (non-commercial outlets) i.e. Datong, Anqing, Hukou, Wuxue, Luxikou and Shashi were stipulated as wharves for a berth. Ships were allowed to berth for loading or unloading passengers and goods.

(7) In the 31st year of Emperor Guangxu's reign, the treaties concerning the three northeast provinces of China stipulated that 16 ports in the northeast of China should be opened and traded voluntarily by China, which was included in the scope of treaty ports in accordance with the present table with * for distinction.

(8) Harbin was originally a Russian subsidiary of the Middle East Railway, and in 1905 it was opened as a treaty port for Japan according to the treaty.

Sources: (1) General Administration of Customs, *Selected Orders of the General Administration of Taxation of the Chinese Customs*, Selected Edition Volume 1 (1861-1910), Beijing: China Customs Press, 2003, pp. 621-625.

(2) Stanley F. Wright, *Hart and the Chinese* Customs (2), Xiamen: Xiamen University Press, 1994, p.586

(3) The Second Historical Archives of China, "Opening Treaty Ports in China in 1921", *Historical Archives*, 1984(4).

(4) Xu Dixin and Wu Chengming, *History of the Development of Capitalism in China* (Volume 2), Beijing: People's Publishing House, 2003, p.53, p.529.

(5) Yan Zhongping, *Selected Statistical Data of Economic History in Modern China*, Beijing: Science Press, 1955, pp. 44-47.

(6) Zhang Hongxiang, *Modern China's Treaty Ports and Concessions*, Tianjin: Tianjin People's Publishing House, 1993, pp. 321-323.

(7) [Japan] Takeshi Hamashita, *A Study of Modern Chinese Economic History: Customs Finance and Trade Port Market Circle in the Late Qing Dynasty*, Nanjing: Phoenix Publishing & Media Network, Jiangsu People's Publishing House, 2006.

(8) Yao Xianhao, *Historical Materials of Modern Foreign Trade in China*, Beijing: Zhonghua Book Company, 1962.

Table 3-2   Opening of national customs during 1860—1910

Name of pass	Date of opening	Location	Notes
Jianghai (Shanghai) Pass	On October 1, 1860 (August 17, the 10th year of Emperor Xianfeng's reign), the pass was opened to levy taxes according to the new regulations.	Shanghai, Jiangsu	Shanghai was opened as a treaty port in accordance with the Treaty of Nanking of 1842 (the 22nd year of Emperor Daoguang's reign). In 1853, when the Knife Club invaded Shanghai, local officials of the Qing Dynasty escaped from their duties. The consulates of Britain, France, and the United States in Shanghai took the opportunity to help with the customs' officers. On June 29, 1854 (the 4th year of Emperor Xianfeng's reign), they concluded an agreement with Wu Jianzhang, agreeing to nominate one person from each consul of the three countries. Wu Jianzhang appointed and assisted Shanghai Customs in tax affairs. The nominated foreigners were called tax commissioners and formed a tax administration committee. On July 12, 2001, Shanghai Customs was reopened and was under consular control of Britain, France, and the United States. After the Treaty of Tientsin in 1858 (the 8th year of Emperor Xianfeng), H.N.Lay, a British, was appointed customs commissioner in chief in 1859 by He Guiqing, Governor of Jiangsu, Anhui and Jiangxi provinces and Minister of Commerce for South China coastal treaty ports, and H. Tutor Davis, a British, was appointed Shanghai customs commissioner in chief in July of the same year. The customs office formally established the customs system and began to collect taxes according to the new regulations in the following year.
Suzhou Pass	On October 1, 1896 (August 25, the 2nd year of Emperor Guangxu's reign), the pass was opened to levy taxes.	Suzhou, Jiangsu	In 1895 (the 21st year of Emperor Guangxu's reign) the Treaty of Shimonoseki between China and Japan stipulated that Suzhou should be opened as a treaty port. The next year, the customs office was set up to levy taxes.

(continued)

Name of pass	Date of opening	Location	Notes
Zhenjiang Pass	On May 10, 1961 (April 1, the 11th year of Emperor Xianfeng's reign), the pass was opened to levy taxes.	Zhenjiang, Jiangsu	In 1858 (the 8th year of Emperon Xianfeng's reign), the Treaty of Tientsin stipulated that Zhenjiang should be opened as a treaty port. In 1861, the customs office was established to levy taxes.
Jinling (Nanjing) Pass	On May 1, 1899 (March 22, the 25th year of Emperor Guangxu's reign), the pass was opened to levy taxes.	Nanjing, Jiangsu	In 1858 (the 8th year of Emperor Xianfeng's reign), the Treaty of Tientsin stipulated that Nanjing should be opened as a treaty port. From 1899, the customs office was established, and Jinling Pass was set up to levy taxes.
Wuhu Pass	On April 1, 1877 (February 18, the 3rd year of Emperor Guangxu's reign), the pass was opened to levy taxes.	Wuhu, Anhui	In 1876 (the 2nd year of Guangxu's reign) the Yantai Treaty between China and Britain stipulated that Wuhu should be opened as a treaty port. In 1877, the customs office was set up to levy taxes.
Jiujiang Pass	The pass was opened to levy taxes on January 1, 1863 (November 12, the 1st year of Emperor Tongzhi's reign).	Jiujiang, Jiangxi	In 1858 (the 8th year of Emperor Xianfeng's reign), the Treaty of Tientsin stipulated that Jiujiang should be opened as a treaty port. In 1863, the customs office was set up to levy taxes.
Jianghan (Hankou) Pass	The pass was opened to levy taxes on January 1, 1863 (November 12, the 1st year of Emperor Tongzhi's reign).	Hankou, Hubei	In 1858 (the 8th year of Emperor Xianfeng's reign), the Treaty of Tientsin stipulated that Hankou should be opened as a treaty port. In 1863, the customs office was set up to levy taxes.
Yuezhou Pass	On December 13, 1899 (November 11, the 25th year of Emperor Guangxu's reign), the pass was opened to levy taxes on January 1, 1900 (November 29, the 25th year of Emperor Guangxu's reign).	Yueyang, Hunan	In 1899 (the 25th year of Emperor Guangxu's reign), the Qing government opened Yuezhou as a treaty port and set up a customs office, which began to levy taxes in 1900.
Changsha Pass	On July 1, 1904 (May 18, the 35th year of Emperor Guangxu's reign), the pass was opened to levy taxes.	Changsha, Hunan	The Sino-British Supplementing Treaty of Commerce and Navigation in 1902 (the 28th year of Guangxu's reign) and the Sino-Japanese Supplementary Treaty of Commerce—Supplementing Treaty of Peking in 1903 (the 29th year of Guangxu's reign) stipulated Changsha should be opened as a treaty port. In 1904, the customs office was set up to levy taxes.
Shashi Pass	On October 1, 1896 (August 25, the 22nd year of Emperor Guangxu's reign), the pass was opened to levy taxes.	Shashi, Hubei	In 1895 (the 21st year of Emperor Guangxu's reign), the Treaty of Shimonoseki between China and Japan stipulated that Shashi should be opened as a treaty port. In 1896, the customs office was set up to levy taxes.

(continued)

Name of pass	Date of opening	Location	Notes
Yichang Pass	On April 1, 1877 (February 18, the 3rd year of Emperor Guangxu's reign), the pass was opened to levy taxes.	Yichang, Hubei	In 1876 (the 2nd year of Emperor Guangxu's reign), the Yantai Treaty stipulated that Yichang should be opened as a treaty port. In 1877, the customs office was set up to levy taxes.
Chongqing Pass	On March 2, 1891 (January 21, the 17th year of Emperor Guangxu's reign), the pass was opened to levy taxes.	Chongqing, Sichuan	In 1890 (the 16th year of Emperor Guangxu's reign), the Additional Articles Re-traffic in Opium-Supplementing Agementing Agreement of Yantai stipulated that Chongqing should be opened as a trading port. In 1891, the customs office was established to levy taxes. In 1895, the Treaty of Shimonoseki re-established Chongqing as a treaty port with concessions.
Hangzhou Pass	On October 1, 1896 (August 25, the 22nd year of Emperor Guangxu's reign), the pass was opened to levy taxes.	Hangzhou, Zhejiang	In 1895 (the 21st year of Emperor Guangxu's reign), the Treaty of Shimonoseki stipulated that Hangzhou should be opened as a treaty port. In 1896, the customs office was established to levy taxes.
Zhejiang (Ningbo) Pass	On January 1, 1861 (November 29, the 10th year of Emperor Xianfeng's reign), the pass began to levy taxes according to the new regulations.	Ningbo, Zhejiang	In 1842 (the 22nd year of Emperor Daoguang's reign), the Treaty of Nanking stipulated that Ningbo should be opened as a treaty port. The Treaty of Tientsin of 1858 stipulated that all ports should be taxed by foreigners according to Shanghai Customs. In 1861, a customs office was established and began to levy taxes according to new regulations.
Ouhai (Wenzhou) Pass	On April 1, 1877 (February 18, the 3rd year of Emperor Guangxu's reign), the pass was opened to levy taxes.	Wenzhou, Zhejiang	In 1876 (the 2nd year of Emperor Guangxu's reign), the Yantai Treaty stipulated that Wenzhou should be opened as a treaty port. In 1877, the customs office was established to levy taxes.
Fujian Passes	Fujian Passes include Fuzhou Pass, Xiamen Pass, and Sandu'ao Branch Pass. Their opening dates are as follows:		
Fuzhou Pass	On July 11, 1861 (June 7, the 11th year of Emperor Xianfeng's reign), the pass began to levy taxes according to the new regulations.	Fuzhou, Fujian	In 1842 (the 22nd year of Emperor Daoguang's reign) the Treaty of Nanking stipulated that Fuzhou should be opened as a treaty port. The Treaty of Tientsin of 1858 stipulated that all ports should be taxed by foreigners according to the Shanghai Customs. In 1861, a customs office was set up to levy taxes according to the new regulations.
Xiamen Pass	On July 1, 1861 (June 7, the 11th year of Emperor Xianfeng's reign), the pass began to levy taxes according to the new regulations.	Xiamen, Fujian	In 1842 (the 22nd year of Emperor Daoguang's reign), the Treaty of Nanjing stipulated that Xiamen should be opened as a treaty port. According to the Treaty of Tientsin of 1858, a Tax Department was established in 1861 to levy taxes according to the new regulations.

(continued)

Name of pass	Date of opening	Location	Notes
Sandu'ao Branch Pass	On October 1, 1899 (August 27, the 25th year of Emperor Guangxu's reign), the pass was opened to levy taxes.	Sandu'ao, Sandu Island, Fujian	In 1899 (the 25th year of Emperor Guangxu's reign), the pass was set up, which was then called the Fuhai Pass.
Taiwan Pass	Taiwan Pass was located at the end of the Danshui Department. On July 18, 1862 (June 22, the 1st year of Emperor Tongzhi's reign), it was opened to levy taxes and set up an outdoor in nearby Keelung. On May 6, 1864 (the first day of April, the 3rd year of Emperor Tongzhi's reign), Dagoukou was set up in Qihou Port, Fengshan County.	Danshui, Taiwan; its exit lies in Keelung and Fengshan County	In 1858 (the 8th year of Emperor Xianfeng's reign), the Treaty of Tientsin opened Taiwan (Tainan) as a treaty port. In 1862, the customs office was established to levy taxes.
Guangdong Passes	Guangdong Passes include Yuezhou, Qionghai, Chaohai, Beihai, Kowloon, Gongbei, Sanshui, Jiangmen, and Ganzhu. Their opening dates are as follows:		
Yuezhou (Guangzhou) Pass	On October 1, 1860 (August 17, the 10th year of Emperor Xianfeng's reign), the pass began to levy taxes according to new regulations.	Guangzhou, Guangdong	In 1842 (the 22nd year of Emperor Daoguang's reign), the Treaty of Nanking stipulated that Guangzhou should be opened as a treaty port. The Treaty of Tientsin of 1858 stipulated that all ports should be taxed by foreigners and a customs office was established in 1860 to levy taxes according to new regulations.
Chaohai (Shantou) Pass	On October 1, 1860 (August 17, the 10th year of Emperor Xianfeng's reign), the pass began to levy taxes according to new regulations.	Shantou, Guangdong	In 1858 (the 8th year of Emperor Xianfeng's reign), Treaty of Tientsin stipulated that Chaozhou should be opened as a treaty port. In 1876, the customs office was established to levy taxes.
Qionghai (Qiongzhou) Pass	On April 1, 1876 (March 7, the 2nd year of Emperor Guangxu's reign), the pass was opened to levy taxes.	Qiongzhou, Guangdong	In 1858 (the 8th year of Emperor Xianfeng's reign), the Treaty of Tientsin stipulated that Qiongzhou should be opened as a treaty port. The customs office was established in 1876 and began to levy taxes.
Beihai pass	On April 1, 1877 (February 18, the 3rd year of Emperor Guangxu's reign), the pass was opened to levy taxes.	Beihai, Guangxi	In 1876 (the 2nd year of Emperor Guangxu's reign), the Yantai Treaty stipulated that Beihai should be opened as a treaty port. In 1877, the customs office was established to levy taxes.

(continued)

Name of pass	Date of opening	Location	Notes
Kowloon Pass	On April 2, 1887 (March 9, the 13th year of Emperor Guangxu's reign), the pass was opened to levy taxes.	Kowloon, Guangdong	In accordance with the Yantai Treaty and the Additional Articles Re-traffic in Opium-Supplementing Agreement of Yantai, China and Britain agreed on September 11, 1886 (August 14, the 12th year of Emperor Guangxu's reign) that China set up a gateway and customs office in Kowloon, which mainly levied foreign drug taxes. Collecting tax under this agreement started in 1877.
Gongbei Pass	On April 2, 1887 (March 9, the 13th year of Emperor Guangxu's reign), the pass was opened to levy taxes.	Gongbeiwan, Macao	In accordance with the Sino-Portuguese Agreement on March 26, 1887 (March 3, the 13th year of Emperor Guangxu's reign), a gateway and customs office should be established in Macao by China, which mainly levied foreign drug taxes.
Sanshui Pass	On June 4, 1897 (May 5, the 23rd year of Guangxu's reign), the pass was opened to levy taxes.	Jianggenxu of Sanshui County, Guangdong	In accordance with the Sino-British Convention Relating to Burmah and Thibet in 1897 (the 23rd year of Emperor Guangxu's reign), Sanshui was opened as a treaty port. In the same year, a customs office was set up to levy taxes.
Jiangmen Pass	On June 4, 1897 (May 5, the 23rd year of Emperor Guangxu's reign), the pass as a branch began to levy tax. In 1904 (January 21, the 30th year of Emperor Guangxu's reign), the pass was formally established to levy taxes.	Xinhui, Guangdong	In 1897, as the division of Sanshui Pass, it began to levy taxes with the Sanshui Pass at the same time. By 1904, Jiangmen was opened as a treaty port in accordance with the Supplementing Treaty of Commerce and Navigation between China and Britain, and a customs office was set up to levy taxes.
Ganzhu Brahch Pass	On July 1, 1897 (June 2, the 23rd year of Emperor Guangxu's reign), the pass began to levy taxes.	Shunde, Guangdong	In 1987, as the division of Sanshui Pass, it began to levy taxes. In 1904, a customs office was set up in Jiangmen, and the Ganzhu Branch Pass was canceled at that time.
Wuzhou Pass	On June 4, 1897 (May 5, the 23rd year of Emperor Guangxu's reign), the pass was opened to levy taxes.	Wuzhou, Guangxi	Wuzhou was opened as a treaty port in accordance with the Sino-British Convention Related to Burmah and Thibet in 1897. In the same year, a customs office was set up to levy taxes.
Nanning pass	On January 1, 1907 (May 3, the 15th year of Emperor Guangxu's reign), the pass was opened to levy taxes.	Nanning, Guangxi	In accordance with the agreement in 1897 (the 24th year of Emperor Guangxu's reign), the pass was opened. In 1907, a customs office was set up to levy taxes.
Zhennan (Longzhou) Pass	On June 1, 1889 (May 3, the 15th year of Emperor Guangxu's reign), the pass was opened to levy taxes.	Longzhou, Guangxi	Longzhou was opened as a trading port in accordance with the Sino-France Supplementing Convention of Commerce in 1887 (the 13th year of Emperor Guangxu's reign). In 1889, a customs office was set up to levy taxes.

(continued)

Name of pass	Date of opening	Location	Notes
Mengzi Pass	On August 13, 1889 (July 28, the 15th year of Emperor Guangxu's reign), the pass was opened to levy taxes.	Mengzi, Yunnan	According to Sino-France Supplementing Convention of Commerce in 1887 (the 13th year of Emperor Guangxu's reign), Mengzi was opened as a trading port. In 1889, a customs office was set up to levy taxes.
Simao Pass	On January 1, 1897 (November 29, the 22nd year of Emperor Guangxu's reign), the pass was opened to levy taxes.	Simao, Yunnan	Simao was opened as a trading port in accordance with the Sino-France Supplementing Convention of Commerce in 1886. In 1897, a customs office was set up to levy taxes.
Tengyue Pass	On May 8, 1902 (April 1, the 28th year of Emperor Guangxu's reign), the pass was opened to levy taxes.	Tengchong, Yunnan	In 1899 (the 25th year of Emperor Guangxu's reign), the British Ambassador, in accordance with the Sino-British Convention Related to Burmah and Thibet in 1897, agreed to set up a new pass in Tengyue to levy taxes. Then in 1902, a customs office was set up in Tengyue.
Jiaohai Pass	In 1899 (the 25th year of Emperor Guangxu's reign), the pass was established to levy taxes.	Qingdao, Shandong	In 1899, the Sino-German Association formulated the Measures of Opening Qingdao Pass and Tax Collection. In the same year, the Jiaohai Pass was established, and a customs office was set up to levy taxes.
Donghai (Yantai) Pass	On August 20, 1861 (July 17, the 11th year of Emperor Xianfeng's reign), the pass was opened to levy taxes.	Yantai, Shandong	Yantai was opened as a trading port in accordance with the Treaty of Tientsin in 1858 (the 8th year of Emperor Xianfeng's reign). In 1861, a customs office was set up to levy taxes.
Jinhai (Tianjin) Pass	On March 23, 1861 (Februay 13, the 11th year of Emperor Xianfeng's reign), the pass was opened to levy taxes.	Tianjin, Hebei	Tianjin was opened as a trading port in accordance with the Beijing Convention in 1860, and a customs office was set up to levy taxes in 1861.
Niuzhuang Pass	The pass was opened to levy taxes on January 1, 1863 (November 12, the 1st year of Emperor Tongzhi's reign).	Niuzhuang, Liaoning	In accordance with the Treaty of Tientsin in 1858, the pass was opened as a trading port. In 1863, a customs office was set up to levy taxes.
Qinhuangdao Pass	On January 1, 1902 (November 22, the 27th year of Emperor Guangxu's reign), the pass was opened to levy taxes.	Qinhuangdao, Hebei	In 1898 (the 24th year of Emperor Guangxu's reign), the pass was opened for business. In 1902, it set up a branch pass and began to levy taxes.
Dalian Pass	On May 30, 1907 (March 19, the 33rd year of Emperor Guangxu's reign), the pass was opened to levy taxes.	Lvda, Liaoning	In 1907, China and Japan agreed on the tax collection measures for Dalian Pass. In the same year, Dalian Pass was established, and a customs office was set up to levy taxes.

(continued)

Name of pass	Date of opening	Location	Notes
Andong Pass	On March 14, 1907 (February 1, the 33rd year of Emperor Guangxu's reign), the pass was opened to levy taxes.	Dandong, Liaoning	Sino-Japanese Supplementary Treaty of Commerce-Supplementing Treaty of Peking in 1903 (the 29th year of Emperor Guangxu's reign) stipulated that China open Dadonggou as a trading port. The Treaty: Commercial Relations between China and the United States in the same year stipulated that China open Andong County as a trading port. In 1907, a customs office was set up in Andong, and branch pass was set up in Dadong gou.
Harbin Pass	Harbin Pass includes: the Manzhouli Branch Pass began to levy taxes on February 5, 1908 (January 4, the 34th year of Emporer Guangxu's reign); Suifenhe Brarch Pass began to levy taxes on February 11 of the same year (January 10, the 34th year of Emporer Guangxu's reign).	Manzhouli and Suifenhe in Heilongjiang	Sino-Japanese Convention Concerning the Three Provinces in Northeast China in 1905 (the 31st year of Emperor Guangxu's reign) stipulated that China should open Harbin as a trading port. In 1907, the Ministry of Foreign Affairs advised North Manzhouli to set up a pass at the junctions in accordance with the China-Russian East Three Provinces Railway Contract. In 1908, it levied taxes in Manzhouli and Suifenhe.

Source: Tang Xianglong, eds., *China's Customs Taxation and Distribution Statistics in Modern Times*, Beijing: Zhonghua Book Company, 1992, pp. 54-60.

3.7 Non–treaty ports in modern China

Modern China's ports opened to the outside world could be divided into two types: the "treaty ports" and the "non-treaty ports" (ports opened voluntarily by China). Unlike the treaty ports, the non-treaty ports were declared by the Qing government or were forced to open to the outside world at the request of foreign agencies in China. The Qing government had the right of decision-making and administration over such ports. When it comes to "non-treaty ports", it is generally defined as "the ports opened voluntarily by China" by Western scholars.

3.7.1 Historical background of the non-treaty ports

After the defeat of the Qing government in the Sino-Japanese War in 1894, the aggression of foreign powers against China deepened, triggering a wave of carving up China. China was facing an unprecedented crisis of national survival, which had a tremendous and profound impact on China's political situation, economy, ideology, and culture. To save the nation from extinction, the Reform Movement was launched. As a means of self-help and trade war, non-treaty commercial ports were a new type of ports opened by modern China in areas with a large population and relatively convenient transportation to ensure sovereignty, stop outsiders from coveting, prevent foreign powers from expanding their aggressive interests, and try to change the situation of loss of rights and humiliation at treaty ports.

In June 1898, the Reform Movement of 1898 entered the stage of "Hundred Days Reform" and "non-treaty ports" were finally implemented as a reform measure. In August of the same year, the Qing government declared to "open more ports", saying that "All trading ports are not allowed to be occupied by any other countries, which is a common practice in Europe. At present, when the sea ban is over, world powers are waiting around in order to seek commercial interest in the treaty ports. Therefore, the only way is to open more ports. In March, as the Premier's Minister of State Affairs proposed, Yuezhou in Hunan, Sandu'ao in Fujian, and Qinwangdao in Zhili (today's Hebei) were opened as ports. Huang Siyong's proposal that officials of all provinces should inspect their local conditions and set up more ports was accepted without the second-round discussion in Yamen (the government office in feudal China), although there was no precedent to refer to. Governors along the Yangtze River or border areas were requested to quickly and carefully plan for the provinces and localities within their jurisdiction. Any places with the necessity to open ports and any merchants who could help in expanding ports could refer their applications to the Yamen and go through the formalities for final approval. It was specified that the localities concerned were not to become foreign concessions, and the interests of all parties were protected. All these stipulations should be made known to other countries". [1] This marked the actual implementation of the policy of "non-treaty ports" planned for many years.

3.7.2 Non-treaty ports in modern China

According to Professor Yang Tianhong [2] and other experts, in the Qing Dynasty, the first non-treaty ports were Wusong, Yuezhou, Sandu'ao, and Qinwangdao. The public opinion at home and abroad responded favorably. The Qing government formally sent instructions to the provinces to "open more ports" and "develop more ports". Then

---

[1] Zhu Shoupeng, *Records of Donghua (East China) in Emperor Guangxu's Dynasty* (Vol.IV), Beijing: Zhonghua Book Company, 1958, p. 5158.

[2] Yang Tianhong, *Port Opening and Social Change—A Study of the Ports Opened Voluntarily by China in Modern Times*, Beijing: Zhonghua Book Company, 2002, pp. 57-82.

in early 1899, Nanning, in Guangxi, was turned into a commercial port. During the Constitutional Reform and Modernization, the number of non-treaty commercial ports was large, and the scale of cities was significantly improved. Wuchang, the capital of Hubei Province, Jinan, the capital of Shandong Province, and Kunming, the capital of Yunnan Province, were opened voluntarily as commercial ports. There were also some cities and towns which had a tradition of trade and merchants or had the potential for commercial development. These cities and towns were open to the outside world after approval. They mainly included Xiangzhou in Xiangshan county of Guangdong, Zhongshan Port, Gongyibu and Tongguwan in Taishan, Weixian county, Zhoucun, Longkou, Jining in Shandong Province, Wusong, Haizhou, Wuxi, Pukou and Xuzhou in Jiangsu Province. Gulangyu in Xiamen, Fujian Province, Changde and Xiangtan in Hunan Province, Zhengxian county and Luoyang in Henan Province, Guihuacheng and Baotou in Suiyuan, Duolun and Zhangjiakou in Chahar Province, Sanmenwan in Zhejiang Province, Bengbu in Anhui Province, Chifeng in Jehol Province, Taonan, Liaoyuan, Jinxian and Zhengjiatun in the three northeastern provinces. Since the beginning of modern times, non-treaty ports have been scattered all over the country, and the boom did not end until 1930.

It should be noted that the three northeastern provinces, in accordance with the Sino-Japanese Treaty on the Matters of the Eastern Provincial Conferences, had stipulated the opening of 16 ports at once such as Fenghuangcheng, Liaoyang, Xinmintun, Tieling, Tongjiangzi, Fakumen, Changchun, Jilin provincial City, Harbin, Ningguta, Hunchun, Sanxing, Qiqihar, Hailaer, Aihui, and Manzhouli. These ports were not only treaty ports in accordance with the contract, but also ports opened voluntarily by China. They have been listed as treaty ports in the preceding article and were no longer included here. In addition, until 1921, Shijiusuo in Shandong Province, Baoshan in Jiangsu Province, Datong in Anhui Province, Xiajiutai and Zhangjiawan in Jilin Province, Jiujiang and Binxingzhou in Jiangxi Province, Songdao Island in Fujian Province, Altay in Xinjiang, Lulintan in Hunan Province and other places were all proposed as open ports, but most failed to be approved. According to incomplete statistics, the number of non-treaty commercial ports approved by China during 1898-1930 should be at least 38 (see Table 3–3).

Table 3–3   Non–treaty ports in modern China (1898–1930)

Serial number	Name of port	Province	Time of approval opening	Time of actual opening	Reasons for opening up
1	Wusong	Jiangsu	April 20, 1898	Not officially open	Proposed by the Customs Commissioner in chief and approved by Yamen in charge of foreign affairs
2	Yuezhou (Yueyang)	Hunan	March 24, 1898	November 13, 1899	Requested by British Consul in charge of foreign affairs, approved by Hunan Governor Duanfang
3	Qinwangdao (Qinhuangdao)	Zhili	March 24, 1898	December 11, 1901	Approved by Yamen in charge of foreign affairs
4	Sandu'ao	Fujian	March 24,1898	May 8,1899	Approved by Zhou Fu, Governor of Liangjiang (Today's Jiangsu, Anhui Shanghai, Jiangxi)
5	Nanning	Guangxi	January 30, 1899	January 1, 1907	Requested by Britain and France, approved by Huang Huaisen, governor of Guangxi
6	Wuchang	Hubei	November 18,1900	Not officially open	Approved by Zhang Zhidong, Governor of Guangdong and Guangxi
7	Gulangyu	Fujian	November 21, 1902	May 1, 1902	Requested by British, Japanese and French Consuls and approved by local administrator of Xinghua-Quanzhou-Yongchun prefecture
8	Jinan	Shandong	May 15, 1904	January 10, 1906	Requested by German Consul and approved by Yuan Shikai
9	Weixian	Shandong	May 15, 1904	January 10, 1906	Requested by German Consul and approved by Yuan Shikai
10	Zhoucun	Shandong	May 15, 1904	January 10, 1906	Requested by German Consul and approved by Yuan Shikai
11	Haizhou (Lianyungang)	Jiangsu	October 24, 1905	April 22, 1921	Approved by local government
12	the capital of Yunnan (Kunming)	Yunnan	May 11, 1905	April 29, 1910	Requested by the French Consul and approved by Ding Zhenduo, the Governor of Yunnan
13	Xiangtan	Hunan	July, 1905	March 16, 1906	Approved by Duanfang, Governor of Hunan
14	Changde	Hunan	1905	It was scheduled to open on July 2, 1906, but didn't open	Approved by Duanfang
15	Zhengxian (Zhengzhou)	Henan	1905	1922	Approved by Chen Kuilong, Governor of Henan

(continued)

Serial number	Name of port	Province	Time of approval opening	Time of actual opening	Reasons for opening up
16	Huludao	Fengtian	1908	January 8, 1914	Approved by the Governor of the Liaoning, Jilin, Heilongjiang
17	Xiangzhou	Guangdong	1908	1909	To be run under the chairmanship of gentry and merchants and approved by the Supervisory Department
18	Gongyibu	Guangdong	1908	1912	With the approval of Guangdong Governor Zhang Renjun
19	Luoyang	Henan	1908	August 27,1909	Approved by Governor of Henan
20	Pukou	Jiangsu	1910	1912	Requested by British and German Consuls and approved by local government
21	Longkou	Shandong	January 8, 1914	October 1, 1915	Notified by the Beiyang Government to open to all countries
22	Taonan	Heilongjiang	January 8, 1914	1914	At the request of the Mission and approved by the Beiyang Government
23	Liaoyuan	Fengtian	January 8, 1914	1914	At the request of the Mission and approved by the Beiyang Government
24	Duolun	Chahar	January 8, 1914	1914	At the request of the Mission
25	Guihuacheng (Hohhot)	Suiyuan	January 8, 1914	1914	At the request of the Mission and approved by the Beiyang Government
26	Chixian (Chifeng)	Jehol	January 8, 1914	1917	Approved by Zhang Shijie and Chixian Governor Ye Dakuang according to regulations
27	Zhangjiakou	Chahar	1914	Not officially open	At request
28	Jinxian (Jinzhou)	Fengtian	February, 1916	1916	Run by local governments
29	Zhengjiatun	Fengtian	1917	1917	At the request of the Japanese Consul
30	Binxingzhou	Jiangxi	1917	1923	Proposed by Jiujiang county governor
31	Sanmenwan	Zhejiang	1919	1920	Proposed by Zou Hui, an overseas Chinese businessman with the approval of the provincial governor
32	Wuxi	Jiangsu	October, 1922	December, 1922	Applied by local government, and approved by the Beiyang Government
33	Xuzhou	Jiangsu	November 15, 1922	1923	Applied by local government, and approved by the Beiyang Government
34	Baotou	Suiyuan	1923	1924	Approved by the Beiyang Government

(continued)

Serial number	Name of port	Province	Time of approval opening	Time of actual opening	Reasons for opening up
35	Jining	Shandong	1921	April 24, 1924	Opened by the Beiyang government at Japan's request
36	Bengbu	Anhui	1923	September 1, 1924	Arranged by Anhui governor Ma Lianjia
37	Tongguwan	Guangdong	September, 1924	Not officially open	Arranged by Chen Yixi, Sun Yat-sen to organize
38	Zhongshan Port	Guangdong	May, 1930	June, 1931	Submitted by Tang Shaoyi to the National Government for verification

Notes: (1) Sixteen ports in Northeast China, which were stipulated in the *Treaty of the Issues on three Eastern Provinces in* 1905, were also opened by China on its own. in accordance with the provisions of the treaty as well as decisions by the Qing government. In this book, they are included in the treaty ports instead of the non-treaty ports.

(2) The provinces in which the ports were located refer to those of the time rather than the actual administrative divisions of today.

Sources: (1) Zhang Hongxiang, *Ports and Concessions in Modern China*, Tianjin: Tianjin People's Publishing House 1993, pp.321-326.

(2) Yang Tianhong, *Port Opening and Social Change—A Study of Modern China's Non-treaty Commercial Ports*, Beijing: Zhonghua Book Company, 2002, pp.112-113.

(3) Yang Tianhong, "The Regional Distribution of Non-treaty Commercial Ports and Its Influence on the Development of Foreign Trade Market Network System in Qing Dynasty", *Journal of Sichuan University*, 1999(2).

(4) The Second Historical Archives of China, "The Commercial Ports China Opened Before 1921", *Historical Archives*, 1984(4).

(5) Xu Dixin, Wu Chengming, *History of the Development of Capitalism in China* (Vol. II), Beijing: People's Publishing House, 2003, pp. 529-530.

3.7.3 Main characteristics of non-treaty ports in modern China

First, because of wide geographical distribution, these non-treaty ports were mostly located in coastal areas (rivers, lakes) and border areas, with few in inland provinces. The reasons for this geographical distribution were complicated. Most located at the entrance of foreign commodities to China or their direct hinterland. The opening of non-treaty commercial ports could make good use of its natural superior geographical location and relatively developed transportation and other convenient conditions with unparalleled social and cultural resources and civilization. Located in coastal areas or railways, highways or intersections, these ports enjoyed convenient transportation. Although the voluntary opening of the ports could ease the pressure of the foreign powers on China to open its treaty ports further and help to increase its fiscal revenue, the Qing government believed that the hinterland was different from the coastal areas. On the premise that the extraterritorial jurisdiction of the coastal ports had not been recovered, in order to protect the sovereignty and the integrity of territory, avoid foreign "entanglement", the mainland did its utmost to avoid foreign involvement in the hinterland. Ports were set up, and trade was allowed. The geographical location of non-treaty commercial ports was important, but political considerations were more important, which was the main reason why the number of non-treaty commercial ports in the mainland was relatively small.

Second, the management of non-treaty ports had their characteristics. Compared with treaty ports, the administrative power of non-treaty commercial ports was not subject to any restrictions, and they bound Chinese and foreign people equally. The permanent rent system of land established by foreigners in concessions in non-treaty commercial ports was abolished, and the ownership of land in the ports was controlled. The legislation and judiciary had maintained independence at non-treaty ports.

Third, due to the existence of a large number of port cities, the choice of cities and towns in modern China where ports were opened voluntarily was limited, and the level of cities in China was relatively low. Since there were no non-treaty ports in cities at the national or regional level, such ports' radiation effect was limited. According to the administrative level and residential population at that time, the largest cities in the commercial ports were provincial capitals and medium-sized regional towns.

Fourth, ports opened voluntarily by China in modern times played a positive role in the times. Since the opening of such ports was within the control of the Chinese customs, the state's fiscal revenue increased. The non-treaty ports promoted the communication between the hinterland markets and the development of modern industry, and the commercialization of production. Besides, the opening of ports for trade stimulated the population growth, trade development, and municipal construction, promoted the modernization process of Chinese cities, and influenced the choice of routes and historical process of China's modernization to a certain extent.

3.8 Major characteristics of open ports in modern China

Since the First Opium War, there had been two different waves of port opening in modern Chinese history. One involved ports that were forced to open by foreign powers, and the other had to do with ports opened voluntarily by the Qing government. Taking the official approval of the opening of commercial ports in the Qing Dynasty as the criteria for the division of different periods of the opening of ports in modern China, we can see that 1840 to 1897, when the economy and society of China changed fundamentally, was the first period of ports opening in modern China; and the second, period was from 1898 to 1948 when the Qing government formally approved the opening of commercial ports till January 1943 before the founding of the People's Republic of China, when the system of China's commercial ports was abolished.

3.8.1 First period of open ports in modern China: 1840-1897

During this period, open treaty ports almost covered China's whole coastline and the major port cities along the Yangtze River and Xijiang River. The northwest of the open port area had penetrated into Jiayuguan, Urumqi and other places, and the Southwest had penetrated into Simao, Longzhou and other places. In the process of opening up, the coastal areas developed from south to north; along the Yangtze River, ports were opened from east to west, and along the border, treaty ports increased from inside to outside. The opening of ports and the extension of hinterland had further expanded the economic radiation capacity of port cities.

It was mainly reflected as follows. First, the treaty ports in China opening to the outside world extended from the coastline of Guangzhou, Xiamen, Fuzhou, Ningbo, and Shanghai in the southeast coastal areas to the north and south, and then the ports of Taiwan, Danshui and Wenzhou in the southeast coastal areas and the ports of Tianjin, Niuzhuang and Dengzhou in the north were opened one after another. The second was treaty ports expanded along the Yangtze River to inland areas. Along the west of the Yangtze River, treaty ports extending from major port cities to the inland to Zhenjiang, Nanjing, Wuhu, Jiujiang, Hankou, Yichang, Shashi and Chongqing, and the Yangtze River waterway between Shanghai and Chongqing were opened. For example, after the Sino-British Treaty of Nanking opened five port cities, i.e., Guangzhou, Xiamen, Fuzhou, Ningbo, and Shanghai along the southeastern coast were opened, meanwhile, the Sino-Japanese Treaty of Shimonoseki opened four port cities along the Yangtze River, including Suzhou, Hangzhou, Shashi (now Shacheng District of Jingzhou), and Chongqing. The third was to expand eastward along the Xijiang River. Since the opening of Guangzhou, Chaozhou, Qiongzhou, Beihai, Gongbei, Kowloon, Sanshui and Wuzhou were opened at different times, and the opening of port cities along the Xijiang River was basically completed. The fourth was the opening of Suzhou and Hangzhou ports along the Beijing-Hangzhou Grand Canal. The fifth was to open ports along the land border. Ili, Tacheng, Kashgar, Kulun, Kyakhta, Gucheng, Uriyasu, Kobdo, Hami, Turpan, Mengzi, Yadong, Hekou, Tengyue, and other ports were opened one after another. The change of the geographical position of the open ports during this period showed that foreign aggression against China had deepened, and the penetration and plunder moved from the coastal areas to the inland, thus significantly deepening the process of semi-colonial and semi-feudal China.

3.8.2　Second period of open ports in modern China: 1898-1948

At the end of the 19th century, the United States proposed to implement the "open door" policy with other western countries in China, and divided their sphere of influence, so as to carve up China. The situation was worrying, and the nation was in danger.

During this period, the opening of ports exposed that the main objective of the invading countries was no longer to expand trade and occupy the market but to export foreign capital and seize power. To some extent, the government implemented the policy of "self-rescue" under the situation of internal and external distress and urgency, including the ports opened voluntarily by the government, in order to save the nation and strive for survival in an attempt to revitalize commerce and preserve sovereignty (see Table 3–4).

Table 3–4　　　Imperialist's "sphere of influence" in the late 19th century

Country	"Sphere of influence"	Occupied or leased land
Russia	North of the Great Wall, Liaoning, Jilin, Heilongjiang and Xinjiang	Forced lease of Lvshun, Dalian, and obtaining the right to construct the Dong-Qing railway south Manzhouli line. Illegally changing the leased land into "Guandong Province", occupying the Liaodong Peninsula and including the whole territory of northeast China into its sphere of influence.
Germany	Shandong	Forced lease of Jiaozhouwan in Shandong province with a term of 99 years, obtaining railway construction right and mining right of Jiaozhouwan.
France	Guangdong, Guangxi, Yunnan, and Hainan	Forced lease of Guangzhouwan.
The UK	Yangtze river basin	Forced lease of New Territories, Weihaiwei.
Japan	Fujian	Occupying Taiwan and Penghu Islands.
The US		At that time, it was too busy expanding into Central and South America, but it did not give up the ambition of invading China. In the autumn of 1899, it proposed an open-door policy of equal opportunities for all countries' interests in China, so as to keep the Chinese market free and open to American goods and protect its interests in China.

Sources: Edited by the author.

During this period, the main features of treaty ports in China and ports opened voluntarily by China were as follows. Firstly, Germany, Britain, Russia, and France occupied and forced the opening of Qingdao, Weihaiwei, Dalian and Guangzhouwan as treaty ports. Other countries followed suit. Secondly, Japan, Russia, the United States, and other countries occupied the Northeast China, and the competition for their interest was intense. Through various means to force the opening of the Northeast China, including the three eastern provinces and Suiyuan, Chahar, and other large areas of Northeast China, the intensity and density of ports open was unprecedented. More than 20 ports were opened. Thirdly, port cities and towns like Anqing, Wanxian, Wusong, Wuchang along the Yangtze River and those along the Xijiang River, such as Jiangmen and Huizhou, were further opened, together with the opening of the economic hinterland of the Yangtze and Xijiang valleys. Fourthly, open ports further spread to coastal areas, border areas, areas along rivers, and inland areas.

Chapter 4
Open Ports in Contemporary China
and Their Development: 1949-1978

History is a chain of time that cannot be cut off. Therefore today's creativity is based on the achievements of yesterday. As observed by Marx, men make their own history, but they do not make it as they please; they do not make it under self-selected circumstances under the circumstances existing already, given and transmitted from the past.[1] The development of China's open ports and their growth have been closely related to the whole country's economic and social development since the founding of the People's Republic of China in 1949. This chapter mainly discusses the development of China's foreign trade as well as the open ports and their development in the period from 1949 to the start of reform and opening up in 1978.

4.1 Economic and social development in early years of the founding of the People's Republic of China

The founding of the People's Republic of China in 1949 marked a new historical stage in China's modernization and economic and social development. However, it should be noted that China had developed under the severe oppression, shackles, and sabotage of the long-term capitalism, imperialism, and feudalism, for more than 100 years since the Opium War in 1840. The Modern economy of China had developed under a long period of imperialist economic aggression and the semi-feudal and semi-colonial background. When the People's Republic of China was founded, it took over a "mess" of a large population with poor education, severe damage to industrial and agricultural production, soaring prices, grave inflation, urban and rural isolation, traffic paralysis, financial difficulties, serious unemployment, and difficult livelihood.

---

[1] The Eighteenth Brumaire of Louis Bonaparte, *Selected Works of Marx and Engels*, Volume 1, Beijing: People's Publishing House, 1995, p.603 .

Looking back on history, from 1840 to 1949, the political and economic development showed the following characteristics:

First, the national economy had been developing very slowly for a long time. The traditional agriculture had been shrinking and depressed, and the development of modern industries had been difficult, seriously lagging and incompatible with each other. The national economy had been destroyed constantly; consumption declining; investment almost exhausted and social wealth had been depleted.

Second, the economic development was extremely imbalanced. The starting point of economic development was low, and the agricultural economy had never been on the road of modernization. Instead, it was in decline. The industrial foundation was weak, the industrial structure was seriously unbalanced, and the development of the heavy industry was weak. Typical "dual economy" had been formed in different areas and between urban and rural areas. Coastal areas had developed rapidly because of favorable transportation conditions, trade ports, and foreign investment. More than 70% of China's industries were concentrated in the eastern coastal areas with an area of less than 12%, and inland areas had long been slow to develop due to inconvenient transportation. What is more, there had never been an integrated market, a unified fiscal and monetary system, a unified industry and commerce; instead, different regions had even been blockaded and destroyed from one another.

Third, the perennial wars had severely damaged the economy and restricted economic operation and social development. The wars had caused severe damage to the urban and rural areas and inflicted losses on all walks of life. In 1949, the output of major industrial products between China and some countries was compared in Table 4–1. It is evident that there was a huge gap between China and the world's economic development.

Table 4–1   A comparison of major industrial products between China and other countries in 1949

Country	Raw coal (10,000 tons)	Crude oil (10,000 tons)	Power generation (100 million kwh)	Raw steel (10,000 tons)	Cement (10,000 tons)	Automobile (10,000 vehicles)	Nitrogen Fertilizer (nitrogen content/ 10,000 tons)	Newsprint (10,000 tons)	Cotton yarn (10,000 tons)
The US	43,316	25,232	3,451	7,074	3,594	625.4	104.8	83.8	171.5
Soviet Union	20,246	3,340	91	2,730	646	27.3	—	19.0	61.3
Canada	1,564	274	509	289	253	29.3	14.4	470.6	8.1
The UK	21,861	15	506	1,580	936	62.9	27.5	48.0	41.7

(continued)

Country	Raw coal (10,000 tons)	Crude oil (10,000 tons)	Power generation (100 million kwh)	Raw steel (10,000 tons)	Cement (10,000 tons)	Automobile (10,000 vehicles)	Nitrogen Fertilizer (nitrogen content/ 10,000 tons)	Newsprint (10,000 tons)	Cotton yarn (10,000 tons)
France	1,120	8	300	915	667	28.4	22.9	25.5	22.8
Japan	3,797	19	410	311	328	2.9	37.8	10.9	15.7
Federal Germany	10,323	84	387	916	846	16.1	43.1	12.7	22.8
Italy	110	1	208	206	404	8.6	13.7	6.5	58.6
Poland	7,408	15	81	231	234	—	6.0	4.6	9.1
Netherlands	1,170	62	—	43	57	—	—	7.1	6.2
India	3,220	25	49	137	213	2.2	1.0	0.2	58.5
Brazil	213	1	27	62	128	—	0.1	3.6	7.68
Mexico	107	871	43	33	123	—	0.4	—	—
Argentina	—	327	41	13	146	1.5	—	—	7.0
Yugoslavia	127	6	22	40	129	0.1	0.4	—	2.9
Egypt	—	228	9	—	89	—	2.8	—	3.4
South Africa	2,549	—	—	64	136	17.3	—	—	—
Australia	1,433	—	91	123	105	—	1.0	3.1	1.2
China	3,200	12	43	16	66	—	0.6	—	32.7
World	111,900	43,500	7,690	13,640	10,800	808	380	788	—
China's output/the world's total output ratio	2.86	0.03	0.56	0.12	0.61	0	0.16	0	—

Sources: Wu Li, ed., *Economic History of the People's Republic of China* (Volume 1), Beijing: China Economic Publishing House, 1999, pp.54-55. Fan Muhan, ed., *Summary of World Economic Statistics*, Beijing: People's Publishing House, 1985, pp.246-493, pp.520-525.

4.2 Fulfillment of China's first Five–Year Plan and the development of economy and foreign trade

The period from the founding of the People's Republic of China in 1949 to the completion of the first Five-year Plan at the end of 1957 marked a period with the most rapid economic development and the most dramatic institutional change in Chinese history. China's national economy was restored during 1949-1952. In just three years, the century-old turmoil in China was ended and the national economy was miraculously restored from the war's ruins. A large-scale economic construction was started in the condition of poverty and backwardness. China completed all the economic tasks of the democratic revolution and mastered the country's economic lifeline and controlled finance, market, and industry. It made remarkable achievements in various fields. The administrative power of the Party and the government was considerably strong, which laid a foundation for the rapid and stable transition of China to the economy under unitary public ownership and planned economy since 1953. With the large-scale economic construction, China embarked on the road of rapid industrialization and the transition to the socialist economy after the model of the Soviet Union. At that time, under the unfavorable internal and external environment of backward economy, lack of funds and shortage of talents, China had to choose an economic development strategy of import substitution, reducing consumption and giving priority to heavy industry, which ensured the smooth completion of the first Five-year Plan and the rapid development of heavy industry, laying a solid foundation for the industrialization of China.

During the period of national economic recovery, the Party and the State had taken the following major measures:

Firstly, the restoration of agriculture was taken as the basis for the recovery of the entire national economy. Through a series of reform measures, such as well-organized land reform in the countryside, construction of water conservancy, improvement of agricultural technology, land reclamation, the elimination of feudal land system and the landlord class and the policy of land to the tillers, the gap between the rich and the poor was dramatically narrowed, the enthusiasm and initiative of the broad masses of farmers were mobilized, and the foundation was laid for the rapid social system reform and large-scale mobilization of social resources.

Secondly, on the basis of "stabilizing prices" and "uniting finance and economy", the state adjusted industry and commerce with an emphasis on adjusting public-private relations, labor relations, production, and marketing relations. The state "utilized, restricted and reformed" the private economy through administrative management, economic leverage, industry self-discipline, and social mobilization so as to make it consistent with macroeconomic plans and social development goals. It was ensured that the state economy was the leading force of all social and economic elements and that various social and economic elements such as the private economy were under the leadership of the state economy. By establishing a state-owned enterprise management system, a robust state-owned economy was established. Through reorganization, preferential treatment and support of cooperatives, a wide range of supply and marketing cooperative economy were set up.

Thirdly, by taking over and reforming the old customs and establishing the new, the key to the gateway of the People's Republic of China was in the people's pockets. By abolishing the imperialist control over China's foreign trade and the privileges and monopolies of foreign enterprises, and fully implementing the import and export trade licensing system and the foreign exchange settlement system, we gradually established a management system of foreign trade plans with mandatory plans as the principle elements and guidance plans as supplements, and a unified foreign trade system with independence, equality and mutual benefit as the principle. By controlling import and export trade and foreign exchange management rights in the hands of the government, we achieved "capital control", "internal and external exchanges" and "trade control". After 1949, China's foreign trade center gradually shifted from western countries to the Soviet Union and other socialist countries in Eastern Europe. At the same time, we actively broke the "blockade" and "embargo" imposed by western countries on China and made great efforts to carry out "barter trade" with western countries, thus rapidly restoring and expanding foreign trade. By 1950, the 70-year unfavorable balance of trade had been ended.

Fourthly, transportation, as one of the key parts of the restoration and development, experienced a relatively quick recovery and construction. At the beginning of the founding of the People's Republic of China, the major means of transportation were livestock wagons and wooden sailboats which were extremely backward. The total mileage of the national railways was only 21,800 kilometers, and half of them were paralyzed. In 1949, more than 8,300 kilometers of railways and 2,715 bridges were repaired. Subsequently, with the increase in mileage, the running route and speed of the railway were improved, the management system was optimized, and the annual turnover of railway freight increased. In 1949, only 54,000 kilometers of roads were accessible in the mainland of China, and more than 60% of them were dirt roads, and the road conditions were deplorable, with 51,000 civil vehicles. Along with the highway reconstruction, the mileage increased gradually, and the traffic condition was improved. Inland waterways were in a natural state when the People's Republic of China was founded. By the end of 1949, there were 757 public and private ships for river and sea transportation with a total transport capacity of 287,733 tons, 69% of which were in the public sector. Among them, seagoing vessels had a transportation capacity of 114,108 tons (91,264 tons in the public sector, accounting for 80% and 22,844 tons in the private sector, accounting for 20%), and most of them were dilapidated vessels. After that, shipping resumed rapidly, the transportation materials were recovered, and the ports and rivers were dredged and improved. Limited by financial resources, civil air transportation officially opened on August 1st, 1950, when there were only 30 aircraft, including 13 passenger aircraft, 17 cargo aircraft, and 12 civil aviation routes. By 1952, the civil aviation mileage was only 13,885 kilometers, with 48 aircraft, 2,409 kilometers of passenger turnover and 1,834 kilotons/kilometer of cargo turnover.

4.3 Development of transportation in China before the reform and opening up

The opening and development of ports relied heavily on the development of transportation. The transportation industry was backward before 1949, which, during the more than 70 years from 1872 when the Qing government established the China Merchants Bureau to the founding of the People's Republic of China, developed at an extremely slow speed. Transportation equipment was worn out, livestock wagons and wooden sailboats were widely used, and transportation layout was very unreasonable. Railways and highways were concentrated along the eastern coast and northeastern regions. In the southwest and northwest region, which accounted for 56% of the country's territory, the length of railway and highway only accounted for 5.5% and 24.3% respectively of the country's total. In Fujian, Guizhou, Gansu, Qinghai, Ningxia, Xinjiang, and Tibet, the railway was not accessible, and travel was very inconvenient, and the communications in vast inland were generally blocked.

From the founding of the People's Republic of China to the beginning of the reform and opening up, China's transportation construction was at an initial stage for restoration and development. Under the planned economic system, transportation was regarded as the priority of national economic recovery and development. The Party and the government took a series of measures to restore transportation, giving support in policy, capital, and other aspects. Transportation construction and development achieved remarkable results. At the end of 1978, China's total volume of transportation line infrastructures (excluding airlines, sea routes, and city roads) increased nearly six times over that of 1949 (see Figures 4–1 to 4–11). During the nearly 30 years from 1949 to 1978 and the period of national economic recovery from 1949 to 1952, damaged transport facilities and equipment and water, land, and air transport were repaired. Since

1953, the state had carried out transportation construction in a planned way. During the first and second Five-year Plan periods and the adjustment period of the national economy (1953-1965), state investment inclined favorably towards transportation. A number of railways, highways, ports, and civil airports were rebuilt and built, major waterways were dredged, and new channels were opened up, together with new international and domestic waterways and air routes and the expanded postal network. The coverage of transport infrastructure and the number of transport equipment increased. During the period from 1966 to 1976, the development of transportation was seriously disrupted, but the scale of facilities and equipment and transportation routes were still increasing, especially in view of the increasingly severe situation of ship-jamming, port-jamming, and cargo-jamming in major coastal ports, which accelerated the construction of port infrastructures. During this period, pipeline transportation was also developed. Table 4–2 and Figure 4–1 show the year-end mileage of various modes of transportation from 1949 to 1978. Table 4–3 and Figure 4–2 show the passenger capacity of various modes of transportation from 1952 to 1978. Table 4–4 and Figure 4–3 show the passenger capacity composition of various modes of transportation from 1949 to 1978. Table 4–5 and Figure 4–4 show the passenger turnover capacity of various modes of transportation from 1952 to 1978. Table 4–6 and Figure 4–5 show the composition of passenger turnover capacity of various modes of transportation from 1952 to 1978. Table 4–7 and Figure 4–6 show the cargo turnover scale of various modes of transportation from 1952 to 1978. Table 4–8 and Figure 4–7 show the composition of the cargo capacity of various transportation from 1952 to 1978. Table 4–9 and Figure 4–8 show cargo turnover of various modes of transportation from 1952 to 1978. Table 4–10 and Figure 4–9 show the composition cargo turnover of various modes of transportation from 1952 to 1978. Table 4–11 and Figure 4–10 show the passenger average transport distance of various modes of transportation from 1952 to 1978. Table 4–12 and Figure 4–11 show the composition of cargo turnover capacity of various modes of transportation from 1952 to 1978.

Table 4–2   Year-end mileage of various modes of transportation
from 1949 to 1978   Unit: 10,000 km

Year	Railway mileage	Highway mileage	Inland waterway mileage	Regular flight mileage	Oil (gas) pipeline mileage
1949	2.18	8.08	7.36	—	—
1950	2.22	9.96	7.36	1.14	—
1951	2.23	11.44	7.36	1.12	—

(continued)

Year	Railway mileage	Highway mileage	Inland waterway mileage	Regular flight mileage	Oil (gas) pipeline mileage
1952	2.29	12.67	9.50	1.31	—
1953	2.38	13.71	9.50	1.40	—
1954	2.45	14.61	9.50	1.52	—
1955	2.56	16.73	9.99	1.55	—
1956	2.65	22.63	10.36	1.91	—
1957	2.67	25.46	14.41	2.64	—
1958	3.02	42.18	15.20	3.30	0.02
1959	3.23	50.79	16.30	3.72	0.02
1960	3.39	51.95	17.39	3.81	0.02
1961	3.45	47.74	17.22	3.91	0.02
1962	3.46	46.35	16.19	3.53	0.02
1963	3.50	47.51	15.72	3.58	0.03
1964	3.69	47.92	15.69	3.85	0.03
1965	3.80	51.45	15.77	3.94	0.04
1966	3.93	54.36	14.72	3.94	0.07
1967	3.86	55.75	14.78	4.45	0.08
1968	3.88	57.17	14.78	4.01	0.09
1969	4.17	60.06	14.81	3.99	0.10
1970	4.37	63.67	14.84	4.06	0.12
1971	4.53	67.54	14.16	4.21	0.20
1972	4.63	69.99	14.06	4.25	0.23
1973	4.66	71.56	13.88	4.54	0.34
1974	4.75	73.79	13.74	8.13	0.42
1975	4.86	78.36	13.56	8.42	0.53
1976	4.91	82.34	13.74	9.78	0.63
1977	5.06	85.56	13.74	13.21	0.67
1978	5.17	89.02	13.60	14.89	0.83

Source: The National Development and Reform Commission, the Ministry of Transport, the National Railway Administration, the Civil Aviation Administration of China, the State Post Bureau, the National Energy Administration and the Transport and Delivery Bureau of the Logistics Support Department of the Central Military Commission, *Year Book of China Transportation & Communications*, Beijing: China Integrated Transport Yearbook Press, 2016, p. 982.

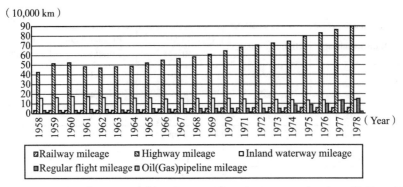

Figure 4-1   Year-end mileage of various modes of transportation from1958 to 1978

Table 4-3   Passenger capacity of various modes of transportation
from 1952 to 1978   Unit: 10,000 passengers

Year	Total	Railway			Highway	Waterway	Civil aviation
		Total	National	Local			
1952	24,518	16,352	16,352	—	4,559	3,605	2
1957	63,821	31,262	31,262	—	23,772	8,780	7
1962	122,154	75,003	74,067	936	30,737	16,397	17
1965	96,334	41,245	40,708	537	43,693	11,369	27
1970	130,056	52,455	51,646	809	61,812	15,767	22
1975	192,969	70,465	69,648	817	101,350	21,015	139
1978	253,993	81,491	80,729	762	149,229	23,042	231

Source: The National Development and Reform Commission, the Ministry of Transport, the National Railway Administration, the Civil Aviation Administration of China, the State Post Bureau, the National Energy Administration and the Transport and Delivery Bureau of the Logistics Support Department of the Central Military Commission, *Year Book of China Transportation & Communication*, Beijing: China Integrated Transport Yearbook Press, 2016, p.986.

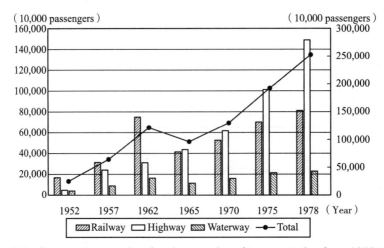

Figure 4-2   Passenger capacity of various modes of transportation from 1952 to 1978

Table 4–4   Passenger capacity composition of various modes
of transportation from 1952 to 1978   Unit: %

Year	Total	Railway	Highway	Waterway	Civil aviation
1952	100.0	66.7	18.6	14.7	0.01
1957	100.0	49.0	37.2	13.8	0.01
1962	100.0	61.4	25.2	13.4	0.01
1965	100.0	42.8	45.4	11.8	0.03
1970	100.0	40.3	47.5	12.1	0.02
1975	100.0	36.5	52.5	10.9	0.07
1978	100.0	32.1	58.8	9.1	0.09

Source: The National Development and Reform Commission, the Ministry of Transport, the National Railway Administration, the Civil Aviation Administration of China, the State Post Bureau, the National Energy Administration and the Transport and Delivery Bureau of the Logistics Support Department of the Central Military Commission, *Year Book of China Transportation & Communications*, Beijing: China Integrated Transport Yearbook Press, 2016, p. 987.

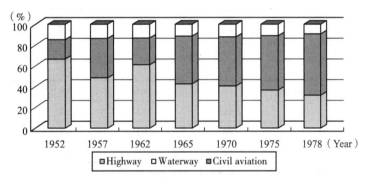

Figure 4–3   Passenger capacity composition of various modes of
transportation from 1952 to 1978

Table 4–5   Passenger turnover capacity of various modes of
transportation from 1952 to 1978   Unit: 100 million passenger-km

Year	Total	Railway	Highway	Waterway	Civil aviation
1952	248.02	200.64	22.64	24.50	0.24
1957	496.55	361.30	88.07	46.38	0.80
1962	1,085.56	859.01	141.46	83.92	1.17
1965	697.04	478.99	168.20	47.37	2.48
1970	1,031.05	718.19	240.06	71.01	1.79
1975	1,434.55	954.09	374.48	90.59	15.39
1978	1,743.06	1,093.22	521.30	100.63	27.91

Source: The National Development and Reform Commission, the Ministry of Transport, the National Railway Administration, the Civil Aviation Administration of China, the State Post Bureau, the National Energy Administration and the Transport and Delivery Bureau of the Logistics Support Department of the Central Military Commission, *Year Book of China Transportation & Communications*, Beijing: China Integrated Transport Yearbook Press, 2016, p.989.

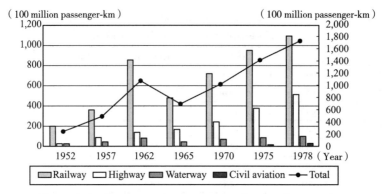

Figure 4–4　Passenger turnover capacity of various modes
of transportation from 1952 to 1978

Table 4–6　　　Composition of passenger turnover capacity of various
modes of transportation from 1952 to 1978　　　Unit: %

Year	Total	Railway	Highway	Waterway	Civil aviation
1952	100.0	80.9	9.1	9.9	0.1
1957	100.0	72.8	17.7	9.3	0.2
1962	100.0	79.1	13.0	7.7	0.1
1965	100.0	68.7	24.1	6.8	0.4
1970	100.0	69.7	23.3	6.9	0.2
1975	100.0	66.5	26.1	6.3	1.1
1978	100.0	62.7	29.9	5.8	1.6

Source: The National Development and Reform Commission, the Ministry of Transport, the National Railway Administration, the Civil Aviation Administration of China, the State Post Bureau, the National Energy Administration and the Transport and Delivery Bureau of the Logistics Support Department of the Central Military Commission, *Year Book of China Transportation & Communications*, China Integrated Transport Yearbook Press, Beijing: 2016, p. 990.

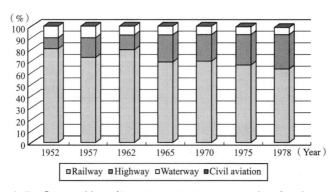

Figure 4–5　Composition of passenger turnover capacity of various modes
transportation from 1952 to 1978

Table 4-7   Cargo capacity of various modes of
                              transportation from 1952 to 1978   Unit: 10,000 tons

Year	Total	Railway	Highway	Waterway	Ocean shipping	Civil aviation	Pipeline
1952	35,605	13,217	17,247	5,141	—	0.2	—
1957	89,990	27,421	46,762	15,806	—	0.9	—
1962	92,185	35,261	38,909	18,013	—	1.8	—
1965	133,253	49,100	59,995	24,155	—	2.5	—
1970	167,913	68,132	72,929	26,848	—	3.7	—
1975	251,593	88,955	117,633	38,968	—	4.7	6,032
1978	319,431	110,119	151,602	47,357	3,659	6.4	10,347

Source: The National Development and Reform Commission, the Ministry of Transport, the National Railway Administration, the Civil Aviation Administration of China, the State Post Bureau, the National Energy Administration and the Transport and Delivery Bureau of the Logistics Support Department of the Central Military Commission, *Year Book of China Transportation & Communication*, Beijing: China Integrated Transport Yearbook Press, 2016, p.992 .

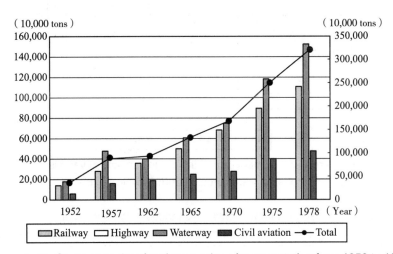

Figure 4-6   Cargo capacity of various modes of transportation from 1952 to 1978

Table 4-8   Composition of the cargo capacity of various modes
                    of transportation from 1952 to 1978   Unit: %

Year	Total	Railway	Highway	Waterway	Ocean shipping	Civil aviation	Pipeline
1952	100.0	37.1	48.4	14.4	—	—	—
1957	100.0	30.5	52.0	17.6	—	—	—
1962	100.0	38.3	42.2	19.5	—	—	—

(continued)

Year	Total	Railway	Highway	Waterway		Civil aviation	Pipeline
					Ocean shipping		
1965	100.0	36.8	45.0	18.1	—	—	—
1970	100.0	40.6	43.4	16.0	—	—	—
1975	100.0	35.4	46.8	15.5	—	—	2.4
1978	100.0	34.5	47.6	14.8	1.1	—	3.2

Source: The National Development and Reform Commission, the Ministry of Transport, the National Railway Administration, the Civil Aviation Administration of China, the State Post Bureau, the National Energy Administration and the Transport and Delivery Bureau of the Logistics Support Department of the Central Military Commission, *Year Book of China Transportation & Communications*, Beijing: China Integrated Transport Yearbook Press, 2016, p.993 .

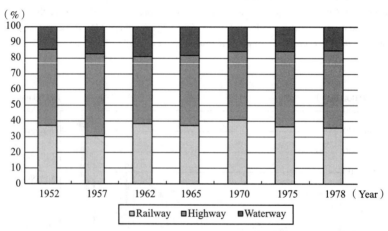

Figure 4–7　Composition of the cargo capacity of various modes of transportation from 1952 to 1978

Table 4–9　　　　Goods turnover of various modes of transportation from 1952 to 1978　　　　Unit: 100 million ton-km

Year	Total	Railway	Highway	Waterway		Civil aviation	Pipeline
					Ocean shipping		
1952	766.97	601.60	19.60	145.75	—	0.02	—
1957	1,825.76	1,345.90	62.39	417.39	—	0.08	—
1962	2,252.29	1,721.08	75.09	455.97	—	0.15	—
1965	3,485.42	2,698.69	110.04	676.44	—	0.25	—
1970	4,590.12	3,495.95	153.95	939.85	—	0.35	—

(continued)

Year	Total	Railway	Highway	Waterway		Civil aviation	Pipeline
					Ocean shipping		
1975	7,594.20	4,255.64	248.12	2,827.83	—	0.60	262.00
1978	9,928.19	5,345.19	350.27	3,801.76	2,487.00	0.97	430.00

Source: The National Development and Reform Commission, the Ministry of Transport, the National Railway Administration, the Civil Aviation Administration of China, the State Post Bureau, the National Energy Administration and the Transport and Delivery Bureau of the Logistics Support Department of the Central Military Commission, *Year Book of China Transportation & Communications*, Beijing: China Integrated Transport Yearbook Press, 2016, p.995 .

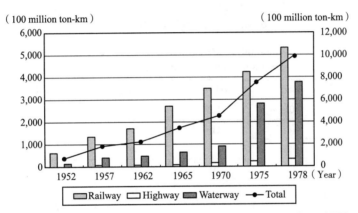

Figure 4–8   Goods turnover of various modes of transportation from 1952 to 1978

Table 4–10   Composition of goods turnover of various modes of
transportation from 1952 to 1978   Unit: %

Year	Total	Railway	Highway	Waterway		Civil aviation	Pipeline
					Ocean shipping		
1952	100.0	78.4	2.6	19.0	—	—	—
1957	100.0	73.7	3.4	22.9	—	—	—
1962	100.0	76.4	3.3	20.2	—	0.01	—
1965	100.0	77.4	3.2	19.4	—	0.01	—
1970	100.0	76.2	3.4	20.5	—	0.01	—
1975	100.0	56.0	3.3	37.2	—	0.01	3.45
1978	100.0	53.8	3.5	38.3	25.0	0.01	4.33

Source: Jointly compiled by the National Development and Reform Commission, the Ministry of Transport, the National Railway Administration, the Civil Aviation Administration of China, the State Post Bureau, the National Energy Administration and the Transport and Delivery Bureau of the Logistics Support Department of the Central Military Commission, *Year Book of China Transportation & Communications*, Beijing: China Integrated Transport Yearbook Press, 2016, p. 996.

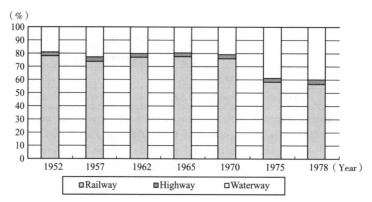

Figure 4-9　Composition of goods turnover of various modes
of transportation from 1952 to 1978

Table 4-11　　　　Passenger average transport distance of various
modes of transportation from 1952 to 1978　　　Unit: km

Year	Total	Railway	Highway	Waterway	Civil aviation
1952	101	123	50	68	1,200
1957	78	116	37	53	1,143
1962	89	115	46	51	688
1965	72	116	38	42	919
1970	79	137	39	45	814
1975	74	135	37	43	1,107
1978	69	134	35	44	1,208

Source: The National Development and Reform Commission, the Ministry of Transport, the National Railway Administration, the Civil Aviation Administration of China, the State Post Bureau, the National Energy Administration and the Transport and Delivery Bureau of the Logistics Support Department of the Central Military Commission, *Year Book of China Transportation & Communications*, Beijing: China Integrated Transport Yearbook Press, 2016, p.998 .

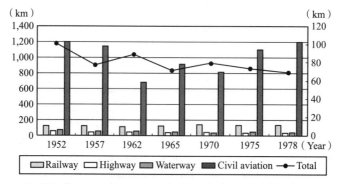

Figure 4-10　Passenger average transport distance of various modes
of transportation from 1952 to 1978

Table 4-12   Composition of goods turnover capacity of various
                    modes of transportation from1952 to 1978 Unit:100 million ton-km

Year	Total	Railway	Highway	Waterway	Ocean Shipping	Civil aviation	Pipeline
1952	215	455	11	284	—	1,000	—
1957	203	491	13	264	—	1,000	—
1962	244	488	19	253	—	833	—
1965	262	550	18	280	—	1,003	—
1970	273	513	21	350	—	951	—
1975	302	478	21	726	—	1,280	434
1978	311	485	23	803	6,797	1,516	416

Source: The National Development and Reform Commission, the Ministry of Transport, the National Railway Administration, the Civil Aviation Administration of China, the State Post Bureau, the National Energy, the Transport and Delivery Bureau of Logistics Support Department of the Central Military Commission, *Year Book of China Transportation & Communications*, Beijing: China Integrated Transport Yearbook Press, 2016, p.999.

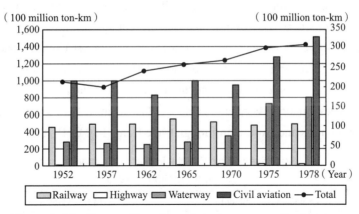

Figure 4-11   Composition of goods turnover capacity of various
modes of transportation from1952 to 1978

4.4 Development of China's foreign trade and the situation of open ports before the reform and opening up

4.4.1 Development of China's foreign trade before the reform and opening up

From 1949 to 1978, under the highly centralized and unified foreign trade system, the state integrated the foreign trade operation and management in an organic whole and was responsible for profits and losses. In the 30 years, the change in China's foreign trade system could be roughly divided into two stages. In the first stage, from 1949 to 1956, the state drew up principles and guidelines of "independence, centralization and unification" for foreign trade, especially the Interim Regulations on the Administration of Foreign Trade promulgated and implemented by the State Council in December 1950. Since then, China's foreign trade had embarked on the road of centralized and unified leadership and management. The second stage was from 1957 to 1978. After the socialist transformation of private enterprises, all import and export businesses in the country were monopolized by state-owned foreign trade specialists and carried out strictly in accordance with the state plan. The state-controlled foreign exchange system carried out the purchasing system for exports, the allocation and delivery system for imports, and the profits and losses were centralized by the state. The state had put an end to the pattern of foreign trade in which enterprises of different ownership coexisted, and established a highly centralized and unified foreign trade system in which government administration mixed up with the enterprise. It could be said that before the reform and opening up, China's foreign trade system followed a typical Soviet model of planned economy and served as an essential part of the country's entire planned economic system. In the 30 years, China's foreign trade with the Soviet Union, Eastern Europe, and other socialist countries accounted for more than 2/3 of the total trade volume, while the import and export trade with Europe, the United States, Japan, and other developed western countries remained very low. Table 4–13 and Figure 4–12 show the statistics of China's total imports and exports in foreign trade from 1950 to 1978.

Table 4–13   Statistics of China's total import and export in foreign trade from 1950 to 1978

Year	In US dollars (100 million)				In RMB (100 million)			
	Total imports and exports	Total exports	Total imports	Balance	Total imports and exports	Total exports	Total imports	Balance
1950	11.3	5.5	5.8	−0.3	41.5	20.2	21.3	−1.1
1951	19.6	7.6	12.0	−4.4	59.5	24.2	35.3	−11.1
1952	19.4	8.2	11.2	−3.0	64.4	27.1	37.5	−10.4
1953	23.7	10.2	13.5	−3.3	80.9	34.8	46.1	−11.3
1954	24.4	11.5	12.9	−1.4	84.7	40.0	44.7	−4.7
1955	31.4	14.1	17.3	−3.2	109.8	48.7	61.1	−12.4
1956	32.1	16.5	15.6	0.9	108.7	55.7	53.0	2.7

(continued)

Year	In US dollars (100 million)				In RMB (100 million)			
	Total imports and exports	Total exports	Total imports	Balance	Total imports and exports	Total exports	Total imports	Balance
1957	31.0	16.0	15.0	1.0	104.5	54.5	50.0	4.5
1958	38.7	19.8	18.9	0.9	128.7	67.0	61.7	5.3
1959	43.8	22.6	21.2	1.4	149.3	78.1	71.2	6.9
1960	38.1	18.6	19.5	−0.9	128.4	63.3	65.1	−1.8
1961	29.4	14.9	14.5	0.4	90.7	47.7	43.0	4.7
1962	26.6	14.9	11.7	3.2	80.9	47.1	33.8	13.3
1963	29.2	16.5	12.7	3.8	85.7	50.0	35.7	14.3
1964	34.7	19.2	15.5	3.7	97.5	55.4	42.1	13.3
1965	42.5	22.3	20.2	2.1	118.4	63.1	55.3	7.8
1966	46.2	23.7	22.5	1.2	127.1	66.0	61.1	4.9
1967	41.6	21.4	20.2	1.2	112.2	58.8	53.4	5.4
1968	40.5	21.0	19.5	1.5	108.5	57.6	50.9	6.7
1969	40.3	22.0	18.3	3.7	107.0	59.8	47.2	12.6
1970	45.9	22.6	23.3	−0.7	112.9	56.8	56.1	0.7
1971	48.4	26.4	22.0	4.4	120.9	68.5	52.4	16.1
1972	63.0	34.4	28.6	5.8	146.9	82.9	64.0	18.9
1973	109.8	58.2	51.6	6.6	220.5	116.9	103.6	13.3
1974	145.7	69.5	76.2	−6.7	292.2	139.4	152.8	−13.4
1975	147.5	72.6	74.9	−2.3	290.4	143.0	147.4	−4.4
1976	134.3	68.5	65.8	2.7	264.1	134.8	129.3	5.5
1977	148.0	75.9	72.1	3.8	272.5	139.7	132.8	6.9
1978	206.4	97.5	108.9	−11.4	355.0	167.6	187.4	−19.8

Source: Wu Li, *Economic History of the People's Republic of China* (Volume II), Beijing: China Economic Press, 1999, pp. 150-151.

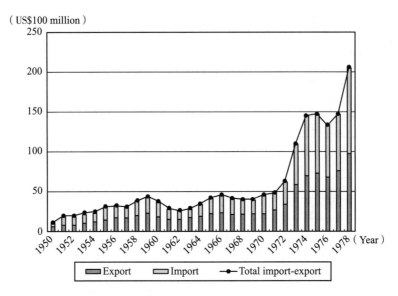

(US$100 million)

Figure 4–12   Statistics of China's total imports and exports in foreign trade
from 1950 to 1978

4.4.2 China's open ports before the reform and opening up

According to statistics, from 1949 when the People's Republic of China was founded to the end of 1978, only 51 ports were open to the outside world. Among them, there were 18 water ports (including 17 sea ports and 1 river port), 16 highway ports, 9 railway ports, and 8 airports.

Geographically, only the waterway ports in the coastal areas and along rivers were open to the outside world, including coastal sea ports in Shanghai, Tianjin, Dalian, Qingdao, Yantai, Wenzhou, Fuzhou, Xiamen, Guangzhou, Zhanjiang, Shantou, Shanwei, Haikou, Basuo, Beihai, Qinhuangdao, Lianyungang and the Heihe river port. Highway and railway ports open to the outside world were confined to border areas between China and its neighboring countries by land. The highway ports included Linjiang, Nanping, Sanhe, Gongbei, Shuikou, Dongxing, Wanding, Ruili, Zhangmu, Pulan, Gyirong, Kaishantun, Khunjerab, Khorgos, Torugart, Youyi Pass. The border railway ports were Dandong, Tumen, Ji'an, Shenzhen, Pingxiang, Hekou, Manzhouli, Suifenhe, Erenhot railway ports. Only the open airports in regional central cities were open to the outside world, namely, Beijing, Shanghai, Guangzhou, Shenyang, Kunming, Nanning, Harbin and Urumqi. These 8 airports with a small network only opened 12 international routes to 13 countries, such as the Soviet Union, North Korea, Pakistan, and France.

Looking back on the development in the nearly 30 years from the founding of the People's Republic of China to the start of the reform and opening up, it could be said that during the specific historical period from 1949 to the mid-1970s, as a result of the comprehensive blockade by the US-led capitalist countries on the new socialist China and the "Cultural Revolution" as well as other domestic and foreign factors, China had been forced to "close" its economy before the reform and opening up. It was contrary to the world economic trend of opening up. Although China made remarkable achievements in economy, transportation, and other aspects, objectively speaking, China became more and more closed during this period. The volume of foreign trade in China was minimal, with fewer ports open to the outside world.

In the late 1970s, with the development of the international economy, the deepening of the international division of labor and the expanding scale of international trade, in addition to the rapid development of capital internationalization, the strengthening of economic integration and international coordination, together with the high socialization and globalization of production, capital, science and technology, most countries regarded the development of foreign economic relations and the implementation of opening up as important propositions for their own development. Opening up to the outside world had become a significant trend of the times. To open new ports and expand the existing open ports had become the first step to promote the development of a region and a town. It can be said that in an open world, it is difficult for a country or a region to succeed in its construction and development by closing its doors. China's development cannot be separated or isolated from the world. Only by adhering to the ideological line of emancipating the mind and seeking truth from facts, and with a forward-looking attitude to coordinate internal and external affairs and keep up with the times in carrying out reform and innovation, can China continue to explore and practice an independent and distinctive road of socialist construction and development with Chinese characteristics.

Chapter 5
Open Ports of Contemporary China and Their Development: 1979-2015

The reform and opening up has been the most significant historical event since the founding of the People's Republic of China. As an overall, revolutionary and strategic social transformation in contemporary China, it is also a national drive to stop China's long-standing poverty and weakness, and change the track of regional development and its people's life. It is related to the future of the country, the nation, and individuals. In December 1978, the Central Committee of the Communist Party of China convened the Third Plenary Session of the Eleventh Central Committee, which was of great historical significance. At the event, it was decided that the focus of the Party's work should be shifted to socialist modernization from 1979, in view of the smooth progress of the Central Committee's work since the Second Plenary Session of the CPC Central Committee.[1] The overall requirements for reform and opening up were also clearly stated. Marked by the convening of the great event, the Communist Party of China has tightly combined Marxism with the reality of China and contemporary characteristics to start a great course of reform and opening up. China has been led to embark on a leap-forward developing path to a stronger nation featuring a market economy, integration into the world and compatibility with domestic reform and opening up where reform has prompted opening up while further opening up has been driving domestic reform. With an unprecedented enterprising spirit and magnificent innovative practice, we have entered the most brilliant historical stage of achievements since modern China and created and developed socialism with Chinese characteristics.

The reform and opening up is the great revolution led by the Party and joined by the people of all ethnic groups. It is the only path for the country to be prosperous and strong, for the nation to be rejuvenated and for the people to be happy. Since the start of the reform and opening up, China has adhered to the basic national policy of opening up

---

[1] Party Literature Research Center of the CPC Central Committee, *Selected Documents Since The Third Plenary Session* (Volume I), Beijing: People's Publishing House, 1982, p.1.

to the outside world, actively promoted free trade, supported an open, transparent, inclusive and non-discriminatory multilateral trading system, and built a mutually beneficial and win-win global value chain. China has been more widely open to the outside world, and its ties with the world economy are getting closer. China's leading role in the global economy, trade, and investment has been increasing. With more contributions to the world economic growth, China has become one of the major engines of economic globalization.

Over the past three decades of the reform and opening up, China has achieved the longest rapid sustainable economic growth since the Second World War. The economic aggregates ranking of China in the world has risen remarkably. At the beginning of the reform and opening up, it ranked the 11th in the world in 1978. However, it began to do well several years later, surpassing France, the UK, Germany, and Japan respectively by ranking fifth in 2005, fourth in 2006, third in 2007 and second in 2009 in the world. According to statistics, from 1982 to 2015, the direct foreign investment by China increased by 28.83% annually, nearly three times over that of the world in the same period. China's opening has provided the world with a broad market, a large amount of capital, abundant products, and valuable opportunities, injecting an essential driving force into the growth of global trade and investment. In a few decades, we have tried to get where it used to take several centuries for developed countries to be, which is a miracle in the history of world economic development. Since China has become the world's second-largest economy, the largest exporter, the second-largest importer and direct foreign investor, the largest foreign exchange reserve country and tourism market, it has become an essential factor affecting the world political and economic landscape, with its weight and status in the world economy and global governance gradually rising. In the history of world economic development, no other country has promoted modernization within such a short time, at such a fast speed, on such a huge scale and with such an open system as China. In the past four decades since the start of the reform and opening up, the open ports of China have developed along with the development of foreign trade to meet the needs of international cooperation and exchanges. In a certain period of time, the open ports should subordinate to and serve the major political, economic and diplomatic policies as well as the overall economic and social development strategy in the same period.

5.1 Coastal areas and coastal ports: leaders in opening up

China's opening up to the outside world was initiated when Guangdong and Fujian provinces were given special economic policies, flexible economic measures and a special economic management system to establish special economic zones.[1]Since the reform and opening up, the development of all regions in the country has been advanced step by step, following the strategic thought of giving priority to the development of eastern coastal areas by speeding up their opening up to the outside world, with understanding and cooperation from the central and western regions. When this first goal was achieved, more resources would then be utilized to help speed up the development of the central and western regions, with support from eastern coastal areas.

5.1.1 Establishment and development of special economic zones

In August 1980, the 15th Meeting of the Standing Committee of the Fifth National People's Congress approved the establishment of special economic zones in Shenzhen, Zhuhai, Shantou, and Xiamen, marking the beginning of China's opening up. The establishment of special economic zones in the four areas is a major decision and breakthrough in China's opening up and has played an important role in economic reform and modernization. The regional gross product of five special economic zones in China from 1980 to 2015 is shown in Table 5–1 and Figure 5–1.

---

[1] Special policies and flexible measures include the following items. (1)The planning system is predominantly determined by the local government, and the economic development plan is predominantly made by the provincial government. The enterprises and institutions that used to be directly under the central government, except railway, post and telecommunications, civil aviation, banking, military production, national defense and scientific research, are all under the jurisdiction of the province. (2) The fiscal system is carried out in an all-inclusive way, dividing revenue and expenditure, and handing in quotas for five years without change. The increased revenue is allocated by the province for economic construction. (3) The province governments' authority for foreign investment is expanded. Under the guidance of the unified foreign trade policy of the state, the two provinces are allowed to arrange and operate their foreign trade. Taking the actual amount of foreign trade export income in 1978 as the base, 30% of the increased income is handed over to the central government with the rest reserved for local use. (4) The financial system is invigorated. The two provinces can set up investment companies to absorb overseas Chinese and foreign investment, borrowing, using and repaying by themselves. (5) The material and commercial systems use the market mechanism, with the amount of 1978 as the base to ensure the transfer in and out by the state, and the rest are flexibly arranged by the province as a whole. (6) The provincial authority for labor wages and price management is expanded. (7) With regard to the establishment of special export zones, overseas Chinese, Hong Kong SAR and Macao SAR businessmen and foreign manufacturers are allowed to invest in factories in the zone, enjoying preferential tax rates.

Table 5–1   Regional gross product of five special economic
                        zones in China from 1980 to 2015   Unit: RMB100 million

Year	Shenzhen	Zhuhai	Shantou	Xiamen	Hainan	Total of special zones	Total of nation	Zone percentage (%)
1980	2.70	2.61	10.79	6.40	19.33	41.83	4,545.60	0.92
1981-1985	88.78	27.36	81.64	56.17	162.65	416.60	32,401.70	1.29
1986-1990	471.85	124.36	262.07	187.67	376.65	1,422.55	73,036.80	1.95
1991-1995	2,414.16	641.83	806.54	739.58	1,255.39	5,857.48	193,030.50	3.03
1996-2000	6,470.57	1,322.89	2,041.93	2,056.37	2,228.02	14,119.75	423,443.50	3.33
2001-2005	17,197.74	2,440.71	2,728.47	3,859.13	3,567.06	29,793.11	708,906.40	4.20
2006	5,813.56	747.70	740.92	1,162.37	1,052.85	9,517.40	211,923.50	4.49
2007	6,765.41	886.84	850.15	1,375.26	1,299.60	11,177.26	249,529.90	4.48
1980-2007	39,224.77	6,194.30	7,522.51	9,442.95	9,961.55	72,345.98	1,896,817.90	3.81
2008	7,786.79	997.16	951.81	1,610.71	1,503.06	12,849.53	316,751.70	4.06
2009	8,201.32	1,038.66	1,035.87	1,737.23	1,654.21	13,677.29	345,629.20	3.95
2010	9,581.51	1,208.60	1,208.97	2,060.07	2,064.50	16,123.65	408,903.00	3.94
2011	11,505.53	1,404.93	1,275.74	2,539.31	2,522.66	19,248.17	484,123.50	3.98
2012	12,950.06	1,503.76	1,425.01	2,815.17	2,855.54	21,549.54	534,123.00	4.03
2013	14,500.23	1,662.38	1,565.90	3,018.13	3,177.56	23,924.23	588,018.80	4.07
2014	16,001.98	1,857.32	1,716.00	3,273.54	3,500.72	26,349.56	636,138.70	4.14
2015	17,502.86	2,025.41	1,868.03	3,466.03	3,702.76	28,565.09	689,052.10	4.15
1980-2015	137,255.10	17,892.52	18,569.84	29,963.17	30,942.56	234,623.00	5,899,557.90	3.98

Note: Regional gross product is calculated at current prices in those years.

Source: National Bureau of Statistics, *China Statistical Yearbook*.

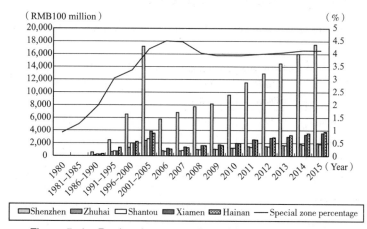

Figure 5–1   Regional gross product of five special economic
                zones in China from 1980 to 2015

Then, in early 1984, Deng Xiaoping inspected three special economic zones of Shenzhen, Zhuhai, and Xiamen, affirming the correct decision to develop and establish the special economic zones and put forward two insightful opinions on opening up to the outside world. He pointed out that releasing instead of controlling is the guiding principle of establishing more special economic zones and carrying out the opening up policy. More places should be opened up, and several port cities should be included to implement preferential policies in China's special economic zones, which were initiated in the early 1980s and developed in the 1990s. By the end of 2015, seven special economic zones had been set up in Shenzhen, Zhuhai, Xiamen, Shantou, Hainan, Kashgar, and Khorgos.

5.1.2 Establishment and development of state-level new areas

After China accelerated its reform and opening up in 1992, the model of special economic zones was upgraded to the state-level new areas. Moreover, some new areas, such as Shanghai Pudong New Area (SPNA), were set up one after another, which became important symbols of China's new round of deepening and expanding reform and opening up. By the end of 2015, 17 new areas had been established, namely Pudong in Shanghai, Binhai in Tianjin, Liangjiang New Area in Chongqing, Zhoushan Archipelago in Zhejiang, and Lanzhou in Gansu, Nansha in Guangdong, Xixian in Shaanxi, Guian in Guizhou, the west coast of Qingdao in Shandong, Jinpu in Liaoning, Tianfu in Chengdu in Sichuan, Jiangbei of Nanjing in Jiangsu, Fuzhou in Fujian, Harbin in Heilongjiang, Dianzhong in Yunnan, Hengqin of Zhuhai in Guangdong, and Xiangjiang in Hunan (see Table 5–2 and Figure 5–2).

Table 5–2   Development statistics of 17 state–level new areas by the end of 2015

Total ranking	New area	Regional gross product in 2015 (RMB100 million)	Regional gross product in 2014 (RMB100 million)	Per capita GDP (RMB)	Time of establishment	Location	Per capita ranking
1	Binhai New Area	9,300	8,760.15	352,933	2015.10	Tianjin	1
2	Pudong New Area	7,200	6,449.51	118,314	1992.10	Shanghai	6
3	Jinpu New Area	3,100	2,870.85	181,699	2014.06	Dalian	2
4	West Coast New Area	2,800	2,470.34	166,555	2014.06	Qingdao	3
5	Liangjiang New Area	2,200	1,860.68	78,796	2010.06	Chongqing	11

(continued)

Total ranking	New area	Regional gross product in 2015 (RMB100 million)	Regional gross product in 2014 (RMB100 million)	Per capita GDP (RMB)	Time of establishment	Location	Per capita ranking
6	Tianfu New Area	1,800	1,594.60	49,065	2014.10	Chengdu	14
7	Jiangbei New Area	1,600	1,385.39	81,494	2015.06	Nanjing	10
8	Fuzhou New Area	1,200	1,041.40	103,559	2015.09	Fuzhou	7
9	Zhoushan Archipelago New Area	1,200	1,021.66	98,237	2011.06	Zhoushan	8
10	Nansha New Area	1,200	1,016.35	160,063	2012.09	Guangzhou	4
11	Xiangjiang New Area	1,076.70	970.00	126,671	2015.04	Changsha	5
12	Harbin New Area	700	599.06	85,582	2015.12	Harbin	9
13	Dianzhong New Area	650	506.50	42,208	2015.09	Kunming	15
14	Xixian New Area	580	446.58	29,772	2014.01	Xi'an	17
15	Lanzhou New Area	110	96.65	51,003	2012.08	Lanzhou	13
16	Hengqin New Area	92.52	58.07	77,488	2009.09	Zhuhai	12
17	Guian New Area	60	44.19	30,688	2014.01	Guiyang	16

Source: Edited by the author.

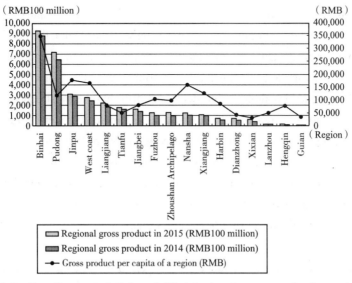

Figure 5–2   Development statistics of 17 state–level new areas by the end of 2015

5.1.3 Port cities: the key to the opening up and development in coastal areas

In the early 1980s, the Central Committee of the CPC and the State Council held that China's economic construction should be gradually promoted and developed from east to west and from coastal areas to inland areas, and stressed the requirement that coastal opening areas should be oriented to the world, open up international markets and expand exports, introducing advanced technology and management methods by absorption, innovation, and applications, then transferring them to inland, to make those coastal opening areas the hub of the two sectors of external and internal radiation.

There are 15 major port cities along the 18,000-kilometer coastline of China. In May 1984, the state decided to open 14 coastal port cities such as Dalian, Qinhuangdao, Tianjin, Yantai, Qingdao, Lianyungang, Nantong, Shanghai, Ningbo, Wenzhou, Fuzhou, Guangzhou, Zhanjiang and Beihai, in addition to Xiamen which was already a special economic zone, rendering them some preferential policies and measures. These port cities are mainly scattered along the southeastern coastal areas with a developed economy, science, technology, and culture, enjoying a favorable geographical location, with ports for international transportation, rivers, and railways for internal transportation. The cargo throughput of coastal ports accounted for 97% of the country's total, making them the main sea passages for China's foreign economic and trade cooperation. Opening the 15 cities meant that the entire coastline and half of China had been opened up to the outside world. Therefore, the international public opinions regarded the strategic decision as "first opening up since the Ming Dynasty in China."

In February 1985, the Central Committee of the CPC and the State Council decided to establish the coastal economic zones in the Yangtze River Delta, the Pearl River Delta, the Xiamen-Zhangzhou-Quanzhou Delta in Southern Fujian, the Jiaodong Peninsula in Shandong and the Liaodong Peninsula. Later, some areas along the coast of Hebei and Guangxi were opened up along the golden coast, forming the most energetic economic belt in China with an area of 420,000 square kilometers, covering more than 310 counties and cities, with a population of nearly 400 million. It extended to Dalianwan in the Liaodong Peninsula in the north and to Hainan Island in the south. Opening the coastal economic areas is another crucial strategy after the foundation of special economic zones and the opening up of 14 coastal port cities. It marked the expansion of China's opening from cities to rural areas and broadly promoted the scale of opening to the outside world.

In August 1987, the State Council put forward a proposal at the 22nd Meeting of the Standing Committee of the 6th National People's Congress to divide Hainan administrative region from Guangdong province and to establish Hainan province separately. In April 1988, the First Session of the 7th National People's Congress passed the proposal to establish Hainan province and establish the largest special economic zone in China, namely Hainan Special Economic Zone.

With the acceleration of reform and opening up, China's rapid restoration and development of industrial and agricultural production, as well as the ever-increasing foreign trade imposed enormous pressure on the coastal ports which mainly undertook the import and export of foreign trade goods (waterborne cargo accounted for 90% of the total volume of foreign trade imports and exports at that time). Delay in goods transportation through ships and ports was common among major ports in the country then. To solve the problem, the state timely opened more waterway ports, effectively alleviating the delay. Since the 1980s, to adapt to the rapid development of "processing and compensation trades" (processing with materials or given samples, assembling supplied components and compensation trade), the state also opened a number of land and water ports in coastal areas, especially in the provinces where the special economic zones are located, as well as the spots for starting shipment, loading and unloading, directly linking Hong Kong SAR and Macao SAR, effectively promoting the development of the local export-oriented economy.

5.2 The Yangtze River Basin: key to promoting opening up and development in inland areas

In the 1980s, the opening up mainly focused on coastal areas. In the 1990s, the most significant move was to open up Shanghai Pudong New Area which, with the main channel of Yangtze River in the east, Wusong Estuary in the north, Huangpu River in the west and Nanhui County in the south, lies in the middle of China's golden coastline where the Yangtze River empties into the sea. Facing the Pacific Ocean and Southeast Asia and backed by the Yangtze River Delta with abundant products and brilliant people, it enjoys very favorable geographical conditions. In April 1990, the State Council officially announced opening up and developing Pudong. This was a crucial step to make full use of the advantages of Shanghai by taking Pudong as the leading city along the Yangtze River, to strengthen its economic central position and international urban functions, and thus to promote the economic development of the Yangtze River Delta basin and the hinterland along the Yangtze River with a population of nearly 300 million, covering an area of more than 1.8 million square kilometers. In the spring of 1992, Deng Xiaoping's south tour talk bringing hope to the whole country and carrying great implications to the world. Since then, China's reform and opening up has entered a new stage of development.

Since the reform and opening up, talents, funds, and resources have been pouring into the southeast of China, resulting in a huge gap between the booming coastal areas and the lagging inland areas. This aroused great attention from the Central Committee of the CPC and the State Council, so they decided to open up inland and border areas further, which are neither near the sea nor the border. In order to fulfill this goal, the first thing was to open and develop the Yangtze River basin.

The Yangtze River, the largest river in China and Asia and the third largest river in the world, originates from Tanggula Mountains in Qinghai Province, across three economic zones in eastern, central and Western China and eventually flows into the East China Sea in Shanghai. With a total length of more than 80,000 kilometers, the main and tributary channels have been the "main artery" of China's east-west shipping and are known as the "golden waterway" since ancient times. The mainstream of the Yangtze River flows through 11 provinces, autonomous regions, and municipalities directly under the central government, including Qinghai, Tibet, Sichuan, Yunnan, Chongqing, Hubei, Hunan, Jiangxi, Anhui, Jiangsu, and Shanghai. Its tributaries extend to parts of eight provinces and autonomous regions, including Guizhou, Gansu, Shaanxi, Henan, Guangxi, Guangdong, Zhejiang, and Fujian. All of these have formed the intermodal water network, connecting the ocean in the east, stretching into Sichuan and Guizhou in the west, reaching Guangxi and Guangdong in the south and Henan and Shaanxi in the north. The navigation mileage of its mainstream and tributaries accounts for 70% of the total inland river navigation mileage in China, and its water transportation accounts for 80% of the total inland river transportation in China. The total area of the river basin is 1.8 million square kilometers, accounting for 18.8% of the territory area of China and 20% of the total land area of China, making it the third-largest river basin in the world. It is the key area for China to integrate with the world economy in an all-round way and the main channel for the world economy to China. It is also one of the core economic areas with the highest productivity and the strongest radiation function to the domestic and foreign economy. In 1992, the State Council decided to open 10 cities along the Yangtze River, including Wuhu, Jiujiang, Yueyang, Wuhan and Chongqing. In the same year, the State Council decided to further open 11 inland provincial capitals such as

Taiyuan, Hefei, Nanchang, Zhengzhou, Changsha, Chengdu, Guiyang, Xi'an, Lanzhou, Xining, and Yinchuan. The opening up of inland areas with the focus on the Yangtze River Basin is of great significance to forming an all-round structure of opening up to the outside world and the gradient transfer of the distribution of productive forces and industrial structure from east to west.

5.3 Opening of border areas: promoting an overall opening up

To strengthen border trade with neighboring countries, since the 1980s, the State Council has approved the plan to open up and give privilege to some border cities such as Manzhouli in Inner Mongolia, Suifenhe in Heilongjiang, Hunchun in Jilin, Dandong in Liaoning, Dongxing in Guangxi and Wanding in Yunnan. Since 1992, with the approval of the State Council, the border economic cooperation zones have been established in border areas like Heihe, Hunchun, Manzhouli, Dandong, Yining, Tacheng, Bole, Pingxiang, Dongxing, Ruili, Wanding, Hekou, Erenhot, and Suifenhe. Together with the border economic cooperation zones, the coastal port cities have further promoted economic and trade exchanges with neighboring countries and good neighborly relations.

Border areas have been taking foreign economic and trade cooperation, prosperous development of border trade as a breakthrough point, turning the "border" of the region into the area that leads in opening up to foreign countries. The northern frontier provinces and autonomous regions are mainly open to Russia and other former Soviet Union countries, Mongolia and Eastern European countries. The southwestern frontier provinces and autonomous regions have been seeking cooperation opportunities in Southeast Asia and South Asia. And the eastern border provinces and autonomous regions are mainly open to Japan and the Korean Peninsula. The reforms have been deepened through opening up to the outside world, attracting foreign investment to develop border areas and people, to develop and form opening border belts gradually. The region of opening to the outside world is gradually moving from coastal areas to inland and border areas. Subsequently, a large number of inland cities and counties as well as border areas have been opened up. So far, China has truly opened up, and a well-coordinated pattern is taking shape. It has entered a period of all-round openness in all regions and areas. The following table is the historical process of opening up in

China since the reform and opening up (see Table 5–3) .

Table 5–3　Historical process of open areas since the reform and opening up

Stage	Time	Open areas
The first stage	July, 1979	The CPC Central Committee and the State Council decided to adopt special policies and preferential measures for the foreign economic and trade activities in Guangdong and Fujian provinces.
	May, 1980	Special economic zones in Shenzhen, Zhuhai, Shantou, and Xiamen were established, marking opening up of China to the outside world.
	May, 1984	Fourteen coastal port cities were opened, such as Dalian, Qinhuangdao, Tianjin, Yantai, Qingdao, Lianyungang, Nantong, Shanghai, Ningbo, Wenzhou, Fuzhou, Guangzhou, Zhanjiang, and Beihai.
	February, 1985	Some cities and counties in the Yangtze River Delta, Pearl River Delta, Xiamen-Zhangzhou-Guanzhou Delta in South Fujian, Liaodong Peninsula, Jiaodong Peninsula, and other coastal areas were opened up gradually.
	April, 1988	Hainan Province was established, and the building of Hainan Special Economic Zone, the largest special economic zone in China, was carried out, enjoying a substantial policy preference.
The second stage	April, 1990	It was decided to develop and open up Pudong in Shanghai and to implement the policies of economic and technological development zones and some special economic zones.
	1991	Four northern ports, namely Manzhouli, Dandong, Suifenhe, and Hunchun were opened, and the State Council approved the establishment of bonded zones including Waigaoqiao in Shanghai, Futian in Shenzhen , Shatoujiao, Tianjin Port and other coastal ports to develop bonded warehousing, bonded processing and transit trade with reference to international practices.
	1992	In the spring of 1992, important speeches were made by Deng Xiaoping during his visit to Wuchang, Shenzhen, Zhuhai, and Shanghai. Taking Pudong in Shanghai as the leader, 6 port cities along the Yangtze River, namely Wuhu, Jiujiang, Huangshi, Wuhan, Yueyang, Chongqing, and the Three Gorges Reservoir Area were opened to the outside world, and economic policies for coastal open cities and regions were implemented. At the same time, four border and coastal provincial capitals of Harbin, Changchun, Hohhot, and Shijiazhuang were opened, as well as the 13 border cities of Hunchun, Suifenhe, Heihe, Manzhouli, Erenhot, Yining, Tacheng, Bole, Ruili, Wanding, Hekou, Pingxiang, and Dongxing.
The third stage	2000	With the implementation of the strategy of developing the western region, the opening up to the outside world has been further extended to the vast western region.
	2001	The entry of China to WTO marked a new stage of China's opening up. And the former regional opening up has been upgraded to an all-around one.

Source: China Development Gateway. http://cn.chinagate.com.cn/reports/ggpg/2008-05/18/Content_15321086.htm.

5.4 Layout and development of major industries and transportation in China

5.4.1 Spatial layout of major industrial sectors in China

In terms of industry, the spatial distribution of major industrial sectors in China shows the following characteristics. Firstly, as for the coal industry whose output ranks first in the world, Shanxi, Inner Mongolia and Shaanxi where the richest coal resources are distributed are the most important coal industrial bases. Secondly, the oil and gas industry is mainly distributed in Songliao Oil Base in northeast China, oil and gas production area in north China and Bohai Rim, Sichuan natural gas base, Xinjiang petroleum and natural gas base, offshore continental shelf oil and gas production area in the offshore continental shelf. Thirdly, thermal power is mainly distributed in leading coal bases and large cities in the north, while hydropower is mainly distributed along the Yangtze River and its tributaries, the Yellow River, the Pearl River, and Lancang River, as well as the upper and middle reaches of the Songhua River. Fourthly, the iron and steel industry is mainly distributed in the Bohai Rim and coastal areas along the Yangtze River, and the leading industrial centers are in Anshan, Baotou, Wuhan, Panzhihua, Shanghai, Taiyuan, and Ma'anshan. Fifthly, as for the machinery industry, large machinery industry bases have been built in Liaoning, Shanghai, Jiangsu, Beijing, Tianjin, and other places. In other provinces, regional machinery industry centers have also been established. Besides, the spatial distribution of high-tech industries shows the following characteristics. Relying on intellectual resources and technological strength, the coastal areas focus on developing high-tech industrial parks. Border areas depend on national development, opening policies, and geographical advantages to develop trade-oriented industries. With advantageous resources and industrial bases, inland areas mainly develop industries closely related to the military industry, the steel industry, and the chemical industry. At present, China has formed four industrial bases, namely Shanghai-Nanjing-Hangzhou Base, Beijing-Tianjin-Hebei Base, Pearl River Delta Base, Central-South Liaoning Base. It has also formed three industrial zones along the eastern coast, along the Yangtze River, and along Longhai-Lanzhou-Xinjiang Lines, as shown in the following table respectively (see Table 5–4 and Table 5–5).

Table 5–4   Brief introduction of the four major industrial bases in China

Item	Shanghai-Nanjing-Hangzhou Base	Beijing-Tianjin-Hebei Base	Pearl River Delta Base	Central-South Liaoning Base
Development conditions	A long history, strong industrial foundation, and technical force; developed transportation; a unified power grid and other facilities	Rich in coal, steel, oil, sea salt, and other resources; convenient transportation; close to Shanxi Energy Base; oil pipelines linking North China and Northeast Oilfields	Near Hong Kong SAR and Southeast Asia; with available foreign capital to develop industries; convenient transportation	Abundant resources; convenient transportation
Status	The largest comprehensive industrial base in China	The Largest comprehensive industrial base in North China	Comprehensive industrial base with light industry as the key part	Heavy industry base
Industrial centers	Shanghai, Nanjing, and Hangzhou	Beijing, Tianjin, and Tangshan	Guangzhou and Shenzhen	Shenyang, Dalian, and Anshan

Source: Edited by the author.

Table 5–5   Brief introduction of the three major industrial zones in China

Item	Eastern coastal industrial zones	Industrial zones along the Yangtze River	Industrial zones along Longhai-Lanzhou-Xinjiang Lines
Range	Coastal special economic zones, coastal open cities and urban open zones	Yangtze River coastal areas	Lianyungang, Xuzhou, Zhengzhou, Luoyang, Xi'an, Lanzhou, and Urumqi, among others
Development conditions	Convenient shipping with many ports and dense railway network; developed agriculture and industry as well as strong financial and technical forces; easy to introduce foreign capital and to develop an export-oriented economy and foreign trade	Well-developed industry and agriculture; a large population and abundant mineral and water resources; convenient water transportation from the coast to the inland	Convenient railway transportation and land-based foreign trade; the Eurasian Continental Bridge as the nearest land passage from Western Europe to Asia and the Pacific; abundant coal, petroleum, and other mineral resources
Major industries	Steel, machinery, electronics, petroleum, chemical, and textile	Iron and steel, as well as light textile in Wuhan, electric power in Yichang and Chongqing, iron and steel in Panzhihua	Coal in Xuzhou, light textile in Zhengzhou, machinery in Luoyang, aircraft manufacturing in Xi'an, Petrochemical industry in Lanzhou, etc.

Source: Edited by the author.

5.4.2   National transportation network and its spatial distribution

The national transportation network is generally densely distributed in the east and sparsely distributed in the west. There are five main lines in the north-south direction in terms of railway transportation: the Beijing-Shanghai Line, the Beijing-Kowloon Line, the Harbin-Beijing-Guangzhou Line, the Jiaozuo-Liuzhou Line, and the Baoji-Chengdu-Kunming Line. There are three main lines in the east-west direction, namely the Beijing-Baotou-Lanzhou Line, the Longhai-Lanzhou-Xinjiang Line, and the Shanghai-Kunming Line. Marine transportation is divided into offshore and ocean routes. As for offshore routes, the north ones are centered on Shanghai and Dalian, and the main seaports are Qinhuangdao, Tianjin, Yantai, Qingdao, Lianyungang, and Ningbo; for the south routes, Guangzhou is the center, and the main ports are Xiamen, Shantou, Zhanjiang, Haikou,etc. The ocean routes are divided into eastbound, westbound, southbound and northbound ones, with the ports of Shanghai, Dalian, Qinhuangdao, Tianjin, Qingdao, Ningbo, Guangzhou and Zhanjiang as the departure ports. Major inland waterway transportation is along the Yangtze River, the Pearl River, the Heilong River, the Huaihe River and the Beijing-Hangzhou Grand Canal. As for air transportation, the main regional air transport centers are Beijing, Shanghai, Guangzhou, Xi'an, Chengdu, Kunming, and Urumqi. The following table shows the difference between the five modes of transportation (see Table 5–6).

Table 5–6　　　　　　Comparison of five modes of transportation

Type of transportation	Advantage	Shortcoming	Goods suitable for transportation
Railway	Large volume, fast speed, low freight, and good continuity	High cost, large land occupation and the high cost of short-distance transportation	Long-distance bulk cargo and passenger transport
Highway	Flexible, quick turnover, easy handling, and adaptability	Small volume, high energy consumption, high cost, and high freight	Short-haul cargo and passenger transportation with a small volume
Waterway	Large volume, low investment, and cost	Slow speed, poor flexibility, and continuity, greatly influenced by natural conditions	Unrestricted bulk or heavy freight or passenger transport
Civil aviation	Fast speed and high efficiency	Small volume, large energy consumption, high freight, large investment, and strict technical requirements	Mainly for passenger transport, and light, precious or urgently needed goods
Pipeline	Low loss, continuity, smoothness, and safety, as well as large volume	Large investment in equipment and poor flexibility	Petroleum, natural gas and so on

Source: Edited by the author.

5.4.3 Transportation development in China since the reform and opening up

Since the reform and opening up, the scale, quality and technical equipment level of the transportation industry in China have undergone tremendous changes and fulfilled outstanding achievements. At present, the country has formed a comprehensive transportation network composed of five transportation modes, namely railway, highway, waterway, civil aviation, and pipeline, which runs across the country. The further construction of the comprehensive traffic corridor with smooth internal and external traffic has laid a solid foundation for further promotion of port opening and the development of the national economy and society of China.

According to statistics, by the end of 2015, the total mileage of various transportation routes in China had reached 10.2512 million kilometers, 58.18 times the length of 1949 (176,200 km). Among them, the railway operation mileage was 121,000 km, 5.55 times the length of 1949 (21,800 km) and 2.34 times the length of 1978 (51,700 km). The total mileage of the highway reached 4.5773 million km, 56.65 times the length of 1949 (80,800 km) and 5.14 times the length of 1978 (890,200 km). The navigation mileage of the inland river reached 127,000 km, 1.73 times the length of 1949 (73,600 km) and 0.94 times the length of 1978 (136,000 km). The mileage of civil aviation routes was 5.3172 million km, 466.42 times the length of 1950 (11,400 km) and 35.71 times the length of 1978 (148,900 km). Pipeline transportation has developed from scratch. At present, oil and gas pipelines have reached 108,700 km. More than 90% of crude oil has been transported through pipelines, which is 543.5 times the volume of 1958 (200 km) and 13.10 times the volume of 1978 (8,300 km) (see Table 5–7 and Figure 5–3).

Table 5–7   Year–end mileage of major modes of transportation in China from 1979 to 2015   Unit: 10,000 km

Year	Railway mileage	Highway mileage	Inland waterway mileage	Regular flight mileage	Oil (gas) pipeline mileage
1979	5.30	87.58	10.78	16.00	0.91
1980	5.33	88.83	10.85	19.53	0.87
1981	5.39	89.75	10.87	21.82	0.97
1982	5.33	90.70	10.86	23.27	1.04
1983	5.46	91.51	10.89	22.91	1.08
1984	5.48	92.67	10.93	26.02	1.10
1985	5.52	94.24	10.91	27.72	1.17
1986	5.58	96.28	10.94	32.31	1.30
1987	5.60	98.22	10.98	38.91	1.38

(continued)

Year	Railway mileage	Highway mileage	Inland waterway mileage	Regular flight mileage	Oil (gas) pipeline mileage
1988	5.62	99.96	10.94	37.38	1.43
1989	5.70	101.43	10.90	47.19	1.51
1990	5.79	102.83	10.92	50.68	1.59
1991	5.78	104.11	10.97	55.91	1.62
1992	5.81	105.67	10.97	83.66	1.59
1993	5.86	108.35	11.02	96.08	1.64
1994	5.90	111.78	11.02	104.56	1.68
1995	6.24	115.70	11.06	112.90	1.72
1996	6.49	118.58	11.08	116.65	1.93
1997	6.60	122.64	10.98	142.50	2.04
1998	6.64	127.85	11.03	150.58	2.31
1999	6.74	135.17	11.65	152.22	2.49
2000	6.87	167.98	11.93	150.29	2.47
2001	7.01	169.80	12.15	155.36	2.76
2002	7.19	176.52	12.16	163.77	2.98
2003	7.30	180.98	12.40	174.95	3.26
2004	7.44	187.07	12.33	204.94	3.82
2005	7.54	334.52	12.33	199.85	4.40
2006	7.71	345.70	12.34	211.35	4.81
2007	7.80	358.37	12.35	234.30	5.45
2008	7.79	373.02	12.28	246.18	5.83
2009	8.55	386.08	12.37	234.51	6.91
2010	9.12	400.82	12.42	276.51	7.85
2011	9.32	410.64	12.46	349.06	8.33
2012	9.76	423.75	12.50	328.01	9.16
2013	10.31	435.62	12.59	410.60	9.85
2014	11.18	446.39	12.63	463.72	10.57
2015	12.10	457.73	12.70	531.72	10.87

Notes: (1) Since 2003, the mileage of inland waterway has been the navigable mileage of inland waterway. (2) Since 2005, the highway mileage has included village roads, which is not comparable to the data of previous years. (3) In 2013, the statistic scope of pipeline transportation had included China National Offshore Oil Corporation (CNOOC) in addition to the China National Petroleum Corporation (CNPC) and the China Petrochemical Corporation (Sinopec Group). In 2012, the pipeline data were adjusted according to the same scope (the same below).

Source: National Development and Reform Commission, Ministry of Transport, National Railway Administration, Civil Aviation Administration of China, State Post Bureau, National Energy Administration, and Transport and Delivery Bureau of Logistics Support Department of Central Military Commission, *Year Book of China Transportation& Communication*, Beijing: China Integrated Transport Yearbook Press, 2016, pp. 982-983.

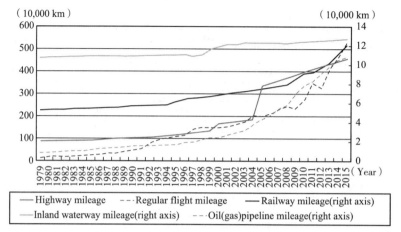

Figure 5-3   Year-end mileage of major modes of transportation in China from 1979 to 2015

Table 5-8   Passenger capacity of major modes of transportation
in China from 1980 to 2015   Unit: 10,000 passengers

Year	Total	Highway			Railway	Waterway	Civil aviation
		Total	National	Local			
1980	341,785	92,204	91,246	958	222,799	26,439	343
1985	620,206	112,110	110,913	1,197	476,486	30,863	747
1986	688,211	108,579	107,358	1,221	544,259	34,377	996
1987	746,422	112,479	111,414	1,065	593,682	38,951	1,310
1988	809,592	122,645	121,595	1,050	650,473	35,032	1,442
1989	791,374	113,805	112,796	1,009	644,508	31,778	1,283
1990	772,682	95,712	94,888	824	648,085	27,225	1,660
1991	806,048	95,080	94,208	872	682,681	26,109	2,178
1992	860,855	99,693	98,788	905	731,774	26,502	2,886
1993	996,634	105,458	104,580	878	860,719	27,074	3,383
1994	1,092,882	108,738	108,009	729	953,940	26,165	4,039
1995	1,172,596	102,745	102,081	664	1,040,810	23,924	5,117
1996	1,245,357	94,797	93,551	612	1,122,110	22,895	5,555
1997	1,326,094	93,308	91,919	659	1,204,583	22,573	5,630
1998	1,378,717	95,085	92,991	629	1,257,332	20,545	5,755
1999	1,394,413	100,164	97,725	528	1,269,004	19,151	6,094
2000	1,478,573	105,073	101,847	519	1,347,392	19,386	6,722
2001	1,534,122	105,155	101,680	558	1,402,798	18,645	7,524
2002	1,608,150	105,606	101,741	516	1,475,257	18,693	8,594
2003	1,587,497	97,260	93,636	412	1,464,335	17,142	8,759

(continued)

Year	Total	Highway			Railway	Waterway	Civil aviation
		Total	National	Local			
2004	1,767,453	111,764	107,346	378	1,624,526	19,040	12,123
2005	1,847,018	115,583	110,651	319	1,697,381	20,227	13,827
2006	2,024,158	125,656	119,728	423	1,860,487	22,047	15,968
2007	2,227,761	135,670	128,712	451	2,050,680	22,835	18,576
2008	2,867,892	146,193	144,452	474	2,682,114	20,334	19,251
2009	2,976,898	152,451	150,798	419	2,779,081	22,314	23,052
2010	3,269,508	167,609	164,761	477	3,052,738	22,392	26,769
2011	3,526,319	186,226	179,199	528	3,286,220	24,556	29,317
2012	3,804,035	189,337	187,863	583	3,557,010	25,752	31,936
2013	2,122,992	210,597	207,541	690	1,853,463	23,535	35,397
2014	2,032,218	230,460	232,381	762	1,736,270	26,293	39,195
2015	1,943,271	253,484	249,558	778	1,619,097	27,072	43,618

Notes: (1) In 2008, the Ministry of Transport organized a special survey on highways and waterways nationwide. The statistic scope was changed, so the data of highway and waterway passengers and freight volumes and turnover volumes were not historically comparable. (2) The statistic scope of highway and waterway transport data in 2013 was adjusted with the special survey on economic statistics of the transportation industry in 2013 (the same below).

Source: National Development and Reform Commission, Ministry of Transport, National Railway Administration, Civil Aviation Administration of China, State Post Bureau, National Energy Administration, and Transport and Delivery Bureau of Logistics Support Department of Central Military Commission, *Year Book of China Transportation & Communications*, Beijing: China Integrated Transport Yearbook Press, 2016, p. 986.

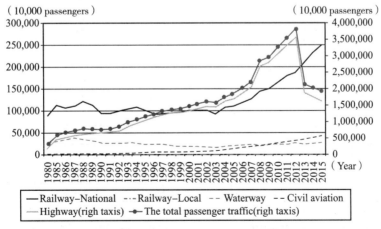

Figure 5–4   Passenger capacity of major modes of transportation
in China from 1980 to 2015

Table 5–9   Passenger capacity Composition of major modes
                   of transportation in China from 1980 to 2015   Unit: %

Year	Total	Railway	Highway	Waterway	Civil aviation
1980	100.0	27.0	65.2	7.7	0.10
1985	100.0	18.1	76.8	5.0	0.12
1986	100.0	15.8	79.1	5.0	0.14
1987	100.0	15.1	79.5	5.2	0.18
1988	100.0	15.1	80.3	4.3	0.18
1989	100.0	14.4	81.4	4.0	0.16
1990	100.0	12.4	83.9	3.5	0.21
1991	100.0	11.8	84.7	3.2	0.27
1992	100.0	11.6	85.0	3.1	0.34
1993	100.0	10.6	86.4	2.7	0.34
1994	100.0	9.9	87.3	2.4	0.37
1995	100.0	8.8	88.8	2.0	0.44
1996	100.0	7.6	90.1	1.8	0.45
1997	100.0	7.0	90.8	1.7	0.42
1998	100.0	6.9	91.2	1.5	0.42
1999	100.0	7.2	91.0	1.4	0.44
2000	100.0	7.1	91.1	1.3	0.45
2001	100.0	6.9	91.4	1.2	0.49
2002	100.0	6.6	91.7	1.2	0.53
2003	100.0	6.1	92.2	1.1	0.55
2004	100.0	6.3	91.9	1.1	0.69
2005	100.0	6.3	91.9	1.1	0.75
2006	100.0	6.2	91.9	1.1	0.79
2007	100.0	6.1	92.1	1.0	0.83
2008	100.0	5.1	93.5	0.7	0.67
2009	100.0	5.1	93.4	0.7	0.77
2010	100.0	5.1	93.4	0.7	0.82
2011	100.0	5.3	93.2	0.7	0.83
2012	100.0	5.0	93.5	0.7	0.84
2013	100.0	9.9	87.3	1.1	1.67
2014	100.0	11.3	85.4	1.3	1.90
2015	100.0	13.0	83.3	1.4	2.20

Source: National Development and Reform Commission, Ministry of Transport, National Railway Administration, Civil Aviation Administration of China, State Post Bureau, National Energy Administration, and Transport and Delivery Bureau of Logistics Support Department of Central Military Commission, *Year Book of China Transportation& Communication*, Beijing: China Integrated Transport Yearbook Press, 2016, p. 987.

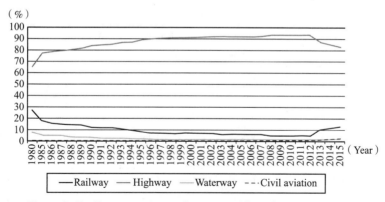

Figure 5–5　Passenger capacity composition of the main modes
of transportation in China from 1980 to 2015

Table 5–10　Passenger turnover capacity of major modes of transportation
in China from 1980 to 2015　Unit: 100 million passenger-km

Year	Total	Railway	Highway	Waterway	Civil aviation
1980	2,281.34	1,383.16	729.50	129.12	39.56
1985	4,435.39	2,416.14	1,724.88	178.65	115.72
1986	4,896.51	2,586.71	1,981.74	182.06	146.00
1987	5,415.47	2,843.06	2,190.43	195.92	186.06
1988	6,209.38	3,260.31	2,528.24	203.92	216.91
1989	6,074.56	3,037.41	2,662.11	188.27	186.77
1990	5,628.35	2,612.64	2,620.32	164.91	230.48
1991	6,178.32	2,828.05	2,871.74	177.21	301.32
1992	6,949.38	3,152.24	3,192.64	198.38	406.12
1993	7,858.00	3,483.30	3,700.70	196.40	477.60
1994	8,591.42	3,636.04	4,220.30	183.50	551.58
1995	9,001.90	3,545.70	4,603.10	171.80	681.30
1996	9,164.80	3,347.60	4,908.79	160.57	747.84
1997	10,055.48	3,584.86	5,541.40	155.70	773.52
1998	10,636.74	3,773.42	5,942.81	120.27	800.24
1999	11,299.74	4,135.94	6,199.20	107.30	857.30
2000	12,261.09	4,532.59	6,657.42	100.54	970.54
2001	13,155.13	4,766.82	7,207.08	89.88	1,091.35
2002	14,125.64	4,969.38	7,805.77	81.78	1,268.70
2003	13,810.50	4,788.61	7,695.60	63.10	1,263.19
2004	16,309.08	5,712.17	8,748.38	66.25	1,782.28

(continued)

Year	Total	Railway	Highway	Waterway	Civil aviation
2005	17,466.74	6,061.96	9,292.08	67.77	2,044.93
2006	19,197.21	6,622.12	10,130.85	73.58	2,370.66
2007	21,592.58	7,216.31	11,506.77	77.78	2,791.73
2008	23,196.70	7,778.60	12,476.11	59.18	2,882.80
2009	24,834.94	7,878.89	13,511.44	69.38	3,375.24
2010	27,894.26	8,762.18	15,020.81	72.27	4,039.00
2011	30,984.03	9,612.29	16,760.25	74.53	4,536.96
2012	33,383.09	9,812.33	18,467.55	77.48	5,025.74
2013	27,571.65	10,595.62	11,250.94	68.33	5,656.76
2014	28,647.13	11,241.85	10,996.75	74.34	6,334.19
2015	30,058.90	11,960.60	10,742.66	73.08	7,282.55

Source: National Development and Reform Commission, Ministry of Transport, National Railway Administration, Civil Aviation Administration of China, State Post Bureau, National Energy Administration, and Transport and Delivery Bureau of Logistics Support Department of Central Military Commission, *Year Book of China Transportation& Communications*, Beijing: China Integrated Transport Yearbook Press, 2016, p. 989.

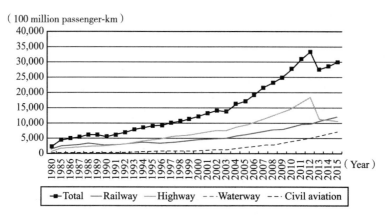

Figure 5–6　Passenger turnover capacity of major modes of transportation in China from 1980 to 2015

Table 5–11　Composition of passenger turnover capacity of major modes of transportation in China from 1980 to 2015　　Unit: %

Year	Total	Railway	Highway	Waterway	Civil aviation
1980	100.0	60.6	32.0	5.7	1.7
1985	100.0	54.5	38.9	4.0	2.6
1986	100.0	52.8	40.5	3.7	3.0
1987	100.0	52.5	40.4	3.6	3.4

(continued)

Year	Total	Railway	Highway	Waterway	Civil aviation
1988	100.0	52.5	40.7	3.3	3.5
1989	100.0	50.0	43.8	3.1	3.1
1990	100.0	46.4	46.6	2.9	4.1
1991	100.0	45.8	46.5	2.9	4.9
1992	100.0	45.4	45.9	2.9	5.8
1993	100.0	44.3	47.1	2.5	6.1
1994	100.0	42.3	49.1	2.1	6.4
1995	100.0	39.4	51.1	1.9	7.6
1996	100.0	36.5	53.6	1.8	8.2
1997	100.0	35.7	55.1	1.5	7.7
1998	100.0	35.5	55.9	1.1	7.5
1999	100.0	36.6	54.9	0.9	7.6
2000	100.0	37.0	54.3	0.8	7.9
2001	100.0	36.2	54.8	0.7	8.3
2002	100.0	35.2	55.3	0.6	9.0
2003	100.0	34.7	55.7	0.5	9.1
2004	100.0	35.0	53.6	0.4	10.9
2005	100.0	34.7	53.2	0.4	11.7
2006	100.0	34.5	52.8	0.4	12.3
2007	100.0	33.4	53.3	0.4	12.9
2008	100.0	33.5	53.8	0.3	12.4
2009	100.0	31.7	54.4	0.3	13.6
2010	100.0	31.4	53.8	0.3	14.5
2011	100.0	31.0	54.1	0.2	14.6
2012	100.0	29.4	55.3	0.2	15.1
2013	100.0	38.4	40.8	0.2	20.5
2014	100.0	39.2	38.4	0.3	22.1
2015	100.0	39.8	35.7	0.2	24.2

Source: National Development and Reform Commission, Ministry of Transport, National Railway Administration, Civil Aviation Administration of China, State Post Bureau, National Energy Administration, and Transport and Delivery Bureau of Logistics Support Department of Central Military Commission, *Year Book of China Transportation& Communications*, Beijing: China Integrated Transport Yearbook Press, 2016, p. 990.

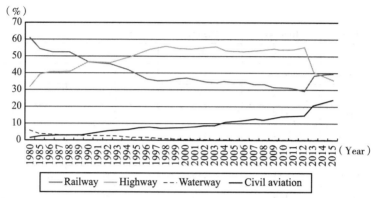

Figure 5-7   Composition of passenger turnover capacity of major modes of transportation in China from 1980 to 2015

Table 5-12   Cargo capacity of major modes of transportation
in China from 1980 to 2015   Unit: 10,000 tons

Year	Total	Railway	Highway	Waterway		Civil aviation	Pipeline
					Ocean shipping		
1980	310,841	111,279	142,195	46,833	4,292	8.9	10,525
1985	745,763	130,709	538,062	63,322	6,627	19.5	13,650
1986	853,557	136,635	620,113	82,962	7,228	22.4	14,825
1987	948,229	140,653	711,424	80,979	7,984	29.9	15,143
1988	982,195	144,948	732,315	89,281	8,530	32.7	15,618
1989	988,435	151,489	733,781	87,493	9,027	31.0	15,641
1990	970,602	150,681	724,040	80,094	9,408	37.0	15,750
1991	985,793	152,893	733,907	83,370	10,567	45.2	15,578
1992	1,045,899	157,627	780,941	92,490	11,191	57.5	14,783
1993	1,115,902	162,794	840,256	97,938	12,508	69.4	14,845
1994	1,180,396	163,216	894,914	107,091	13,421	82.9	15,092
1995	1,234,938	165,982	940,387	113,194	15,251	101.1	15,274
1996	1,298,421	171,024	983,860	127,430	14,213	115.0	15,592
1997	1,278,218	172,149	976,536	113,406	20,287	124.7	16,002
1998	1,267,427	164,309	976,004	109,555	18,892	140.1	17,419
1999	1,293,008	167,554	990,444	114,608	22,621	170.4	20,232
2000	1,358,682	178,581	1,038,813	122,391	22,949	196.7	18,700
2001	1,401,786	193,189	1,056,312	132,675	27,573	171.0	19,439
2002	1,483,447	204,956	1,116,324	141,832	29,896	202.1	20,133
2003	1,564,492	224,248	1,159,957	158,070	34,002	219.0	21,998

(continued)

Year	Total	Railway	Highway	Waterway	Ocean shipping	Civil aviation	Pipeline
2004	1,706,412	249,017	1,244,990	187,394	39,469	276.7	24,734
2005	1,862,066	269,296	1,341,778	219,648	48,549	306.7	31,037
2006	2,037,060	288,224	1,466,347	248,703	54,413	349.4	33,436
2007	2,275,822	314,237	1,639,432	281,199	58,903	401.8	40,552
2008	2,585,937	330,354	1,916,759	294,510	42,352	407.6	43,906
2009	2,825,222	333,348	2,127,834	318,996	51,733	445.5	44,598
2010	3,241,807	364,271	2,448,052	378,949	58,054	563.0	49,972
2011	3,696,961	393,263	2,820,100	425,968	63,542	557.5	57,073
2012	4,100,436	390,438	3,188,475	458,705	65,815	545.0	62,274
2013	409,800	396,697	3,076,648	559,785	71,156	561.3	65,209
2014	4,167,296	391,334	3,113,334	598,283	74,733	594.1	73,752
2015	4,175,886	335,801	3,150,019	613,567	74,685	629.3	75,870

Notes: (1) Since 1984, the cargo volume of road transportation has included private transport sectors, and since 2008 the statistic scope of road transportation has been in principle commercial vehicles. (2) The statistic scope of waterway transport covers ships that have been examined and approved by the transportation authority, kept as records, and engaged in the production of commercial passenger and cargo transport (the same below). (3) The index scope of railway cargo transportation has been adjusted to increase the volume of luggage and parcel transport since 1993 (the same below). (4) Since 2012, the historical data of highway and waterway cargo volume before 1980 have been adjusted according to the department scope (the same below).

Source: National Development and Reform Commission, Ministry of Transport, National Railway Administration, Civil Aviation Administration of China, State Post Bureau, National Energy Administration, and Transport and Delivery Bureau of Logistics Support Department of Central Military Commission, *Year Book of China Transportation& Communications*, Beijing: China Integrated Transport Yearbook Press, 2016, p. 992.

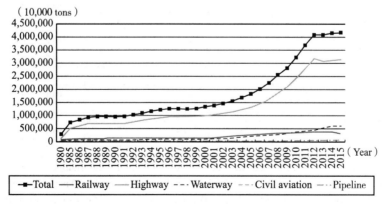

Figure 5–8　Cargo capacity of major modes of transportation in China from 1980 to 2015

Table 5–13   Composition of cargo capacity of major modes
of transportation in China from 1980 to 2015   Unit: %

Year	Total	Railway	Highway	Waterway		Civil aviation	Pipeline
					Ocean shipping		
1980	100.0	35.8	45.7	15.1	1.4	—	3.4
1985	100.0	17.5	72.1	8.5	0.9	—	1.6
1986	100.0	15.9	72.7	9.7	0.8	—	1.7
1987	100.0	14.8	75.0	8.5	0.8	—	1.6
1988	100.0	14.7	74.6	9.1	0.9	—	1.6
1989	100.0	15.4	74.2	8.9	0.9	—	1.6
1990	100.0	15.6	74.6	8.3	1.0	—	1.6
1991	100.0	15.5	74.4	8.5	1.1	—	1.6
1992	100.0	15.1	74.7	8.8	1.1	—	1.4
1993	100.0	14.6	75.3	8.8	1.1	0.01	1.3
1994	100.0	13.8	75.8	9.1	1.1	0.01	1.3
1995	100.0	13.4	76.1	9.2	1.2	0.01	1.2
1996	100.0	13.2	75.8	9.8	1.1	0.01	1.2
1997	100.0	13.5	76.4	8.9	1.6	0.01	1.3
1998	100.0	13.0	77.0	8.6	1.5	0.01	1.4
1999	100.0	13.0	76.6	8.9	1.7	0.01	1.6
2000	100.0	13.1	76.5	9.0	1.7	0.01	1.4
2001	100.0	13.8	75.4	9.5	2.0	0.01	1.4
2002	100.0	13.8	75.3	9.6	2.0	0.01	1.4
2003	100.0	14.3	74.1	10.1	2.2	0.01	1.4
2004	100.0	14.6	73.0	11.0	2.3	0.02	1.4
2005	100.0	14.5	72.1	11.8	2.6	0.02	1.7
2006	100.0	14.1	72.0	12.2	2.7	0.02	1.6
2007	100.0	13.8	72.0	12.4	2.6	0.02	1.8
2008	100.0	12.8	74.1	11.4	1.6	0.02	1.7
2009	100.0	11.8	75.3	11.3	1.8	0.02	1.6
2010	100.0	11.2	75.5	11.7	1.8	0.02	1.5
2011	100.0	10.6	76.3	11.5	1.7	0.02	1.5
2012	100.0	9.5	77.8	11.2	1.6	0.01	1.5
2013	100.0	9.7	75.1	13.7	1.7	0.01	1.6
2014	100.0	9.2	74.7	14.4	1.7	0.01	1.8
2015	100.0	8.0	75.4	14.7	1.8	0.02	1.8

Source: National Development and Reform Commission, Ministry of Transport, National Railway Administration, Civil Aviation Administration of China, State Post Bureau, National Energy Administration, and Transport and Delivery Bureau of Logistics Support Department of Central Military Commission, *Year Book of China Transportation& Communications*, Beijing: China Integrated Transport Yearbook Press, 2016, p. 993.

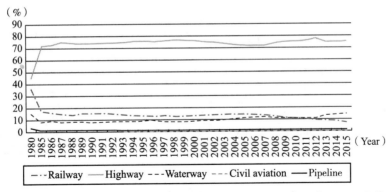

Figure 5-9　Composition of cargo capacity of major modes of transportation
in China from 1980 to 2015

Table 5-14　　　　　Cargo turnover of major modes of transportation
in China from 1980 to 2015　　　Unit: 100 million ton-km

Year	Total	Railway	Highway	Waterway		Civil aviation	Pipeline
					Ocean shipping		
1980	11,628.64	5,717.53	342.87	5,076.49	3,532.00	1.41	491.00
1985	18,365.11	8,125.66	1,903.00	7,729.30	5,329.00	4.15	603.00
1986	20,147.44	8,764.78	2,118.00	8,647.90	5,948.00	4.76	612.00
1987	22,228.51	9,471.49	2,660.40	9,465.10	6,576.00	6.52	625.00
1988	23,825.71	9,877.59	3,220.40	10,070.40	6,966.00	7.32	650.00
1989	25,591.71	10,394.18	3,374.80	11,186.80	7,689.00	6.93	629.00
1990	26,207.56	10,622.38	3,358.10	11,591.90	8,140.86	8.18	627.00
1991	27,986.49	10,971.99	3,428.00	12,955.40	8,990.40	10.10	621.00
1992	29,217.57	11,575.55	3,755.40	13,256.20	9,034.00	13.42	617.00
1993	30,646.81	12,090.90	4,070.50	13,860.80	9,133.90	16.61	608.00
1994	33,435.48	12,632.00	4,486.30	15,686.60	10,267.70	18.58	612.00
1995	35,908.88	13,049.48	4,694.90	17,552.20	11,938.00	22.30	590.00
1996	36,589.79	13,106.16	5,011.20	17,862.50	11,254.00	24.93	585.00
1997	38,384.69	13,269.88	5,271.50	19,235.00	14,874.70	29.10	579.21
1998	38,088.71	12,560.08	5,483.38	19,405.80	14,920.28	33.45	606.00
1999	40,567.64	12,910.30	5,724.30	21,262.80	17,014.40	42.34	627.90
2000	44,320.51	13,770.49	6,129.40	23,734.20	17,073.00	50.27	636.15
2001	47,709.94	14,694.14	6,330.44	25,988.89	20,873.00	43.72	652.75
2002	50,685.85	15,658.42	6,782.46	27,510.64	21,733.00	51.55	682.78
2003	53,859.18	17,246.65	7,099.48	28,715.76	22,304.77	57.90	739.39
2004	69,445.04	19,288.77	7,840.86	41,428.69	32,255.00	71.80	814.92

(continued)

Year	Total	Railway	Highway	Waterway		Civil aviation	Pipeline
					Ocean shipping		
2005	80,258.10	20,726.03	8,693.19	49,672.28	38,552.00	78.90	1,087.70
2006	88,839.85	21,954.41	9,754.25	55,485.75	42,577.30	94.28	1,551.17
2007	101,418.81	123,797.00	11,354.69	64,284.85	48,686.00	116.39	1,865.89
2008	110,300.49	25,106.29	32,868.19	50,262.74	32,850.60	119.60	1,943.68
2009	122,133.31	25,239.17	37,188.82	57,556.67	39,524.12	126.30	2,022.42
2010	141,837.42	27,644.13	43,389.67	68,427.53	45,999.00	178.90	2,197.19
2011	159,323.62	29,465.79	51,374.74	75,423.84	49,355.40	173.91	2,885.44
2012	173,804.46	29,187.09	59,534.86	81,707.58	53,412.10	163.89	3,211.04
2013	168,013.80	29,173.89	55,738.08	79,435.65	48,705.37	170.29	3,495.89
2014	181,667.69	27,530.19	56,846.90	92,774.56	55,935.06	187.77	4,328.28
2015	178,355.90	23,754.31	57,955.72	91,772.45	54,236.09	208.07	4,665.35

Source: National Development and Reform Commission, Ministry of Transport, National Railway Administration, Civil Aviation Administration of China, State Post Bureau, National Energy Administration, and Transport and Delivery Bureau of Logistics Support Department of Central Military Commission, *Year Book of China Transportation& Communications*, Beijing: China Integrated Transport Yearbook Press, 2016, p. 995.

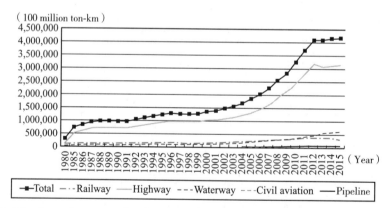

Figure 5–10　Cargo turnover of major modes of transportation in China from 1980 to 2015

Table 5–15　　　　Composition of cargo turnover of major modes
of transportation in China from 1980 to 2015　　　　Unit: %

Year	Total	Railway	Highway	Waterway		Civil aviation	Pipeline
					Ocean shipping		
1980	100.0	49.2	2.9	43.7	30.4	0.01	4.22
1985	100.0	44.2	10.4	42.1	29.0	0.02	3.28
1986	100.0	43.5	10.5	42.9	29.5	0.02	3.04

(continued)

Year	Total	Railway	Highway	Waterway	Ocean shipping	Civil aviation	Pipeline
1987	100.0	42.6	12.0	42.6	29.6	0.03	2.81
1988	100.0	41.5	13.5	42.3	29.2	0.03	2.73
1989	100.0	40.6	13.2	43.7	30.0	0.03	2.46
1990	100.0	40.5	12.8	44.2	31.1	0.03	2.39
1991	100.0	39.2	12.2	46.3	32.1	0.04	2.22
1992	100.0	39.6	12.9	45.4	30.9	0.05	2.11
1993	100.0	39.5	13.3	45.2	29.8	0.05	1.98
1994	100.0	37.8	13.4	46.9	30.7	0.06	1.83
1995	100.0	36.3	13.1	48.9	33.2	0.06	1.64
1996	100.0	35.8	13.7	48.8	30.8	0.07	1.60
1997	100.0	34.6	13.7	50.1	38.8	0.08	1.51
1998	100.0	33.0	14.4	50.9	39.2	0.09	1.59
1999	100.0	31.8	14.1	52.4	41.9	0.10	1.55
2000	100.0	31.1	13.8	53.6	38.5	0.11	1.44
2001	100.0	30.8	13.3	54.5	43.7	0.09	1.37
2002	100.0	30.9	13.4	54.3	42.9	0.10	1.35
2003	100.0	32.0	13.2	53.3	41.4	0.11	1.37
2004	100.0	27.8	11.3	59.7	46.4	0.10	1.17
2005	100.0	25.8	10.8	61.9	48.0	0.10	1.36
2006	100.0	24.7	11.0	62.5	47.9	0.11	1.75
2007	100.0	23.5	11.2	63.4	48.0	0.11	1.84
2008	100.0	22.8	29.8	45.6	29.8	0.11	1.76
2009	100.0	20.7	30.4	47.1	32.4	0.10	1.66
2010	100.0	19.5	30.6	48.2	32.4	0.13	1.55
2011	100.0	18.5	32.2	47.3	31.0	0.11	1.81
2012	100.0	16.8	34.3	47.0	30.7	0.09	1.85
2013	100.0	17.4	33.2	47.3	29.0	0.10	2.08
2014	100.0	15.2	31.3	51.1	30.1	0.10	2.38
2015	100.0	13.3	32.5	51.5	30.4	0.12	2.62

Source: National Development and Reform Commission, Ministry of Transport, National Railway Administration, Civil Aviation Administration of China, State Post Office, National Energy Administration, and Transport and Delivery Bureau of Logistics Support Department of Central Military Commission, *Year Book of China Transportation& Communications*, Beijing: China Integrated Transport Yearbook Press, 2016, p. 996.

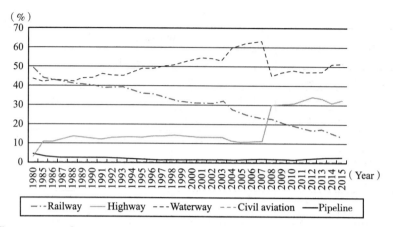

Figure 5–11　Composition of cargo turnover of major modes of transportation in China from 1980 to 2015

Table 5–16　　　Average passenger travel distance of major modes of transportation in China from 1980 to 2015　　　Unit: km

Year	Total	Railway	Highway	Waterway	Civil aviation
1980	67	150	33	49	1,153
1985	72	216	36	58	1,563
1986	71	238	36	53	1,466
1987	73	253	37	50	1,441
1988	77	266	39	58	1,501
1989	77	267	41	59	1,456
1990	73	273	40	61	1,388
1991	77	297	42	68	1,383
1992	81	316	44	75	1,407
1993	79	330	43	73	1,412
1994	79	334	44	70	1,366
1995	77	345	44	72	1,331
1996	74	353	44	70	1,346
1997	76	384	46	69	1,374
1998	77	397	47	59	1,391
1999	81	413	49	56	1,407
2000	83	431	49	52	1,444
2001	86	453	51	48	1,450
2002	88	471	53	44	1,476
2003	87	492	53	37	1,442

(continued)

Year	Total	Railway	Highway	Waterway	Civil aviation
2004	92	511	54	35	1,470
2005	95	524	55	34	1,479
2006	95	527	54	33	1,485
2007	97	532	56	34	1,503
2008	81	532	47	29	1,497
2009	83	517	49	31	1,464
2010	85	523	49	32	1,509
2011	88	516	51	30	1,548
2012	88	518	52	30	1,574
2013	130	503	61	29	1,598
2014	141	488	63	28	1,616
2015	155	472	66	27	1,670

Source: National Development and Reform Commission, Ministry of Transport, National Railway Administration, Civil Aviation Administration of China, State Post Bureau, National Energy Administration, and Transport and Delivery Bureau of Logistics Support Department of Central Military Commission, *Year Book of China Transportation& Communications*, Beijing: China Integrated Transport Yearbook Press, 2016, p. 998.

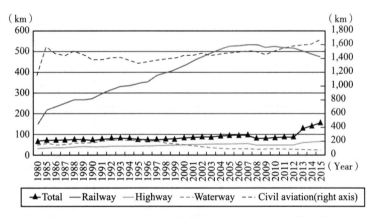

Figure 5-12   Average passenger travel distance of major modes of transportation
in China from 1980 to 2015

Table 5-17   Average cargo transport distance of major modes
of transportation in China from 1980 to 2015   Unit: km

Year	Total	Railway	Highway	Waterway	Ocean shipping	Civil aviation	Pipeline
1980	374	514	24	1,084	8,229	1,580	467
1985	246	622	35	1,221	8,041	2,129	442

177

(continued)

Year	Total	Railway	Highway	Waterway		Civil aviation	Pipeline
					Ocean shipping		
1986	236	646	34	1,042	8,229	2,126	413
1987	234	673	37	1,169	8,236	2,182	413
1988	243	681	44	1,128	8,166	2,236	416
1989	259	686	46	1,279	8,518	2,237	402
1990	270	705	46	1,447	8,653	2,211	398
1991	284	718	47	1,554	8,508	2,234	399
1992	279	734	48	1,433	8,073	2,335	417
1993	275	743	48	1,415	7,302	2,394	410
1994	283	774	50	1,465	7,650	2,241	406
1995	291	786	50	1,551	7,828	2,206	386
1996	282	766	51	1,402	7,918	2,168	366
1997	300	771	54	1,696	7,332	2,334	362
1998	301	764	56	1,771	7,898	2,388	348
1999	314	771	58	1,855	7,522	2,485	310
2000	326	771	59	1,939	7,440	2,555	340
2001	340	761	60	1,959	7,570	2,556	336
2002	342	764	61	1,940	7,270	2,551	339
2003	344	769	61	1,817	6,560	2,643	336
2004	407	775	63	2,211	8,172	2,595	329
2005	431	770	65	2,261	7,941	2,572	350
2006	436	762	67	2,231	7,825	2,698	464
2007	446	757	69	2,286	8,265	2,896	460
2008	427	760	171	1,707	7,757	2,934	443
2009	432	757	175	1,804	7,640	2,833	453
2010	438	759	177	1,806	7,923	3,177	440
2011	431	749	182	1,771	7,767	3,120	506
2012	424	748	187	1,781	8,115	3,007	516
2013	410	735	181	1,419	6,845	3,034	536
2014	436	722	183	1,551	7,485	3,161	587
2015	427	707	184	1,496	7,262	3,306	615

Source: National Development and Reform Commission, Ministry of Transport, National Railway Administration, Civil Aviation Administration of China, State Post Bureau, National Energy Administration, and Transport and Delivery Bureau of Logistics Support Department of Central Military Commission, *Year Book of China Transportation& Communications*, Beijing: China Integrated Transport Yearbook Press, 2016, p. 999.

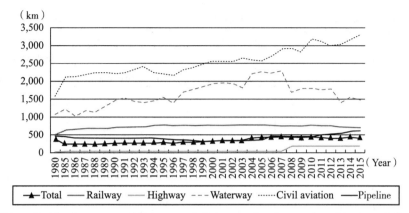

Figure 5–13　Average cargo transport distance of major modes of transportation
in China from 1980 to 2015

5.5　Approval, cleaning up and rectification of Category–2 ports in China

5.5.1　Situation of Category-2 ports before cleaning up and rectification

Since the reform and opening up, in order to better promote the development of the provincial and regional export-oriented economy, the State Council delegated power to provincial governments to examine and approve the establishment of Category-2 ports. According to Provisions of the State Council on the Opening of Ports, the ports in China are divided into 2 categories according to the examination and approval authority. Category-1 ports refer to ports approved by the State Council (including ports administered by the central government and some by provinces, autonomous regions, and municipalities directly under the central government). Category-2 ports refer to ports approved by the provincial people's government for opening and management. Since the reform and opening up, Category-2 ports approved by the provincial people's government have served as a supplement to Category-1 ports, playing a positive role in further improving the local investment environment and promoting the local development export-oriented economy. Table 5–18 shows the numbers of Category-2 ports in each province by June 30, 1995.

Table 5–18   Numbers of Category–2 ports in each province (by June 30, 1995)

Number	Province	Total	Land transport Railway	Highway	Waterway	Hong Kong and Macao SARs vehicle checking point
		350	25	37	238	50 (administrated as Category-2 ports)
1	Beijing	2	1	1		
2	Shanghai	0				
3	Tianjin	8			8	
4	Hebei	2	1		1	
5	Shanxi	0				
6	Inner Mongolia	4		4		
7	Liaoning	10			10	
8	Jilin	5		3	2	
9	Heilongjiang	0				
10	Jiangsu	3			3	
11	Zhejiang	12			12	
12	Anhui	3	2		1	
13	Fujian	31			31	
14	Jiangxi	1	1			
15	Shandong	6		2	4	
16	Henan	5	3	2		
17	Hubei	5	2		3	
18	Hunan	0				
19	Guangdong	207	6	1	150	50
20	Guangxi	11		9	2	
21	Hainan	10			10	
22	Sichuan (including) Chongqing)	4	3		1	
23	Guizhou	1	1			
24	Yunnan	8		8		
25	Shaanxi	3	3			
26	Gansu	1	1			
27	Ningxia	0				
28	Qinghai	0				
29	Xinjiang	5	1	4		
30	Tibet	3		3		

Notes: (1) Up to the time when the data were counted, Chongqing had not yet been listed as a municipality directly under the central government, and the relevant data were classified as those of Sichuan Province. (2) Up to the time when the data were counted, Shanghai, Heilongjiang, Shanxi, Hunan, Ningxia, and Qinghai had not yet opened the Category-2 ports.

Source: *Ports in China*, 1995(5), p. 47.

According to statistics, by the end of 1997, there were 331 Category-2 ports in China. There were 234 waterway ports, 32 border highway ports, and 65 inland railway and highway ports. These Category-2 ports were not distributed in balance. Except for Ningxia, Qinghai, Gansu, Hunan, Heilongjiang, Shanghai and Tianjin, there were Category-2 ports in all other provinces. Guangdong Province ranked first with 141 ports, followed by Fujian with 39. In Shandong, Liaoning, Hainan, Zhejiang, Guangxi, Xinjiang, Yunnan and Hubei provinces, there were more than ten Category-2 ports respectively (see Figure 5–14). Due to the excessive number and unreasonable layout of the Category-2 ports approved and opened by the provinces, the redundant construction problems, difficult supervision, and nonstandard management were becoming increasingly prominent.

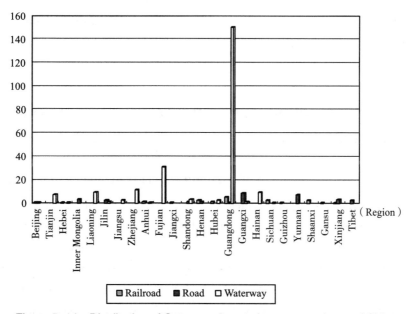

Figure 5–14   Distribution of Category–2 ports in some provinces of China

5.5.2 The situation of Category-2 ports after cleaning up and rectification

In 1998, in order to standardize port management, promote the well-coordinated distribution of ports and further improve the comprehensive utilization, the State Council decided to clean up and rectify Category-2 ports nationwide and made it clear that the provincial government would no longer examine and approve Category-2 ports. In line with the principle of "seeking truth and facts and achieving significant benefits, reasonable layout and effective supervision," 43 Category-2 ports were revoked, and 47

Category-2 ports with unreasonable layout were consolidated by the end of 2000 after more than two years of cleaning up and rectification. Moreover, 65 inland railway ports and highway ports that did not meet the requirements of Provisions of the State Council on the Opening of Ports were no longer managed as the Category-2 ports. Instead, they were all operated in accordance with the follow-up supervision and inspection of the open ports.

150 Category-2 ports remained in China after the rectification, and most of them located in counties and cities along the coasts, borders, and rivers without the were Category-1 ports approved by the state. There are two Category-2 ports in a few developed counties and cities, while there is only one port in most counties and cities with conditions to open ports. After the rectification, the number of open ports in China has been significantly reduced, with an balanced layout. The management of ports has been standardized, with the existing port resources being further optimized and integrated, and the comprehensive utilization and benefits of open ports further enhanced.

5.6 Development of import and export trade at ports in China since the reform and opening up

5.6.1 Overall achievements of import and export trade development of ports

According to statistics, the efficiency of ports in China increased year by year from 1978 to 2015, The total volume of imports and exports increased from US$20.64 billion to US$3,958.64 billion, an increase of 190.7 times. The cargo volume of imports and exports increased from 70.33 million tons to 3.184 billion tons, an increase of 45.3 times. The number of inbound and outbound vehicles increased from 325,000 ships/times (sorties, train trips, and vehicle trips) to 26.338 million ships/times (sorties, train trips, and vehicle trips), an increase of 80.1 times. The number of exit and entry passengers increased from 5.658 million person-time to 522.22 million person-time (excluding persons with border passes), an increase of 91.3 times. Since the reform and opening up, China has made remarkable achievements in open ports. With the continuous expansion of port opening, ports in China have developed rapidly, which play a vital role in promoting economic and social development as well as the level of opening up (see Table 5–19,Table 5–20, Figure 5–15 to 5–22).

Table 5–19 Statistics of total imports and exports of foreign trade in different years after the founding of People's Republic of China

Unit: US$100 million

Year	Total imports and exports	Total exports	Total imports
Recovery Period	50.31	21.32	28.99
1950	11.35	5.52	5.83
1951	19.55	7.57	11.98
1952	19.41	8.23	11.18
1st Five-year Plan Period	142.57	68.22	74.35
1953	23.68	10.22	13.46
1954	24.33	11.46	12.87
1955	31.45	14.12	17.33
1956	32.08	16.45	15.63
1957	31.03	15.97	15.06
2nd Five-year Plan Period	176.6	90.79	85.81
1958	38.71	19.81	18.90
1959	43.81	22.61	21.20
1960	38.09	18.56	19.53
1961	29.36	14.91	14.45
1962	26.63	14.9	11.73
Adjustment Period	106.23	57.93	48.30
1963	29.15	16.49	12.66
1964	34.63	19.16	15.47
1965	42.45	22.28	20.17
3rd Five-year Plan Period	214.32	110.68	103.64
1966	46.14	23.66	22.48
1967	41.55	21.35	20.20
1968	40.48	21.03	19.45
1969	40.29	22.04	18.25
1970	45.86	22.6	23.26
4th Five-year Plan Period	514.37	261.11	253.26
1971	48.41	26.36	22.05
1972	63.01	34.43	28.58
1973	109.76	58.19	51.57
1974	145.68	69.49	76.19
1975	147.51	72.64	74.87
5th Five-year Plan Period	1,163.48	560.67	603.80
1976	134.33	68.55	65.78
1977	148.04	75.9	72.14
1978	206.38	97.45	108.93

(continued)

Year	Total imports and exports	Total exports	Total imports
1979	293.33	136.58	156.75
1980	381.4	181.2	200.20
6th Five-year Plan Period	2,523.95	1,200.43	1,323.52
1981	440.22	220.07	220.15
1982	416.06	223.21	192.85
1983	436.16	222.26	213.90
1984	535.49	261.39	274.10
1985	696.02	873.5	422.52
7th Five-year Plan Period	4,863.97	2,325.24	2,538.73
1986	738.46	309.42	429.04
1987	826.53	394.37	432.16
1988	1,027.84	475.16	552.68
1989	1,116.78	525.38	591.40
1990	1,154.36	620.91	533.45
8th Five-year Plan Period	10,143.47	5,183.13	4,960.34
1991	1,356.34	718.43	637.91
1992	1,655.25	849.4	805.85
1993	1,957.03	917.44	1,039.59
1994	2,366.21	1,210.06	1,156.15
1995	2,808.64	1,487.8	1,320.84
9th Five-year Plan Period	17,739.19	9,616.86	8,122.33
1996	2,898.81	1,510.48	1,383.33
1997	3,251.62	1,827.92	1,423.70
1998	3,239.49	1,837.12	1,402.37
1999	3,606.3	1,949.31	1,656.99
2000	4,742.97	2,492.03	2,250.94
10th Five-year Plan Period	45,578.65	23,852.01	21,726.65
2001	5,096.51	2,660.98	2,435.53
2002	6,207.66	3,255.96	2,951.70
2003	8,509.88	4,382.28	4,127.60
2004	11,545.54	5,933.26	5,612.29
2005	14,219.06	7,619.53	6,599.53
11th Five-year Plan Period	116,814.04	63,990.97	52,823.08
2006	17,604.38	9,689.78	7,914.61
2007	21,761.75	12,200.6	9,561.15
2008	25,632.55	14,306.93	11,325.62
2009	22,075.35	12,016.12	10,059.23
2010	29,740.01	15,777.54	13,962.47

(continued)

Year	Total imports and exports	Total exports	Total imports
12th Five-year Plan Period	159,683.75	84,998.52	74,696.67
2011	36,418.64	18,983.81	17,434.84
2012	38,671.19	20,487.14	18,184.05
2013	41,589.93	22,090.04	19,499.89
2014	43,003.99	23,437.53	19,577.89
2015	39,569	22,749	16,820

Sources: (1) The number of imports and exports through the ports before 1979 in this table is the statistical data of foreign trade. The data after 1980 is the annual statistical data of imports and exports of the customs. (2) General Administration of Customs, P. R. China, Department Statistics and Analysis, *Yearly Report on China's Foreign Trade 2015*, Beijing: China Customs Press, 2015. (3) Data sources of 2015: Ministry of Transport, *China Shipping Development Annual Report 2015*, Beijing: China Communications Press Co., Ltd., 2016.

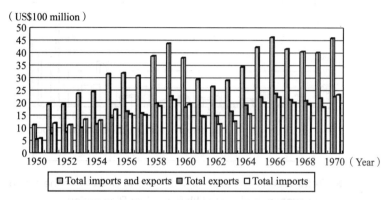

Figure 5–15　Total imports and exports of all ports in China from 1950 to 1970

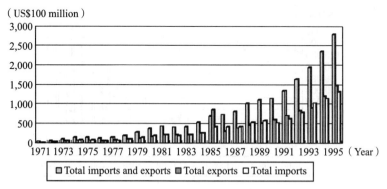

Figure 5–16　Total imports and exports of all ports in China from 1971 to 1995

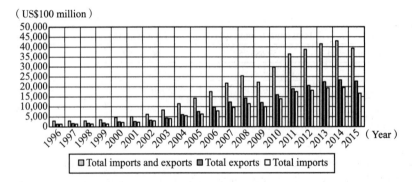

Figure 5–17   Total imports and exports of all ports in China from 1996 to 2015

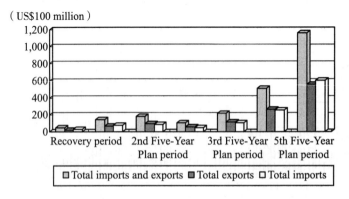

Figure 5–18   Total imports and exports of all ports in China from the economic recovery period to the fifth Five–Year Plan period

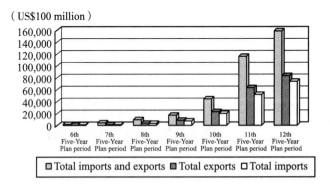

Figure 5–19   Total imports and exports of China from the sixth Five–Year Plan period to the twelfth Five–Year Plan period

Table 5–20   Statistics on the growth rate of foreign trade after the
founding of the People's Republic of China

(calculated by US dollar, previous year=100)

Year	Total imports and exports	Total exports	Total imports
Recovery Period			
1950			
1951	17.2	37.1	105.5
1952	−0.7	8.7	−6.7
1st Five-Year Plan Period	9.8	14.2	6.1
1953	22.0	24.2	20.4
1954	2.7	12.3	−4.4
1955	29.3	23.2	34.7
1956	2.0	16.5	−10.2
1957	−3.3	−3.1	−3.6
2nd Five-Year Plan Period	−3.1	−1.4	−4.9
1958	24.8	24	25.5
1959	13.2	14.1	12.2
1960	−13.1	−17.9	−7.9
1961	−22.9	−19.7	−26.0
1962	−19.3	0.0	−18.8
Adjustment Period	16.8	14.4	19.8
1963	9.5	10.7	7.9
1964	18.8	16.2	22.2
1965	22.6	16.3	30.4
3rd Five-Year Plan Period	1.6	0.3	2.9
1966	8.7	6.2	11.5
1967	−9.9	−9.8	−10.1
1968	−2.6	−1.5	−3.7
1969	−1.2	4.8	−6.2
1970	13.8	2.5	27.5
4th Five-Year Plan Period	26.3	26.3	26.3
1971	5.6	16.6	−5.2
1972	30.2	30.6	29.6
1973	74.2	69.0	80.4
1974	32.7	19.4	47.7
1975	1.3	4.5	−1.7
5th Five-Year Plan Period	20.9	20.1	21.7
1976	−8.9	−5.6	−12.1
1977	10.2	10.7	9.7
1978	39.4	28.4	51.0

(continued)

Year	Total imports and exports	Total exports	Total imports
1979	42.1	40.2	43.9
1980	30.0	32.7	27.7
6th Five-Year Plan Period	12.8	8.6	16.1
1981	15.4	21.5	10.0
1982	−5.5	1.4	−12.4
1983	4.8	−0.4	10.9
1984	22.8	17.6	28.1
1985	30.0	4.6	54.1
7th Five-Year Plan Period	10.6	17.8	4.8
1986	6.1	13.1	1.5
1987	11.9	27.5	0.7
1988	24.4	20.5	27.9
1989	8.7	10.6	7.0
1990	3.4	18.2	−9.8
8th Five-Year Plan Period	19.5	19.1	19.9
1991	17.6	15.8	19.6
1992	22.0	18.1	26.3
1993	18.2	8.0	29.0
1994	20.9	31.9	11.2
1995	18.7	23.0	14.2
9th Five-Year Plan Period	11.0	10.9	11.3
1996	3.2	1.5	5.1
1997	12.2	21.0	2.5
1998	−0.4	0.5	−1.5
1999	11.3	6.1	18.2
2000	31.5	27.8	35.8
10th Five-Year Plan Period	24.6	25.0	24.0
2001	7.5	6.8	8.2
2002	21.8	22.4	21.2
2003	37.1	34.6	39.8
2004	35.7	35.4	36.0
2005	23.2	28.4	17.6
11th Five-Year Plan Period	15.9	15.7	16.2
2006	23.8	27.2	19.9
2007	23.5	25.7	20.8
2008	17.8	17.3	18.5
2009	−13.9	−16.0	−11.2
2010	34.7	31.3	38.7

(continued)

Year	Total imports and exports	Total exports	Total imports
12th Five-Year Plan Period			
2011	22.5	20.3	24.9
2012	6.2	7.9	4.3
2013	7.5	7.8	7.2
2014	3.4	6.1	0.4
2015	−8.0	−2.8	−14.1

Sources: (1)General Administration of Customs, P. R. China, Department of Statistics and Analysis, *Yearly Report on China's Foreign Trade 2015*, Beijing: China Customs Press, 2015. (2) Data for the growth rate of foreign trade imports and exports in 2015 were quoted from the website of the Ministry of Commerce of the P.R. China Comprehensive Department. http://zhs.mofcom.gon.cn/article/Nocategory/20165/20160501314688.shtml.

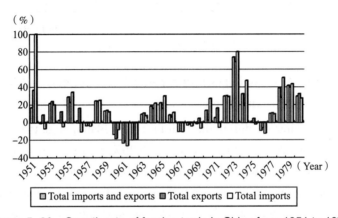

Figure 5-20 Growth rate of foreign trade in China from 1951 to 1979

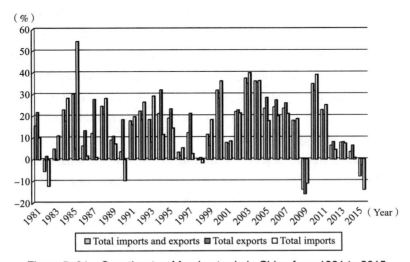

Figure 5-21 Growth rate of foreign trade in China from 1981 to 2015

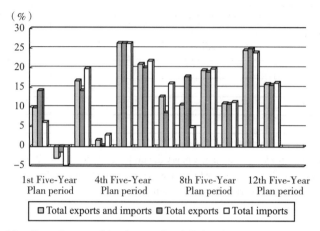

Figure 5–22　Growth rate of foreign trade of China from the 1st Five–Year Plan period to the 12th Five–Year Plan period

5.6.2　Development of passenger and cargo volume at ports in China since the 11th Five-Year Plan period

According to statistics, during the 11th Five-year Plan period, the average growth rate of foreign trade cargo volume in China was 9.26% per year, and the average annual growth of entry-exit personnel number was 2.35%. From 2006 to 2010, the volumes of cargo directly passing through the open ports were as follows. In 2006, the total cargo volume at all ports in China reached 1.35373 billion tons, including 1.28074 billion tons by waterway, 46.93 million tons by railway, 21.48 million tons by highway, and 4.58 million tons by air. In 2007, the total cargo volume at all ports in China reached 1.475 billion tons, including 1.395 billion tons by waterway, 48 million tons by railway, 28 million tons by highway, and 4 million tons by air. In 2008, the total cargo volume of all ports was 1.496 billion tons, including 1.413 billion tons by waterway, 44 million tons by railway, 34 million tons by highway, and 5 million tons by air. In 2009, the total cargo volume of all ports got to 1.768 billion tons, including 1.687 billion tons by waterway, 44 million tons by railway, 32 million tons by highway, and 5 million tons by air. In 2010, the total cargo volume of all ports came up to 1.929 billion tons, including 1.822 billion tons by waterway, 47 million tons by railway, 55 million tons by highway and 6 million tons by air (see Table 5–21 and Figure 5–23).

Table 5–21 Statistics of inbound and outbound cargo by transportation modes at
ports in China during the 11th Five–Year Plan period

Unit: 10,000 tons

Year	Total cargo volume	Waterway	Railway	Highway	Civil aviation
2006	135,373	128,074	4,693	2,148	458
2007	147,500	139,500	4,800	2,800	400
2008	149,600	141,300	4,400	3,400	500
2009	176,800	168,700	4,400	3,200	500
2010	192,900	182,200	4,700	5,500	600

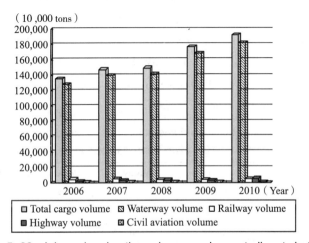

Figure 5–23   Inbound and outbound cargo volume at all ports in China
during the 11th Five–Year Plan period

During the 12th Five-year Plan period (2011-2015), the average growth rate of China's foreign trade cargo volume was 13.01% per year, and the average annual growth of entry-exit personnel number was 4.51%. During this period, the volumes of cargo directly passing through the open ports of each year were as follows. In 2011, the total cargo volume at all ports in China reached 2.009 billion tons (an increase of 4.1% over the same period of the previous year—1.929 billion tons in 2010), including 1.905 billion tons by waterway, 40 million tons by railway, 58 million tons by highway and 6 million tons by air. In 2012, the total cargo volume at all ports in China reached 2.847 billion tons, including 2.698 billion tons by waterway, 49 million tons by railway, 92 million tons by highway, and 8 million tons by air (different from the previous year, the statistical data of the year was cargo throughput of foreign trade, including both the volume of goods directly imported and exported through the port and the volume of cargo transferred from the port). In 2013, the total cargo volume of ports of China was up to 3.099 billion tons, an increase of 8.9% over the same period of the previous year. In the year-on-year terms, among them, 2.941 billion tons was by waterway, an increase of 9%; 52 million tons by railway, rising 6.1%; 98 million tons by highway, an increase of 6.5%; 8 million tons by air, which remained the same as the previous year. In 2014, the total cargo volume of ports of China reached 3.277 billion tons, an increase of 5.7% over the same period of the previous year. Compared with the volume of the previous year, 3.131 tons were carried by waterway, an increase of 6.5%; 43 million tons by railway, a decrease of 17.3%; 94 million tons by highway, a reduction of 4.1%; 9 million tons by air, an increase of 12.5%. In 2015, the total cargo volume of ports of China reached 3.184 billion tons, a decrease of 2.8% over the same period of the previous year. In the year-on-year terms, the cargo volume by waterway was 3.051 billion tons, a decrease of 2.6%; 36 million tons by railway, decreasing by 16.3%; 89 million tons by highway, reducing by 5.3%; 8 million tons by air, a decrease of 11.1% (see Tables 5–22 to 5–25 and Figures 5–24 to 5–27).

Table 5–22   Statistics of cargo volume at all ports in China during the
12th Five–Year Plan period   Unit: 10,000 tons

Year	Total volume	Waterway	Railway	Highway	Civil aviation
2011	200,900	190,500	4,000	5,800	600
2012	284,700	269,800	4,900	9,200	800
2013	309,900	294,100	5,200	9,800	800
2014	327,700	313,100	4,300	9,400	900
2015	318,400	305,100	3,600	8,900	800

Table 5–23   Statistics of cargo volume by transportation modes at
all ports in China from 2005 to 2015

Year	Total volume (10,000 tons)	Ratio (YOY) (%)	Waterway (10,000 tons)	Ratio (YOY) (%)	Railway (10,000 tons)	Ratio (YOY) (%)	Highway (10,000 tons)	Ratio (YOY) (%)	Civil Aviation (10,000 tons)	Ration (YOY) (%)
2005	116,700	—	110,000	—	4,400	—	2,000	—	300	—
2006	135,373	16.00	128,074	16.43	4,693	6.66	2,148	7.40	458	52.67
2007	147,500	8.96	139,500	8.92	4,800	2.28	2,800	30.35	400	−12.66
2008	149,600	1.42	141,300	1.29	4,400	−8.33	3,400	21.43	500	25.00
2009	176,800	18.18	168,700	19.39	4,400	0.00	3,200	−5.88	500	0.00
2010	192,900	9.10	182,200	8.00	4,700	6.82	5,500	71.88	600	20.00
2011	200,900	4.10	190,500	4.56	4,000	−14.89	5,800	5.45	600	0

(continued)

Year	Total volume (10,000 tons)	Ratio (YOY) (%)	Waterway (10,000 tons)	Ratio (YOY) (%)	Railway (10,000 tons)	Ratio (YOY) (%)	Highway (10,000 tons)	Ratio (YOY) (%)	Civil Aviation (10,000 tons)	Ration (YOY) (%)
2012	284,700	41.71	269,800	41.63	4,900	22.50	9,200	58.62	800	33.33
2013	309,900	8.85	294,100	9.00	5,200	6.12	9,800	6.52	800	0

Source: Complied by the author according to *China's Ports-of-Entry Yearbook 2005-2016.*

Table 5–24 Entry–exit passenger capacity by transportation modes at all ports in China from 2005 to 2015

Year	Passenger number (10,000 person-time)	Raito (YOY) (%)	Waterway (10,000 person-time)	Raito (YOY) (%)	Railway (10,000 person-time)	Raito (YOY) (%)	Highway (10,000 person-time)	Raito (YOY) (%)	Civil Aviation (10,000 person-time)	Raito (YOY) (%)
2005	29,900	—	1,400	—	800	—	23,500	—	4,200	—
2006	33,996	13.70	3,350	139.29	379	-52.63	25,501	8.52	4,766	13.48
2007	34,442	1.31	1,970	-41.19	462	21.90	26,523	4.01	5,487	15.13
2008	34,976	1.55	1,853	-5.94	459	-0.65	27,442	3.47	5,222	-4.83
2009	34,682	-0.85	1,376	-25.74	552	20.26	27,299	-0.52	5,455	4.46
2010	38,377	10.65	1,646	19.62	771	39.67	29,340	7.48	6,720	23.19
2011	41,087	7.06	1,669	1.40	771	0	31,072	5.90	7,572	12.68
2012	43,103	4.91	2,000	19.83	499	64.72	32,273	3.87	8,331	10.02
2013	45,066	4.55	2,097	4.85	472	-5.41	33,235	2.98	9,262	11.18
2014	49,005	8.74	3,562	69.86	544	15.25	34,619	4.16	10,280	10.99
2015	52,222	6.56	2,260	-36.55	502	-7.7	37,663	8.79	11,798	14.77

Source: Complied by the author according to *China's Ports-of-Entry Yearbook 2005-2016.*

Table 5–25 Statistics of vehicles by transportation modes at all ports in China from 2005 to 2015

Year	Total vehicles (10,000 times)	Ratio (YOY) (%)	Ship (10,000 times)	Ratio (YOY) (%)	Train (10,000 times)	Ratio (YOY) (%)	Vehicle (10,000 times)	Ratio (YOY) (%)	Plane (10,000 times)	Ratio (YOY) (%)
2005	1,978.11	—	49.08	—	73.25	—	1,822.88	—	32.90	—
2006	2,067.00	4.49	65.00	32.44	9.00	-87.71	1,955.00	7.25	38.00	15.50
2007	2,174.00	5.18	58.00	-10.77	7.00	-22.22	2,066.00	5.68	43.00	13.16
2008	2,165.00	-0.41	57.00	-1.72	7.00	0.00	2,071.00	0.24	30.00	-30.23
2009	2,153.00	-0.55	48.00	-15.79	6.00	-14.29	2,058.00	-0.63	41.00	36.67
2010	2,398.50	11.40	46.30	-3.54	6.70	11.67	2,297.00	11.61	48.40	18.05

(continued)

Year	Total vehicles (10,000 times)	Ratio (YOY) (%)	Ship (10,000 times)	Ratio (YOY) (%)	Train (10,000 times)	Ratio (YOY) (%)	Vehicle (10,000 times)	Ratio (YOY) (%)	Plane (10,000 times)	Ratio (YOY) (%)
2011	2,482.40	3.50	49.60	7.13	5.60	−16.42	2,374.30	3.37	52.90	9.30
2012	2,523.20	1.60	51.10	3.02	6.50	16.07	2,407.20	1.39	58.40	10.40
2013	2,573.80	2.00	44.40	−13.12	6.30	−3.08	2,459.50	2.17	63.60	8.90
2014	2,591.10	0.70	43.30	−2.48	5.60	−11.11	2,472.20	0.52	70.00	10.06
2015	2,633.80	1.60	42.80	−1.15	4.80	−14.28	2,507.90	1.44	78.30	11.43

Source: Complied by the author according to *China's Ports-of-Entry Yearbook 2005-2016.*

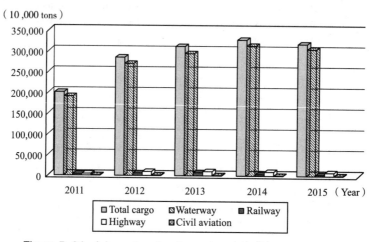

Figure 5–24　Inbound and outbound cargo volume at all ports in China during the 12th Five–Year Plan period

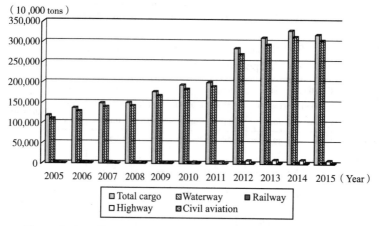

Figure 5–25　Export and import cargo volume by transportation modes at all ports in China from 2005 to 2015

194

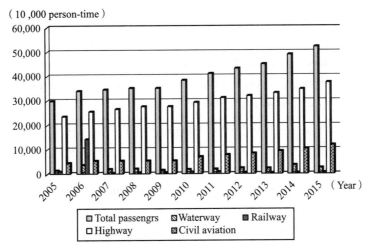

Figure 5–26   Entry–exit passenger capacity by transportation modes
at all ports in China from 2005 to 2015

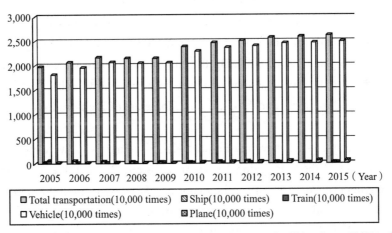

Figure 5–27   Inbound and outbound vehicles at all ports in China from 2005 to 2015

5.7 Major achievements of the opening and development of ports in China since the start of the reform and opening up

5.7.1 Cargo volume and transport capacity of waterway ports: ranking among the tops in the world

At present, the leading open coastal ports are developing toward larger specialized ports with deep-water berths. The key ports have strengthened their multifunction of gathering and transferring transportation, information transmission, and customs clearance, accelerated the construction of electronic port information platform to further promote the development of port logistics industry and foreign trade transportation and to improve customs clearance efficiency. Waterway ports have become a modern logistics hub. The cargo throughput of foreign trade at ports above the national scale has increased from more than 50 million tons in 1978 to 3.59 billion tons in 2014 (3.267 billion tons through coastal ports and 323 million tons through inland ports). The waterway port cargo throughput has increased by 71 times, accounting for more than 75% of the import and export freight volume in China. Ningbo-Zhoushan, Shanghai, Tianjin, Tangshan, Guangzhou, Qingdao, Dalian, Rizhao, Yingkou, Qinhuangdao, Yantai, Shenzhen, Xiamen, Zhanjiang, and other leading ports have played an active role in the world cargo throughput. Among the top 20 ports of global cargo throughput in 2014, 13 of them belong to ports of the Chinese mainland. Ningbo-Zhoushan Port and Shanghai Port respectively continued to be the first and second largest ports in the world; Tangshan Port soared from the 8th to the 5th; and Rizhao Port, Hong Kong Port, Yantai Port rose by one place respectively. By the end of 2015, there were more than 2,100 berths for ships of 10 thousand tons or above in coastal ports, with a total handling capacity of 7.9 billion tons, and 13.6 million kilometers of high-grade standard inland waterways.

Table 5–26 and 5–27, as well as Figure 5–28, 5–29 and 5–30, were the statistics of cargo throughput of the major global ports in 2014 and 2015. Table 5–28 shows the cargo throughput of foreign trade at the major coastal ports from 2006 to 2014. Table 5–29 displays the statistics of cargo throughput of the major coastal ports from 2007 to 2015. Table 5–30 is the container throughput of foreign trade at the major ports in China from 2006 to 2014.

In addition, relying on the coastal ports, the state has established a number of bonded logistics parks[1] in Waigaoqiao in Shanghai, Tianjin, Ningbo, Wuhan, Dalian, Qingdao, Xiangyu in Xiamen, Fuzhou, Yantian in Shenzhen and Zhangjiagang, as well as 14

---

[1] Bonded logistics park refers to the special area of customs supervision, which is approved by the State Council and established in the planned area of the bonded area or in the specific port area adjacent to the bonded area, specializing in the development of modern international logistics industry. Its business scope covers international transfer, import and export trade, storage of imports and exports, international procurement, allocation, and distribution, as well as other international logistics business approved by customs.

bonded port areas[1] in Yangshan in Shanghai, Dongjiang in Tianjin, Lianglucuntan in Chongqing, Dayaowan in Liaoning, Yangpu in Hainan, Meishan of Ningbo in Zhejiang, Qinzhou in Guangxi, Haicang of Xiamen in Fujian, Qianwan of Qingdao in Shandong, Qianhaiwan in Shenzhen and Nansha of Guangzhou in Guangdong, Zhangjiagang in Jiangsu, Yantai in Shandong, Fuzhou in Fujian. The port logistics demonstration area, featuring the interconnection of bonded logistics park and bonded port areas, has laid a good foundation for China's port operation to be oriented to the outside world, so as to undertake the transfer of world manufacturing and international modern service industries, and accelerate the regional economic and social development.

Table 5-26   Cargo throughputs of major ports in the world in 2014

Ranking	Ports	Country	Cargo throughputs (100 million tons)	Comparison with the volume in 2013 (%)
1 (1)	Ningbo–Zhoushan	China	8.73	7.9
2 (2)	Shanghai	China	7.55	−2.6
3 (31)	Singapore	Singapore	5.81	3.9
4 (4)	Tianjin	China	5.40	7.9
5 (8)	Tangshan	China	5.01	12.2
6 (5)	Guangzhou	China	4.82	5.9
7 (6)	Suzhou	China	4.78	5.2
8 (7)	Qingdao	China	4.68	4.0
9 (9)	Rotterdam	Netherlands	4.45	0.8
10 (10)	Dalian	China	4.23	3.9
11 (11)	Hedland	Australia	4.04	23.9
12 (12)	Busan	South Korea	3.46	6.5
13 (14)	Rizhao	China	3.35	8.3
14 (13)	Yingkou	China	3.31	3.3

---

[1] Bonded port area refers to the special customs supervision area with functions of port, logistics, and processing, which is established in the port area opening to the outside world and in the specific area connected with it, with the approval of the State Council. The functions of the bonded port area include warehousing logistics, foreign trade, international procurement, allocation and distribution, international transfer, inspection and after-sales service maintenance, product display, research and development, processing, manufacturing, and port operation, Bonded port areas enjoy tax and foreign exchange management policies related to bonded areas, export processing zones and bonded logistics parks, including bonded entry zones for foreign goods; customs declaration for domestic sales of goods entering and leaving port zones according to relevant provisions on import of goods; bonded port zones have tax and foreign exchange policies overlapped with bonded zones and export processing zones, which enjoy more obvious advantages in location, function, and policy.

(continued)

Ranking	Ports	Country	Cargo throughputs (100 million tons)	Comparison with the volume in 2013 (%)
15 (16)	Hong Kong	China	2.98	7.9
16 (15)	Qinhuangdao	China	2.74	0.5
17 (17)	South Louisiana	America	2.65	9.6
18 (18)	Gwangyang	South Korea	2.51	6.9
19 (20)	Yantai	China	2.38	7.3
20 (19)	Shenzhen	China	2.23	−4.6

Note: The number in the bracket on the right of the rank is the rank of 2013.

Source: Ministry of Transport, *Report on China's Shipping Development 2014*, Beijing: China Communications Press Co., Ltd., 2015, p. 63.

Table 5–27   Cargo throughputs of major ports in the world in 2015

Ranking	Ports	Country	Cargo throughputs (10,000 tons)	Comparison with the volume in 2014 (%)
1 (1)	Ningbo–Zhoushan	China	88,929	1.8
2 (2)	Shanghai	China	71,740	−5.0
3 (3)	Singapore	Singapore	57,585	−0.9
4 (4)	Tianjin	China	54,051	0.1
5 (7)	Suzhou	China	53,990	13.0
6 (6)	Guangzhou	China	50,053	3.8
7 (5)	Tangshan	China	49,285	−1.6
8 (8)	Qingdao	China	48,453	3.5
9(9)	Rotterdam	Netherlands	46,636	4.9
10(11)	Hedland	Australia	45,255	7.3
11(10)	Dalian	China	41,482	−2.0
12(12)	Busan	South Korea	35,897	3.6
13(14)	Yingkou	China	33,849	2.3
14(13)	Rizhao	China	33,707	0.6
15(17)	South Louisiana	America	26,566	0.3
16(15)	Hong Kong	China	25,656	−13.8
17(18)	Gwangyang	South Korea	26,168	4.2
18 (16)	Qinhuangdao	China	25,309	−7.6
19(19)	Yantai	China	25,163	5.9
20 (---)	Zhanjiang	China	22,036	8.9

Note: The number in the bracket on the right was the ranking of 2014.

Source: Ministry of Transport, *Report on China's Shipping Development 2015*, Beijing: China Communications Press Co., Ltd., 2016, p. 61.

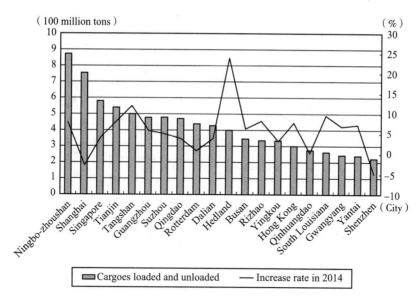

Figure 5–28   Comparison between cargo throughputs and growth rates of major ports in the world in 2014

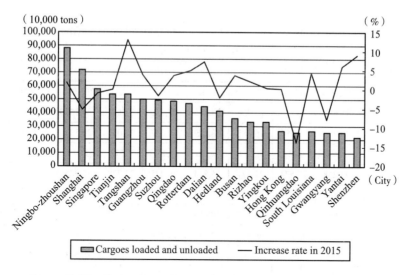

Figure 5–29   Cargo throughputs of major ports in the world in 2015

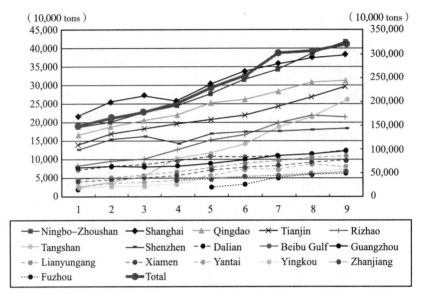

Figure 5–30　Foreign trade throughputs of major coastal ports in China from 2006 to 2014

Note: The thickest line corresponds to the secondary axis (right) and the rest ports correspond to the primary axis (left).

Table 5–28　　Foreign trade throughputs of major coastal ports in China from 2006 to 2014　　Unit: 10,000 tons

Ports	2006	2007	2008	2009	2010	2011	2012	2013	2014
Total	145,827	165,631	178,271	197,922	226,938	252,318	303,053	302,431	320,839
Ningbo-Zhoushan	18,631	20,236	23,057	24,515	27,738	31,611	34,350	38,416	41,882
#Ningbo	14,769	15,785	16,888	18,179	20,337	23,034	24,533	27,628	29,723
#Zhoushan	3,862	4,451	6,169	6,336	7,401	8,577	9,816	10,788	12,159
Shanghai	21,268	25,574	27,377	25,814	30,225	33,778	35,825	37,706	38,232
Qingdao	16,833	19,011	20,665	22,205	25,541	26,394	28,502	30,963	31,094
Tianjin	13,966	16,803	18,245	19,633	20,709	22,162	24,326	26,738	29,493
Rizhao	8,185	9,517	9,980	12,687	15,204	16,690	19,832	21,908	21,608
Tangshan	2,851	3,963	5,477	10,171	11,395	14,329	18,941	21,582	26,254
#Jingtang	1,752	1,975	2,334	4,308	4,125	4,189	7,313	8,284	9,755
#Caofeidian	1,099	1,987	3,143	5,864	7,270	10,140	11,628	13,298	16,499
Shenzhen	12,709	15,354	16,200	14,344	17,106	17,503	17,707	18,174	18,397
Dalian	7,017	8,214	8,585	9,778	10,830	10,672	11,018	11,767	12,531
Beibu gulf	—	—	—	5,870	7,195	8,906	10,517	11,548	12,773
#Fangcheng	2,236	2,634	2,968	4,956	5,662	6,611	7,276	10,561	8,896
Guangzhou	7,727	8,051	7,942	8,357	8,992	9,914	10,968	11,329	11,957

(continued)

Ports	2006	2007	2008	2009	2010	2011	2012	2013	2014
Lianyungang	4,481	4,983	5,508	6,606	7,804	9,158	9,688	10,599	11,036
Xiamen	—	—	—	—	—	8,035	8,486	9,375	10,199
#Former Xiamen	4,188	4,629	5,394	5,635	7,082	7,963	8,442	9,245	9,741
Yantai	1,916	3,404	3,792	4,461	5,697	7,421	7,246	8,707	7,907
Yingkou	2,308	2,775	2,685	3,441	4,868	5,415	5,066	6,222	7,230
Zhanjiang	—	—	—	4,587	4,760	5,464	5,730	5,974	6,457
Fuzhou	—	—	—	—	2,720	3,319	5,281	5,956	6,455

Note: The # mark refers to the port that used to be included before incorporating.

Source: Ministry of Transport, *Report on China's Shipping Development 2014*, Beijing: China Communications Press Co., Ltd., 2015, p.87.

Table 5–29   Cargo throughputs of major coastal ports in
                    China from 2007 to 2015   Unit: 10, 000 tons

Ports	2007	2008	2009	2010	2011	2012	2013	2014	2015
Total	388,200	429,599	475,481	548,358	616,292	665,245	728,098	769,557	784,578
Ningbo—Zhoushan	47,336	52,048	57,684	63,300	69,393	74,401	80,978	87,346	88,929
# Ningbo	34,519	36,185	38,385	41,217	43,339	45,303	49,592	52,646	51,004
# Zhoushan	12,818	15,862	19,300	22,084	26,054	29,099	31,387	34,700	37,925
Shanghai	49,227	50,808	49,467	56,320	62,432	63,740	68,273	66,954	64,906
Tianjin	30,946	35,593	38,111	41,325	45,338	47,697	50,063	54,002	54,051
Guangzhou	34,325	34,700	36,395	41,095	43,149	43,517	45,517	48,217	50,053
Tangshan	6,759	10,853	17,559	24,609	31,263	36,505	4,620	50,075	49,285
#Jingtang	4,570	7,645	10,541	12,017	13,757	17,002	20,102	21,503	23,298
#Caofeidian	2,009	3,209	7,018	12,591	17,506	19,503	24,518	28,572	25,987
Qingdao	26,502	30,029	31,546	35,012	37,230	40,690	45,003	46,802	48,453
Dalian	22,286	24,588	27,203	31,399	33,691	37,426	40,746	42,337	41,482
Yingkou	12,207	15,085	17,603	22,579	26,085	30,107	32,013	33,073	33,849
Rizhao	13,063	15,102	18,131	22,597	25,260	28,098	30,937	33,502	33,707
Qinhuangdao	24,893	25,231	24,942	26,297	28,770	27,099	27,260	27,403	25,309
Yantai	10,129	11,189	12,351	15,033	18,029	20,298	22,157	23,767	25,163
Zhanjiang	—	—	11,838	13,638	15,539	17,092	18,006	20,238	22,036
# Former Zhanjiang	6,075	6,682	7,090	7,635	8,889	8,541	8,511	9,518	9,827
Shenzhen	19,994	21,125	19,365	22,098	23,325	22,807	23,398	22,324	21,706
Xiamen	—	—	—	—	15,654	17,227	19,088	20,504	21,023
#Former Xiamen	8,117	9,702	11,096	12,728	14,153	15,513	17,157	18,864	19,580

(continued)

Ports	2007	2008	2009	2010	2011	2012	2013	2014	2015
Beibu gulf	—	—	—	—	15,331	17,438	18,674	20,189	20,482
#Fangcheng	—	—	—	—	9,024	10,058	10,561	11,501	11,504
Lianyungang	8,507	10,060	10,843	12,739	15,627	17,367	18,898	19,638	19,756
Huanghua	8,333	7,980	8,374	9,438	11,267	12,630	17,103	17,551	16,658
Dandong	—	—	—	—	—	—	12,019	13,758	15,022
Fuzhou	6,433	6,703	8,094	7,125	8,218	11,410	12,759	14,391	13,967
Quanzhou	6,215	7,224	7,666	8,455	9,330	10,372	10,804	11,201	12,241
Humen	—	—	—	—	—	8,434	10,293	11,935	12,089
Zhuhai	3,713	4,086	4,407	6,056	7,170	7,745	10,023	10,703	11,209

Note: The # mark refers to the port that used to be included before incorporating.

Source: Ministry of Transport, *Report on China's Shipping Development 2015*, Beijing: China Communications Press Co., Ltd., 2016, p.81.

Table 5–30   Cargo throughputs of major inland ports in China from 2006 to 2014

Unit: 10,000 tons

Ports	2006	2007	2008	2009	2010	2011	2012	2013	2014
Total	12,061	14,009	14,288	18,296	21,025	23,967	26,831	29,961	32,091
Suzhou	4,149	4,718	4,570	6,084	8,137	9,846	10,463	10,949	12,302
Nantong	966	1,882	2,439	2,860	2,961	3,114	3,867	4,538	4,814
Zhenjiang	1,216	1,351	1,162	1,370	1,546	1,841	2,133	2,653	2,313
Foshan	—	—	—	2,178	2,267	2,206	2,134	2,247	2,250
Nanjing	709	726	702	672	833	1,062	1,742	2,204	1,974
Taizhou	448	399	304	463	803	983	1,047	1,280	1,630
Jiangyin	888	1,082	1,099	1,669	192	1,353	1,433	1,477	1,333
Wuhan	171	262	320	379	402	417	496	587	706
Yangzhou	265	298	327	296	371	353	397	404	636
Changzhou	229	180	202	322	342	391	391	534	557
Chongqing	—	—	—	277	288	350	409	448	507
#Former Chongqing	188	217	252	194	239	296	21	256	407
Huangshi	146	129	117	143	185	245	266	324	441
Jiangmen	—	—	—	—	312	338	381	428	408
Zhaoqing	—	—	—	—	150	199	273	272	308
Yueyang	—	—	—	—	121	167	226	218	240
Wuhu	104	154	173	110	139	163	156	190	224
Jiujiang	—	—	—	—	—	—	—	187	202

(continued)

Ports	2006	2007	2008	2009	2010	2011	2012	2013	2014
Zhongshan	—	—	—	—	242	203	172	185	198
Wuzhou	—	—	—	—	—	106	151	168	123

Note: The # mark refers to the port that used to be included before incorporating.

Source: Ministry of Transport, *Report on China's Shipping Development 2014*, Beijing: China Communications Press Co., Ltd., 2015, p. 88.

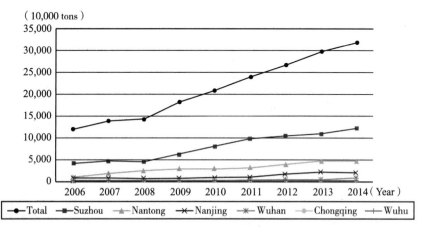

Figure 5–31　Foreign trade throughputs of major inland ports in China from 2006 to 2014

Table 5–31　Foreign trade throughputs of major inland ports in China from 2007 to 2015

Unit: 10,000 tons

Ports	2007	2008	2009	2010	2011	2012	2013	2014	2015
Total	138,208	159,481	221,678	261,822	295,522	312,228	336,793	349,246	361,804
Suzhou	18,377	20,348	24,634	32,877	38,006	42,801	45,435	47,792	53,990
Nantong	12,339	13,214	13,641	15,070	17,331	18,526	20,494	21,599	21,827
Nanjing	10,859	11,125	12,146	14,719	17,333	19,197	20,201	21,001	21,454
Taizhou	2,128	2,592	7,467	9,890	12,038	13,210	15,425	15,822	16,803
Chongqing	—	—	8,612	9,668	11,606	12,502	13,676	14,665	15,750
# Former Chongqing	1,317	1,470	1,727	1,886	2,049	2,084	2,267	2,661	3,057
Yueyang	4,100	6,539	7,822	8,170	9,037	10,396	10,873	12,021	13,144
Zhenjiang	7,824	8,705	8,713	10,634	11,806	13,460	14,098	14,061	13,010
Jiangyin	7,218	8,740	10,103	12,522	12,934	13,248	12,590	12,462	12,228
Wuhu	4,681	5,514	5,710	6,609	7,473	8,260	9,313	10,847	12,009
Jiujiang	—	—	—	—	—	4,827	6,030	8,036	10,425
Hangzhou	5,550	5,299	7,605	8,753	8,929	9,097	9,382	10,084	9,372

(continued)

Ports	2007	2008	2009	2010	2011	2012	2013	2014	2015
Ma'anshan	3,684	4,697	4,191	4,826	5,306	6,809	7,489	8,101	9,205
Xuzhou	4,379	4,738	4,708	6,308	6,662	7,208	8,226	9,202	9,030
Wuhan	5,278	5,592	5,409	6,620	7,602	7,632	7,701	8,150	8,455
Huzhou	4,204	4,241	14,945	14,357	14,668	17,840	15,312	8,487	8,052
Tongling	2,860	2,872	3,157	3,914	4,729	5,507	5,905	7,045	8,011
Huai'an	—	—	—	—	—	—	6,508	7,101	8,004
Wuxi	—	—	—	—	8,081	8,030	8,291	8,452	7,637
Yangzhou	—	—	—	—	4,370	4,841	6,189	7,866	7,345
Shanghai	—	—	—	—	—	—	—	—	6,834
Foshan	—	—	—	—	5,423	5,253	5,474	5,907	6,147

Note: The # mark refers to the port that used to be included before incorporating.

Source: Ministry of Transport, *Report on China's Shipping Development 2015*, Beijing: China Communications Press Co., Ltd., 2016, p. 82.

Table 5–32   Container throughputs of major ports in China from 2006 to 2015

Unit: 10,000 TEU

Ports	2006	2007	2008	2009	2010	2011	2012	2013	2014	2015
Total	8,563	10,450	11,610	10,991	13,112	14,596	15,752	16,902	18,084	18,808
Shanghai	2,172	2,615	2,801	2,500	2,907	3,174	3,253	3,362	3,529	3,654
Shenzhen	1,847	2,110	2,142	1,825	2,251	2,257	2,294	2,328	2,404	2,420
Ningbo-Zhoushan	714	943	1,093	1,050	1,315	1,472	1,618	1,735	1,945	2,063
# Ningbo	707	935	1,085	1,042	1,300	1,451	1,567	1,677	1,870	1,982
Qingdao	770	946	1,002	1,026	1,201	1,302	1,450	1,552	1,658	1,744
Guangzhou	666	926	1,100	1,120	1,255	1,425	1,455	1,531	1,639	1,740
Tianjin	595	710	850	870	1,009	1,159	1,230	1,301	1,406	1,411
Dalian	321	381	453	458	526	640	806	1,002	1,013	945
Xiamen	—	—	—	—	—	647	720	801	857	918
# Former Xiamen	401	463	504	468	582	647	719	799	854	917
Yingkou	101	137	204	254	334	403	485	530	561	592
Lianyungang	130	200	300	303	387	485	502	549	501	501
Humen	—	—	—	—	—	—	—	—	—	288
Rizhao	105	125	153	140	154	171	185	215	242	281
Yantai	—	—	—	—	106	140	175	203	236	245
Fuzhou	101	120	118	122	147	166	183	198	224	243

(continued)

Ports	2006	2007	2008	2009	2010	2011	2012	2013	2014	2015
Quanzhou	84	102	121	125	137	157	170	170	188	202
Dandong	—	—	—	—	—	—	—	151	167	183
The statistics above are for major coastal container ports, and the following statistics are for major inland container ports.										
Total	636	809	964	1,217	1,459	1,725	1,937	2,040	2,048	2,222
Suzhou	124	190	257	272	364	469	586	531	445	510
Foshan	—	—	—	292	306	292	267	275	290	302
Nanjing	80	106	129	121	145	184	230	267	276	294
Chongqing	—	—	—	52	56	68	80	91	101	101
# Former Chongqing	27	35	44	52	42	51	56	66	75	71
Wuhan	35	39	47	56	65	72	77	85	101	106
Zhaoqing	—	—	—	—	45	61	71	70	72	70
Nantong	36	43	44	35	46	54	50	60	71	76
Jiangmen	—	—	—	—	45	50	50	57	64	65
Yangzhou	—	—	—	—	—	40	40	51	55	61

Note: The # mark refers to the port that used to be included before incorporating.

Sources:(1) Ministry of Transport, *Report on China's Shipping Development 2014*, China Communications Press Co., Ltd., 2015 edition, p. 89. (2) Ministry of Transport, *Report on China's Shipping Development 2015*, Beijing: China Communications Press Co., Ltd., 2016, p. 86.

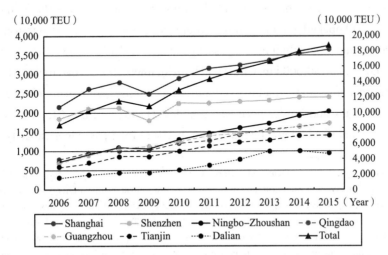

Figure 5–32   Container throughputs of major coastal ports in China from 2006 to 2015

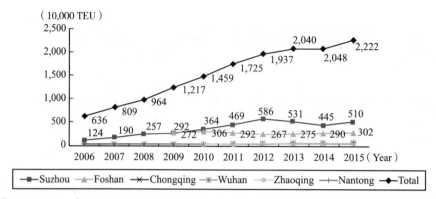

Figure 5–33   Container throughputs of major inland ports in China from 2006 to 2015

5.7.2   Great improvement in border highway ports and international road transport

China borders North Korea, Russia, Mongolia, Kazakhstan, Kyrgyzstan, Tajikistan, Afghanistan, Pakistan, India, Nepal, Sikkim, Bhutan, Myanmar, Laos, Vietnam and so on. According to the statistics from the Ministry of Transport[1], after the signing of the first bilateral automobile transport agreement with Mongolia in 1991, China signed 16 bilateral and multilateral agreements on the road, transit, and transport facilitation with 15 counties, such as Russia, Mongolia, Pakistan, Nepal, Myanmar, Laos and Vietnam, among others, by the end of 2016. Besides, 356 international roads for passenger and cargo transport had been opened through 73 highway and waterway ports. By the end of 2016, China had opened 356 international routes for passenger and cargo transport with neighboring countries, including 178 passenger routes and 178 cargo routes, with a total length of more than 150,000 km. China had built an international road transport network covering border areas and radiating to neighboring countries, with major cities along the border as its hubs and border ports as its nodes. By the end of 2015, China and its neighboring countries had completed an international road passenger capacity of 7.13

---

[1] Sources: (1) National Development and Reform Commission, Ministry of Transport, National Railway Administration, Civil Aviation Administration of China, State Post Bureau, National Energy Administration, and Transport and Delivery Bureau of Logistics Support Department of Central Military Commission, *Year Book of China Transportation& Communications*, Beijing: China Integrated Transport Yearbook Press, 2014, p. 180. (2) National Development and Reform Commission, Ministry of Transport, National Railway Administration, Civil Aviation Administration of China, State Post Bureau, National Energy Administration, and Transport and Delivery Bureau of Logistics Support Department of Central Military Commission. *Year Book of China Transportation & Communications 2015*, Beijing: China Integrated Transport Yearbook Press, 2016. (3) "Promoting Interconnection and Building and Developing Ties— An Exclusive Interview of Li Xiaopeng with Minister of Transport by the *People's Daily* Reporter", *China Transport News*, May 13, 2017.

million and passenger turnover of 465 million passenger-km in addition to international road cargo of 37.47 million tons and cargo turnover of 2.466 billion ton-km. During the 12th Five-year Plan period, the passenger capacity and cargo volume increased by 3% and 22% respectively. There were 58 main highway ports and 17 waterway ports for international road transport, of which 47 are for Northeast Asia, 18 for South Asia, and 10 for Central Asia.

In recent years, in order to implement the Belt and Road Initiative with the development of the Silk Road Economic Belt and the 21st Century Maritime Silk Road as its core, the state and governments at all levels have been actively promoting the construction of major international land passages and sea routes, and further promoting connectivity, international transportation and facilitation of infrastructures such as cross-region transportation and ports. Aiming at enhancing international road transport interconnection and service, the investment in infrastructure construction such as highway ports and cross-border roads has steadily increased. This has greatly promoted the rapid development of China's highway ports and international road transport and enhanced the transport capacity of international roads at borders.

According to the statistics of the Ministry of Transport, China and its neighboring countries have transported passengers of 6.704 million person-time through international roads in 2014, which decreased by 0.9% over the same period of the previous year. Passenger turnover was about 469 million passenger-km, an increase of 13% over the same period of the previous year. On a year-on-year basis, the volume of international road cargo transportation reached 39.579 million tons, an increase of 10.7%, and the cargo turnover of highway was 2.728 billion ton-km, increasing by 23.5%. In 2015, the international road passenger capacity completed by China and its neighboring countries reached 7.129 million person-time, an increase of 6.3% over the same period of the previous year. Passenger turnover volume was about 470 million passenger-km, a decrease of 0.8% over the same period of the year before. The volume of international road cargo transportation was 37.468 million tons, a year-on-year decrease of about 5.3%, and the cargo turnover through highway was 2.47 billion ton-km, a decrease of about 9.6% over the same period of the previous year (Table 5–33, 5–34 and Figure 5–34 represent passenger capacity of international highway transportation and proportion of China from 2010 to 2015).

According to statistics of the Ministry of Transport, 178 international passenger routes and 178 freight routes had been opened in China by the end of 2015. In the international transportation completed by Chinese and foreign carriers through China border ports in 2015 (excluding transport between the mainland and Hong Kong SAR, the mainland and Macao SAR), the passenger cargo was up to 7.1294 million, an increase of 6.3% over the previous year; the passenger turnover was 465 million passenger-km, a decrease of 0.8%; the cargo volume was 37.468 million tons, a decrease of 5.3%, and the cargo turnover was 2.466 billion ton-km, decreased by 9.6%. As for passenger and cargo transportation, the passenger capacity by Chinese carriers reached 3.6142 million, an increase of 11.9%, and the cargo volume was 12.5334 million tons, a decrease of 0.9%. The reduction of passenger turnover was mainly due to the decrease in passenger capacity between China and Kazakhstan (long distance) at Khorgos Port. In 2015, passenger capacity between the mainland, Hong Kong SAR and Macao SAR was 14.0296 million, a decrease of 1.1%. Passenger turnover was 3.496 billion passenger-km, an increase of 0.2%; cargo volume reached 148 million tons, an increase of 16%; and cargo turnover came up to 23.252 billion ton-km, a rise of 7.5%.

Table 5–33　Passenger capacity of international highway transportation and the proportion of China from 2010 to 2015

Volume and proportion	2010	2011	2012	2013	2014	2015
Passenger traffic (10,000 person-time)	780.1	815.9	854.2	676.7	670.4	712.9
China's proportion (%)	43.4	48.0	46.8	47.9	48.2	50.7

Sources: (1) Ministry of Transport, *National Report on Road Transport Development (2014)*, Beijing: China Communications Press Co., Ltd., 2015, p. 54. (2) Ministry of Transport, *National Report on Road Transport Development (2015)*, Beijing: China Communications Press Co., Ltd., 2016, p. 57.

Table 5–34　Cargo volume of international road transport and the proportion of China from 2010 to 2015

Volume and proportion	2010	2011	2012	2013	2014	2015
Cargo volume (10,000 tons)	2,963.1	3,531.7	3,371.6	3,573.2	3,957.9	3,746.8
China's proportion (%)	52.3	41.2	25.3	30.1	32.0	33.4

Sources: (1) Ministry of Transport, *National Report on Road Transport Development (2014)*, Beijing: China Communications Press Co., Ltd., 2015, p.54. (2) Ministry of Transport, *National Report on Road Transport Development (2015)*, Beijing: China Communications Press Co., Ltd., 2016, p. 57.

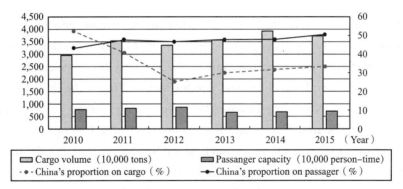

Figure 5–34 Passenger capacity and freight volume of national road transport and China's proportion from 2010 to 2015

5.7.3 Rapid development of passenger capacity and cargo volume of railway ports

Railway transportation is the basic industry of the national economy. As a bridge between the Asia-Pacific and the Eurasian economic circles, China has opened international railway transport corridors such as the North-South Passage of the Eurasian Continental Bridge, the Trans-Asian Railway Passage, the Asia-Europe International Railway Transport Corridor, and the China-Europe International Freight Line, enabling the cross-border railways and railway ports to play an increasingly important role in enhancing communication with neighboring countries and implementing development initiatives such as the Belt and Road Initiative. By the end of 2016, the construction of 11 cross-border railways had been accomplished in China, and the Sino-European trains had been shuttling back and forth across the vast Eurasian continent. The international railway transport and postal cooperation have been carried out and an international logistics brand is taking shape. In recent years, great development has been achieved in the volume of imports and exports at the national railway ports.

Among China's existing railway ports, in addition to Beijing, Shanghai, Guangzhou, Zhengzhou, Harbin, Shenzhen, Foshan, Zhaoqing, Dongguan, and other inland railway ports, there are railway ports located in the border areas, such as Manzhouli, Suifenhe, and Hunchun railway ports connected with Russia; Erenhot Railway Port linked to Mongolia; Alashankou and Khorgos Railway Ports connected with Kazakhstan; Dandong, Tumen, Ji'an Railway Ports connected with North Korea, Pingxiang, Hekou Mountain Railway Ports connected with Vietnam.

Among all the railway ports opening to the outside world, the top four in passenger capacity and freight volume are Manzhouli, Alashankou, Erenhot, and Suifenhe. As for the four major railway ports' division and positioning, Manzhouli Railway Port mainly undertakes the freight transportation from Northeast China to Europe and Eurasia, and from Northeast China, East China, and South China to Russia, the three countries of Baltic Sea and the Nordic countries. Alashankou Railway Port mainly undertakes freight transportation from Northwest China, Southwest China, Central China to Europe (including Russia) and Central Asia; from East and South China to Central Asia, Europe, and other European countries except Russia, in addition to the three countries of the Baltic Sea and the Nordic countries. Besides, Japan, South Korea, and other East Asian countries also transit goods to Europe and Central Asia through this port. Erenhot Railway Port mainly undertakes the freight transportation from domestic regions to Mongolia and from North China to Russia, the three coastal countries of the Baltic Sea and the Nordic countries. Suifenhe Railway Port mainly carries part of the cargo transportation from Northeast China to Europe and Central Asia, from the domestic regions to the coastal areas of Eastern Russia. At present, China-Europe freight trains pass through Manzhouli and Alashankou Railway Ports.

5.7.4 Leap-forward growth of international passenger capacity and freight volume at airports

In 1978, the total turnover of air transport on international routes was only 74.5 million ton/km, the passenger capacity 110,000 people, the freight and postal transport volume 5,262 tons, and the navigation mileage 55,000 kilometers.

According to statistics from the Ministry of Transport, by the end of 2015, China had signed 118 bilateral air transport agreements with other countries or regions, 2 more than that signed at the end of 2014. Among them, 43 agreements were signed with Asian countries (including ASEAN), 24 with African countries, 36 with European countries, 9 with the American countries and 5 with Oceanian countries. At present, an air transport network connecting domestic and foreign cities has been built up with airports of Beijing, Shanghai, and Guangzhou as the hubs, airports of the provincial capitals and tourist cities as its nodes, and other city airports as the branches.

According to statistics from the Ministry of Transport, there are 3,326 scheduled flights, including 2,666 domestic routes (including 109 ones to Hong Kong SAR, Macao SAR, and Taiwan region) and 660 international routes. According to the repetitive distance calculation, the route mileage is 7.866 million km, including 4.964 million km of domestic routes (including 178,000 km of routes to Hong Kong SAR,

Macao SAR and Taiwan region) and 2.902 million km of international routes. In the light of the non-repetitive distance calculation, the route mileage is 5.317 million km, including 2.923 million km of domestic routes (including 172,000 km of routes to Hong Kong SAR, Macao SAR and Taiwan Region) and 2.394 million km of international routes. Navigable cities have been up to 204 (not including Hongkong SAR, Macao SAR and Taiwan region). In China, the international scheduled flights fly to and from 137 cities of 55 countries, and the domestic scheduled flights arrive at Hong Kong SAR from 38 mainland cities, Macao SAR from 12 mainland cities, and Taiwan Region from 43 mainland cities.

By the end of 2015, the total turnover of air transportation in China was 85.165 billion ton-km, an increase of 13.8% over the previous year. Also, on a year-on-year basis, the passenger turnover was 72.8255 million passenger-km, an increase of 15.0%, and 20.807 billion ton-km of cargo and mail, an increase of 10.8%. The total turnover via domestic routes was 55.904 billion ton-km, an increase of 10.0% over the previous year, among which the turnover of the routes to Hong Kong SAR, Macao SAR and Taiwan Region was 1.622 billion ton-km, an increase of 0.3%. The total turnover via international routes was 29.261 billion ton-km, an increase of 21.9%. The total passenger capacity was 436.18 million person-time, a rise of 11.3%. The passenger capacity via domestic routes was 394.11 million person-time, an increase of 9.4%, among which the passenger capacity via the routes to Hong Kong SAR, Macao SAR and Taiwan region was 10.2 million person-time, an increase of 1.4%. The passenger capacity via international routes was 42.07 million person-time, an increase of 33.3%.

By the end of 2015, the civil aviation industry had transported 6.293 million tons of cargo and mail, an increase of 5.9% over the previous year. 4.424 million tons of cargo and postal transport had been transported via the domestic routes, an increase of 3.9%, among which 221,000 tons were via Hong Kong SAR, Macao SAR, and Taiwan region routes, a decrease of 1.0%. 1.868 million tons of cargo and postal transport were completed via the international routes, an increase of 10.9%. The national civil aviation airports had completed a passenger throughput of 915 million person-time, an increase of 10%. Among them, the passenger throughput reached 502 million person-time in East China, 55 million person-time in Northeast China, 90 million person-time in Central China, and 269 million person-time in West China. The cargo and postal throughput of civil airports in China reached 14.094 million tons, an increase of 3.9% over the previous year. The cargo and postal throughput in east China was 10.6288 million tons, 4.887 million tons in northeast China, 8.589 million tons in Central China, and 2.1176 million tons in west China.[1]

By the end of 2015, 8.5655 million sorties had taken off and landed at civil aviation airports in China, an increase of 8.0% over 2014. There were 70 airports with an annual passenger throughput of more than one million person-time, among which Beijing, Shanghai, and Guangzhou airports accounted for 27.3% of the total throughput. There were 51 airports with annual cargo and postal throughput of more than 10,000 tons, among which Beijing, Shanghai, and Guangzhou airports accounted for 50.9% of the total. In 2015, Beijing Capital International Airport completed the passenger throughput of 90 million person-time, ranking second in the world for six consecutive years. Shanghai Pudong International Airport achieved a cargo and postal throughput of 3.275 million tons, ranking third in the world for eight consecutive years.

China is the second largest aviation market in the world after the US. China's domestic routes are mainly distributed in the east of the Harbin-Beijing-Xi'an-Chengdu-Kunming line, with Beijing, Shanghai, and Guangzhou triangle zone as the most densely distributed areas. On the whole, the domestic routes are mostly distributed in the north-south direction, and the route density gradually decreases from east to west. In addition, some routes extend from coastal areas to inland areas, in the east-west direction. Globally, international aviation routes are generally distributed in the east-west direction. The main international routes are concentrated in the middle latitudes of the northern hemisphere, forming a circular airline belt. In addition, the latitudinal airline belt spreads towards north and south from North America, East Asia, Europe, and other areas with the densest airlines, forming a particular meridional airline distribution. The international flights of China-centered on Beijing are radiating eastward, westward, and southward via the airport ports of Shanghai, Guangzhou, and the major airports of Urumqi, Shenyang, Chengdu, Xi'an, Kunming, and Xiamen, forming three major air routes. The main international air routes linking Japan, North America, and other countries in the east, the Middle East and Europe in the west, have become an essential part of the Asia-Pacific air transport network and the northern hemisphere air belt.

At present, passenger and cargo transport via air ports in China are growing rapidly,

---

[1] East China refers to Beijing, Shanghai, Shandong, Jiangsu, Tianjin, Zhejiang, Hainan, Hebei, Fujian, and Guangdong. Northeast China refers to Heilongjiang, Liaoning, and Jilin provinces. Central China refers to Jiangxi, Hubei, Hunan, Henan, Anhui and Shanxi provinces. West China refers to 12 provinces (autonomous regions and municipalities) of Ningxia, Shaanxi, Yunnan, Inner Mongolia, Guangxi, Gansu, Guizhou, Tibet, Xinjiang, Chongqing, Qinghai, and Sichuan.

and the passenger composition has changed significantly. The ranking of the total turnover of cargo transport, passenger turnover, cargo, and postal volume turnover, as well as navigation mileage of scheduled flights, have increased significantly among International Civil Aviation Organization (ICAO) contracting states. Up to now, the rank of total air transport turnover in China has soared from the 31st in 1978 to the world's second for many years and the ranking of total international air transport turnover has risen from the 37th in 1978 to the top 10 in the world. The port routes network has also been greatly improved, with routes extending to Asia, Europe, North America, South America, Oceania, Africa, and other continents. Beijing, Shanghai, and Guangzhou have been playing an increasingly prominent role as three major air hubs. The annual average entry-exit personnel via Shanghai, Beijing and Guangzhou airports accounts for more than 70% of the total number at all air ports in China. Beijing Capital International Airport has the second largest passenger throughput in the world after Atlanta International Airport in the US, and Pudong International Airport in Shanghai has become the world's third largest airport in terms of passenger throughput after Hong Kong International Airport and Memphis International Airport.

5.8 Competition and cooperation among open ports in China

Waterway ports are the pioneers and "main force" of open ports in China. At present, waterborne ports account for more than 50% of all open ports. To a large extent, the development of waterway ports reflects the development of open ports in China.

5.8.1 Present competition and cooperation among major clusters of waterway ports in China

After the founding of the People's Republic of China in 1949, especially through the rapid development of reform and opening up in the past four decades, China has formed an all-round, multi-level and three-dimensional distribution of ports with the main hub ports as the focus, important regional ports as the secondary, and local small and medium-sized ports as the supplement. At present, the coastal ports in China as a whole have formed five regional port clusters with a reasonable layout, clear structure, and specific functions. From north to south, there are respectively the port cluster of Bohai Sea Rim, the port cluster in Yangtze River Delta, the port cluster in southeastern coastal areas, the port cluster in the Pearl River Delta, and the port cluster in southwestern coastal areas. These regional port clusters provide logistics services for the common hinterland. They restrict and complement each other in terms of development scale and nature, and are geographically adjacent to or close to each other. They should maintain not only a reasonable scale but also strengthen the competition and cooperation between each other. It is the general trend to establish a benign competition and cooperation mechanism. The development scale of port clusters should be compatible with the economic development needs of its radiation areas.

(1) *Port Cluster of the Bohai Sea Rim*

This cluster is mainly composed of coastal ports in Liaoning, Tianjin, Hebei, and Shandong. The Bohai Sea Rim covers nearly half of China and is the major industrial area of the country, especially for the heavy industry. The hinterland of the harbor covers the northeast, north, and northwest areas. With abundant energy and mineral resources, it is the base of coal and crude oil production, the base of heavy chemical industry such as metallurgy, petrochemical and machinery manufacturing, and the agricultural production base. At present, there are more than 60 ports of different sizes, which form a most densely distributed port cluster in China and the world. The port cluster aims to build an important international shipping center in Northeast Asia, with the ports of Dalian, Tianjin, Yingkou, Qinhuangdao, Yantai, Qingdao, and Rizhao as the main ports, and the ports of Dandong, Jinzhou, Caofeidian, Huanghua, and Weihai as the supplementary ports. The distinctive port cluster with well-structured characteristics mainly serves the social and economic development of the coastal and inland areas of North China. Liaoning coastal port cluster is centering on Dalian Northeast Asia International Shipping Center and Yingkou Port, Tianjin-Hebei coastal port cluster centering on Tianjin Northern International Shipping Center and Qinhuangdao Port, and Shandong coastal port cluster centering on Qingdao, Yantai, and Rizhao Port.

(2) *Yangtze River Delta port cluster*

In this area, the port cluster relies on Shanghai International Shipping Center, with Shanghai hub port as the leading port, and Jiangsu, and Zhejiang as the two wings for development. It has formed a container transportation layout with Shanghai Port, Ningbo-Zhoushan Port serving as the main line ports, Lianyungang, Suzhou, Nanjing, Nantong, Zhenjiang, and Wenzhou Ports as the branch line ports and other ports as the feeder ports. With the ports of Shanghai, Ningbo-Zhoushan, Zhapu, Wenzhou, Nanjing, Zhenjiang, Nantong, Lianyungang, Zhangjiagang, Jiangyin, Yangzhou, Taizhou, Changshu, and Taicang and the cooperation of the cities and hinterlands, the port group mainly serves the economic and social development of the Yangtze River Delta and the areas along the Yangtze River.

(3) *Port cluster in southeast coastal areas*

With the ports of Xiamen, Quanzhou, and Fuzhou as the main ports, Putian and Zhangzhou ports as the branch line ports, this port cluster in southeast coastal areas focuses on container transportation, transportation between land and island, and passenger and freight transport across the Taiwan Straits. Mainly serving the economic and social development of Fujian Province and some inland provinces such as Jiangxi Province and meeting the needs of the "Three Direct Links" between China's mainland and the Taiwan region, it has made great contributions to the building of the Western Taiwan Straits Economic Zone.

(4) *Pearl River Delta port cluster*

The port cluster consists of ports in eastern Guangdong and the Pearl River Delta region, with Hong Kong International Shipping Center as the hub, the ports of Hong Kong, Shenzhen and Guangzhou as the main ports, taking the advantages of Hong Kong SAR as the economic, trade, financial, information and international shipping center. While consolidating Hong Kong SAR's position as an international shipping center, the ports of Guangzhou, Shenzhen, Zhuhai, and Shantou are the main ports, with corresponding development of ports of Shanwei, Huizhou, Humen, Maoming and Yangjiang to serve parts of south and southwest regions in China and strengthen exchanges of Guangdong Province with inland areas, Hong Kong SAR and Macao SAR.

(5) *Port cluster in southwest coastal areas*

The port cluster in this area consists of the ports of western Guangdong, Guangxi coastal areas, and Hainan Province. It mainly centers on the ports of Zhanjiang, Fangchenggang, and Haikou, and correspondingly develops the ports of Beihai, Qinzhou, Yangpu, Basuo, and Sanya to serve the development of the western areas as the main channel for the cargo transport from Southwest China to the Southeast Asian market, and guarantee the expansion of the cargo transport between Hainan Province and other areas. As an important node, industrial base and product distribution center of Pan-Beibu Gulf economic corridor, the port cluster plays a vital supporting role in regional economic development.

Nowadays, these major port clusters have yet formed the effective dynamics of competition and cooperation. The competition among them is extremely fierce, leading to not only a waste of resources but also further intensified vicious competition. Moreover, the functional division of regional ports is not reasonable, coupled with the seriously duplicate construction. The coordinated development among trunk ports, branch ports, and feeding ports has not been realized. The five major port groups should start with an analysis of their respective functions, locations, development potentials, hinterland resources, industrial distribution, and cluster characteristics, making clear of their own overall positioning, with international and domestic shipping market as the orientation, and make overall planning and reasonable layout. The aim is to develop a group of well-structured modern port clusters featuring complete functions, smooth flow of information, high quality and safety, as well as convenience and efficiency with environment friendliness, so as to meet the demands of regional economic and social development and the trend of economic globalization.

5.8.2 Implications and classifications of competition and cooperation between open ports

In terms of the development orientation and major functions, ports can be roughly divided into hub ports of global routes, transshipment ports of regional routes, sub-regional transshipment ports and small and medium-sized harbors with cargo ship berths. Competition and cooperation among ports are a win-win strategy adopted by ports with the same or overlapping economic hinterland in a particular region for the overall development strategy. The strategic alliance between ports can improve the ports' overall competition, and moderate competition is the driving force of port development. The trend of economic globalization and the development of the shipping alliance call for long-term win-win cooperation between ports to avoid destructive and malicious competition while improving the capability of ports to resist risks and realize market penetration. Through combining and joint use of their resources, management capabilities and core competence, the market viability and overall competitiveness of the ports will be enhanced.

There are many different ways to divide competition between ports. First, they can be divided according to the contents of the competition, namely price competition, service quality competition, terminal construction competition, and other competitions. Second, they can be divided according to the level of competition and the region in which it is located. They are mainly competitions at the international hub port level, which means the competition between the main port clusters in China and overseas port clusters and shipping centers. The competition among the port clusters in the Pearl River Delta, Yangtze River Delta, Bohai Sea Rim, Southeast Coast, and Southwest Coastal is moderate, but the competition between international hub ports is fierce. For example, the Pearl River Delta port cluster with Singapore port clusters, the Yangtze River Delta and Bohai Sea Rim port clusters with the Pacific coastal port clusters in Japan and Busan in South Korea. The competition among the same port cluster is mainly between the leading international hub ports or shipping centers, especially the leading operators (port enterprises). Competition between hub ports in the same region will weaken their international competitiveness to a considerable extent. The competition between Shanghai Port and Ningbo-Zhoushan Port in the Yangtze River Delta, and the competition between ports in the Bohai Bay region (such as Tianjin Port, Dalian Port, and Qingdao Port, etc.) are cases in point. It also includes the competition between the hub port and the surrounding small and medium ports and competition among port enterprises within the same port. The third kind of competition is divided according to the competitive industry. It can be divided into competition within the port industry as well as competition between the port and other transport industries (such as railway, highway, and civil aviation).

5.8.3 Major patterns of competition and cooperation among regional ports

In order to avoid blind and vicious competition and to promote common prosperity and development, port operators and enterprises often realize competition and cooperation through alliance. Because of the various forms of joint port strategies, regional port competition and cooperation patterns are also different. According to the classification of Professor Wang Chuanxu with Shanghai Maritime University, the patterns of competition and cooperation between regional ports are mainly divided into horizontal and vertical ones.

(1) *Horizontal competition and cooperation pattern among regional ports*

This pattern is mainly embodied in the pattern of competition and cooperation among ports to maximize their common interests. In China, the horizontal competition and cooperation pattern between regional ports can be roughly divided into three forms. The first is competition and cooperation in port investment and construction. Generally speaking, in order to further expand the existing and developing space, the large-scale ports will invest in the construction of self-operated port areas in their neighboring small ports due to limited construction resources, inadequate port shoreline, and inadequate water depth of port area or port waterway. Alternatively, to break the limits of administrative divisions, the large-scale ports will build self-operated port areas with other neighboring ports. For example, Ningbo-Zhoushan Port was established in 2006 to optimize and integrate the port resources in Zhejiang Province and compete with

Shanghai Port. At the same time, Ningbo Port and Zhoushan Port developed the container deep-water port area in Jintang Island to further strengthen port cooperation. There are also many examples of joint investment in other regional ports.

The second form is cooperation in port integration. With the implementation of domestic port management system reform, the principle of "one city, one port" and "one place, one port" has been put into practice. According to this principle, local governments should integrate several ports that used to be relatively independent in their respective jurisdictions into a unified port, and the regional port integration strategy mainly relies on administrative means. In order to mobilize the enthusiasm of all parties in the port and make use of the competition within the port to improve the overall competitiveness of the ports, the management system of the department of affairs can be adopted, which means to set up a port investment and construction group on the basis of the original several independent ports and to establish a number of subsidiaries. The group does not interfere in its subsidiaries' specific production and operation but adjusts its structure through investment to achieve the goal of rational utilization of resources. Determining the market position of each port according to its location will promote the effective integration of regional ports.

The third form is the establishment of port alliances. On the premise of not changing their property rights, ports belonging to different administrative regions within the same regional port cluster establish a port alliance organization to achieve complementary advantages, resources sharing, coordinated development, and to avoid vicious competition, duplicate construction and waste of resources. The purpose of establishing port alliances is to allocate transport and services effectively, maximize port capacity utilization and port services while minimizing port user costs. The usual form of regional port alliances is joint ports.

In the above horizontal competition and cooperation patterns, port investment and construction are prevailing among regional port clusters. The main reason is that this pattern can complement each other and achieve mutual benefit. Due to the disparity of strength and status between the two ports, it is impossible for them to become competitors. Horizontal competition promotes not only the development of regional port groups but also their overall competitiveness.

(2) *Vertical competition and cooperation pattern between regional ports*

This pattern mainly aims to build a perfect logistics transportation network among ports. For example, the port invests in the construction of its branch ports or feeding ports and builds a transport network with other means of transportation. To construct a multimode transport network and become its center, a trunk port or hub port often needs to form a vertical competition and cooperation relationship with other ports in the region. In order to realize competitive and cooperative development, the trunk ports can adopt the strategy of investing in constructing of the branch ports and form the alliance of the transit ports and the branch ports. For example, Shanghai Port has implemented the investment strategy in other ports in the Yangtze River Delta region due to its limited port resources and started cooperation at different levels in Chongqing, Wuhu, Yangzhou, Anqing, Ningbo, Nanchang, and Changsha.

Vertical competition and cooperation among regional ports have played an important role in improving the logistics transportation network and increasing transit cargo sources. However, in terms of the regional port vertical competition and cooperation pattern, there are risks in trunk ports, or hub ports' investment in the construction of small and medium-sized ports. These ports can serve as feeding ports for trunk ports or hub ports when the cargo sources are insufficient. However, with the economic development of the hinterland of small and medium-sized ports and the increasing supply of cargo sources, the port may gradually open up near-sea routes and become a branch port. This may lead to that the cargo source of the near-sear shipping line will no longer pass through the original trunk port and may divert some ocean shipping cargo sources from trunk ports, if the cargo supply of small and medium-sized ports continues to increase and when the port has sufficient cargo sources and opens up ocean shipping routes. In that case it may be further upgraded to a trunk port, which will not only affect the original trunk port cargo source but also become a competitor of the original trunk port.

5.9 Spatial statistical analysis of passenger capacity and cargo volume at provincial open ports in China

In spatial statistics, the nature of spatial aggregation (concentration) of similar things or phenomena is called spatial autocorrelation. Waldo Tobler's definition of "the first law of geography" is that "all attribute values on a geographic surface are related to each other, but closer values are more strongly related than distant ones". The correlation or relevance in space is one of the main reasons for the existence of order and pattern in nature. In geography, everything (phenomenon) in a spatial position has the characteristics of being different from other things (phenomena). This difference is called spatial heterogeneity.

In reference to the predecessors' research results and under the guidance of the principle of spatial statistical analysis, the author analyzed the inbound and outbound traffic data of all ports in 31 provinces (autonomous regions and municipalities directly under the central government) from 2007 to 2015, and used the exploratory spatial data analysis method to calculate the statistics of Global Spatial Autocorrelation Analysis (Moran's I) and the Local Indicators of Spatial Association(LISA), and drew Moran scatter plot, and the following conclusions were reached accordingly.

Firstly, generally speaking, from 2007 to 2015, the volume of inbound and outbound cargo in China has maintained rapid growth. The average annual growth of total import and export cargo was 10.94%, 11.15% at harbor ports, 10.30% at air ports and 7.17% at land ports (including highway and railway ports). The volume of inbound and outbound freight at ports of all provinces in China maintained a relatively rapid growth from 2007 to 2015, but that of each province was significantly different. The volume of inbound and outbound cargo in eastern coastal provinces was significantly larger than that in central and western regions. Among them, the volume of inbound and outbound cargo of Shandong has always been in the first place and Jiangsu Province has grown rapidly in recent years, from the fifth place in 2008 to the second place in 2015. Of the provinces with the lowest annual inbound and outbound cargo ranking, Qinghai, Ningxia, and Gansu have achieved a breakthrough from scratch, but their total volume is far less than these of the eastern coastal provinces.

Secondly, as for the relationship between the inbound and outbound cargo at ports and the province they are located, the empirical analysis shows that there is a positive spatial correlation between the total volume of inbound and cargo freight and the volume of inbound and outbound cargo at ports of various provinces in China. That means spatial agglomeration and its effect is increasing in regions with a high volume of inbound and outbound cargo represented by harbor ports. In contrast, the air ports and land transport ports show no obvious spatial agglomeration.

Thirdly, as for waterborne ports, Shandong, Zhejiang, Jiangsu, Tianjin, Shanghai, Hebei, Fujian, and other provinces have larger inbound and outbound cargo volume, and so do that of the neighboring regions. The above provinces are located in the Yangtze River Delta, the Bohai Sea Rim, and the southeast coastal areas with densely distributed ports of foreign trade. In recent years, the volume of import and export cargo in Guangdong, Liaoning, and Guangxi were large, but that of the surrounding ports was relatively small. Most of the central and western provinces in China (accounting for about 50% of the provinces in the country) have a quite small volume of inbound and outbound cargoes. This reflects the spatial autocorrelation and heterogeneity of inbound and outbound cargo volume of ports in various provinces and regions in China. The regional spatial agglomeration characteristics are obvious, highlighting the uneven development of port freight volume between coastal areas and mid-western regions.

Fourthly, in terms of air ports, from 2007 to 2015, the inbound and outbound cargo volume of each province's air ports was relatively stable. This is concentrated in Beijing, Shanghai, and Guangdong. Capital International Airport, Guangzhou International Airport, and Shanghai International Airport are the hub air ports in China.

Fifthly, in terms of land ports, the inbound and outbound cargo volume at land ports of most provinces was small, and that at land (highway and railway) ports is mainly concentrated in border areas. The majority of land transport highway and railway ports, as well as the most inbound and outbound cargo volume, were concentrated in Inner Mongolia, Xinjiang, Guangdong, Heilongjiang and Yunnan. Especially in recent years, Xinjiang has been enjoying a rapid growth in this respect.

5.10 Challenges in the opening up and development of ports

Effective management and making good use of the open ports and constantly improving their traffic capacity is vital for promoting the open economy's development and opening up to the outside world. After the founding of the People's Republic of China, especially since the reform and opening up, the opening and development of ports have made tremendous achievements. Meanwhile, it should be noticed that with the continuous improvement of opening up to the outside world, there is the bigger volume of foreign trade and more international exchanges, and port work becomes much more demanding with heavier tasks under new circumstances. The deep contradictions and problems of port layout, operation efficiency, exertion of functions, resource matching, access and exit and legal system construction in the process of opening and development of ports have been emerging. Attention should be made to address these problems and efforts should be made to solve them.

5.10.1 Disparities in transport volume standards and operational benefits between different ports

During the 11th Five-year Plan and the 12th Five-year Plan periods, the state set specific requirements for the standard of annual passenger capacity and cargo volume of different types of ports. Accordingly, the annual foreign trade cargo volume at the seaport in three years after the opening would be no less than 500,000 tons, and that at river port no less than 200,000 tons, the annual foreign trade cargo volume of boundary river port more than 50,000 tons or passenger capacity of more than 10,000 person-time. Before the opening of air ports, there were only some 20 domestic scheduled flights, and in three years after the opening, the volume of inbound and outbound freight would be no less than 30,000 tons or the number of entry-exit passengers no less than 50,000 person-time. The inbound and outbound freight volume was expected to achieve no less than 100,000 tons, or the number of entry-exit passengers no less than 100,000 person-time. The inbound and outbound cargo volume would be no less than 50,000 tons or the person capacity no less than 50,000 person-time after three years of the opening of land highway ports. The above annual passenger capacity and cargo volume standards remained the same at different ports during the 11th Five-year Plan and the 12th Five-year Plan periods. The ports approved by the State Council and opened for less than three years were not included in the statistical scope of the national port operations of the year.

Comparing the annual passenger capacity and cargo volume of open ports in China from 2005 to 2015, the standard-meeting rate of open ports in all provinces and regions in China was about 80%. Waterway ports had the highest standard-meeting rate, with an average annual rate of 85%, highway ports 84%, railway ports 77% and air ports 65%. On one hand, corresponding to the differences in regional economic development and environmental and geographical conditions, the operational benefits of all ports in China also indicated the gradient inequality between the coastal, inland and border areas. Among them, coastal ports had obvious advantages in operational benefits and profits, followed by the port in border areas in terms of standard-meeting rate of passenger traffic and freight volume. The inland ports had a heavy task of reaching the standard, and the operation benefits need to be further improved. On the other hand, there was a big gap between the operational benefits of ports of the same type, and the development gap between provinces was obvious. Those with better port development benefits were mainly located in the coastal areas and the strategic areas along the border. Comparatively speaking, operational benefits of some ports in inland and highway ports along the border did not reach the standard.

5.10.2 Big gap in the functioning of all types of open ports

Generally speaking, according to the classification and comparison of transportation modes, the operational efficiency of waterway and railway ports were better than that of highway ports, with the efficiency of air ports being the lowest. This was because more air ports were opened. With relatively limited passenger sources, the more ports divert, the less port traffic there is, and the more intense the competition among air ports is. In addition, most of the air ports with small radiating range are short-haul routes to the neighboring countries and cities, and most Chinese and foreign passengers choose to transfer abroad, which has reduced the passenger sources of inter-continental long-haul flights of the domestic airlines, leading to the hub port traffic decline and, to a certain extent, causing resources to be idled and wasted.

According to the classification and location of ports, the operational benefits of ports in coastal areas are generally higher than inland ones and those in border areas. The function of some hub ports and regional key ports will be further fulfilled to undertake the main task of passenger and cargo transport among similar ports in China and play an outstanding role in the country and even in the world. Also, the uneven development of ports in different regions is prominent. In some provinces, some ports have had a small volume of passengers and cargoes or no traffic in recent years, and the functions of ports can hardly be brought into full play.

5.10.3 Imbalanced distribution of provincial and inter-provincial ports

Open ports are the result of the economic and social development of a country and a region at a particular historical stage and belong to the historical category. The laws and track of opening ports are usually found with a specific historical imprint. Since the reform and opening up, the port opening has been progressively promoted with the gradient development of the regional economy. The selection of locations to open ports and the decision of the number of ports to open are related not only to the process of opening up, economic laws, natural laws, but also to many factors like the needs of local governments to develop an export-oriented economy, their achievement view to guide the local development and their assessment system. At present, as for the overall location of open ports in China, waterway ports are mostly distributed in the eastern coastal areas and areas along the Yangtze River, land highway and railway ports mostly in the northeast, northwest and southwest border areas, and air ports mainly in the eastern coastal areas, provincial capitals and cities with rich tourism resources.

At present, in terms of the number of ports opening to the outside world, by the end of 2015, there were 11 provinces with more than 10 ports respectively approved by the State Council, namely Guangdong(58 ports), Heilongjiang (25 ports), Jiangsu (25 ports), Guangxi (18 ports), Xinjiang (18 ports), Yunnan (17 ports), Inner Mongolia (16 ports), Jilin (16 ports), Shandong (16 ports), Liaoning (13 ports) and Fujian (11 ports).

More specifically, in addition to the ports approved by the State Council for opening up, there are still some former Category-2 ports in Guangdong, Fujian, Guangxi, Zhejiang, Yunnan and other provinces and autonomous regions which have been cleared up and rectified by the State Council and remain to be further classified and handled. In Guangdong Province, there are about 80 former Category-2 ports. Now those ports usually exist as customs follow-up supervision areas. In addition, there are entry-exit vehicle inspection centers and border passages established with the approval of the governments of Guangdong and Yunnan provinces and supervised by the local port check and inspection institutions. Local governments have included the former Category-2 ports, checkpoints for inbound and outbound vehicles and border passages with sizable volumes of passengers and cargoes into the port control. In contrast, some provinces in the central and western regions have only one port such as Sichuan, Guizhou, Shaanxi, Shanxi, Ningxia, and Qinghai, where only an airport has been established in the provincial capital city. Beijing, Jiangxi, Chongqing, and Gansu have only two or three ports, one of which is the capital city airport.

In China, if a coordinated approach of taking the country as a whole is adopted and the actual overall situation of economic and social development of each province and region is considered; and if the existing port resources of the whole country, especially the port clusters of key regions are optimized and integrated, the function of the open ports will be better played. However, the classified management, optimization, and integration on a national scale have not been carried out, resulting in a waste of port resources and affecting the overall efficiency of ports. Attention should be paid to the imbalance and unreasonable layout of ports in different provinces.

Things are more serious in some cities and their adjacent cities where there are two or more air ports within 300km, which do not meet the requirements of reasonable navigation distance of more than 500km. Generally speaking, short-distance transportation within 400km prefers road transport, the medium-distance transportation between 400km and 800km prefers railway transport, and long-distance transportation over 800km prefers air transportation. In some provinces, many water ports have been set up in one prefecture-level administrative region. The ports are located where the municipal institutions are located, the subordinate counties and municipalities, and even villages and towns. As a result, there are ports in cities, counties, and municipalities, and even in towns and townships with in the same administrative region, which is not in line with the concept of development of "one city, one harbor and one port", but also likely to waste the administrative law enforcement and human resources to a certain degree, increase administrative costs and lead to homogeneous vicious competition.

5.10.4   Inefficiency between resources and benefits of ports

Generally speaking, when the State Council approves or further expands the opening of ports, it will check the staffing of inspection institutions of a certain level, such as immigration inspection, customs, entry-exit inspection and quarantine and maritime (harbor port only) and a certain number of administrative law enforcement personnel. The more ports approved by the State Council are opened in provincial areas, the more check and inspection institutions and the staff there will be. As long as the ports are not canceled, integrated or optimized, the examination and inspection institutions and staffing at the ports are rarely adjusted. This has resulted in an uneven workload of personnel in different regions and different port examination and inspection institutions. Some ports along the coast may work for a whole week, day and night and even for 24-hour customs clearance. Some ports in the central and western regions and border areas may have much less annual business, and some ports are open for half a year and closed for another half because of their altitude, climate, traffic, and other conditions. We should not only be aware of this particular situation but also think of practical solutions.

The mismatch of port resources and benefits mainly lies in two aspects. On the one hand, the establishment and opening of ports are not only related to national interests but also directly related to local economic and social development. In order to open wider to the outside world, improve the environment to attract investment and promote the development of the export-oriented economy, much attention has been paid to the opening, construction, and development of ports. Some local governments take into account factors such as performance appraisal, so they actively apply for the construction of ports and expand the opening of ports. Some have unilaterally pursued the opening of ports and neglected the operational quality and efficiency of ports. As a result, some ports have not been put into operation for a long time or have had little transport volume and some others have not achieved satisfactory benefits. The port resources were wasted, and the port layout was not reasonable. Some ports had a small business volume and made a small profit for a long time. Some ports have not completed construction and received inspection for a long time after being approved by the state for opening up, and have not been put into operation or have not been operated for a long time with poor benefits, unable to fulfill their due functions. On the other hand, some ports with large transport volume and benefits are short of human resources, especially in developed coastal areas where the transport volume has kept increasing, while the construction of port infrastructure and supporting facilities and the personnel of administrative law enforcement are inadequate. These ports have long been overloaded.

5.10.5 Urgent demand for a dynamic management mechanism of port access and exit

The 11th Five-year Plan and the 12th Five-year Plan for the development of ports put forward specific requirements for the optimization and integration as well as access and exit of ports. Ports within the jurisdiction of provinces (autonomous regions and municipalities directly under the central government) that have not yet been opened for operation within three years since the date of the State Council's approval for opening up, will automatically start the exit mechanism, and when it is necessary to open again, the local government must re-apply for opening up and report in accordance with the approval procedures for the new port. At the same time, the application and opening of new ports in these areas should be strictly controlled.

However, the dynamic access and exit management mechanism has yet to be implemented. The main reason is that the entrance of ports generally needs a bottom-up application. The main body of the port's opening and exit is the local provincial government. Local governments including the provincial government where the ports are located are unwilling to apply for closing or revocation of the port in consideration of their performance appraisal, investment and output of construction funds for port opening, the personnel arrangement of port check and inspection institutions, and the follow-up problems of port revocation. Even if the competent national ports authority applies to closing the port according to the authorization, it should generally obtain the provincial government's consent where the port is located, and the competent national port inspection authorities. If they fail to reach a consensus, it is difficult to report it to the State Council for examination and approval. As a result, Once opened, the ports will never be closed. The problem that the performance of ports is not the decisive factor for opening or closing has been outstanding. At the same time, some ports that have been approved by the State Council for opening have not really opened up for many years, and some ports' functions have been declining with inefficiency. However, it is still difficult to close and adjust them timely. If the dynamic management mechanism of port access and egress is not implemented, it is different to achieve a balanced layout of the ports.

5.10.6　Prominent problem of the lagging legal system of ports

Since the reform and opening up, there is no special legal basis for the port opening, construction, operation and management in China except for only two administrative regulations respectively, namely, Provisions of the State Council on the Opening of Ports and The Notice of Port Leading Group on the Interim Provisions on the Scope of Responsibilities of Local Administrative Organs for Port Affairs. Most contents of these two regulations have lagged behind port management's practice because they were made a long time ago. In recent years, this has attracted the attention of the State Council and all sectors of society.

The opening, construction, and operation of ports throughout the country have lacked laws to regulate the relationship between the various departments of the ports, which has not only caused a gap and deficiency in the process of the rule of law in the country but also caused the inadequate effectiveness in the existing administrative regulations and normative documents on port management and finally resulted in many problems in practical work:

Firstly, the documents guiding port opening, acceptance inspection and investment are the old ones issued by the State Council shortly after the reform and opening up, which have not been revised in due course, and some of the contents failed to meet the actual needs now. Especially when the present port investment and financing system has undergone profound changes, the subjects of port construction and operation have been diversified. Therefore there is the problem that the responsibilities do not match the financial resources.

Secondly, the functions of institutions overlap with each other, and the effective linkage between departments is not enough. Port check and inspection institutions, immigration inspection, customs, entry-exit inspection and quarantine, and maritime departments have their own laws, and the laws and regulations implemented by the port inspection departments are overlapping and repeated which have increased the burden on enterprises. There are re-declarations and repeated inspections in customs clearance because the customs, inspection and quarantine institutions and even immigration inspection institutions have the rights to inspect import and export goods according to law. As a result, there are cases in which a batch of goods is repeatedly opened for checking.

Thirdly, as new forms of the port opening are constantly emerging, the scale of the opening is constantly expanding, the access and exit mechanism of ports are imperfect, and the layout of ports should be optimized and adjusted. Indeed, there is an urgent need for the rule of law. At the Third and Fourth Plenary Sessions of the 18th Central Committee of the CPC, new requirements have been put forward for port work and legal system construction. The port development should be strengthened under legal guarantee. At the same time, it is an urgent need to sum up the successful practices and experience of port work since the reform and opening up, so as to ensure improved institutions as well as rules and regulations. All these problems above need to be solved through legal system building.

5.10.7 Difficulties of coordination caused by decentralization of port management authorities

Port management involves not only immigration inspection, customs, entry-exit inspection and quarantine, maritime and other ports check and inspection institutions which belong to the central vertical management, but also local government port management departments, port service guarantee departments, entry-exit personnel, import and export enterprises, and other subjects. It involves different departments, industries and sectors. Besides, there is a strong interdependent relationship between the management bodies, which determines that the ports relevant departments must cooperate and effectively avoid port management fragmentation. At present, there are two main problems in the coordination of ports.

Firstly, the cooperation and coordination between port management institutions have not been smooth, and there is room for improvement. Each port inspection institution carries out its work according to its own laws, regulations and statutory responsibilities, and has strong independence. However, in fact, each institution must cooperate to accomplish the task better. The lack of mutual support and cooperation will directly affect the overall port traffic efficiency. If a port inspection institution introduces a reform measure, and other port inspection institutions fail to take supporting measures timely, the customs clearance efficiency will be affected to an extent. There is a need to strengthen further cooperation and coordination between port inspection and examination institutions. Local government departments in charge of ports should play an active role in ensuring the safe and smooth operation and management of ports and the effective play of the overall efficiency through collaboration.

Secondly, the management of ports involves many units at different levels, and the decentralization of central and local port management authorities makes it difficult to coordinate. The port's management should be fulfilled by the central government and the local governments respectively with different emphasis. According to the current division of port management, port planning and approval for opening, inspection and supervision and other management are concentrated in the central government, while the local government mainly undertakes port construction and operation management. The interwoven authorities have increased the difficulty of coordination, and the comprehensive management of ports needs to be further improved.

5.10.8   Lack of stable input and fixed channels of investment in port facilities construction

At present, there is a striking contradiction between insufficient investment in the construction and transformation of port check and inspection facilities and the sustained and rapid growth of port traffic. The reasons are as follows:

Firstly, the construction of port inspection facilities and maintenance lack long-term input mechanism and stable channels of investments. After the local government stopped levying port management fees in 1998, some ports which had opened earlier were short of funds for maintenance, renovation, and transformation. The aging and outdated facilities lagged behind the demands of port development.

Secondly, the construction standard of the national port check and inspection supporting facilities implemented nowadays were formulated in the 1990s, which has not been revised and improved, and the national port check and inspection facilities construction standards have not yet been promulgated and implemented. The competent departments of port inspection under the State Council, namely the Ministry of Public Security, the General Administration of Customs and the General Administration of Quality Supervision, Inspection and Quarantine, have promulgated their respective department rules and standards. Local governments have difficulties in implementing these different standards and requirements.

Thirdly, port check and inspection facilities lack integration. There exists the problem of duplicated and repeated inspection facilities construction of the port. To take the information construction of ports for example, different inspection departments at the ports have developed information systems suitable for them respectively, lacking business and resource integration at the national level, and failing to establish a well-organized information management operating system and a well-functioning public application platform.

Some of the above problems are left over from history, some are caused by the inadaptability of working mechanism and management system to the port development, and some by the lag of port legal construction and inadequate reform and innovation.

Through the analysis above in this chapter, it should be admitted that since the reform and opening up, China has made remarkable achievements in the opening, construction, and development of all kinds of ports, and the efficiency of ports has been improved year by year. Judging from its classification, the freight volume and international shipping capacity of waterway ports have risen to the forefront of the world. The opening of highway ports has promoted a good relationship with neighboring counties and the development of international road transport. The opening of railway ports has brought about a rapid development of international passenger and cargo transport, and the opening of air ports has realized the mutual promotion of international air transport. However, while we hail the achievements, we should admit that there are still problems in the aspects of operation efficiency, function exertion, reasonable layout, resource matching, access and exit of ports in the country, which need to be studied and solved as a whole.

Chapter 6
Opening Mechanism and Management System of Ports in China

As far as China's ports' opening mechanism is concerned, the power of examination and approval of open ports belongs to the central government in which the State Council or departments authorized have the authority of examination and approval. Open ports can be divided into two categories: official and temporary. The official opening ports include newly open ports and expanded open ports. When it comes to the management system of China's open ports, after the founding of the People's Republic of China, especially since the reform and opening up, the management system of ports, inspection institutions, and the overall management system have undergone a transformation with the national structural reform.

6.1 Examination and approval mechanism of open ports in China

Generally speaking, whether or not a country (region) opens its ports, airports, stations and cross-border passages to the outside world is affected by internal and external factors. These factors include the specific geographical location and transportation convenience of ports, air ports, railway stations, and cross-border channels to be opened, the reasonable distribution of ports within the city and provincial administrative region, the present situation of the local export-oriented economic development and the anticipated needs, and endogenous demands like the existing and expected passenger and cargo volume. It also includes exogenous requirements such as the status and role of the specific projects to be opened in the overall political, economic and diplomatic framework of the country and in the development of regional economy and society, the assessment and examination opinions of the relevant departments of the state's port administration on the projects to be opened, the construction of the ports to be opened, and the bottom-line control of operating costs. The complexity of the factors affecting open ports determines the complexity of the examination and approval mechanism. The declaration subject, examination and approval subject and examination and approval mechanism of China's officially open ports and temporary ones are different.

6.1.1 Approval mechanism for officially open ports in China

In accordance with the current administrative regulations on port administration Provisions of the State Council on the Opening of Ports, ports to open shall follow the following procedures.

(1) *Application.* The provincial governments or relevant state departments are to submit a written application to the State Council for setting up new ports or expanding open ports in accordance with the needs of export-oriented economic development. The following material should be attached to the application for open ports: the feasibility study report on the ports' opening up, and materials concerning the basic conditions, passenger and cargo volume, economic benefits and development prospects during the past three years; plans for institutional setup and staffing in check and inspection based on passenger and cargo transport; inspection sites, plans for facilities of office and living, as well as investment budgets and funding sources.

(2) *Examination.* Examinations on whether the project has been listed in the national five-year development plan for ports and the annual examination plan for ports' opening up. If it has been included in both of the plans, the trial procedure may be initiated. If it has been listed in the national five-year development plan for ports but not in the annual examination plan for ports' opening up, the trial can be started only after it is added to the latter during the five-year plan period. For projects that have not yet been included in the national five-year development plan for ports, the trial procedures shall not be initiated unless the project is added into both plans.

(3) *Audit and evaluation.* In conjunction with the relevant departments of the state, the state port administration shall examine emphatically the contents and basis of the documents submitted by the provincial people's governments for the project in trial procedure. The audit mainly focuses on: Whether the county-level administrative area where the port project is located is an area for opening up approved by the State Council; whether it is in line with national military and national defense requirements; whether the optimization and integration scheme, concrete measures, and implementation schedule have been formulated for the same type of ports in the same provincial administrative region; whether the infrastructure of the port project has been examined

and approved in accordance with the procedures of the construction of the state, and whether the production and safety facilities conform to the state regulations; whether the feasibility study on economic and social benefits of ports' opening has been completed and whether the standard of the transport volume of the open port can be reached. Moreover, before international aviation routes are to be opened, there should be no less than 10 domestic scheduled flights in inland and border airports and no less than 15 domestic scheduled flights in coastal airports; whether the projects of border highway and railway open ports have been listed in the agreements between the governments of the two countries on the border ports and their management systems or agreed via diplomatic channels; whether a plan for the construction of check and inspection facilities in the port has been stipulated and the source of funds has been definite; whether a solution to inspection personnel required by port inspection and supervision has been worked out.

(4) *Report for approval.* If the port opening projects are fully qualified, the state department in charge of ports shall submit them to the State Council for examination and approval according to the procedure.

(5) *Organizing acceptance inspection.* After the State Council approves or expands the opening of a particular port, the state port administrative department shall organize the state acceptance inspection.

(6) *Announcement.* After the state has accepted a port opening project, the provincial people's government or the department in charge of the transportation industry in the locality entrusted by the state port authority shall declare the ports' formal opening up to the outside world.

6.1.2 Examination and approval mechanism for a temporary opening

According to the Provisions of the State Council on the Opening of Ports, temporary entry-exit of personnel, goods, and means of transport into or out of China's non-open areas shall be subject to the approval of relevant state authorities.

The examination and approval authority for temporary opening is as follows: Firstly, for vessels of Chinese and foreign nationality temporarily entering and leaving China's closed ports and coastal waters, the competent transportation department shall, in conjunction with the relevant state departments, examine and approve the application made by the port administrative department of the provincial government or the provincial maritime departments. Secondly, for Chinese and foreign civil aircraft taking off and landing temporarily from China's non-open airports, as well as Chinese and foreign personnel, vehicles, goods, and articles temporarily entering and leaving China's non-open land border areas, according to the application of the provincial government's port management departments, the state port management departments, in conjunction with the relevant state departments, shall conduct the examination.

Considering that the temporary opening requires prior coordination of the inspection of entry-exit, the application for the temporary opening should be approved by the check and inspection institutions and relevant departments directly under the stationed port. In principle, the time limit for the temporary opening of a single batch shall not exceed six months. If a subsequent continuous temporary entry-exit is necessary, it should be approved according to the procedure.

6.2 Restructuring and development of China's port management system

After the founding of the People's Republic of China, especially since the start of reform and opening up, China's port management system has experienced several restructuring. At present, there are port management agencies at the national and provincial levels. At each entry-exit port approved by the State Council for opening up, there are usually port check and inspection institutions directly administered by the central government such as immigration inspection, customs, entry-exit inspection and quarantine, and maritime agencies (only at water ports). From the perspective of institutional transformation, the formation and development of China's current port management system has its specific historical background and reasons. There are significant differences between the periods before and after the reform and opening up.

6.2.1 Miscellaneous cross-border management departments before reform and opening up

Before the reform and opening up, due to the relatively small import and export volume, a comprehensive management agency and functional departments hadn't been set up at China's open ports, which were mainly managed by relevant departments in implementation of professional management with separate responsibility. Port management departments involved many professional institutions such as immigration inspection, customs supervision, sanitation and quarantine, animal and plant quarantine, commodity inspection, food inspection, port supervision, ship inspection, etc. At the same time, they also needed the coordination and cooperation of many other departments such as foreign trade management, port handling, transportation, logistics service and so on. Since these institutions mechanisms involved the central, the local, and the military systems, an independent and unified management system for port inspection has not been formed. In the process of customs clearance management, due to the overlapping management scope and inspection items, customs supervision and management of the ports were independent, leading to contradictions and adverse impact to the outside world. In some cases, low loading and unloading efficiency of foreign trade ports, stagnant cargo ships, poor port services occurred from time to time.

The Central Committee of the CPC and the State Council have been attaching great importance to port work. As early as February 1973, the State Council issued On Situations and Improvement of Port Work in which suggestions for the improvement of the existing problems in port work and the working principle of "centralized leadership, active cooperation, and unified external relations" were put forward. In the early days of reform and opening up when the door was first opened to the outside world, with the development of export-oriented economy, acceleration of foreign economic and trade cooperation, and cultural and technological exchanges with foreign countries, it was imperative for open ports, especially coastal open ports, to be operated safely and smoothly, otherwise import and export goods would be stranded and jammed, and contract would be breached, which would undoubtedly affect the reform and opening up. In order to draw lessons from foreign port management experience, the State Economic Commission (SEC) carried out domestic and overseas investigations of port work and put forward policies and suggestions, which were highly valued by the leadership of the Central Committee of the CPC and the State Council. Effective measures have been taken to solve the existing problems and strengthen the organization, leadership, and comprehensive management of port work.

6.2.2 Gradual implementation of vertical management by port inspection institutions since reform and opening up

Since the start of the reform and opening up, professional port management institutions, which perform the functions of inspection, supervision, monitoring, examination, and quarantine, have resumed the vertical management system and a specialized management model was implemented. The practice has been carried out as follows:

Firstly, national customs has implemented vertical management. In February

1980, the State council promulgated the Decision on the Reform of the Customs Administration System, which puts the national customs system under the central government's unified administration. Base on the Customs Administration Bureau of the Ministry of Foreign Trade, the General Administration of Customs (the sub-ministerial level) was re-established as an agency directly under the State Council, practicing unified management of the national customs houses, staff and operations. Since then, customs agencies throughout the country have been under the unified leadership of the General Administration of Customs, and their affiliations are not subject to administrative regions.

Secondly, the national commodity inspection authorities have gradually implemented a unified vertical management system. In February 1980, the State Council approved the State administration of Import and Export Commodity Inspection as a state-level administration under the Ministry of Foreign Trade to replace the Commodity Inspection Bureau of the Ministry of Foreign Trade. As subordinate organizations of the State Administration, the import and export commodity inspection institutions in various localities are subject to the dual leadership of both the State Administration and provincial governments. In 1994, the State Administration of Import and Export Commodity Inspection was upgraded to a Vice-ministerial State Bureau implementing a line management system.

Thirdly, the State has set up the Animal and Plant Quarantine Agencies at major ports. In November 1980, the State Council approved the establishment of Animal and Plant Quarantine offices at major national ports to be directly affiliated to the Ministry of Agriculture and under the dual leadership of both the Ministry of Agriculture and provincial governments. In February 1982, the Ministry of Agriculture established the State General Institute of Animal and Plant Quarantine. In 1994, with the approval of the State Council, the Institute was renamed the State Animal and Plant Quarantine Bureau, managing all animal and plant quarantine agencies stationed at various ports throughout the country.

Fourthly, a harbor supervisory administration under the management of transportation departments has been set up. In 1984, the Ministry of Communications established a special water safety regulatory agency—the Port Authority—to implement vertical management.Thereafter, the State decided to reform the supervision and management system of water safety by integrating the functions of the Harbour Supervisory Bureau and the Ship Inspection Bureau under the Ministry of Communications, and transferred the management to the Maritime Security Administration.

Fifthly, in 1985, the armed police forces that undertook border inspection and management were transferred from the armed police forces to the Frontier Defense Bureau of the Ministry of Public Security.

Sixthly, in May 1988, the State Council approved the proposal put forward by the Ministry of Public Health to establish the National Public Health and Quarantine General Office, and reassigned the public health and quarantine institutions established at major ports throughout the country to the line management of Ministry of Public Health.

Seventhly, after 1998, the State Council decided to establish the State Entry-Exit Inspection and Quarantine Bureau under the administration of the General Administration of Customs with a merge of inspection on sanitation, animals and plants, and commodities. Later on, the State Entry-Exit Inspection and Quarantine Bureau were merged with the State Administration of Quality Supervision to form the General Administration of Quality Supervision, Inspection and Quarantine at the ministerial level directly under the State Council.

6.2.3 Restructuring of the state and local port management agencies after reform and opening up

Firstly, in the early years of reform and opening up, in view of the actual situation of import and export and port management in foreign trade, in order to attach importance to and strengthen the leadership of port work from the national level and ensure the smooth collection and distribution of coastal ports, the State Council issued the Notice on Strengthening the Leadership of Port Organizations in 1978 and set up the State Council Port Leading Group and its office. The group and its office determined the policy, scope, and model of comprehensive management of ports with a requirement that all open coastal ports set up offices under the unified leadership of local governments with responsibility for the unified management of port work.

Secondly, a comprehensive reinforcement of the organization and leadership in port work began. To better promote domestic reform and opening up to the outside world, in January 1984, the State Council issued the Notice on Further Strengthening the Leadership of Port Work, renaming its leading group of harbors and ports as the leading group of ports. The group leader was Li Peng, then Vice Premier of the State Council. Later, according to the division of work among the State Council leaders, Li Lanqing and others directly led the port work. Correspondingly, the comprehensive management and coordination service functions of ports were strengthened at the national and local levels during the period. From 1978 to 1993 when the State Council Leading Group and its offices were functioning, the local people's governments where the ports were opening up established the Port Management Committees (Port Office), and some vice-governors (vice-chairmen and vice-mayors) of provincial governments in charge of port work also directly served as directors of Port Management Committees.

Thirdly, there was gradually reinforcement of the construction of the legal system at ports. In September 1985, the State Council promulgated Provisions of the State Council on the Opening of Ports, which clearly defined the ports, the specific criteria for the division of the first and second types of ports, the opening and closing of ports, set the relevant requirements for the establishment of port check and inspection institutions, specified the procedures for the approval and acceptance inspection of the opening of ports, and established the examination of temporary entry-exit to the non-opening areas of China and funding sources of port inspection and facilities construction. In April 1987, the General Office of the State Council issued the Circular of the General Office of the State Council Concerning Transmission of the Interim Provisions of the Leading Group of Ports on Functions of Local Administrative Organs for Port Affairs, which clarified the specific responsibilities of local port administrations, the principles for coordinating arbitration and the rights and obligations for local port administrations to perform, legally supporting the implementation of responsibilities for local port administrations. The two regulatory documents of the State Council mentioned above were later defined as administrative rules and regulations, and are still effective and have made important contributions to the development of China's port opening up. In addition, in order to strengthen the specialized management of ports, the state has enacted, promulgated, revised and improved laws and regulations such as The Customs Law, The Law on Entry-Exit Administration Law, The Law on Import and Export Commodity Inspection, The Frontier Health and Quarantine Law, The Law on the Entry and Exit Animal and Plant Quarantine, Regulations on Frontier Inspection and the detailed supporting provisions or methods in implementation. Therefore, port management gradually stepped into the track of legislation.

Fourthly, after the institutional reform of the State Council in March 1998, the state and local governments abolished the separate port management agencies. At the national level, after the cancellation of the National Port Office, its functions of port planning and examination were assigned to the General Administration of Customs, and the Port Planning Office was set up in the General Administration of Customs. In the subsequent reform of local government organizations, with the abolition of the National

Port Office, the local port management institutions have been adjusted, weakened or abolished. The port management departments of provinces, autonomous regions, and municipalities nationwide were of different attributions and levels. The functions, institutions, and staffing of the port management have been assigned to other departments. Only a few places have retained the independent management system of ports.

Fifthly, the State has further strengthened the management, guidance and coordination of port work, since the beginning of the 21st century, especially since China's accession to the World Trade Organization (WTO), in order to fully participate in the process of economic globalization, and to further improve the efficiency of customs clearance of ports. In May 2006, the State Commission Office of Public Sectors Reform approved the renaming of the Port Planning Office of the General Administration of Customs as the National Office of Port Administration and gave it the functions of guiding and coordinating the work of local government ports. By then, the state port administration department had been reestablished after its revocation for nearly ten years. In recent years, with the reestablishment of national port management agencies, provincial governments and major port cities have resumed the establishment of specialized agencies or agencies affiliated to internal agencies under the port management institution.

6.2.4 Division of major responsibilities of port management and inspection institutions at the present stage

At present, the main divisions of responsibilities of port management functional departments and port check and inspection institutions are: according to the principle of graded management, the state port management department, as the national port management institution, is responsible for: the study and proposal of the overall planning of all kinds of open ports and the specific measures for port regulations and their implementation; according to the general needs of the State Council, organizing and coordinating relevant departments in the customs clearance at ports guide local governments in port affairs. The administrative departments of the local governments at or above the county level, as the administrative organizations of the local ports, are mainly responsible for the work of the ports within their respective areas. The primary duties are: managing and coordinating port work in the region; implementing the principles, policies and regulations of the Central Committee of the CPC and the State Council on port work, and formulating detailed rules for implementation in accordance with the specific conditions of the local ports; the declaration and opening up of ports in the region; organizing the goods collecting and distributing to ensure smooth operation. They are also responsible for supervising and urging the check and inspection units at the ports to supervise, inspect and quarantine entry-exit personnel, means of transport, cargoes and articles in accordance with their respective duties and regulations; guiding and coordinating the port work of local government at lower levels, and the working relations among the relevant units at the ports; checking and urge the organization and implementation of port planning, construction and restructuring in the region.

The inspection institutions of each port independently perform their duties according to respective laws and regulations. Border inspection agencies are mainly responsible for the certification and inspection of entry-exit personnel at ports. Customs agencies are mainly responsible for the supervision and inspection of entry-exit goods, articles and means of transport at ports. The entry-exit inspection and quarantine institutions are mainly responsible for quarantine inspection of entry-exit personnel and goods at ports. Established at waterborne ports, the maritime agencies are mainly responsible for the entry-exit foreign ships, the supervision, and management of port waters in China, ship supervision, and navigation management.

6.3 Experimental results and implications of the port management system reform in Shenzhen

6.3.1 Background of the port management system reform in Shenzhen

Since the start of reform and opening up in Shenzhen, especially since the establishment of special economic zones, the opening and construction of Shenzhen port have been developing at high speed. Shortly before Hong Kong's return to the motherland, the Shenzhen port work has made fruitful achievements. However, a careful examination and comparison with the Hong Kong port management showed that the port management model established under the planned economic system in Shenzhen was incompatible with the development of the market economy and the demand for opening up. At that time, contradictions had arisen. For instance, some businesses in port check and inspection departments were overlapping with repeated inspection, charges and inspection links, which aggravated the burden of import and export enterprises, affecting the efficiency of customs clearance and reducing the competitiveness of the port. The Ministry of Communications and Guangdong Province had set up two sets of regulators with the same function in the same waters. The coexistence of "one water area with two supervisors", i.e. the ministry and the province, made the administrative relationship complicated and was not conducive to unified management. The substandard caliber and malpractices of a small number of staff members in the entry-exit links of the ports hurt the image of the opening up to the outside world. These problems had not only restricted Shenzhen's further development and opening up, but also made it impossible to meet the needs of Hong Kong's return to the motherland in 1997 and a better cooperation between Shenzhen and Hong Kong SAR.

In early 1993, the Shenzhen Port Authority, after in-depth investigation and study, submitted the Survey Report on Restrictions on Port Development to the State Council. Li Lanqing, then Vice Premier of the State Council, attached great importance to the report and made important instructions for the pilot reform of the port management system in Shenzhen. In order to implement the deployment requirements of the State Council, the Shenzhen Port and Port Management Mechanism Reform Team was formed at the national level in early 1994, including the State Commission for Restructuring the Economic System, the State Economic and Trade Commission, the Ministry of Communications and the Shenzhen Municipal Government.

6.3.2 Partial structural reform of Shenzhen ports and the steady progress of the pilot program

The management system reform at Shenzhen ports started from the structural reform, and gradually expanded to other fields. In September 1993, the National Port Office issued The Notice on A Trial Scheme for Simplifying the Inspection Procedures in Yantian Port. The plan proposed that when international ships enter the port, inspection units generally do not check on board; telecommunications quarantine is implemented in international ships from non-epidemic areas; the transit containers will not be opened for inspection if the boxes are undamaged with good seals and in normal conditions. Import and export containers can be submitted for prior check and inspection in the mainland of China, which dramatically simplifies inspection procedures.

In February 1994, the General Office of the State Council transmitted the State Economic and Trade Commission's Opinions on Improving the Management of Shenzhen Land Transport Ports. It required that centralized customs declaration and inspection, one sampling, joint inspection of flowing operations and one-stop check and inspection service be carried out on a trial basis. Cargo inspection was gradually reduced from 4 stops to 2 stops. All check and inspection units at ports implemented unified charges. Two cargo corridors were opened at Huanggang port with 24 hours customs clearance.

In order to simplify the customs clearance process, on May 1, 1995, Huanggang Port Health Inspection took the lead in withdrawing the inspection passage, and implemented pre-declaration visa in health quarantine. The partial reform of the port and land port management system in Shenzhen has achieved remarkable results and evoked positive social responses.

On the basis of local reform and rigorous investigation and demonstration, the State Commission for Restructuring the Economic System and the State Economic and Trade Commission drew up the Pilot Scheme on Management Structural Reform at Shenzhen Port (hereinafter referred to as the Pilot Scheme), which was approved by the State Council. In July 1995, the General Office of the State Council transmitted the pilot scheme. According to the scheme, the reform aimed to establish a port management mechanism that is legitimate, effective, and easily accessible, featuring good service, coordinated management, reasonable charge and international practices, with a port operation mechanism separating government functions from enterprise management, to ensure unification and coordination, fair competition and high efficiency. Therefore, Shenzhen's opening up and economic development could be promoted to a better role as a special economic zone.

The Pilot Scheme proposed 11 suggestions: straightening out the work relationship in the inspection; developing a pilot project of professional immigration inspectors; reforming the management system of health inspection, animal and plant inspection and commodity inspection; simplifying the inspection procedures; improving work efficiency; reforming the port charge system; strengthening the building of a clean government and establishing a binding mechanism; reforming port administrative institutions; reforming the management system of port supervision; reforming pilotage management system; implementing a modern port enterprise system; gradually opening the service market in its ports to the outside world.

6.3.3 Active promotion of comprehensive port management system reform

In July 1995, the State Commission for Restructuring the Economic System and the State Economic and Trade Commission held a work meeting on the pilot reform of the Shenzhen port management system. The event marked the pilot project of the structural reform on management at Shenzhen Ports has entered the stage of comprehensive reform.

In accordance with the overall requirements of the Pilot Scheme, relevant departments of the State Council and of Guangdong and Shenzhen made arrangements for implementation. In August of the same year, the National Port Office formulated the Implementation Plan for Structural Reform on Management at Shenzhen Port Pilot Scheme, working out the corresponding supporting measures and clear division of labor and the specific reform schedule, with a monthly work inspection and coordination meeting on the agenda. Shenzhen municipal government attached great importance to this reform and took it as the most important task in its work. At the same time, the State Commission Office of Public Sectors Reform, the National Development and Reform Commission, the Ministry of Finance, the Ministry of Public Security, the Ministry of Communications, the General Administration of Customs, the National Office of Port Administration, the State Sanitation Inspection Bureau, the State Animal and Plant Inspection Bureau, the State Commodity Inspection Bureau and other departments worked out supporting reform measures with relevant departments in Shenzhen and the check and inspection points stationed in Shenzhen.

In December 1995, the State Commission for Reconstructing Economic System and the State Economic and Trade Commission convened a meeting to examine and implement the pilot scheme of Shenzhen port management mechanism reform, summarized the progress of the pilot project, and put forward suggestions and work arrangements for the next step. In June 1996, Li Lanqing received a report on the progress of the Shenzhen port management mechanism reform. In view of the existing problems in the reform and the future focus, he stressed that the final results of the Shenzhen port pilot reform should be extended to the whole country. By the end of 1997, 18 supporting measures for the reform of the Shenzhen port management mechanism had been issued, and all the reform measures were implemented, reaching the anticipated goals.

6.3.4　Major achievements in the Shenzhen port management system reform

After three years of practice and exploration, achievements have been made in Shenzhen port management system reform.

Firstly, port inspection procedures were streamlined and simplified to improve the overall efficiency. Through the reform, we have streamlined the inspection work relationship among the "three inspections" including health inspection, animal inspection, and commodity inspection, and made a beneficial exploration for the "three inspections in one" in the future practice. The mode of "on-the-spot supervision at ports in which the immigration inspectors inspect people, the customs controls the goods, the health inspection, the animal and plant inspection do not work on the ports by keeping the on-site workshops with the strengthened follow-up supervision, and cooperation with the immigration inspection and the customs control." The mode was in conformity with international practices and achieved the preliminary goal of both strictly guarding the national gates and the work objectives of focusing on efficiency.

Secondly, measures were taken to reform port charges and further standardize the charging policy. Port charges were managed by the central government following the two lines of "revenue and expenditure." The merger and reduction of the charges of "three inspections" to alleviate the burden on import and export enterprises and cargo owners and increase the efficiency were well received by all circles of society.

Thirdly, immigration inspection professionals were brought in on a trial basis. Immigration inspection staff was transferred from active service soldiers to professional police and incorporated into the management of national civil servants, which laid a good foundation for the future exploration of professional immigration inspection.

Fourthly, the port management system was straightened out to gradually improve the efficiency of port operation. The Shenzhen Water Safety Supervision Bureau under the Ministry of Communications was set up. The Shenzhen Port Authority was included in the local government, and the history of "one water area with two supervisions" (harbor affairs and harbor supervision) in Shenzhen waters came to an end. Competition mechanism was introduced into the port service market and gradually opened to the outside world. Some drawbacks brought about by the monopoly of the industry were being solved.

Fifthly, advanced technologies were made good use of in improving the service of port supervision. In the course of the pilot reform, with the support of the higher authorities and the local government, the check and inspection points at Shenzhen ports have improved their human resources and efficiency with the development of science and technology, which significantly improved the overall level of supervision and service as well as their work efficiency.

6.4 Comparison of the opening mechanism and the management system of China's ports with other countries

6.4.1 Comparison of port opening mechanism between China and other countries

(1) Major similarities are reflected in three aspects: Firstly, the right to examine and approve the opening of ports is in the central authority, and the central government decides whether to open up the ports to the outside world. Secondly, highway ports, railway ports, waterborne ports, and cross-border passages at the border should be included in the agreements between the governments of the two countries on border ports and their management policies, or the two countries concerned have reached complete agreement at the diplomatic level. After the two sides have reached a consensus, competent authorities of the respective national ports shall take the lead in fulfilling the national examination and approval procedures. With the approval and consent of the respective central government and the confirmation and completion of the construction of the diplomatic channels between the two countries, they would announce the opening-up operation. Thirdly, according to the laws of various countries, persons, goods, articles, and means of the transport entering and leaving the country through land (railway, highway) ports, air ports, and water ports should be subject to inspection, examination, and supervision.

(2) Major differences are reflected in three aspects: Firstly, special port management agencies are established in China at the national level with different duties and tasks. At present, apart from China, other countries have not set up special port management institutions. It should be noted that before March 2016, the Russian central government established a special port management agency—the Russian Border Construction Agency, which was mainly responsible for the national port planning, opening up, border port construction and restructuring. The agency was revoked in 2016 due to the reform of the Russian central government institutions and its function was assigned to the Ministry of Transport in Russia. Other countries have not set up special national port management agencies, and the relevant departments act its function as the port management authorities.

Secondly, organizations responsible for examination and approval for open ports are different. China, like Russia, Kazakhstan, Vietnam, Mongolia, and other neighboring countries, the right for examination and approval of official opening of ports to the outside world is in the central government. In the United States, France, and some other countries, the opening of ports (harbors, airports) does not need to be approved by the central government.

Thirdly, the state inspection institutions stationed at ports are different in their responsibilities and tasks. China's entry-exit ports are usually stationed with frontier inspection (equivalent to immigration bureaus in foreign countries), customs, entry-exit inspection and quarantine agencies, and maritime agencies (only water ports) and other port check and inspection institutions. Russia's frontier ports retain two agencies: immigration inspection and customs enforcement. Immigration inspection is mainly responsible for the supervision of entry-exit personnel, while customs are mainly responsible for the supervision of entry-exit goods, means of transport, and baggage and other goods carried by entry-exit personnel. In addition, the customs also performs the functions of port transport supervision. Kazakhstan's frontier ports also retain immigration inspection and customs agencies. The customs agency performs the functions of port transportation, health, and animal and plant quarantine supervision. In some European countries, there are only immigration bureaus and customs agencies at ports. Check and inspection departments do not enforce the law at the ports, and their functions are performed by the customs.

6.4.2　Main characteristics and implications of port management systems in other countries

(1) Notable characteristics of port management systems in other countries. Firstly, many countries' border and port management mainly follow the principle of "Customs in change of the supervision of goods, and Immigration/Border Defense Bureau of people," which optimizes the integration of border regulatory agencies and port check and inspection institutions. Efforts are made to minimize the costs of administrative law enforcement and maximize the sharing of law enforcement resources through port management, reorganization of law enforcement agencies, and cooperation in law enforcement across agencies and departments. On the premise of safeguarding national security and national interests, the port should be operated safely, smoothly and efficiently so as to better promote economic and trade cooperation, people exchanges and trade facilitation.

Secondly, more attention is paid to the intensification of port management functions. After the "9·11 Terrorist Attacks", the United States implemented the reform of the port management system with the establishment of the Customs and Border Protection Agency (CBP), realizing the unification of border management and protection, which transformed the traditional respective function of different departments to integrated management at the national level with maximization of the effectiveness of resources. In this aspect, the move adopted by the US has set an example for other countries to follow in port management.

(2) Implications from overseas port management systems. By analyzing and comparing China's and foreign port management systems and the establishment and responsibilities of check and inspection institutions, the following implications can be drawn: on the one hand, we should further promote the implementation of the Decision of the Central Committee of the Communist Party of China on Some Major Issues Concerning Comprehensively Deepening the Reform, particularly in the aspect of the administrative law enforcement system. The third Plenary Session of the 18th Central Committee of the CPC stressed that it is necessary to learn from advanced management experience of other countries, deepen the reform and innovation of port management and port inspection system, which still has room for improvement and great potentials to explore. At the same time, under the existing port management system, we should continue to push forward the reform in coordination, breaking down the barriers of port management departments and administrative divisions, strengthening the organization, leadership and overall coordination of port work of the central government, facilitating the cooperation among ports departments, and strengthening a more systematic, integrated and coordinated port reform and innovation to promote synergy generation and the overall effect.

On the other hand, we should see that functional integration is the trend for development of port management system reform. According to the practice of port management in the EU Member States and other countries, most ports are under the policy of "Customs in charge of supervision of goods, and Immigration/Border Defense Bureau of people." The US, the UK, Canada, and other countries have carried out consolidated supervision of entry-exit ports by a comprehensive law enforcement department, truly realizing the "single window" and "one-stop" service among entry-exit links, significantly improving the level of port supervision services. It is worthy of deep thinking about how to learn from advanced foreign experience to promote the overall design and scientific construction of the restructure of the port entry-exit process and optimize the functions of port check and inspection institutions.

Chapter 7
Theory, Practice, Experience, and Implications of Development of Open Ports in China

Since the founding of the People's Republic of China, China's port opening and development has experienced three periods: gradually opening after the founding of the People's Republic of China in 1949, reform and opening up after the Third Plenary Session of the 11th Central Committee of the CPC in 1978, and the deepening reform and opening up in an all-round way after the 18th National Congress of the CPC in 2012, each of which has its distinct characteristics of the times and its own thoughts of opening. Since the 18th National Congress of the CPC, under the correct guiding principles from the CPC General Secretary Xi Jinping's major speeches and his new ideas, thinking, and strategies for governance of China, the port work has been closely centered on the overall task of serving the country by comprehensive implementation of the new development philosophy, adapting to and addressing the new normal in economic development. Efforts have been made to put into practice the general principle of pursuing progress while ensuring stability, focusing on supply-side structural reform and pushing ahead reform and innovation and practical exploration, through which new achievements have been made, new experiences have been accumulated and new inspirations are gained.

7.1 Major opening–up thoughts of China in different periods

Great times forge great people; great moves create great history;great ideas promote great changes, and great strategies contribute to the great cause. Reform and opening up is a revolution in which the Communist Party of China leads the Chinese people of all ethnic groups to forge ahead in the new era. It is the only way for the

248

country to be prosperous and strong, the nation to be rejuvenated and the people to be happy. It is the most distinctive feature of the times and the greatest dividend for the long-term development of contemporary China. It is also the decisive factor for the bright future of China, the realization of China's Two Centenary Goals and the great rejuvenation of the Chinese nation.

7.1.1 China's opening-up thoughts from the founding of the People's Republic of China to the start of reform and opening up

After the founding of the People's Republic of China, the country's opening up ideas were mainly from Mao Zedong thought. With distinct characteristics of the times, dialectical, consistent, and strongly political, it is built on the basis of inheriting Marx, Engels and Lenin's thoughts on opening to the outside world and gradually formed and developed along with China's new democratic revolution and socialist construction practice. Politically, it is based on Marxist theory and draws lessons from experiences and specific systems of Western capitalist countries; economically, it proposes to absorb and utilize foreign and overseas Chinese funds, to advocate "doing business" with foreigners, to develop foreign economic and trade relations, to learn science and technology and management experience from foreign countries; culturally, it criticizes two wrong tendencies—blind exclusion of or copying from foreign culture, and suggests learning from advanced foreign cultures. Zheng Guorui divides it into three levels, namely, the logical starting point originates from Marx's "world history" theory, the practice from Lenin's "new economy" policy, and the historical inspiration from Sun Yat-sen's "Three Principles of People".[1] Mao Zedong thought of opening up to the outside world is rich in its content, covering almost all fields related to politics, economy, culture, and society. In particular, he always insists and emphasizes the importance of independence, self-reliance, and "making foreign things serve China," which is still of great guiding significance to China's opening up today. In the author's opinion, Mao Zedong's thought of opening up to the outside world includes at least the following aspects:

(1) Insisting on opening up to the outside world. Great importance is attached to the need for continuous and intensified learning, drawing lessons from all the things beneficial to us, and opposing isolation and blind exclusion. All nations and countries

---

[1] Zheng Guorui, "The Theoretical Origin of Mao Zedong Thought of Opening to the Outside World", *Truth Seeking*, 2009.

have their strengths and weaknesses, thus they all need to develop their strengths and avoid their weaknesses by learning from each other. Whether it was in the era of revolutionary wars or the period of building and development after the founding of the People's Republic of China, Mao Zedong resolutely opposed self-defense and self-arrogance. He insisted on learning from the Soviet Union and the West in order to seek a path for China's modernization on the basis of maintaining Chinese characteristics. He also emphasized the need to remove "the panic of lack of ability,"[1] advocating "learning from foreign countries," and not closing the door" with a view of "learning the advanced technology of the West to resist the West."[2] Mao Zedong was an advocate of opening up to the outside world and absorbing the advanced achievements of other civilizations, in order to develop, innovate, catch up with and surpass the advanced level of the world.

In April 1956, Mao Zedong put forward and emphasized his view of "the relationship between China and foreign countries" in his *On Ten Relations*: "Our policy is that we should learn the strengths of all nations and countries and all beneficial things in politics, economy, science, technology, literature, and art. However, we must learn analytically and critically rather than learn blindly and copy and use everything mechanically."[3] "In the future, when China is rich and strong, we will still uphold the revolutionary stand, be modest and prudent, learn from others, and not be proud. Not only should we learn from others during the first Five-year Plan Period, but also we should learn from them after dozens of five-year plans. We will learn from them for even after ten thousand years! Why not?" He points out: "There are two kinds of learning attitudes. One is a dogmatic attitude, which means to copy both applicable and inapplicable things regardless of the situation of our country, and obviously, this is not a good attitude. The other one is to use your mind when you study, to learn something that suits the situation of our country, that is, to absorb experience that is useful for us. What we need is such an attitude."[4] "Learning from ancient sages is for living people of today,

---

[1] In 1939, Mao Zedong once said: There is a panic in our people. It is not an economic nor a political panic, but a panic of lack of ability. In the past, only a little bit of learning was done. If we use them everyday, it is running out very soon. It's like running a shop where the goods are not enough to be sold. If we want to run our shop in the long run, we must keep a stock. The so-called "stock" is reading.

[2] Wei Yuan, Qing Dynasty, *Complete Works of Wei Yuan*, Changsha: Yuelu Book Company, 2004, p.1.

[3] Mao Zedong, "On Ten Relations", published in the 7th volume of *Mao Zedong's Anthology*, Beijing: People's Publishing House, 1999, pp. 41-44.

[4] *Selected Works of Mao Zedong*, Beijing: People's Publishing House, 1986, p.798.

and learning from foreigners is for today's China"[1] In particular, he stresses that we should not only pay attention to study Western science and technology but also learn advanced experience and management methods from other countries. We can first imitate and follow those technologies that we do not have, and then digest them. We can do without them when we fully understand them.

(2) Emphasizing the basic principle of opening up to the outside world based on independence and self-reliance, supplemented with foreign aid. Mao Zedong points out: "We Chinese have the courage to fight till the end against our enemies, the determination to restore the past on the basis of self-reliance, and the ability to stand proudly among the world nations. However, it does not mean that we don't need international assistance. International assistance is requisite for the revolution of all nations and all modern countries."[2] The history and practical experience since the founding of the People's Republic of China have repeatedly proved that adhering to the policy of opening up to the outside world based on independence and self-reliance with supplement of foreign aid will enable China to take the initiative and be in a favorable position in its foreign relations. This is an important magic weapon for the victory of China's revolution and construction.

After the founding of the People's Republic of China, the Chinese people became the master of their own fate. However, what the Communists had to face at that time was a fragile economy on the verge of collapse. In 1949, the country's output was only 158,000 tons of steel, 120,000 tons of crude oil, 32.4 million tons of raw coal, 1.89 billion cubic meters of timber and 6,000 tons of agricultural fertilizer. The per capita income of farmers was only RMB43.8, and that of urban residents was less than RMB100, which was only equivalent to the level of Britain during the Industrial Revolution 200 years ago. Compared with 1936, the decrease in heavy industrial production was by about 70%, light industrial production by about 30%, and agricultural production by about 25%. In the early days of the founding of the PRC, China was faced with problems at home such as shrinking production, soaring prices, rampant speculation, serious unemployment, and low living standards. Internationally, China had a tense surrounding environment with sharp contradictions. The anti-China forces of the western countries, led by the United States, politically isolated China, economically blocked and militarily encircled China, and such long-term "blockade"

---

[1] *Selected Works of Mao Zedong*, Beijing: People's Publishing House, 1986, p.752.

[2] *Mao Zedong's Anthology*, Volume I, Beijing: People's Publishing House, 1991, p.161.

and "embargo" aimed to strangle the People's Republic of China in its cradle. How difficult was it to develop "internal and external exchanges" at that time? According to a survey by Amartya Sen (1933-), an Indian economist who won the Nobel Prize in Economics, the international blockade, and internal and external pressures confronted by the People's Republic of China were much greater than those experienced by India which gained independence almost at the same time. However, due to the fundamental improvement in the living and welfare conditions of the grass-root people in China, the number of Chinese people who died during 1948-1976 was 100 million less than India. It was precisely this complicated and dangerous situation that forged the Chinese people's will power of working tenaciously and facing problems without fear, and cast the character of independence and self-reliance and the ability to cope with crises and overcome difficulties.

According to statistics, during the First Five-year Plan period, the Soviet Union sent 3,000 technical experts, and China sent 7,000 students and 5,000 interns to the Soviet Union; the 156 key construction projects under the "Five-year Plan" were built, most of which belonged to new industries that China had never established before. By the end of 1957, 135 key projects had been started, and 68 of them had been completed or partially completed and put into operation. During this period, German Democratic Republic, Czechoslovakia, Poland, Hungary, Romania, Bulgaria, and other socialist countries have also offered aids to China in the building of the 68 projects.

7.1.2 Thoughts of opening up to the outside world after the third plenary session of the 11th CPC Central Committee

After the Third Plenary Session of the 11th Central Committee of the Communist Party of China, the Central government inherited and developed Mao Zedong Thought of opening up to the outside world by combining Marxism's universal truth with the concrete practice of China. The historical lessons of China's long-standing stagnation and backwardness were summed up to observe the world from a broader perspective. The important policy of opening up to the outside world was put forward, which was defined as a basic national policy that must be adhered to and unshakable on a long-term basis.

Deng Xiaoping's theory of opening up to the outside world is based on how to speed up the development of contemporary China and realize modernization as soon as possible in an open world. He systematically clarified a series of important theoretical and practical problems, such as the inevitability, main contents, principles and the basic pattern of China's opening up, and expounded how to handle the main relations in this process correctly. He established China's strategic goal of three-step development and formed a set of opening-up theory systems suitable for China's reality, which has raised Marx's theory of opening up to the outside world to a new level. In early 1979, Deng Xiaoping was selected "Person of the Year 1978" by the first issue of *Time* in 1979. The Journal commented: "Deng Xiaoping made a great turn of 180 degrees in a very short time for a country with a large population, which is a magnificent and unique feat in human history." The author holds that Deng Xiaoping's thought of opening up to the outside world includes the following main aspects:

(1) Emphasis that opening to the outside world is a basic national policy that China should stick to for a long time. Deng Xiaoping stresses that, "No country can develop in isolation, with its doors closed; it must increase international contacts, introduce advanced methods, science and technology from developed countries and use their capital."[1] "By the opening up policy we mean opening up to all other countries, irrespective of their social systems. "[2] "A closed-door policy prevents any country from developing. We suffered from isolation, and so did our forefathers".

"The present world is open. One important reason for China's backwardness after the industrial revolution in Western countries was its closed-door policy."[3] "This is because we are acting according to our own concrete realities and conditions and mainly relying on ourselves. Now that we are on the right track, our people are happy and we are confident. Our policies will not change. Or if they do, it will be only for the better. And our policy of opening to the outside world will only expand. The path will not become narrower and narrower but wider and wider. "[4] Opening up to the outside world is a long-term and lasting policy, which should not be changed in this century or in the first 50 years of the next century. China will be more closely linked to foreign countries economically in fifty years."[5]

(2) Emphasis that independence is the fundamental principle for China's opening up. Deng Xiaoping makes a special point that: "China's foreign policy is independent and truly non-aligned."[6] "Therefore, while pursuing the policy of opening to the outside

---

[1] Deng Xiaoping, "Developing Democracy Politically and Implementing Reform Economically (April 15, 1985)", *Selected Works of Deng Xiaoping* Volume III, Beijing: People's Publishing House, 1993, p.177.

[2] Deng Xiaoping, "The Step of Reform Should Be Accelerated (June 12, 1987)", Volume 3, *Selected Works of Deng Xiaoping*, Beijing: People's Publishing House, 1993, p. 237.

[3] Deng Xiaoping, *Selected Works of Deng Xiaoping* Volume III, Beijing: People's Publishing House, 1993, p.90.

[4] Deng Xiaoping, *Selected Works of Deng Xiaoping* Volume III, Beijing: People's Publishing House, 1993, p.64.

[5] Deng Xiaoping, *Selected Works of Deng Xiaoping* Volume III, Beijing: People's Publishing House, 1993, p.29.

[6] Deng Xiaoping, *Selected Works of Deng Xiaoping* Volume III, Beijing: People's Publishing House, 1993, p.57.

world, we must stick to the principle of relying mainly on our own efforts, a principle consistently advocated by Chairman Mao Zedong since the founding of the PRC. We must seek help from outside on the basis of self-reliance, depending mainly on our own hard work."[1] " But independence does not mean shutting the door on the world, nor does self-reliance mean blind opposition to everything foreign."[2] The ideas of opening to the outside world, external cooperation, and independence and self-reliance are complementary to each other.

(3) Making it clear that opening up to the outside world is an all-round, multi-level and wide-ranging opening up, and it is a combination of the external and internal opening. Deng Xiaoping emphasizes that "Opening to the outside world is our unswerving national policy. We are now opening up insufficiently rather than excessively. In order to further widen the opening up, we must be bold, move faster and implement the policy of 'wide opening up'."[3] " By the open policy we mean opening to all other countries, irrespective of their social systems."[4] "On the one hand we shall open to the outside world, and on the other we shall invigorate our domestic economy. Reform means invigorating the economy. And doing that means opening up at home, which is another aspect of the same policy."[5]It can be seen that opening up includes opening up not only to other countries but also an opening to the domestic market and the invigorating domestic economy. He also formulates a specific strategic plan for an opening to the outside world from the overall situation of the country. The opening up would be carried out progressively from the establishment of special economic zones, opening coastal port cities to gradually promoting the development of coastal, border, and inland areas. In the field of opening up, the emphasis should be expanded from economic and trade sectors to other fields, such as politics, diplomacy, science and education, culture, health, art, and sports. In terms of the way of opening up, through "crossing a river by feeling the stones," we should select the breakthrough point of reform and opening up, conduct pilot projects boldly, summarize the experience of pilot projects in time, gradually expand the scope of pilot projects according to local conditions, and constantly improve the way of opening up.

---

[1] Deng Xiaoping, *Selected Works of Deng Xiaoping* Volume III, Beijing: People's Publishing House, 1993, p.406.

[2] Deng Xiaoping, *Deng Xiaoping's Anthology* Volume II, Beijing: People's Publishing House, 1993, p. 91.

[3] Deng Xiaoping, "Emancipating the Mind, Deepening Reform and Expanding Opening—A Record of the Talks to Central Leading Comrades", *China Comment*, 1992(4).

[4] Deng Xiaoping, *Selected Works of Deng Xiaoping* Volume III, Beijing: People's Publishing House, 1993, p. 237.

[5] Deng Xiaoping, *Selected Works of Deng Xiaoping* Volume III, Beijing: People's Publishing House, 1993, p. 98.

(4) Emphasizing the importance of courage, responsibility, and flexibility while opening up to the outside world. Deng Xiaoping emphasizes that, "Our policy is to be bold and steady, to go one step at a time. Our policy is unswerving and unshakable. We must continue to work on it. It is important to sum up our experience after a period of time."[1] At the beginning of 1992, he stressed in one of his talks during his inspection tour to the south of China, , "We should pluck up courage in reform and opening up and be open-minded to experiment, and not act timidly and conservatively. We should dare to blaze a new trail and do experiments once we make up our mind. Without a pioneering and enterprising spirit, we cannot find a good and new road, and we cannot go in for a new cause."[2]

7.1.3 Opening-up thoughts since the 18th CPC National Congress

The 18th National Congress of the Communist Party of China (CPC) in 2012 marked a "new historic starting point" for China's development and the beginning of a new stage for China's reform and opening up—a stage of comprehensively deepening reform. The collective leadership of the CPC Central Committee, with Xi Jinping as its core, has been delivering on the Two Centenary Goals and realization of the Chinese Dream of national rejuvenation, keeping in mind both internal and international imperatives as well as the great cause and great project.

Efforts have been made to fully implement the overall plan for promoting economic, political, cultural, social, and ecological progress, for a more coordinated development of socialism with Chinese characteristics. The 4Cs Strategic Blueprint has been carried out, namely, comprehensive development of a moderately prosperous society; comprehensive deepening of reforms; comprehensive implementation of the rule of law and comprehensive enforcement of Party discipline. Measures have been taken to pull China's strength with the Chinese Dream and to boost the spirit of the whole Party by improving its conduct. Reform initiatives have been encouraged to improve governance, and practical actions are taken to forge ahead. A new vision of innovative, coordinated, green, open and shared development has been firmly established and implemented in response to the new normal of the economy.

In adherence to the general principle of pursuing progress while ensuring stability, importance has been attached to improving the quality and efficiency of development

---

[1] Deng Xiaoping, *Selected Works of Deng Xiaoping* Volume III, Beijing: People's Publishing House, 1993, p. 113.
[2] Deng Xiaoping, *Selected Works of Deng Xiaoping* Volume III, Beijing: People's Publishing House, 1993, p. 372.

and the supply-side structural reform as our primary task to accelerate the two-way opening up at home and abroad. We have been pursuing a win-win opening policy to accelerate the construction of a new open economic system by coordinating domestic and foreign demands for balanced imports and exports. Equal importance has been given to bringing in investment, technology, and talented people from abroad and going global. Coordinated efforts have been made to maintain steady growth, accelerate reform, adjust economic structure, improve people's living standards, fend off risks, and actively participate in global economic governance and the supply of public goods. All this has not only effectively coped with the complicated changes in the world's political and economic environment but also achieved a medium-high growth rate under adverse external conditions. Remarkable reform achievements have been made in key areas such as the overall strategic blueprint, the top-level design, the regulation of government power, and the role of the market, with breakthroughs in the governance of the country, which won applause from home and abroad. This is the basic backdrop for deepening reform and opening up in contemporary China.

Xi Jinping, as the leader and core of the contemporary Chinese Communist Party and the People's Republic of China, has a vision for the world and the future with a forward-looking attitude. Following the trend of history, Xi Jinping takes the initiative to seize opportunities to formulate a strategic blueprint for the sustainable development of contemporary China.

He attaches great importance to speed up reform and opening up, emphasizing time and again the importance of deepening reform in an all-round way and expanding opening up to the outside world. He regards reform dividends and innovation drive as the new engine of China's sustainable development, making a series of insightful observations and important speeches closely around comprehensively deepening reform. He profoundly analyzes major theoretical and practical problems China faces in its reform, development, and stability, and puts forward a series of new concepts, ideas, strategies, and initiatives for governing the country, advancing the theoretical exploration and practical innovation of the Communist Party of China and contemporary China's reform and opening up. All these fully demonstrate his integral personality and charismatic leadership style of caring for the country and the people, his aspirations and political wisdom as a Marxist statesman, and his great foresight and outstanding ability as a strategist.

Since the 18th National Congress of the CPC, Xi Jinping has expounded on many occasions at home and abroad important statements that China will adhere to an all-round opening up. These insightful words not only point out the direction for the development of China's sustainable opening but also indicate that China will strive to lead the economic globalization into a new era with the open development. The author holds that Xi Jinping's statement of opening to the outside world includes at least the following aspects:

(1) Implementing a more proactive strategy of opening up and improve the mutually beneficial, win-win, multi-balanced, safe and efficient open economic system. In 2013, Xi Jinping stressed at the first phase of the G20 Summit that:" China will adhere to the mutually beneficial and win-win strategy of opening up, deepen the reform of investment and trade systems, improve laws and regulations, create a legal environment for fair operation of enterprises in China, and resolve trade disputes with relevant countries through dialogue." [1] In the same year, he further stressed at the APEC CEO Summit: "We will adopt a more proactive and open strategy to improve an open economy that is mutually beneficial, multi-balanced, safe, and efficient, and promote the complementary advantages of coastal, inland and border areas, so as to develop open region that leads in international economic cooperation and competition, as well as pace-setters in regional development. We should continue to pay attention to exports and imports and promote balanced development of foreign trade. Efforts should be made to 'bring in' and 'go global' to promote international investment cooperation. We should deepen the reform of investment and trade systems, improve laws and regulations, and create a legal environment for enterprises in China to operate fairly. We will coordinate bilateral, multilateral, regional and sub-regional open cooperation, accelerate the implementation of the free trade zone strategy, and promote interconnection with neighboring countries." [2] These important expositions profoundly demonstrate that Xi Jinping accurately grasps the trend of the times and the international situation, stresses the implementation of a more proactive opening strategy, and improves the mutually beneficial, win-win, multi-balanced, safe and efficient open economic system. This is a new historical starting point for further clarifying whether China will continue to open up to the outside world, in what direction it will open up, and how to deepen the opening up. Only by adhering to the more active strategy of

---

[1] Xi Jinping, Jointly Maintaining and Developing—An Open World Economy Speech on the World Economic Situation at the First Phase of the G20 Summit, *People's Daily*, Sep. 6, 2013.

[2] Xi Jinping, Playing Asia-Pacific Leadership in Maintaining and Developing an Open World Economy—Speech on the Global Economic Situation and the Multilateral Trade System at the First Phase of the APEC Leaders' Meeting, *People's Daily*, Oct. 8, 2013.

opening to the outside world, promoting reform through opening up, promoting development through reform and deepening the reform and opening up in an all-round way, can we better build a new open economic system, promote the modernization of national governance and realize the goal of building a well-off society in an all-round way.

(2) Proposing major development strategies. Today, China's opening up is no longer a one-way opening to some countries, but a two-way opening to the outside world. We should not only "bring in" but also "go global" to promote sustainable development through the two-way opening. The CPC Central Committee with Xi Jinping as its core has grasped the general trend of China's and the world's economic development and changes. With a far-reaching global and strategic vision, it has put forward the national strategies of "Yangtze River Economic Belt", "the coordinated development of the Beijing-Tianjin-Hebei region" as well as international cooperation programs like the Belt and Road Initiative. The three development plans provide a great potential for internal and external development and a strong driving force for development in China's shifting of economic development speed. They have the economic significance of coordinating regional development, promoting sustainable development, and realizing common prosperity, as well as the political significance of maintaining social stability, promoting ethnic unity and safeguarding national security. Diplomatically, they help seek the greatest common interests of all countries and expand the meeting point of common interests for building a community with a shared future for mankind and realizing a mutual benefit and win-win situation. They can be said to be China's best national development strategies and regional coordination strategies so far.

In December 2014, Xi Jinping emphasized in his speech at the central economic work conference that: "The central leadership has decided to implement three initiatives: the Belt and Road Initiative, the Coordinated Development of Beijing, Tianjin and Hebei, and the Yangtze River Economic Belt. Their common feature is that they cross administrative divisions and promote balanced development between regions. I hope you will compare notes and reach consensus and carry them out, and strive for a good start next year. The Belt and Road Initiative offers good development opportunities to the eastern, central and western regions and especially to some marginal areas in the west which will become centers with great development potential as soon as they are interconnected with neighboring countries. In the future, a key point of our policies on regional development will be to unify the large domestic market, which is both a problem to be addressed and an important challenge facing fiscal and taxation reforms. We should break regional barriers and vested interests through reform and innovation, so as to comprehensively improve the efficiency of resource allocation."[1]

Through the long-term implementation of the Belt and Road Initiative as well as the coordinated development of Beijing-Tianjin-Hebei region and Yangtze River Economic Belt, we will deepen and expand the opening up of coastal areas and inland border areas, to improve the strategic layout and form a new system of opening up. At home, we will create a new and globally oriented open landscape that promotes both land and maritime opening, eastern and western development, and internal and external connectivity, Externally, we will promote policy communication, connectivity of infrastructure, unimpeded trade, capital financing and people-to-people communication, from reshaping China's economic geography to helping reshape the world's economic geography, and build a more open, inclusive, balanced, inclusive, mutually beneficial and win-win cooperation platform, better promote regional coordination under the new normal in economic development, mutually beneficial cooperation at home and abroad and the early realization of national prosperity and rejuvenation, and bring development wisdom and experience to other countries and regions.

(3) Proposing the new development concept of innovation, coordination, green, openness and sharing. The new concept of development is the innovative theoretical achievement of the Party Central Committee, with Xi Jinping as its core, in the course of practical exploration. It is an important and fundamental principle that must be adhered to on a long-term basis in promoting China's economic and social development. It is the direction of overall, fundamental, and long-term management. It has strategic, programmatic and leading importance. In January 2016, Xi Jinping emphasized at the 30th collective study session of the Political Bureau of the CPC Central Committee, the new philosophy of development is like the baton and the traffic lights. The whole Party should unify its ideas and actions with the new development philosophy, strive to improve its ability and the level of overall implementation of the philosophy. We should immediately adjust, correct and completely abandon any behavior or practices that are inappropriate, not suited to, or even runs counter to the new development philosophy.

In the new development philosophy, open development includes active opening, two-way opening, fair opening, all-round opening and win-win opening, focusing on how to connect with world development, how to boost domestic reform and

---

[1] Xi Jinping's speech at the Central Conference on Economic Work, Dec. 9, 2014.

development by opening to the outside world, pursuing development in the context of a closer relationship with the rest of the world and focusing on making good use of both international and domestic markets and resources. It emphasizes that we must conform to the trend of China's deep economic integration into the world's economy, pursue a win-win opening and further strengthen the impact of opening. A deeper, wider and better-quality opening up has been carried out for a higher level of open economy to develop a new dynamic of comprehensive opening up with connectivity of the land and the sea, and the East and the West; while actively participating in global economic governance and public goods supply to enhance China's international presence and build a wide range of interest, responsibility and a community with a shared future.

(4) Emphasizing that reform and opening up has been a game-changing move in making China what it is today; which is important for us to achieve China's "Two Centenary Goals" and the great rejuvenation of the Chinese nation. In December 2012, Xi Jinping left Beijing on a fact-finding tour for the first time after assuming the post of General Secretary of the CPC Central Committee. He selected Guangdong Province which was at the forefront of reform and opening up, and reviewed the historical process of China's reform and opening up and paid tribute to the statue of Deng Xiaoping, the "chief architect" of China's reform and opening up in order to declare China's firm determination to continue its reform and opening up.

During his inspection in Guangdong, Xi Jinping stressed: "The Eighteenth National Congress of the Party has issued a new declaration and mobilization order to deepen the reform and opening up to the whole Party and the whole country. All the Chinese people should firmly follow the road of building China into a powerful country through reform and opening up, pay more attention to a more systematic, integral, and coordinated reform, keep the reform and opening up on going, and make concerted efforts to build a well-off society in an all-round way and accelerate our socialist modernization".[1] He emphasizes on many occasions that: "Reform and opening up is a great awakening in the history of our Party, and it is this great awakening that gives birth to the great creation from theory to practice in the new period. The practice has proved that reform and opening up is the source of vitality for the development and progress of contemporary China, is an important magic weapon for our Party and people to catch up with the pace of the times. It is the only way to adhere to and develop socialism with Chinese characteristics. Practice and development are never-ending, the emancipation

---

[1] Xinhua News Agency, Guangzhou, Dec. 11, 2012.

of the mind is never-ending, reform and opening up are never-ending; there is no way out for pauses and retrogression."[1]He stresses: "Now that China's reform has entered a critical period of attack and a deep-water zone, we must deepen reform in important areas with greater political courage and wisdom. To deepen reform and opening up, we must strengthen confidence, build consensus, plan, and advance together."[2] These important expositions profoundly show that only by adhering to seeking truth from facts, emancipating the mind, advancing with the times, reforming and opening up, and forging ahead bravely, can we achieve the Two Centenary Goals and the great rejuvenation of the Chinese nation at an early date.

(5) Emphasizing that reform is never-ending. Opening up is the only way for China's economic prosperity and development. It is also an inevitable choice for the prosperity and development of the world economy. There is no limit to the development of practice. There is no limit to emancipating our minds. China's economy is closely related to the world economy. In order to achieve comprehensive, coordinated, and sustainable development of China's economy, we must consistently adhere to the basic state policy of opening up to the outside world. In December 2012, when Xi Jinping presided over the second collective study session of the 18th Central Political Bureau, he stressed: "Reform and opening up is a long-term and arduous undertaking, which must be carried on from generation to generation." He emphasized: "Reform and opening up is ongoing and not completed. Without reform and opening up, there will be no China today, and there will be no tomorrow for China. Contradictions in reform and opening up can only be resolved through reform and opening up." [3]"In order to implement the major reform and opening-up plan established at the 18th National Congress of the Party, we must carefully review and thoroughly summarize the course of reform and opening up, more deeply understand the historical inevitability of reform and opening up, more consciously grasp the laws of reform and opening up, and more firmly shoulder the major responsibility of deepening reform and opening up."[4] In November 2013, when meeting with foreign representatives of the 21st Century Council in Beijing, Xi Jinping stressed that: "China will adhere to reform and opening

---

[1] *People's Daily*, Jan. 22, 2012.

[2] Xi Jinping's talk on Reform in Guangdong: Daring to break through the barriers of ideas and interests, published in the *Beijing News* on Dec. 12, 2012.

[3] Xi Jinping's speech at the second collective study session of the 18th Central Political Bureau.

[4] Xi Jinping's speech at the second collective study session of the Political Bureau of the CPC Central Committee, Jan. 2, 2013.

up. The more open China is, the more open China will be." In March 2017, general secretary Xi Jinping stressed again when he participated in the deliberations of the Shanghai delegation of the two sessions of The National People's Congress(NPC) and The Chinese People's Political Consultative Conference(CPPCC), "The door of China's opening up will not be closed. We should adhere to all-round opening up and continue to promote trade and investment liberalization and facilitation."These important expositions profoundly show that only by unswervingly complying with the basic state policy of reform and opening up, deepening reform and opening up to the outside world, can we develop and build socialism with Chinese characteristics better and broaden the path of socialism with Chinese characteristics.

(6) Emphasizing that open development leads to economic globalization into a new era. History has proved that openness brings progress, and closeness leads to backwardness. For a long time, economic globalization has become an irresistible historical trend, providing a strong driving force for world economic growth. Although economic globalization is a "double-edged sword", which means it has remarkable positive effects and problems and shortcomings, it cannot stop the historical development trend of economic globalization.

China has entered a new stage of interaction with and in-depth opening to the world. Xi Jinping emphasizes that: "Mankind has become a community with a shared future in which we are all intertwined, and our interests are highly integrated. To make the process of economic globalization more dynamic, more inclusive and more sustainable is the responsibility of the leaders of our times, and the expectations of the people of all countries. China will upgrade an open economy in a wider range, broader scope, and at a deeper level. We should unswervingly develop an open world economy, share opportunities and interests in opening up, and achieve mutual benefit and a win-win situation. We need to make great efforts to develop global interconnection so that all countries in the world can achieve joint growth and achieve shared prosperity". While attending the 2015 annual meeting of the Boao Forum for Asia, Xi Jinping, reiterated that "China will become more and more open, China's policy of utilizing foreign capital will not change, the protection of the legitimate rights and interests of foreign-invested enterprises will not change, and the direction of providing better services for foreign enterprises to invest in China will not change." [1]

---

[1] Xi Jinping, China's Policy on Increasing Openness and Utilization of Foreign Capital Will Not Change, published in China.com, Mar. 30, 2015.

These insightful words profoundly show that only by clearly understanding the development trend of the world economy, moving on with the times, and taking the initiative to innovate with courage can we make full use of all opportunities to cope with all challenges in coordination and vigorously develop a higher level of the open economy. Only by innovating in the opening up and developing in the innovation, and continually pushing forward liberalization and facilitation of trade and investment, as well as an orderly flow of domestic and international factors and efficient allocation of resources, can we better promote China's continuous development and growth, while striving to jointly lead the sustained and healthy development of economic globalization, making it a more dynamic and innovative momentum to achieve deeper integration and interaction between China and the world economy in its open development, to benefit the Chinese people and the people of the world.

In addition to the above important expositions of Xi Jinping on reform and opening up, he has also put forward a series of strategic ideas for deepening reform and opening up in an all-round way. He not only depicts a new systematic blueprint, a new vision, and a new goal for deepening reform, but scientifically brings together new ideas, new judgments, and new measures for deepening reform. All these will play an important guiding role and have a far-reaching historical impact in deepening China's overall reform and promoting healthy and sustainable economic and social development in the future.

7.2 Major courses of opening up and development of China's ports

Since the founding of the People's Republic of China in 1949, marked by the Third Plenary Session of the 11th Central Committee of the CPC held in 1978, the south tour talks by Deng Xiaoping, the "chief architect" of China's reform and opening up in 1992, and the 18th National Congress of the CPC held in 2012, the development of China's port opening can be divided into four stages.

7.2.1 Before the reform and opening up (1949-1978)

During this period, the planned economic system was in its infancy and shaping, and the policy of opening up and development was mainly "one-sided". During the period from the founding of the People's Republic of China to the time before the start of the reform and opening up, due to the special political and economic situation at home and abroad, the main features of the opening up were as follows: first, the country was in a closed and semi-closed economic state, with a single economic structure and a low level of production, and implemented rationing under a planned economic system. The second was the 1949 Common Programme of the Chinese People's Political Consultative Conference which stipulated: "the implementation of foreign trade control and adoption of a protective trade policy." After 1956, the planned economic system was established in an all-round way, and an independent, exclusive, highly closed, single-planned, unified foreign trade system and management system were established. The state integrated foreign trade operation and management, and imports and exports were carried out strictly in accordance with the state plan. As for the acquisition system, the system of transfer was adopted, and the state unified the profit and loss. Thirdly, in accordance with the policy of economic construction, which was based on self-reliance and supplemented by foreign aid, foreign trade was regarded as a supplementary means of social expansion and reproduction, and was limited to the exchange of needed goods, adjustment surplus and foreign aid. The main export commodities were primary products such as agricultural and sideline products, mineral products, and trade relations were restricted by foreign affairs. A "one-sided" development strategy of opening up to the outside world was implemented for socialist countries such as the Soviet Union. The state has made some practical explorations in utilizing foreign funds and foreign economic assistance.

During the period from the late 1950s to the early 1960s, many colonial countries in Asia, Africa, and Latin America won national independence. The People's Republic of China established and developed extensive trade relations of equality, mutual benefit and exchange of needs with them, and carried out some activities such as barter trade, border trade, accounting trade, and spot trade. In 1960, the primary target of China's foreign trade was shifted from socialist countries such as the Soviet Union to capitalist countries such as Japan and Western Europe. By 1965, the proportion of China's foreign trade with Western countries in the total foreign trade volume of China rose to more than 50%. In the early 1970s, after China resumed its legitimate seat in the United Nations, its foreign relations improved rapidly, and diplomatic relations with Japan, Germany, and the United States were established one after another, which provided preliminary preparations for China's reform and opening up in the 1970s.

From 1949 to 1978, China's ports opened to the outside world were compatible with foreign economic and trade cooperation and personnel exchanges. The number of ports open to the outside world was small. By the end of 1978, only 51 ports were open to the outside world, including 18 water ports (17 sea ports, 1 river ports), 16 highway ports, 9 railway ports, and 8 air ports. The open air ports were mainly concentrated in the regional central cities, the open water ports in the coastal and river-side areas, and the open highway and railway ports in the key land border areas.

7.2.2 Period of initiation and exploration of reform and opening up (1978-1992)

During this period, the foreign trade system was reformed rapidly. Under the highly centralized planned economic system, the opening to the outside world was expanded from coastal areas to inland areas. The main characteristics of this stage of opening up were: firstly, the Third Plenary Session of the 11th Central Committee of the CPC established the guiding ideology of emancipating the mind and seeking truth from facts, with the strategic policy of shifting the focus of work to the socialist modernization drive and implementing the reform at home and opening up to the outside world, which brought about a fundamental change from "an obsession with the class struggle" to taking economic development as the center, from rigidity and semi-rigidity to comprehensiveness. With the historical transformation from being closed and semi-closed to opening up, China entered a new stage of practical exploration and has since embarked on the correct road of building socialism with Chinese characteristics. Secondly, four special economic zones were established in Shenzhen, Zhuhai, Shantou, and Xiamen, a number of port cities and development zones along the coast opened up, with more flexible and preferential special policies being experimented with import and export management, and foreign exchange policies. Foreign trade had developed rapidly, and processing trade in coastal areas had flourished, undertaking the transfer of labor-intensive international industries, and driving the development of domestic industries. These practices also promoted the optimization and upgrading of export commodity structure to realize the transformation of foreign trade exports from primary products and resource-based products to industrially manufactured products, expanding the export of labor-intensive products. Foreign direct investment influx and the establishment of special economic zones had injected great vitality into the development of China's foreign trade and economic relations. Thirdly, China has carried out a series of reforms in its foreign trade system, including the readjustment of the state's unified foreign trade management system established in the early days of the founding of the People's Republic of China to the central foreign trade leading body, the establishment of a number of industrial and trade companies under the management of industrial departments, the unified revenue and expenditure, and the unified responsibility for profits and losses, which have simplified the contents of the foreign trade plan and implemented dual exchange rate system and import and export license system. Moreover, the introduction of foreign capital, technology and management experience, the attraction of investment and utilization of external funds had broken the domestic market separatism under the planned economy, promoted the free flow of production factors and commodities at home, made rapid progress in foreign economic and trade cooperation, and enhanced the economic strength of the country. From 1978 to 1991, the total import and export volume increased from US\$20.64 billion to US\$135.63 billion, with an average annual growth rate of 16.6% and 14.6%. However, by the early 1990s, China's economic system reform and opening up to the outside world were still facing difficulties. Economic development and reform and opening up came to a historical juncture. Finally, under the strong impetus of Deng Xiaoping's south tour talks, the opening up to the outside world entered a new stage.

From 1979 to 1992, the state approved 121 new open ports, with an annual average increase of 8.64. Among them, 40 ports were approved to open to the outside world during the 6th Five-year Plan period (1981-1985), and 8 ports were added annually. During the 7th Five-year Plan period (1986-1990), 42 ports were approved, with an annual average increase of 8.4 new ports. In the early stage of reform and opening up, there were few ports opening to the outside world. The infrastructure of ports was generally backward, and the traffic capacity was seriously insufficient, which hindered the development of foreign economy and trade to a certain extent. In order to speed up the development of China's economic construction from east to west, and from coastal to border areas in the hinterland, the state first opened up 14 coastal port cities in Dalian, Qinhuangdao, Tianjin, Yantai, Qingdao, Lianyungang, Nantong, Shanghai, Ningbo, Wenzhou, Fuzhou, Guangzhou, Zhanjiang, and Beihai on the basis of establishing four special economic zones, granting them preferential policies and measures. Subsequently, the state opened up the Yangtze River Delta, the Pearl River Delta, the Xiamen-Zhangzhou-Quanzhou Delta in Southern Fujian, Jiaodong Peninsula in Shandong and Liaodong Peninsula as coastal economic open areas, as well as areas along the coast of Hebei and Guangxi, and established the largest special economic zone, Hainan Province, and all the key coastal port cities were open to the outside world. Taking the development and the opening up of Pudong in Shanghai as the lead to promote the opening up of the Yangtze River Basin, 10 port cities along the Yangtze River, such as Wuhu, Jiujiang, Yueyang, Wuhan and Chongqing, were all open to the outside world. Some cities along the coast and river have opened more water ports to construct the most vigorous open coastal economic belt across China's north and south. More land crossings, water ports, and supervision points connecting Hong Kong and Macao SARs were opened in the 5 special economic zones. The inland provincial capitals of Taiyuan, Hefei, Nanchang, Zhengzhou, Changsha, Chengdu, Guiyang, Xi'an, Lanzhou, Xining, and Yinchuan opened to the outside world. The border counties and cities of Manzhouli, Erenhot, Hunchun, Suifenhe, Heihe, Dandong, Dongxing, Pingxiang, Ruili, Wanding, Hekou, Yining, Tacheng, Bole, etc. opened to the outside world one after another together with some border railways and highway ports. The opening of ports had progressively moved from coastal areas to inland areas along the border.

7.2.3 Period of rapid reform and opening up and initial improvement (1992-2012)

During this period, foreign trade developed rapidly, and the socialist market economy was explored. Opening up to the outside world expanded from regional to national. The main characteristics of this stage of opening up are: firstly, Deng Xiaoping's south tour talks in 1992 completely solved the controversy of whether the opening system belonged to capitalism or socialism, and the whole country accelerated the solid pace of reform and opening up in accordance with the principle of "3Fs (namely determining whether what we do is favorable to growing the productive forces in a socialist society, whether what we do is favorable to increase the overall strength of the socialist state, and whether what we do is favorable to raise people's living standards)". Second, the 14th National Congress of the CPC in 1993 established the goal of socialist market economy reform. Foreign trade changed from the exchange of needed goods and surplus to full use of both domestic and foreign market resources under the market economy conditions, and actively participated in the international division of labor and competition and cooperation, giving full play to comparative advantages. Thirdly, the state put forward and promoted major measures of opening up to the outside world, such as market diversification, big economy and trade, the combination of "bringing in" and "going global", encouragement of "win-through-quality", the invigoration of trade through science and technology, active participation in regional economic cooperation, and the establishment of a multilateral trading system. Especially since 1999, the "going global" strategy has been implemented. Since then,

China's non-financial foreign direct investment has been developing at high speed almost every year, driving the export of technology and equipment, while overseas investment has provided a useful supplement to protect domestic resources supply. Fourthly, China joined the World Trade Organization (WTO) in 2001 after 15 years of arduous negotiations and has gained tremendous potentials of international development since then. Taking this as a milestone, China has actively participated in economic and trade cooperation under the multilateral trading system, vigorously implemented trade liberalization and facilitation. Basically a foreign trade system has been established that is compatible with the market economy and conforms to international practices, which further improves the mutually beneficial cooperative relations between China and other countries by participating in the formulation of international economic and trade rules. By safeguarding the national sovereign interests, the legitimate rights, and interests of enterprises, and the legitimate rights and interests of citizens, and truly integrating into the world economy, China has achieved rapid and sustainable development in foreign trade, and the country's overall competitiveness has been further enhanced. Fifthly, from the perspective of opening up to the outside world in all regions of the country, opening up has shifted from a regional to a comprehensive and deepening stage. The Yangtze River Delta basin, including Pudong, has been further developed and opened to the outside world. Five cities along the Yangtze River, such as Chongqing, 18 inland provincial capitals, including Chengdu and 13 border cities, such as Manzhouli, have been opened to the outside world. The opening up has been fully implemented.

From 1993 to 2012, the state approved a total of 83 new open ports, with an annual average of 4.15 new open ports. After Deng Xiaoping's south tour talks in 1992, there was a great enthusiasm for accelerating the pace of opening up to the outside world by applying for the opening of new ports and widening the opening of existing ports in many places. During the 8th Five-year Plan period (1991-1995), 78 ports were approved to be opened or more widely opened, and 15.6 ports were opened annually (including new or expanded ports). Since the 9th Five-year Plan (1996-2000), China's open ports had been put into planning and management in accordance with the principle of "rational layout and priority of benefits." During this period, 16 new ports were opened, with an average of 3.2 ports being opened annually. During the 10th Five-year Plan period (2001-2005), 10 new ports were opened, with an average increase of 2 ports per year. Compared with the 9th Five-year Plan period, the overheating situation at ports was effectively controlled. During the 11th Five-year Plan period (2006-2010), in order to cope with the impact of the international financial crisis, the state and local governments continued to promote opening up vigorously and actively participate in the process of globalization. Efforts were made to create an optimized open environment, expand the scale of foreign trade, accelerate the pace of foreign economic cooperation, and open new ports across the country. Twenty-five new ports were opened, an average of 5 each year.

In the past 20 years, especially since China's accession into the WTO, the opening up has entered a new stage to cover all regions in the east, central and western regions. Through a gradient opening, the eastern coastal areas have constructed a frontier zone of opening to the outside world. The coastal ports and the port cities have opened one after another, effectively playing their roles as gateways to the outside world. Subsequently, inland areas, especially the provinces and major cities in the Yangtze River Basin, have been opened to the outside world. With the rapid development of border trade, barter trade and cross-border tourism in the border areas, the state has opened up land border towns, more land border railways, intersections, trade zones, and trade points along the northeast, northwest, and southwest border areas, as well as a number of air, water and land ports accordingly. The opening of ports and regional economic and social development are mutually promoted.

7.2.4 Period of deepening reform and opening up (2012 to the present)

This is a period when China has been actively constructing a new open economic system and fully engaged in government administration's modernization drive, and entered the decisive stage of building a well-off society in an all-around way. The main characteristics of this stage of opening up are:

Firstly, China has entered a new stage of deepening the reform and opening more widely to the outside world since the 18th National Congress of the CPC. Internationally, the world economy is in a period of deep adjustment. The long-term prosperity of the global economy for more than 30 years has become a low-speed growth at present and in the future. The trends of "de-globalization" and trade protectionism are on the rise,so is the trend of politicization of trade frictions. The low-speed growth of world trade in goods has become a new normal. From the domestic point of view, China's economic development has also stepped into a "new normal", showing new characteristics in terms of economic growth rate, structural optimization and adjustment, and shift of development drivers. However, the three interwoven problems have posed a great many difficulties and challenges to China's economic and financial development as well. The

CPC Central Committee, with General Secretary Xi Jinping as its core, accurately grasps the trend of peace, development, cooperation and win-win situation of the times and the world, and has decision-making from the strategic height of the overall layout of the cause of socialism with Chinese characteristics, and from the historical dimension of realizing the great rejuvenation of the Chinese nation. He stresses the importance of deepening reform in an all-around way at home and expanding opening up to the outside world to promote reform, development and innovation, and speed up the building of China as an open and strong economy. This will be of mutual benefit for China and the world.

Secondly, starting from the system and mechanism, China has been taking a problem-oriented approach in the reform to optimize the market environment and actively adapt to new changes in the domestic and foreign environment and new requirements of domestic reform and development. Obstacles in the system and mechanism of prominent problems in economic and social development are to be solved by actively innovating and opening up the economic system, further promoting a new round of two-way opening to the outside world, and cultivating the main body of the market, releasing the reform dividends and making the market play a decisive role in the allocation of resources. In this way, the government plays a better role to form a new system of opening to the outside world and accelerate the cultivation of new advantages in international competition, so as to realize the new development of opening up to the outside world.

Thirdly, based on mutual benefit and win-win approaches, we have been making efforts to contribute China's wisdom, adhere to the spirit of peace and cooperation, openness and tolerance, as well as mutual learning and mutual benefit to promote the development of the Silk Road Economic Belt and the 21st Century Maritime Silk Road. We have been upholding the principle of mutual consultation, joint contribution, and shared benefits to improve the open economic system of internal and external interaction, mutual benefit, and win-win situation, security and efficiency, to actively participate in global economic governance. China has been trying its best to take corresponding international responsibilities and obligations to promote the establishment of a fair, reasonable and transparent system of international economic, trade and investment rules with the orderly flow of factors of production, efficient allocation of resources, and deep integration of domestic and foreign markets, as well as the establishment of equality and justice. The new international economic order of cooperation and the win-win situation should help create a platform for cross-regional cooperation with Chinese characteristics and inclusiveness so as to drive economic and social development by innovation. While China's economy has achieved sustained and rapid development, it will also bring new opportunities and growth potentials for world development.

Fourthly, we have been firmly adhering to the basic state policy of reform and opening up to deeply implement the development concept of innovation, coordination, green, opening up and sharing, constantly adapt, grasp and lead the new normal of economic development to actively promote the structural reform on the supply side and focus on promoting the modernization of the national governance system and governance capacity. Hard work has been done to modernize China's governance system and capacity to effectively transform the functions of governments at all levels and deepen the reform of the administrative system. Efforts are made to further separate government administration from the management of enterprises, public institutions, communities, and state assets. Major reform and innovation measures have been taken to streamline administration, delegate more powers, strengthen regulation, and improve services. An intelligent, scientific, well-structured, clean, efficient and service-oriented government that meets the people's needs is being built. At present, China has embarked on the decisive journey of building a well-off society in an all-around way. Standing at a new historical starting point, we will not slow down or stop. We will continue to expand and deepen opening up, injecting strong positive energy into the development of China and the world.

According to statistics, by the end of 2016, there had been 300 ports opened with approval by the State Council, including 136 ports (81 sea ports and 55 river ports), 73 air ports, 20 railway ports, and 71 highway ports. In addition, there were more than 100 ports of former regional ports approved by the provincial people's government since the reform and opening up, which have been reserved in the clearing up and rectification by the State Council in 1998. At present, the whole country has formed densely distributed coastal and border waterborne ports which have basically covered major open and tourist cities in various provinces. The railway and highway ports in the border areas are open at multiple points in an all-around, multi-level and three-dimensional way.

7.3 New practices of development of China's ports since the 18th CPC National Congress

Since the 18th National Congress of the CPC, the CPC Central Committee and the

State Council have attached great importance to the work of ports, and further strengthened its organizational leadership and top-level design at the national level. Focusing on promoting the construction of "mutual information sharing, mutual oversight recognition and mutual law-enforcement assistance" (referred to as "3Ms") for greater customs clearance among port management departments, we have strengthened communication and coordination among port departments, work together to promote trade facilitation and improve the overall efficiency of port traffic. Focusing on the Belt and Road Initiative, we have conscientiously implemented the 12th Five-year Plan and the 13th Five-year Plan for the development of national ports, deepened the opening of ports in the coastal areas, expanded the opening of ports along the inland border areas, and optimized the adjustment of the opening layout of ports throughout the country. Construction of intelligent ports, particularly of "single window" in international trade has been actively promoted to upgrade intelligent port information management level. We have implemented the reform and strategic plan of the State Council on "Streamlining administration, delegating government power, strengthening regulations and improving services" to promote the pilot work of the Zhuhai Port inspection mechanism innovation; strengthen the construction of the rule of law at ports, increase efforts to promote the pace of port management legislation, and promote the early promulgation of port management regulations and rules. Efforts are made to strengthen comprehensive port management with more attention to port safety management, ensure the smooth and efficient operation of ports so as to serve better and promote the country's comprehensive deepening of reform, expand opening up, and make a positive contribution to maintain the overall situation of development and stability.

7.3.1 Organization, leadership and top-level design for strengthening port work at the national level

In order to strengthen the organizational monopoly of port work, strengthen the cooperation among departments and further enhance the efficiency of port work, in June 2015, the State Council approved the establishment of a joint inter-ministerial meeting system for port work under the State Council. The then Vice Premier of the State Council Wang Yang, was the convenor of the joint inter-ministerial meeting, with the Minister of the General Administration of Customs and the Deputy Secretary-General of the State Council who assisted in the port work as the deputy convenors, and 21 central departments as members of the joint meeting. The main function of the joint conference was to coordinate the work of the whole country under the leadership of the State Council and to study, determine and promote the implementation of major port reform programs and policies and measures. It also discussed how to coordinate and solve major issues in the reform and development of national ports; how to promote cooperation and coordination among various departments in port clearance; how to guide and coordinate the construction of national and local digital ports, and how to complete other tasks assigned by the State Council. The joint meeting was to be convened regularly or irregularly according to the needs of the work.

7.3.2 Further strengthening legal system building at ports

In recent years, the State Council has attached great importance to port work, promulgated some important documents on port work, such as the Notice on Issuing the Scheme for Reforms and Implementation of Mutual Exchange of Information, Mutual Recognition of Regulation and Mutual Assistance in law Enforcement of Port Administration to Promote Construction of Greater Customs Clearance and of Opinions on Improving Port Administration to Support Foreign Trade Development, pointing out the correct direction for the reform and development of ports at present and in the future. The General Administration of Customs (National Office of Port Administration), as the competent department of state ports, has attached great importance to the legalization, standardization, and institutionalization of ports. On the basis of an in-depth investigation and extensive consultation with relevant ministries and commissions and the competent departments of local governments at various provincial levels, the General Administration of Customs has taken the lead in drafting "Port Management Regulations", which has sped up the legislative work of regulations on port management. At the same time, we have further strengthened the construction of rules and regulations for port administration. By steadily strengthening the construction of the port legal system, the port work has become more institutionalized and standardized.

7.3.3 Accelerating the construction of "single window" for international trade

Since the 18th National Congress of the CPC, the CPC Central Committee and the State Council have made a series of decisions and arrangements for the construction of China's "Single Window" for international trade, which is not only one of the core measures advocated by the United Nations to promote the global trade facilitation strategy, but also a common practice of all countries to promote trade facilitation. It is also a way for China to promote the construction of "3 Ms" Greater Customs Clearance[1] at ports by streamlining the process of customs clearance, reducing the cost of enterprise for customs clearance, and optimizing port clearance. The important service measures have helped promote the steady development of foreign trade and a new round of high-level opening up.

China's "Single Window" practice began in early 2014, when the national port authorities, together with the competent authorities of port inspection agencies, selected Shanghai Pilot Free Trade Zone to carry out the pilot practice, and in the same year, gained valuable experience that could be replicated and spread. In 2015, the practice was applied from the Shanghai Pilot Free Trade Zone to coastal ports. The "Single Window" in 11 coastal provinces, such as Shanghai, Tianjin, Fujian, Guangdong, Shandong, Liaoning, Zhejiang, Jiangsu, Hainan, Guangxi, and Hebei, were built and put into operation. In 2016, the "Single Window" coverage was conditionally extended to central and western provinces. In September of that year, the Second Plenary Session of the Joint Inter-Ministerial Meeting of the State Council on Port Work deliberated and adopted them for implementation. The top-level design of the "Single Window" practice at the national level was further strengthened. According to the deployment of the State Council, by the end of 2017, in order to lay a foundation for the facilitation of trade and investment, all ports across the country have to build a "Single Window."

At present, China's "Single Window" practice will follow the path of enforcing the law at ports first, then expand to trade services and internationalization steadily. It will achieve the goal of a unified portal, unified data and unified certification to effectively simplify the declaration procedures, improve efficiency, and realize one-point access and "one-stop" for enterprises. Business processing, data entry and submission, multiple sharing and reuse have laid a good foundation and for relevant government departments of ports to achieve the " 3 Ms". Through the "Single Window" to give feedback of processing results and share data information, port departments can effectively break the "isolated island" of information, eliminate the "blockage" of the system, and improve the efficiency and transparency of supervision and service. Big data support has been provided for the efficiency of enterprise declaration, joint law

---

[1] The so-called "3 Ms" customs clearance refers to the reform measures of mutual information sharing, mutual oversight recognition and mutual law-enforcement assistance among relevant departments of border control, customs, inspection, and quarantine. The information, supervision, and law enforcement among port departments are interconnected and cooperated. The imports and exports only need to be accepted once, and the goods only need one customs clearance to complete the inspection.

enforcement, port security and control, social integrity, government decision-making, and management. Moreover, we can effectively improve the modernization of port management and supervision and service level.

7.3.4   Further optimization of the layout of the opening ports nationwide

In the past decades of reform and opening up, the number of China's ports has increased from 51 in 1978 to 300 at the end of 2016, forming an all-around, multi-level and three-dimensional dynamic of port opening. Among the 300 ports, 136 are mainly distributed in the eastern coastal areas and the economically developed areas along the Yangtze River. The 73 air ports are in the eastern and central cities and areas rich in tourist resources, covering the provincial capital cities and other major cities. There are 20 railway ports and 71 highway ports in the border areas, distributed in the northeast, northwest and southwest border areas. According to geographical classification, there are 152 ports in coastal areas, 27 in inland areas, and 121 in border areas.

Since the 18th National Congress of the CPC, the number and size of port opening have been greatly increased, and the infrastructure and inspection facilities improved. The layout of functions and the traffic environment have been continuously optimized, and the ability and level of serving the major national development strategy and the overall political, economic and diplomatic situation have been further enhanced, which have adapted to the national development of an open economy. The system's development needs meet the actual needs of the rapid growth of population, commodities, goods, and means of transport entering and leaving the country. Taking the 12th Five-year Plan period for example, China's ports have completed a total of 15.21 billion tons of cargo imports and exports, with a value of US$19.9 trillion, 2.308 billion person-time, and 128 million vehicles (planes, trains, and ships), providing a strong guarantee for China's foreign economic and trade cooperation, personnel exchanges and cross-border interconnection.

7.3.5   Active promotion of port management reform and innovation

Since the 18th National Congress of the CPC, the reform and innovation of port management at the national level has been represented by the pilot project of Zhuhai Port inspection mechanism innovation. This work is a major reform and innovation project in the port area in accordance with the requirements of the Notice of the State Council on Issuing the scheme for Reforms and Implementation of Mutual Exchange of Information, Mutual Recognition of Regulations and Mutual Assistance in Law

Enforcement of Port Administration to Promote Construction of Greater Customs Clearance and the State Council's Deployment. It is a concrete measure to deepen the innovation of port mechanism and further promote the facilitation of customs clearance in the Zhuhai-Macao region. The innovative pilot work includes promoting the separation of front and back-stage inspection of Zhuhai Port's tourist inspection corridor, strengthening the law enforcement cooperation mechanism at Zhuhai-Macao Port, implementing the "Single Window" practice for international trade, accelerating the "Greater Customs Clearance" of inspection links, strengthening the unified coordination of local governments, and coordinating the staffing of inspection personnel.

With the joint efforts of all parties, the one-year Zhuhai Port Inspection Mechanism Innovation Pilot Work has been completed and achieved desirable results. New breakthroughs have been made in the areas of combining top-level design with local implementation, exploring the mode of "cooperative inspection, one-time release in one pass," constructing digital ports and "Single Window" and informatization of inspection; it has stepped up the implementation of the "3 Ms" Greater Customs Clearance construction, Zhuhai-Macao port cooperation, and the use of human resources. New progress has been made in the separation of foreground and background inspection at Zhuhai Port and in the cooperation of law enforcement at Zhuhai-Macao Port. The construction of Zhuhai Digital Port and "Single Window" went online as scheduled and the construction of "Great Customs Clearance" in Zhuhai was further promoted, and the human resources of the port inspection were released. In the meantime, Zhuhai set up the first national port work committee to coordinate the overall situation and vigorously promote the pilot work. It has played a positive role in strengthening the comprehensive management of the ports and coordinating the working relationship of the various port inspection agencies. It has created conditions for the reform of the law enforcement and customs clearance of the port inspection agencies and has been able to negotiate and resolve problems in pilot work problems in a timely manner. At present, the customs clearance environment at Zhuhai-Macao port has been further improved, and the level of customs clearance has been further improved.

7.3.6 Active implementation of policies and measures to reduce burdens and increase efficiency of import and export enterprises

The port management departments have conscientiously implemented the State Council's reform measures and policies of "streamlining administration, delegating government power, strengthening regulation and improve services" as well as "benefiting enterprises" so as to promote trade security and convenience as the grasp point, to standardize international traffic regulations, to focus on simplifying and coordinating port customs management and procedures for the reduction of institutional costs and customs clearance procedures. We have been actively carrying out the work of exempting foreign trade enterprises from inspection of lifting, shifting and warehousing expenses and further reducing the burden on import and export enterprises to promote the stable development of foreign trade. Efforts are made to create a good overall customs clearance environment at ports to lay a solid foundation for promoting a new round of opening up and speeding up the development of a new open economy system.

7.3.7 Closer international cooperation of ports

China has 22,000 kilometers of land borders and 18,000 kilometers of coastline, bordering 14 countries' land areas and separated by the sea with six countries. For a long time, the General Administration of Customs (National Office of Port Administration) has attached great importance to strengthening cooperation and exchanges with the competent ports of the surrounding countries. At present, long-term bilateral port cooperation mechanisms have been established with Russia, Kazakhstan, Vietnam, Mongolia, and other neighboring countries, and cooperation mechanisms in the field of port development have been established with the Russian and Mongolian ports authorities. Closely centered on the country's overall political, economic and diplomatic situation, the reciprocal opening of ports has been promoted. Meanwhile, the construction of facilities, optimization of port operation and management, enhancement of the port entry efficiency, and active service of the Belt and Road Initiative together with the six major economic corridors and the China-Europe Cargo Railways have been put into operation and achieved practical results.

At the same time, in accordance with relevant United Nations initiatives and deployment requirements of the national "Internet+," we have actively promoted the "Single Window" practice of international trade cooperation and exchanges with foreign countries and achieved good results. Through the cooperation and exchanges of "off-line" substantive bilateral and multilateral ports in multi-channel, multi-level and multi-fields and the cooperation and exchanges of "on-line" foreign ports with "Single Window" as the main content, foreign cooperation has been further expanded, so that we can more effectively serve the overall situation of the country and promote the development of foreign trade.

7.4 Basic experience of the opening and development of China's ports

The course of China's port opening and development is closely related to the overall development of the country's economy and society. Since the reform and opening up, especially since the 18th National Congress of the CPC, China's port opening has made not only great progress but also accumulated valuable experience in practice and gained useful implications which can be summed up in the following aspects.

7.4.1 Adherence to the correct guidelines

At present and for the period to come, the port work should firmly establish and always adhere to the guiding concept of emancipating the mind, seeking truth from facts, advancing with the times and reform, and implement the new development philosophy of innovation, coordination, green, opening up and sharing. The correct guiding concept determines the final result of social practice. The new concept of development is the baton and the traffic light of the port work. Only by adhering to the correct guiding ideology and highly uniting the action with the new concept can we do everything better from the reality of the port work, and accurately grasp the direction and focus of the port work in serving the economic and social development. That is the way to constantly deepen the corresponding port work, better understand the working rules, take the initiative to integrate into the overall situation of national development, and gather the strength and wisdom of all parties to promote the sound and rapid development of ports in China.

7.4.2 Adherence to the principle of obeying and serving the overall situation of the country

As an old saying goes: "If we do not approach from an overall point of view, we cannot manage one single area well." To do a good job and achieve outstanding achievements, we must first understand and grasp the overall situation, taking into account and commanding the overall situation based on political awareness and holistic points of view. We can judge the situation from a broad perspective, grasp the situation as a whole, and coordinate efforts to achieve the desired objectives. To this end, we must firmly establish the overall concept and awareness, carrying out port work under the correct guidance of the work policy of the state at home and abroad and adhering to the objective law. Handling the relationships between the part and the whole, the country and a region, home and abroad and many other aspects is the premise and basis for doing a good job in port work. At present, port work should be subordinated to further serve the needs of the national political, economic and diplomatic situation, the Belt and Road Initiative, the coordinated development of Beijing-Tianjin-Hebei region, the Yangtze River Economic Belt and other national development strategies, and earnestly safeguard the overall interests of the country, taking into account local interests, and vigorously promoting port services and the country's foreign trade and economic cooperation. At the same time, with an open mind and strategic vision, we should focus on simplifying customs formalities, reducing costs for customs clearance procedures and promoting trade facilitation by actively drawing on advanced experience and mature practices of foreign port management. We should steadily promote international port cooperation and exchanges, jointly enhance the level of port opening and customs services, and promote bilateral and multilateral economic and trade cooperation.

7.4.3 Adherence to innovation and development in the reform

The endogenous impetus of port work lies in reform and innovation and should be carried out step by step around the objectives with step by step breakthroughs. There are no fixed jobs, no fixed management patterns, and no fixed system and mechanism. Looking back on the course of port opening and development, we can see that in different historical stages, the major tasks, objectives, approaches and realization paths of port work may be different, which depends on the specific needs of the development of the times, if we want to achieve comprehensive, coordinated and sustainable development of the port work in the long run. In that case we must meet international standards and draw lessons from experiences, find out weaknesses in China's port management institutions, customs clearance modes, service levels, efficiency and other aspects for improvement. We should take reform and innovation as the driving force for the sustainable development of the port work, keep pace with the times, make clear the objectives, and find out what could be done better. Problems and counter measures should be studied so as to promote innovation of port management mode and system mechanism. We should unremittingly push forward the modernization of port management and "Mutual Sharing of information, mutual recognition of control and mutual assistance of enforcement" to speed up the transformation of government functions, promote simplification and decentralization of port work, and innovate port inspection and supervision model, so as to maintain the vitality of the vigorous development of the port.

7.4.4　Adherence to the principle of supremacy of national interests

National interests are always on the primary. On the premise of ensuring national interests, we should actively coordinate and promote cross-sectoral, cross-regional and cross-industry cooperation that is mutually beneficial for a win-win outcome. Port work involves multi-level, multi-sectoral and multi-regional work, involving not only the interests of the central and the local, governments but also the interests of enterprises and individuals. Among these interests, ensuring the interests of the state is the primary principle. On this basis, reasonable interests of all parties should be fully considered to give full play to relevant ports. Functions and comparative advantages of institutions and departments should be strengthened to achieve mutually beneficial cooperation and a win-win situation.

7.4.5　Equal importance to top-level design and grass-root practice

Given the complexity of the port work, it is necessary to strengthen the top-level design, overall planning, scientific management, classification, and guidance, paying attention not only to strategic planning but also to practical work. In accordance with the overall plan of national economic and social development and the specific needs of coordinated development of regional economy, attention should be paid not only to the reality of demand-side, but also to the intensification of structural reform on the supply-side with a view from overall planning, rational distribution, and scientific management. Importance should also be attached to the priority of benefits, adaptation to local conditions, classified guidance, with the elaborate and conscientious formulation. We should implement the Five-year Development Plan for National Ports, promote port opening in an orderly manner, rationally integrate port resources, constantly optimize port layout, and realize the optimal allocation of port resources and the complementary and coordinated development of ports in eastern, central, and western regions.

7.4.6 Adherence to the construction of legal system and modern management

With the great achievement since the start of reform and opening up, the construction of the port legal system has been lagged behind, and this has become one of the major factors affecting and restricting the further development of ports. Therefore, port work should, in accordance with the overall requirements of the CPC Central Committee on comprehensively deepening reform, adhere to the principle of addressing both the symptoms and root causes of problems, so as to continuously improve the capability of supervision, service and modern governance. Nothing can be accomplished without rules and standards. Adhering to the rule of law is the institutional guarantee for doing an excellent job in port work and the solid foundation for the healthy development of port undertakings. We should accelerate legislation on port administration and take measures to make our laws and regulations more responsive, systematic, relevant, and effective. We should deepen the reform of the administrative law enforcement system and mechanism innovation to further improve institutions, rules and regulations, and well-defined procedures of the enforcement of port laws. At the same time, with a view to port security, efficiency, harmony, and smoothness, the work concept of checking in according to law, effective supervision, convenient entry-exit, good services, scientific management, harmony, and efficiency should be carried out throughout the whole process, so as to create a good customs clearance environment actively, continuously enhance the overall efficiency of the port, further improve the service quality and promote the healthy development of ports.

7.5 Implications

"People who have a keen insight into the situation are wise men, while people who can command the historical trend are winners." This ancient Chinese wisdom tells us that the man who governs the country must respond appropriately to the situation and take advantage of it. The history of Chinese and foreign development practice has proved that opening up to the outside world concerns the survival of a nation, and is the inevitable choice for the prosperity and revival of a country or a region. In the past 40 years since China's reform and opening up, along with the rapid economic and social development, port opening has gone through a gradual growth in number and size, from passive opening to proactive planning, from coastal border to inland areas, from emphasis on quantity to priority on scientific layout planning. In the past 40 years, with the strengthening in the construction of port infrastructure, the improvement in traffic capacity, and the management system, the overall layout has become more reasonable, the customs procedures have been optimized, the comprehensive functions have been further strengthened, and the traffic efficiency has been further improved. Reflecting on the development and the practical exploration of China's reform and opening up, especially the ports' opening up, the author concludes the following implications:

7.5.1 Sticking to the basic national policy of reform and opening up as the core of prosperity and development of various undertakings in China

The practice has proved that opening up to the outside world is the right way for China to choose and the long-term way to revitalize. Since the reform and opening up, China has made remarkable achievements. The rapid growth of the national economy, the remarkable improvement of people's living standards, the sustained and rapid growth of foreign trade have created a "Chinese miracle" in the global economic history with an average annual growth rate of nearly 10% over the past 30 years. At present, China's total economic volume has leaped to the second place in the world, and the foreign exchange rate has increased significantly. Foreign reserves, total trade imports and exports, and manufacturing output have ranked first in the world, all of which have been achieved through reform and opening up. By continuously expanding the opening to the outside world, China has opened its doors for accelerating the development of an open economy, thus successfully realizing a great historical turning from closed and semi-closed to all-round opening. If we had not started or firmly carried out reform and opening up, we would not have made such remarkable achievements. Facts have eloquently proved that reform and opening up is a great new revolution led by the Party to the people of all ethnic groups in the new era. It is the most distinctive feature of contemporary China, the key choice to determine the future of contemporary China, and the only way to develop socialism with Chinese characteristics and realize the Chinese Dream of the rejuvenation of the Chinese nation. The opening and development of China's ports will inevitably be accompanied by the accelerated process of China's opening up and continuous development, and prosperity.

7.5.2 Implementing two-way opening as the inevitable choice to continuously enhance the comprehensive national strength under the economic new normal

Different from the initial stage of reform and opening up, China has entered a new stage of opening up. The economy has shown a new normal of slowing down the growth rate, optimizing the industrial restructuring, changing of the driving force of economic growth, and the mode of resource allocation, with inclusive sharing of economic well-being. In order to adapt to the new situation of economic globalization and participate in international economic cooperation and competition in a broader range and at a higher level, we should insist on the overall planning of domestic and foreign demand and the balance of imports and exports, seize more actively the current and future strategic opportunities, pay more attention to making full use of the international and domestic markets and resources. More attention should be paid to both opening up at home and opening up to the outside world, attracting investment and introducing wisdom. More attention should be paid to the better integration of "bringing in" and "going global", ensuring the security of the country's politics, economy, culture, information, science and technology, and resources. We should further expand the space for strategic development, and constantly improve China's overall competitiveness, soft power and make its voice better heard. In particular, we should adhere to innovative development, coordinated development, green development, open development, and shared development, resolutely remove all obstacles to the system and mechanism of opening up to improve the quality interconnectivity the level of opening up. We should further improve the internal and external interconnectivity, mutual benefit and win-win mode to ensure a secure and efficient open economic system, and actively promote international production. Greater efforts should be made to cultivate and strengthen new advantages in international economic and trade cooperation, and attach greater importance to enhancing independent innovation capability. We should work hard to turn China from a big country in economy and manufacture to a great country strong in sustainable development, smart manufacturing, and innovation. We should promote orderly and free flow of domestic and international elements to ensure efficient allocation of resources and an in-depth market integration, so as to better realize the healthy and sustainable development of the economy and society.

7.5.3 Adhering to overall planning and implementing as an important guarantee for deepening the reform in an all-around way

Preparedness ensures success and unpreparedness foretell failure. In accordance with the overall national strategy, the blueprint of the "economic, political, cultural, social and ecological progress" should be comprehensively promoted with a broad vision of the country and the world, as well as great aspirations, strategic planning and determination, so as to build a well-off society in an all-around way with a strong sense of political responsibility and historical mission. We should comprehensively promote the "Four-pronged Comprehensive" strategic layout of administering the country according to law and strengthening Party self-discipline. We should further strengthen the top-level design and institutional arrangements for the new round of opening up, properly handle the relationships between the "domestic and international interests"[1] of opening up and regional development, the deepening of the reform and expanding the opening up simultaneously to the east and to the west to make the Belt and Road Initiative and the strategy of "going global" benefiting China and the world. We will further improve the layout of opening to the outside world, deepen the opening up of coastal areas, expand the opening of the inland border areas, and promote the complementary advantages, resources, and mutual development of the coastal and inland border areas. We should create a more law-based, international and convenient business environment and open China wider to the outside world, making it possible for more people to enjoy the benefits of the deepening and all-around reform. We should work hard to overcome difficulties, make progress, firmly promote the great practice of comprehensive reform, and expand the path of socialism with Chinese characteristics.

---

[1] Deng Xiaoping emphasized on September 12, 1988: To speed up the opening up of the coastal areas with 200 million people to the outside world so as to promote the better development of the inland area is a matter of great importance to the overall situation. The inland area should take account of this overall situation. On the other hand, when it develops to a certain extent, it requires the coastal areas to exert more power to help the development of the inland, which is also an overall situation in China on which the coastal area should be based. Published in Volume 3 of *Selected Works of Deng Xiaoping*, Beijing: People's Publishing House, 1993, pp. 277-278.

Bibliography

[1] An Husen, *A Textbook of Spatial Economics*, Beijing: Economic Science Press, 2006.

[2] Andrew S. Erickson, Lyle J. Goldstein, Carnes Lord, translated by Dong Shaofeng, Jiang Daichao, *China Goes to Sea*, Beijing: China Ocean Press, 2015.

[3] Angus Madison, translated by Wu Xiaoying, Ma Debin, *Chinese Economic Performance in the Long Run: 960-2030 AD*, Shanghai: Shanghai People's Publishing House, 2008.

[4] Bai Shouyi, *History of Transportation in China*, Beijing: Unity Press, 2011.

[5] Beijing Institute of Foreign Trade, *Marx, Engels, Lenin and Stalin on International Trade*, Beijing: Renmin University of China Printing Factory, 1959.

[6] Cai Fang, Du Yang, "Convergence and Divergence of Regional Economic Growth in China—Implications of the Western Development Strategy, *Economic Research Journal*, 2000(10).

[7] Cai Fang, Wang Dewen, "Comparative Advantages: Differences, Changes and Their Impact on Regional Disparity", *Social Sciences in China*, 2002(5).

[8] Cai Guowei, *Analysis on the Decisive Factors of Regional Economic Growth in China*, Beijing: Science Press, 2010.

[9] Chen Cai, Xiu Chunliang, "On Re-understanding of Mechanism Responsible for the Formation and Development of the Northeast's Economic Regional System", *Scientia Geographica Sinica*, 1995(1).

[10] Chen Changchun, "Probing into Northeast China's Participation in the Economic Cooperation in Northeast Asia", *Human Geography*, 1996(2).

[11] Chen Guodong, *One Thousand Years History of East Asian Seas: China Maritime and Foreign Trade in History*, Jinan: Shandong Pictorial Publishing House,

2006.

[12] Chen Qiuxi, *Essays in Port Management*, Haikou: Nan Hai Publishing Co., 1991.

[13] Chen Shibin, "Developmental Strategic Pattern of the Economic Regional System of Open Ports in Heilongjiang Province", *China's Borderland and History and Geography Studies*, 1999(1).

[14] Chen Xiushan, *Regional Issues in China*, Beijing: The Commercial Press, 2005.

[15] Chen Xiushan, Zhang Keyun, *Theory of Regional Economic Development*, Beijing: The Commercial Press, 2003.

[16] Chen Zhenjiang, *Concise Modern Chinese History*, Beijing: Zhonghua Book Company, 2013.

[17] China Association of Ports, *A Practical List of Chinese Ports*, Beijing: China Customs Press, 2003.

[18] China Association of Ports, *China Ports and Reform and Opening Up*, Beijing: China Customs Press, 2002.

[19] China Association of Ports, *Ports in China: 2001*, Beijing: China Customs Press, 2002.

[20] China Association of Ports, *Ports in China: 2003*, Beijing: China Customs Press, 2004.

[21] China Association of Ports, *Ports in China: 2004*, Beijing: China Customs Press, 2005.

[22] China Association of Ports, *Ports in China: 2005*, Beijing: China Customs Press, 2006.

[23] China Association of Ports, *Ports in China: 2006*, Beijing: China Customs Press, 2007.

[24] China Association of Ports, *Ports in China: 2007*, Beijing: China Customs Press, 2008.

[25] China Association of Ports, *Ports in China: 2008*, Beijing: China Customs Press, 2009.

[26] China Association of Ports, *Ports in China: 2009*, Beijing: China Customs Press, 2010.

[27] China Association of Ports, *Ports in China: 2010*, Beijing: China Customs Press, 2011.

[28] China Association of Ports, *Ports in China: 2011*, Beijing: China Customs

Press, 2012.

[29] China Association of Ports, *Ports in China: 2012*, Beijing: China Customs Press, 2013.

[30] China Association of Ports, *Ports in China: 2013*, Beijing: China Customs Press, 2014.

[31] China Association of Ports, *Ports in China: 2014*, Beijing: China Customs Press, 2015.

[32] China Association of Ports, *Ports in China: 2015*, Beijing: China Customs Press, 2015.

[33] China Association of Ports, *Ports in China: 2016*, Beijing: China Customs Press, 2016.

[34] China Office of Ports of Entry and Exit, *Collection of National Second-Tier Port*, 1996.

[35] China Port Magazine, *Selected Papers on Port Management*, Hefei: Anhui Renmin Press, 1996.

[36] Chinese Academy of International Trade and Economic Cooperation, Ministry of Commerce, *History of Chinese Foreign Trade*, Beijing: China Commerce and Trade Press, 2015.

[37] Dai Angang, *Development and Gaps—A Comparative Study on the Economic Development Process between the East and the West in Modern China*, Shanghai: Fudan University Press, 2006.

[38] Dai Angang, *Port, City and Hinterland–A Historical Survey on the Economic Relationship Between Shanghai and Yangtze River Basin (1843-1913)*, Shanghai: Fudan University Press, 1998.

[39] Dong Fan et. al., *Establishing an International Economic Cooperation Belt Along the Western Border of China: Scientific Programs for Strategic Adjustment in China's Spatial Economy in the Next 50 Years*, Dalian: Dongbei University of Finance and Economics Press, 2004.

[40] Dou Zhiwu, Li Hongwei, Xiong Qi, "Evaluation of Port-logistics Capacity based on Entropy Weight Method and BP Neural Network", *Computer Science*, 2015(7).

[41] Du Yu, *The History of Chinese Borderland*, Beijing: China International Broadcasting Press, 2011.

[42] Editorial Board of *Encyclopedia of China Customs*, *Encyclopedia of China Customs*, Beijing: Encyclopedia of China Publishing House, 2004.

[43] Editorial Board of General Administration of Customs of China, *Selected General Decrees of the General Administration of Taxation of the Old China Customs*, Beijing: China Customs Press, 2003.

[44] Editorial Board of *General Records of China Customs*, *General Records of China Customs (Vol.1-Vol.6)*, Beijing: China Local Records Publishing House, 2013.

[45] Editorial Department of *Study Times*: *The Glory of the Sunset: The Glorious Age of Kangxi and Qianlong in the Global Change of the 17th/18th Centuries*, Beijing: Central Party School Press, 2001.

[46] Editorial Team, *Coaching Book on Decision of the Central Committee of the Communist Party of China on Some Major Issues Concerning Comprehensively Deepening Reform*, Beijing: People's Publishing House, 2013.

[47] Fan Baichuan, *Rise of China's Shipping Industry*, Chengdu: Sichuan People's Publishing House, 1985.

[48] Fan Weiguo, "Central and Unified Port Markets in Modern China", *Social Sciences*, 2001(10).

[49] Fan Weiguo, "Market Features in Modern Shanghai and Formation of Port Economy", *Quarterly Journal of the Shanghai Academy of Social Sciences*, 1994(2).

[50] Fei Chengkang, *History of Leased Territory in China*, Shanghai: Shanghai Academy of Social Sciences Press, 1991.

[51] Feng Tianyu, Mao Lei, Xu Renzhang, *History of China's Opening Up*, Wuhan: Hubei People's Press, 1996.

[52] Fuzhou Customs, *A Brief Introduction on Society and Economy in Modern Fuzhou and East Part of Fujian Province*, Beijing: Hua Yi Publishing House, 1992.

[53] G. L. Clark, M.P. Feldman, M.S. Gertler, Translated by Liu Weidong, Wang Zhici, Li Xiaojian, et. al., *Oxford Handbook of Economic Geography*, Beijing: The Commercial Press, 2005.

[54] Ge Jianxiong, *China in History*: *The Evolution of China's Territory*, Shanghai: Shanghai Literature and Art Publishing House, 2007.

[55] Gong Yingyan, Liu Hengwu, *Maritime Silk Road Studies in 20th Century China*, Hangzhou: Zhejiang University Press, 2011.

[56] Gu Jiegang, Shi Nianhai, *The Evolution of China's Territory*, Beijing: The Commercial Press, 2015.

[57] Gu Zuyu, *Summary of Reading History* (Vol.1–Vol.12), Beijing: Zhonghua Book Company, 2005.

[58] Guangzhou Local Chronicle Editorial Committee, Guangzhou Customs

Chronicle Editorial Committee, *An Economic and Social Survey of Modern Guangzhou Ports—Collection of Guangdong Customs Reports*, Guangzhou: Jinan University Press, 1995.

[59] Guo Laixi, "Distribution of Ports in China", *Acta Geographica Sinica*, 1994(1).

[60] Guo Laixi, *A Study of Dehong Prefectures Opening up and Port System*, Beijing: China Science and Technology Press, 1993.

[61] Han Yuhai, *Beneath the Skies: An All-inclusive China*, Beijing: Jiuzhou Press, 2012.

[62] Han Yuhai, *Who Made the History of Past 500 Years*? Beijing: Jiuzhou Press, 2011.

[63] Hangzhou Customs District P.R.China, *Economic and Social Survey of Zhejiang Trading Ports in Modern Times—Integration of Zhejiang Customs, Wenchou Customs and Hangzhou Customs*, Hangzhou: Zhejiang People's Publishing House, 2002.

[64] Hangzhou Customs Records Compilation Committee, *Hangzhou Customs Records*, Hangzhou: Zhejiang People's Publishing House, 2003.

[65] Hansen, Susan, *The Geography of Urban Transportation*, Beijing: The Commercial Press, 2014.

[66] Hao Xiajun, Mao Lei, Shi Guangrong, *Comparison Between West and East in the Past 500 Hundred Years*, Beijing: China Workers Press, 1989.

[67] Hong Aimei, "Interdependence Between Port and City Economy Based on Grey Relation Analysis", *Market Weekly*, 2013(11).

[68] Hou Angyu, *Wind from the Sea: on China's Modern Marine Ideas*, Beijing: Military Science Publishing House, 2014.

[69] Hu Angang, Wang Shaoguang, Zhou Jianming, Han Yuhai, *Insights into China*, Beijing: China Renmin University Press, 2011.

[70] Hu Axiang, *Crucial Places for Military: Outline of China's History, Military, and Geography*, Haikou: Hainan Publishing House, 2007.

[71] Hu De, *Process of Rights Space and Development of Regional Economy*, Nanjing: Southeast University Press, 2014.

[72] Hu Jiangyun, *Exploring the Path of Open Economy in China*, Beijing: China Fortune Press, 2015.

[73] Hu Naiwu, *Macroeconomic Management*, Beijing: China Renmin University Press, 2007.

[74] Hu Naiwu, *Study on Unbalanced Development of China's Economy*, Taiyuan: Shanxi University Association Press, 1994.

[75] Hu Sheng, *From the Opium War to May 4th Movement*, Beijing: People's Publishing House,1997.

[76] Hu Yuanzi, Xue Xiaoyuan, *Globalization and China*, Beijing: Central Compilation & Translation Press, 1998.

[77] Hu Zhaoliang, Han Maoli, *Introduction to Regional Development in China*, Beijing: Peking University Press, 2008.

[78] Huang Guosheng, *The Customs in China's Four Southeastern Provinces Before the Opium War*, Fuzhou: Fujian People's Publishing House, 2000.

[79] Huang Qichen, *The Maritime Silk Road in Guangdong's History*, Guangzhou: Guangdong Economy Publishing House, 2003.

[80] Huang Shengzhang, "Southeast Asia Trade Ports and Chinese Merchant Ships and Overseas Chinese in the Late Ming Dynasty", *Collections of Essays on Chinese Historical Geography*, 1993(3).

[81] Huang Wei, *Foreign Trade at the Initial Stage of Shanghai Port Opening*, Shanghai: Shanghai People's Publishing House, 1961.

[82] Huntington, Samuel, *The Clash of Civilizations and the Remaking of World Order*, Beijing: Xinghua Publishing House, 2013.

[83] Institute of Economics, Shanghai Academy of Social Sciences, *Shanghai Foreign Trade (1840-1949)*, Shanghai: Shanghai Academy of Social Sciences Press, 1989.

[84] [Japan] Ozaki, Haruo, *China's Strong Power Strategy*, Beijing: The Oriental Press, 2012.

[85] Jean-Paul Rodgigue, Claude Comtois, Brian Slack, *The Geography of Transportation Systems*, Beijing: China Communications Press, 2014.

[86] Jia Heting, *A Thorough Analysis of Port Management*, Shenzhen: Shenzhen Publishing House, 1998.

[87] Jia Jinye, *Comprehensive Management of Ports in Guangdong*, Port Office of Guangzhou Government, 2014.

[88] Jiang Xiuping, *Oriental Dialogue Towards Modernization—A Comparison Between Westernization Movement and Meiji Reform*, Beijing: China Social Sciences Press, 1993.

[89] Jing Yinan, *China's Attitude Towards World's Landscape*, Beijing: Beijing United Publishing Co., Ltd., 2015.

[90] Kissinger, Alfred Henry, *Does America Need a Foreign Policy?* Haikou: Hainan Publishing House, 2009.

[91] Kissinger, Henry, *Does America Need a Foreign Policy*, Haikou: Hainan Publishing House, 2009.

[92] Kissinger, Henry, *On China*, Beijing: China CITIC Press, 2012.

[93] Krugman, Paul, *Development, Geography, and Economic Theory*, Beijing: Peking University Press, 2000.

[94] Lechager, James, R. Kelly Pace, Translated by Xiao Guang'en, Yang Yong, et al., *Introduction to Spatial Econometrics*, Beijing: Peking University Press, 2014.

[95] Li Bizhang, *An Overview of the Development of Modern Foreign Trade and Economy in Shanghai: Trade Reports of British Consular of Shanghai (1854-1898)*, Shanghai: Shanghai Academy of Social Sciences Press, 1993.

[96] Li Mingjie, Shen Wenzhou, *The Past and Present of China's Seas*, Beijing: China Intercontinental Press, 2014.

[97] Li Shuxi, *Chill Northern Wind–A Historical Survey of China from Division to Unification*, Beijing: The Chinese Overseas Publishing House, 2007.

[98] Li Wannan, "Opportunities, and Challenges to China's Construction of the '21st Century Maritime Silk Road': with Responding Measures", *Journal of China's Neighboring Diplomacy*, 2015(1).

[99] Li Xiaojian, *Economic Geography*, Beijing: Higher Education Press, 2008.

[100] Li Yan, *Ports in Ancient China: Evolution of Economy, Culture and Space*, Guangzhou: Guangdong Economy Publishing House, 2014.

[101] Lian Xinhao, *Chinese Customs and Foreign Trade*, Changsha: Yuelu Press, 2004.

[102] Liang Minyi, "On Foreign Trade and Its Characteristics after the Opening of Sandu'ao Port in Modern Fujian Province", *Journal of Jiangxi Normal University*, 2000(4).

[103] Liang Minyi, "On the Motivation of the Development of Social Economy in Northeast Fujian after the Voluntary Opening of Sandu'ao Port: Historical Status and Historical Utility of the Voluntarily-opened Commercial Port System in Modern China", *The Journal of Chinese Social and Economic History*, 2002(3).

[104] Liang Minyi, He Ruihu, "On the Active Opening of Sandu'ao Port and the Rise and Fall of Shipping of Northeast Fujian in Modern times", *Journal of Jiangxi University of Finance and Economics*, 2000(5).

[105] Lin Yifu, "Development Strategy, Viability and Economic Convergence",

China Economics Quarterly, 2002(2).

[106] Liu Wei, Huang Guitian, Li Shaorong, *A Course in Economics*, Beijing: Peking University Press, 2010.

[107] Liu Xiaoling, "On Relationship Between Port and Industry Based on Grey Relational Analysis and Comprehensive Evaluation Model", *Port & Waterway Engineering*, 2011(5).

[108] Long Guoqiang, Hu Jiangyun, *China's New Regional Opening-up Strategy*, Beijing: China Development Press, 2010.

[109] Long Guoqiang, Hu Jiangyun, *Strategic Opportunities for China in the Wake of Global Crisis*, Beijing: China Development Press, 2011.

[110] Lu Dahu, *Following the General Secretary to Read History*, Beijing: Central Party School Press, 2014.

[111] Lu Feng, Xu Jianhua, "Exploratory Spatial Data Analysis of the Regional Economic Disparities in China", *Journal of East China Normal University*, 2007(2).

[112] Lu Han, *Chronology of Unequal Treaties in Modern China*, Beijing: Foreign Languages Press, 2012.

[113] Lu Ming, *The Power of Space*, Shanghai: Truth & Wisdom Press, Shanghai People's Publishing House, 2013.

[114] Luan Ling, "Prediction of Cargo Throughput in Shanghai Port: Based on Neural Network", *Market Weekly: Theory Research*, 2015(1).

[115] Meng Fanren, *A Brief History of the Silk Road*, Beijing: Social Sciences Academic Press (China), 2011.

[116] Meng Zhijun, *The Historical Inspirations and China Road of Opening Up*, Beijing: Guangming Daily Press, 2012.

[117] Morse, Hosea Ballou, Translated by Zhang Huiwen, *The International Relation of the Chinese Empire*, Shanghai: Shanghai Bookstore Publishing House, 2000.

[118] Murphey, Rhoads, *Shanghai, Key to Modern China*, Shanghai: Shanghai People's Press, 1986.

[119] National Office of Port Administration, *Manual of Port Work*, 2013.

[120] Office of the Financial and Economic Committee of the National People's Congress, Department of Development Planning of the National Development and Reform Commission, *A Compilation of Important Documents of the Five-Year Plan for National Economic and Social Development Since the Founding of the People's Republic of China*, Beijing: China Democratic and Law Press, 2008.

[121] Paul Kennedy, translated by Chen Jingbiao, Wang Baocun, Wang Zhanghui, Yu Changkai, *The Rise and Fall of the Foreign Powers*, Beijing: International Cultural Press, 2008.

[122] Peng Zheyi, *Evolution of China's Society and Economy*, Beijing: China Financial & Economic Publishing House,1990.

[123] Qi Yanchen, *The Hangover Dynasty—the 30 Years of Late Qing Dynasty from 1860 to 1889*, Beijing: Jiuzhou Press, 2005.

[124] Qin Yucai, Zhou Guping, Luo Weidong, *Interpreting the Belt and Road Initiative*, Hangzhou: Zhejiang University Press, 2015.

[125] Quanzhou Customs, *Quanzhou Customs Records*, Xiamen: Xiamen University Press, 2005.

[126] "Recommendations on the 13th Five-Year Plan for Economic and Social Development by the Central Committee of the Communist Party of China (Adopted by the Fifth Plenary Session of the 18th Central Committee of the Communist Party of China on October 29, 2015)", *People's Daily*, Nov. 4, 2015.

[127] Ren Hongsheng, *Between the Hegemonies: The World System and the Development of Eurasia Steppes*, Beijing: Peking University Press, 2006.

[128] Ren Ming, *China's Major Railway Ports and Foreign Trade*, Beijing: China Minzu University Press, 2007.

[129] Research Center of History and Geography of Fudan University, *Trade Ports and Their Hinterland and the Course of China's Modernization*, Jinan: Shandong Qilu Press Co., Ltd., 2005.

[130] Schram, Stuart R, *The Thought of Mao Tse-tung*, Beijing: China Renmin University Press, 2005.

[131] Sha Yu, *The History of Ancient Chinese Navigation*, Beijing: Liaohai Publishing House, 2012.

[132] Shen Jinjian, Chen Jiaqin, "Opening up Ports along the Belt and Road and Building a Community with the Shared Future", *Globalization*, 2015(7).

[133] Shen Jishi, *The Silk Road*, Beijing: Zhonghua Book Company, Shanghai: Shanghai Classics Publishing House, 2010.

[134] Shi Yonggang, Zou Ming, *China Era:1900-2000*, Beijing: The Writers Publishing House Co., Ltd., 2009.

[135] Shigeki, Tōyama, *Modern History of Japan*, Beijing: The Commercial Press, 1983.

[136] Shu Hongfeng, *Competition Between Ports—Dynamic of Container*

Development in Ports, Beijing: China Communications Press Co., Ltd., 2007.

[137] Sun Jiuwen, *An Empirical Study of Regional Economy in China*, Beijing: China Light Industry Press, 1999.

[138] Sun Qingchao, *Ports in Heilongjiang Province*, Harbin: Heilongjiang People's Publishing House, 1999.

[139] Sun Yutang, Wang Jingyu, *Materials of Industry History in Modern China*, Beijing: Sciences Press, 1957.

[140] Tang Chongnan, Wang Miao, Qiang Guo, Han Wenjuan, *The Rise and Fall of the Japanese Empire*, Beijing: World Affairs Press, 2005.

[141] Tang Jin, *The Rise of Great Nations*, Beijing: People's Publishing House, 2006.

[142] Tang Ling et al., *Active-opened Trading Ports and Economic Evolutions in Modern China*, Nanning: Guangxi People's Publishing House, 2002.

[143] Tang Xianglong, *Statistics of Customs Duty and Distribution in Modern China*, Beijing: Zhonghua Book Company, 1992.

[144] Tang Xiaoguang, Sun Yanjie, He Zhijun, *Port Administration Dictionary*, Yanji: YanBian University Press Limited Liability Company, Beijing: Police Education Press, 1991.

[145] Tang Xiaoguang, Zhao Yiren, *Survey of Ports in China*, Beijing: Economy & Management Publishing House, 1992.

[146] Teng Yong, *Port Administration*, Beijing: People's Daily Press, 1989.

[147] The Compilation Committee of *Ningbo Customs Records*, *Ningbo Customs Records*, Hangzhou: Zhejiang Science and Technology Publishing House, 2000.

[148] The Second Historical Archives of China, "The Opened Trading Ports in 1921", *Historical Archives*, 1984(4).

[149] The Second Historical Archives of China, *Historical Materials of Old Customs of China*, Beijing: Jinghua Publishing House, 2001.

[150] Theory Department of People's Daily, *In-depth Study of the Essence of Xi Jinping's Speeches*, Beijing: People's Publishing House, 2013.

[151] Wan Ling, *The Modernization Road of Changzhou: A Case Study of Modernization of Non-Treaty Port City in the Areas of Southern Cities of Yangtze River*, Hefei: Anhui Educational Publishing House, 2002.

[152] Wang Bo, *Suifen River Road Port Logistics Forecast and Development Plan in Heilongjiang Province*, Master's Degree Thesis, Harbin: Northeast Forestry University, Jun. 2010.

[153] Wang Chuanxu, *Cooperation and Competition in Regional Port and Logistical System*, Shanghai: Shanghai Jiao Tong University Press, 2010.

[154] Wang Dingjie, "The History of World War II: National Strategies of the Great Powers: Japan (Part I)", *World Military Affairs*, 2015(14).

[155] Wang Ermin, *Turbulent Situations of Five Trading Ports*, Guilin: Guangxi Normal University Press, 2006.

[156] Wang Fangzhong, *China's Economic History: 1842-1949*, Beijing: China Renmin University Press, 2014.

[157] Wang Guimin, *Multi-dimension Interpretation of Open Economy: Theory Foundation and Practical Application*, Beijing: China Social Sciences Press, 2014.

[158] Wang Guoping, "Treaty Port Coverage and the Infraction of Powers in Modern China", *Jianghai Academic Journal*, 2001, No.4.

[159] Wang Jie, Li Baoming, Wang Li, *A Brief History of Sailing in China*, Beijing: Social Sciences Academic Press, 2012.

[160] Wang Jingyu, "On the Closure of the Sea in the Early Qing Dynasty", *The Journal of Chinese Social and Economic History*, 1983(2).

[161] Wang Jingyu, *The Economic History of Modern China*, Beijing: People's Publishing House, 2000.

[162] Wang Qingxi, Jiang Ye, Chen Zhuoyong, *Practical Methods of Regional Economy Research: on the Basis of ArcGIS, GeoDa, and R*, Beijing: Economic Science Press, 2014.

[163] Wang Tieya, *A Compilation of Old Treaties Between China and Foreign Countries*, Beijing: SDX Joint Publishing Company, 1957.

[164] Wang Xianming, *The Modern History of China*, Beijing: China Renmin University Press, 2011.

[165] Wang Xiaolu, Fan Gang, "Analysis on the Regional Disparity in China and the Influential Factors", *Economic Research Journal*, 2004(1).

[166] Wang Xing, *Non-parametric Statistics*, Beijing: China Renmin University Press, 2002.

[167] Wang Xueqing, Chen Yuan, Liu Bingsheng, "Exploratory Spatial Data Analysis about the Development Level of the Regional Real Estate Economy in China— Based on Global Moran'I Moran Scatter Plots and LISA Cluster Map, *Journal of Applied Statistics and Management*, 2014(1).

[168] Wang Yipin, *Open Gradient Theory: A Study on the Unbalanced Development of Open Economy*, Beijing: China Economic Publishing House, 1995.

[169] Wang Yuanfei, He Honglin, *Methods of Spatial Data Analysis*, Beijing: Science Press, 2007.

[170] Wang Yuanlin, *Ancient Roads Between Land and Sea–the Connection Between the Land Silk Road and Maritime Silk Road*, Guangzhou: Guangdong Economy Publishing House, 2015.

[171] Wang Yuru et al., *Institutional Change and Industrialization in Modern China*, Xi'an: Shaanxi People's Publishing House, 2000.

[172] Wang Yuru, *Growth, Development and Change: Research on Modern Economic Development in China*, Beijing: China Logistics Publishing House, 2004.

[173] Wei Hao, Wang Chen, "Research on Spatial Agglomeration and Its Determinants of Foreign Trade in China", *The Journal of Quantitative & Technical Economics*, 2011(11).

[174] Wei Houkai, "Thoughts on Several Theoretical Issues of Current Regional Economic Development, *Economic Research Journal*, 2007(1).

[175] Wei Houkai, *Modern Regional Economics*, Beijing: Economy & Management Publishing House, 2006.

[176] Wei Liqun, *Hot Issues of China's Reform and Development* (2016), Beijing: The Commercial Press, 2016.

[177] Wei Liqun, *Hot Issues of China's Reform and Development* (2017), Beijing: The Commercial Press, 2017.

[178] Wei Liqun, *Road to Building Think Tanks*, Beijing: People's Publishing House, 2014.

[179] Wei Liqun, *Selected Essays of Wei Liqun on Economy*, Beijing: China Modern Economic Publishing House, 2011.

[180] Wei Liqun, *The 4Cs: New Blueprint and New Aspirations*, Beijing: People's Publishing House, 2015.

[181] William, Skinner. G, Translated by Wang Xu, *The City in Late Imperial China*, Changsha: Jilin Education Publishing House,1992.

[182] Wright, Stanley F, Translated by Chen Caicai, Lu Zhuocheng, Li Xiufeng, *Robert Hart and China Customs*, Xiamen: Xiamen University Press, 1994.

[183] Writing Group of the Book, *100 Questions and Answers on Decision of the Third Plenary Session of the Eighteenth Central Committee of the Communist Party Central Committee of China*, Beijing: Party Building Books Publishing House, Xuexi Publishing House, 2013.

[184] Wu Songdi, *A Centennial Economic Mosaic of China: Port Cities,*

Hinterland and China's Modernization, Jinan: Shandong Pictorial Publishing House, 2006.

[185] Wu Songdi, Fan Rusen, Chen Weizhong, Yao Yongchao, Dai Angang, *Port Cities and Their Hinterland and Economic Change in North China: 1840-1949*, Hangzhou: Zhejiang University Press, 2011.

[186] Wu Songdi, Fan Rusen, *Evolution of the Economic and Geographical Patterns of Northern China in Modern Times*, Beijing: People's Publishing House, 2013.

[187] Wu Yuming, Xu Jianhua, "A Spatial Analysis on Regional Economic Growth Clustering", *Scientia Geographica Sinica*, 2004(6).

[188] Xi Jinping, "Notes on the 13th Five-Year Plan for Economic and Social Development of the Central Committee of the Communist Party of China", *People's Daily*, Nov. 4, 2015.

[189] Xi Jinping, *The Governance of China*, Beijing: Foreign Languages Press, 2014.

[190] Xia Yidong, *The Pacific Hegemony in the Past 500 Years*, Beijing: Xinhua Publishing House, 2013.

[191] Xiamen City Chronicle Compilation Committee, Xiamen Customs Chronicle Editorial Committee, *Xiamen Social and Economic Survey in Modern Times*, Xiamen: Lujiang Publishing House, 1990.

[192] Xiao Gang, "Politics and Philosophy of Japan's Cross-century Strategies to China", *Journal of Foreign Affairs College*, 1999(3).

[193] Xie Hangsheng, *Official Silver Numbers in the Late Qing Dynasty: Social and Economic Changes in China*, Beijing: Chinese Financial & Economic Publishing House, 1990.

[194] Xie Lingfeng, et al., *Port Development Patterns in the Pearl River Delta*, Beijing: China Ocean Press, 2014.

[195] Xu Deyou, Liang Qi, "Spatial Correlation Analysis of County Export Trade: A Case Study of Jiangsu Province", *Journal of Finance and Economics*, 2011(5).

[196] Xu Dixin, Wu Chengming, *History of the Development of Capitalism in China (Vol.1): The Germination of Capitalism in China*, Beijing: People's Publishing House, 2003.

[197] Xu Dixin, Wu Chengming, *History of the Development of Capitalism in China (Vol.2): Chinese Capitalism in the Period of the Old Democratic Revolution*, Beijing: People's Publishing House, 2003.

[198] Xu Dixin, Wu Chengming, *History of the Development of Capitalism in China (Vol.3): Chinese Capitalism in the Period of New Democratic Revolution*, Beijing: People's Publishing House, 2003.

[199] Xu Lili, *China's Borderland and Security (Vol.1)*, Beijing: Social Sciences Academic Press (China), 2015.

[200] Xu Xiyun, *A Contrast Between Chinese and Western Civilizations*, Hangzhou: Zhejiang People's Publishing House, 2013.

[201] Xu Xueyun et al., *A Survey of Social and Economic Development in Modern Shanghai (1882-1931)–Translating and Editing of the 10-Year Report of the Customs*, Shanghai: Shanghai Academy of Social Sciences Press, 1985.

[202] Xu Zhongyue, *The Rise of Modern China*, Beijing: World Publishing Corporation, 2013.

[203] Xue Litai, *China's Grand Strategy for Engaging an Uncertain World*, Beijing: The Oriental Press, 2014.

[204] Yan Genqi, *Ancient Navigation History of the South China Sea*, Beijing: China Ocean Press, 2016.

[205] Yan Zhongping et al., *Selected Statistical Data of Economic History in Modern China*, Beijing: Science Press, 1955.

[206] Yang Cuibai, *Legal Studies on China's Sovereignty over NANSHA Islands*, Beijing: The Commercial Press, 2015.

[207] Yang Jinsen, *A Brief History of the Rise and Fall of Marine Powers*, Beijing: China Ocean Press, 2014.

[208] Yang Peng, *Channel Economy*, Beijing: China Economic Publishing House, 2012.

[209] Yang Tianhong, "Establishment of Modern Enterprises and Industrialization in Non-treaty Ports", *Journal of Sichuan University (Philosophy and Social Sciences Edition)*, 2002(2).

[210] Yang Tianhong, "Establishment of Non-treaty Ports in New Policy Period of Late Qing Dynasty", *Journal of Sichuan Normal University (Social Sciences Edition)*, 2002(6).

[211] Yang Tianhong, "Financing and Expenditure of Non-treaty Ports in the Qing Dynasty", *The Journal of Chinese Social and Economic History*, 1999(2).

[212] Yang Tianhong, "First Non-treaty Ports in the Qing Dynasty", *Historical Research*, 1998(2).

[213] Yang Tianhong, "Review of Studies of Non-treaty Ports in Modern China",

Journal of Sichuan Normal University (Social Sciences Edition), 2001(6).

[214] Yang Tianhong, "Setting up and Operating System of Customs of Non-treaty Ports in the Qing Dynasty", *Social Science Research*, 1998(3).

[215] Yang Tianhong, "The Regional Distribution of Non-treaty Ports and the Extension of Foreign Trade in the Qing Dynasty", *Journal of Sichuan University (Philosophy and Social Sciences Edition)*, 1999(2).

[216] Yang Tianhong, *Port Opening and Social Change: Non-Treaty Ports in Modern China*, Beijing: Zhonghua Book Company, 2012.

[217] Yang Wenhe, Tao Boyong, *Oceans and Modern China*, Beijing: China Ocean Press, 2014.

[218] Yao Xianhao, *Historical Data of Modern Trade in China*, Beijing: Zhonghua Book Company, 1962.

[219] Yao Yongchao, Wang Xiaogang, *Sixteen Lectures on the History of Chinese Customs*, Shanghai: Fudan University Press, 2014.

[220] Ye Jian, "Reflections on the Opening of China's Ports", *Management World*, 1998(1).

[221] Ye Jian, *An Overview of China's Ports*, Beijing: Economy & Management Publishing House, 1996.

[222] Yin Haiwei, Kong Fanhua, *Lab Manual* for *Spatial Analysis in Urban and Regional Planning*, Beijing: Southeast University Press, 2014.

[223] Yuan Weipeng, *Aggregation and Diffusion: China's Modern Industrial Distribution*, Shanghai: Shanghai University of Finance & Economics Press, 2007.

[224] Yun Zhongtian, *The Great Navigation in Chinese History*, Beijing: China Three Gorges Publishing House, 2007.

[225] Zeng Peiyan, *New China's Economy in 50 Years (1949-1999)*, Beijing: China Planning Publishing House, 1999.

[226] Zhang Dan, "Chongqing Port Logistics and Urban Industry Based on Grey Relation Analysis", *Urban and Rural Planning* (*City Geography Edition*), 2014(4).

[227] Zhang Hongxiang, *Modern Chinese Trade Ports and Concessions*, Tianjin: Tianjin People's Publishing House, 1993.

[228] Zhang Jinzong, Zhu Yuxin, Zhou Jie, "Prediction of Population Spatial Distribution in Shandong—Based on BP ANN and Spatial Statistical Analysis", *Science of Surveying and Mapping*, 2009(6).

[229] Zhang Junguo, *On Reform and Opening Up and Economic Globalization*, Beijing: National Defense University Press, 2009.

[230] Zhang Li, *Accessibility and Regional Spatial Structure*, Beijing: Science Press, 2010.

[231] Zhang Weidi, Xiao Chuanguo, *Evolution of Japan's National Strategy Since Modern Times*, Beijing: Current Affairs Press, 2013.

[232] Zhang Wenmu, *Geopolitical Theory of China*, Beijing: China Ocean Press, 2015.

[233] Zhang Xun, *Collation and Annotation of Record of Buddhistic Kingdoms and Maritime Traffic in Ancient China*, Shanghai: Fudan University Press, 2015.

[234] Zhang Yan, Niu Guanjie, *Fifteen Lectures on the History of Qing Dynasty*, Beijing: Peking University Press, 2004.

[235] Zhang Zhongli, Pan Junxiang, "On the Internal Causes of Transformation and Development of Shanghai's Economic Modernization", *Researches in Chinese Economic History*, 1992(3).

[236] Zhang Zhongli, *Selected Translations of Works on History of Modern Chinese Economy*, Shanghai: Shanghai Social Sciences Academy Press, 1987.

[237] Zhang Zhongli, *Southeast Coastal Cities and China's Modernization*, Shanghai: Shanghai People's Publishing House, 1996.

[238] Zhang Zhongmin, *Urban Development and Comprehensive Competitiveness of Modern Shanghai*, Shanghai: Shanghai Academy of Social Sciences Press, 2005.

[239] Zhao Bing, *Port Competitiveness Evaluation Based on BP Neural Network*, Master's Degree Thesis, Dalian: Dalian Maritime University, June 2008.

[240] Zhao Jinping, et al., China's *Opening Up: New Breakthroughs in Key Areas*, Beijing: China Development Press, 2015.

[241] Zhao Jun, *Broken Lever: A Comparative Study of New Policies in Late Qing Dynasty and Meiji Restoration*, Changsha: Hunan Publishing House, 1992.

[242] Zhao Wei et al., *The Opening up Effects of Regional Economics on Institutional Transition and Economic Growth in China*, Beijing: Economic Science Press, 2011.

[243] Zhao Yanyun, Hu Ruipeng, "Analysis of Spatial Distribution of Rural Residents' Consumption in Provincial Areas of China", *Consumer Economics*, 2014(1).

[244] Zhao Yanyun, *Statistical Analysis of Macroeconomy*, Beijing: China Renmin University Press.

[245] Zhao Zuoquan, *Statistics of Spatial Pattern and Analysis of Spatial Economy*, Beijing: Science Press, 2014.

[246] Zhen Feng, et, al, *Economy of African Ports and Urban Development*,

Nanjing: Nanjing University Press, 2014.

[247] Zheng Bijian, Kissinger, et al., *In Search for a Path of Common Prosperity*, Beijing: China CITIC Press, 2013.

[248] Zheng Youzheng, *Foreign Trade and Industrial Development in China: 1840-1948*, Shanghai: Shanghai Academy of Social Sciences Press, 1984.

[249] Zheng Zhong, "On Characteristics of the Development of Modern China's Treaty Port Cities Compared with Non-treaty Cities, *Jianghai Academic Journal*, 2001(4).

[250] Zhou Renwei, *Rise from Stagnation: Modernization of Cities Along the Yangtze River in Anhui*, Hefei: Anhui Educational Publishing House, 2002.

[251] Zhu Buchong, "Chinese Maritine Road in the Age of Classical Globalization", *Life Weekly*, 2015(30).

[252] Zhu Buchong, "Maritime Silk Road: the Age of Classical Globalization", *Life Weekly*, 2015(30).

[253] Zhu Buchong, "Starting from Guangzhou, Chinese Sailing to the Sea", *Life Weekly*, 2015(30).

[254] Zhu Zhen, *The Plutonomic Analysis on China's Opening of Ports*, Beijing: China Economic Publishing House, 2016.